Harold the Haunted Doll

Harold the Haunted Doll

The Terrifying, True Story of the
World's Most Sinister Doll

Anthony Quinata

Copyright © 2015 Anthony Quinata
All rights reserved.

ISBN: 1516840062
ISBN 13: 9781516840069

The story you are about to read is true. It is based on real events - my personal experiences since winning eBay's most infamous haunted doll in an auction in June of 2004, as well as what has happened to those who have had encounters with the doll.

I've also adapted the texts and Facebook messages of those claiming to have been affected by the doll. Many of the names have been changed to protect the privacy of those involved.

This book is dedicated to -
My friend, Tereva, and to my fur baby, Chance.
Both of whom are victims in my war with the doll.
I'm so sorry.
I miss you both beyond words.

ACKNOWLEDGEMENTS

There are so many people I want to thank, but who have in all honesty asked me not to… at least, publicly. As one of my friends said to me, "I don't want to take the chance of attracting the attention of whatever is in the doll."

But you know who you are. And I thank you.

Most, but not all, of the names in this book have been changed.

To everyone whose story I share in this book, and to those whose stories I haven't included, I want to say both, "Thank you for sharing your story with me; and I'm sorry."

FOREWORD

*I*f you have ever researched or looked into haunted dolls on the web, chances are you have come across Haunted Harold. With that being said, Harold has an extensive history. The doll was manufactured around the turn of the century and is made of composite particles, plaster and water. The manufacturer is unknown at this time. You can tell the doll has been, and forgive my pun, through hell and back. The doll has been owned by people around the world. All of the previous owners have reported strange occurrences, such as voices, slight movement and changes in facial expression. Headaches, migraines, back pain and unexplained injuries have also been reported while in its presence. The doll has also been blamed for the death of two people. The doll being responsible for these deaths is still up to speculation, the truth may never be known....

Harold's current owner, Anthony Quinata, bought the doll on eBay in 2004. After experiencing some paranormal activity, Anthony put the doll in storage from 2005-2013. We were contacted by Anthony to provide an understanding of what type of entity inhabits the doll. After an initial interview we decided to go to an undisclosed location and perform an EVP/Ovilus session. During the investigation, the Ovilus had numerous hits on the words "worry" and "guilt." Our EVP picked up on many different voices accompanied by screaming and laughter.

While reviewing a short EVP session we conducted on our first meeting with Harold, our lead investigator became ill. Plagued with a migraine headache, severe lower back pain, and the feeling of being disorientated, the investigator had reason to believe he was being attacked. After our lead recovered, it was decided to delay the release of the evidence that was collected on Harold. It was also determined not to further pursue any other investigations with Harold and Anthony at this time.

There is reason to believe the doll is inhabited by many spirits. Due to the evidence collected, we believe there is a malevolent entity that may be attached to the doll, disguising itself as many spirits. Anthony was informed of our findings and we wish him the best of luck with Harold.

Hopefully, Harold will find his peace....

Lockdown Paranormal
www.lockdownparanormal.com

PROLOGUE

My name is "Jane." I live in Australia with my husband and two sons, the oldest of whom, "Vincent," is moderate to severely autistic.

I was not, and still am not, the slightest bit interested in anything having to do with the paranormal. I was interested in learning how to sew cloth toys, so I went onto YouTube to find a tutorial on how to do just that.

God knows how I got on to the weird side of YouTube, but Annabelle was where I ended. I had never even heard of her before that but felt compelled to click and watch a short story on her. Then, at the side, I saw Harold!

He sure grabs your attention and draws you in. I think it was almost a sense of pity…, but also a feeling of wanting to know more. A need to know his story. He's not a kind of thing you look at once on a page and move on. He makes you stop and look twice.

I clicked on the video clip, but to be honest I didn't really listen to it too much (it was one with just a still picture of Harold). After that, I'm not sure… I think the phone rang or [my husband] came home, but I forgot about it and carried on with the day. Come to think of it, I don't think my computer has worked properly since.

It would have been a few hours after I first seen the clip that Vincent saw it as well. I don't really remember how we both got to being back in front of the screen. I think he wanted to play reading eggs or something, but I know his reaction was instant. He just stopped in his tracks, looked, did a double take, and looked again, which is unusual for him with his autism. Then he became instantly upset.

I didn't know it at the time, but that moment was the beginning of what would be a roller coaster of events that would make my family's life a living hell. It was like watching a programme on the television. As Anthony likes to say, "A real life nightmare," only you're awake. People may not believe, or think it's real, but until it consumes you, and becomes your life, you have no idea.

I think, this experience with the doll, it's made not just me but all of us [in my family] that little more aware. There is a lot more to this world than we know and understand.

I'm still trying to get my head around what happened. It all feels so surreal.

Nothing in our lives will ever be the same or taken for granted. Yeah, I still keep looking at my two beautiful boys, hugging them that little bit tighter!

"Jane" (name changed at her request)

INTRODUCTION

When this doll was offered on eBay, back in 2003, I wasn't aware of the infamous "Haunted Harold." I didn't know about the claims made by Greg, the original seller of the doll, that were so bizarre and outrageous, Harold was discussed on Art Bell's Coast to Coast AM radio show. Paranormal websites were discussing this doll around the world. At least one news article was written about the doll.

Years later, Greg admitted that he made up the things he wrote in his listing hoping to make a few more dollars. In other words, the whole thing was a hoax.

What Greg wrote may have been the product of his fertile imagination, but the story you're about to read is true. It starts from the time I won the doll on eBay in 2004, and continues to this day, in 2015.

One question I'm often asked is, "What proof do you have that what you're saying about the doll is true?"

I usually answer that question with one of my own, "How do you define proof?"

Dictionary.com defines the word as - *Evidence sufficient to establish a thing as true, or to produce belief in its truth.*

2. Anything serving as such evidence:

Now let's take a look at the definition of the word, "evidence."

That which tends to prove or disprove something; ground for belief; proof.

Something that makes plain or clear; an indication or sign.

A video of the doll "moving" would be, to many people, proof that the doll is haunted. A video could also be a camera trick, fishing line, or "invisible thread."

I've seen magicians (entertainers) do it. Does that mean that what I'm seeing is "proof" of a haunting? Of course not.

Things move, appear, and disappear, during poltergeist cases. Parapsychologists will tell you that in those cases, "ghosts" aren't the source of the activity. The human mind is.

In the "Philip Experiment," a table they were using to conduct séances on literally moved on its own, chasing one of the experimenters in full view of others with no one near it. Is that proof that there was a "spirit" present? No, because the ghost was a creation, made up in the minds of the experimenters.

I haven't shared much of the "evidence" I've collected concerning Harold before now. I wanted to avoid the so-called, "Philip effect."

Another reason is that I was constantly getting people's (especially psychic's) opinions all of the time. Unless what they said lined up with what I knew to be true, I wasn't accepting it. When I asked two psychics how I can verify what they were telling me they both said that I simply needed to agree to take their assessment at face value. Thanks, but no thanks.

So called "scientific investigations" of hauntings often use technology that was never designed to detect ghosts in the first place. And those devices that were designed to do so are "experimental" and designed for research purposes, at best.

Hauntings are human encounters. An anomalous reading on an EMF, without a human experience is just that… an irregularity. It's not "proof," or even "evidence," of a ghost. So the question isn't, "Can I prove Harold is haunted?" but, "Am I trying to prove the doll is haunted?"

The answer to the first question is, "It depends on how you define the word 'haunted.'"

My response to the *second question* is, "No." I'm *not* trying to prove that it's haunted—to anyone. I *do* have enough evidence to convince me that *something* is going on. The question in my mind is, "What?"

Is the doll really haunted?

Is it cursed?

Is it possessed?

All of the above?

Whatever is going on, how did what caused this to happen… happen?

Ultimately, the question in my mind is, "What I can do to stop what's apparently going on?"

I have personally been attacked by the energy contained in the doll, and have been an eyewitness to the things that happened to others. I'll also share a few of the many stories told to me in person, emails, and texts, by the people who experienced them, in this book.

Another question I'm often asked is why I wanted the doll in the first place. I didn't. I'll share with you how I ended up with the doll. I will tell you this however—if I'd known then what I know now, I would have left well enough alone. I would never have bid on that doll in the first place.

Finally, I want to say that in many of the chapters, especially those involving a family in Australia, what I'm going to share with you is from messages I received on Facebook Messenger. If that's the case, I've *italicized* the text in order to keep the tone of what was said intact, and in "real time."

I did rephrase messages, making corrections for spelling, grammar, and reading ease.

For purposes of privacy, many of the names in this book have been changed.

"CAN SOMEONE HELP ME WITH THIS?"

Phyllis was an R.N. in the psychiatric ward of a large hospital in Southern California. Because of the patients Phyllis worked with, she and her staff were permitted to wear costumes on Halloween, but they were not allowed to wear masks.

Halloween night, 2003, she had a small digital camera with her and was taking pictures of her nursing team in their costumes. An LPN walked by, whom she only knew well enough to say "hello" to in passing. Phyllis asked her to take a photo of the entire group. The nurse agreed, took a couple of pictures of the group, handed the camera back, and walked away. When Phyllis took a look at the images, she was stunned to see someone was wearing a disguise.

"Who has the mask?" she demanded to know. Whoever it was wasn't admitting it, so she searched the women's purses, and made the men show her that they weren't concealing one. It turns out they were telling the truth. But *someone* was wearing one. Whoever it was could clearly be seen in the picture peering over the shoulder of one of the male nurses.

She posted the picture on the Internet, asking, "Can someone help me with this?" I wrote to her saying that, to me, it was pretty obvious what happened. Someone walked by as the picture was being taken and stopped to include themselves in the picture.

Within minutes she wrote back. "The doorway that figure is in doesn't lead to a hallway," she wrote, "but a small office. There's no way anyone could have snuck in behind us without us seeing them."

"That's weird," I thought, so I wrote her back asking if she would send me copies of the images so I could look at them. To make sure she'd do it, I told her that I'd be happy to reimburse her for the amount it cost to mail them to me. A few days later, a large manila envelope came in the mail from California; inside were copies of the pictures she had posted online. She included a note saying that I was the only person who responded to her request.

One of the first things I noticed was that in most of the pictures, everyone posed in front of the clock on the wall in the small office area. I could see the clock in the photos that the LPN had taken. The entire time between the first photo and the last one was around 11 minutes, so the pictures were taken one after another.

I took the images to a local photography store and had the photo with the masked faced enlarged so I could see it better. I also asked that the image be reversed, so it would be the equivalent of a "negative." Examining the enlarged versions, I could see the skin folds under the eyes. I ruled out the possibility of it being a mannequin's head. I was stunned to see that there was no sclera (white) in the eyes. I could see the pupils of its eyes, but the areas surrounding the pupils were dark.

The mask itself reminded me of the monster in the movie, "The Creature from the Black Lagoon." It was clearly a mask, but had a reptilian look to it. The nurse he was standing behind was dressed in a vampire costume and had his right arm extended, holding up his cape. All that could be seen was the mask and part of his neck.

Since I have family out in the Los Angeles area, I decided to pay them a visit, with the idea of killing two birds with one stone. I contacted Phyllis, told her of my plan and asked if I could come by while I was out there. I told her that I wanted to talk to her, and her staff. She agreed, as long as I was discreet about it. I assured her I would be and booked a flight to Los Angeles.

When I arrived at the hospital, Phyllis told me that she was told by her supervisor that she was driving everyone crazy, talking about what happened that night and taking pictures hoping to capture whatever it was on that pic again. She was told to stop or risk losing her job. Unfortunately, because of this, no one on her staff was too keen about talking to me, except for one—Tony. He was wearing the vampire outfit with a gold costume jewelry necklace that had a red "crystal" in the middle.

"Do you think what showed up in the picture had anything to do with the necklace I was wearing?" he asked me. "After all, it was standing next to me."

I asked him about it. He told me he borrowed it from a friend of his who was an antiques dealer. The merchant purchased the necklace from an estate sale during the early 1960s, and believed it was from the 1940s.

I had heard of objects being haunted before, but hadn't investigated one, so I was intrigued. "It's possible," I told him, "but I won't know until I do an investigation of it. Do you think she'd sell it to me?"

"I'll ask her," he said, and called her on the phone. "She said she'll sell it to you. If it's haunted, she doesn't want it anyway." Tony and I laughed.

I asked him if she said how much she wanted.

$100.

Deal.

On my way back home, my flight was delayed so I wanted to ask someone at the gate how long the wait would be. I had the trinket with me in my backpack. There was someone in front of me, and the woman behind the counter was all smiles, and extremely helpful. After she was done helping that passenger, and he walked away, I walked up to the counter. She looked up at me and scowled. Without a word, she walked away.

There was another line next to me, but I didn't want to go to the back of *that* line, and have to wait all over again. I might as well have because apparently the woman who walked away was on a break. She didn't return for about 15 minutes. Instead of asking me, "How may I help you?" she looked at me and said, "What do *you* want?"

I chalked it up my newly acquired piece of jewelry, whatever energy it might be holding. I hoped for the best when I finally did get on the plane.

THE THIRD BRIDGE

Back in Denver, Melissa, a member of my ghost hunting team, asked me to check out "The Third Bridge" with her. It was supposedly the site where Indians massacred several settlers living in the area. I wasn't really interested, but when she told me that no one else she knew had the guts to go there, I agreed.

A full moon lit the sky, making it easier to see, but every time the clouds would overshadow the moon, the region around us became pitch black. As soon as I got out of the car, I felt a deep chill that had nothing to do with the air, so I took a picture. The moon was behind the clouds. In the flash, I could clearly see that there was nothing in front of me. In the LCD I saw what appeared to be a woman carrying a baby on her hip. The baby looked like it had a green Mohawk.

A few more occurrences happened that night. I heard the sound of footsteps walking towards me, from behind, crunching the gravel of the bridge I was standing on. I thought it was Melissa, but when I turned around, no one was there.

A little later, I heard a female behind me, asking me what I was looking at. Thinking it was Melissa, I turned around. There was no one there. Melissa was sitting in my car, a good quarter of a mile away. I walked down to the car and told her what just happened. She said that she heard someone too, but it was a male voice. She thought it was me talking to her and replied, "I'm looking at the pictures I just took," before looking up and seeing I wasn't standing in front of her.

Despite all of that, it didn't take long before I became bored, losing complete interest in why we were there. I did think the night sky was so beautiful that I decided to take a few pictures of the full moon and the clouds that surrounded it. I also shot a couple of images in "negative" mode.

Before I went home that night I bought a meal at a hamburger place and was looking at the pictures on the camera's LCD, deleting most of them. I did keep pictures of the moon I thought were "artistic." I noticed on a couple of images what appeared to be a dot I couldn't explain next to the moon. I was curious as to what the speck was, so I kept them to view later on my computer. When I did I was stunned to clearly see the angry face of a Native American with a Mohawk, looking toward his left. I could even see pock marks in his face.

The next image, which I shot as a "negative," showed the terrified face of an older Caucasian male, looking towards his right. I went outside and took more pictures of the moon that night, but I was never able to replicate those images.

It made me wonder if the pendant was somehow able to, psychokinetically, imprint images simply thought about into digital pictures. It would explain the picture of the "man" in the mask that appeared on Halloween.

—⚡—

A few nights later, I was meeting with members of the team I founded, "The Rocky Mountain Ghost Hunters Alliance," for dinner. We were going to investigate a school that was supposedly haunted later that night. I showed them the images I had captured earlier, and shared my theory regarding the pendant.

"Have any of you seen the haunted painting on eBay?" Melissa asked.

"There's a haunted picture on eBay?" I asked, stunned. I'd been on eBay many times buying collectible coins, but this was the first time I had ever heard of anything "haunted" being auctioned. I couldn't believe it. To me this changed the game... after all, what is a haunted house, other than a huge haunted, *object?*

"Instead of me going to where hauntings were supposedly happening, I could bring them to me!" I thought to myself.

The next day I went onto eBay, put the word "haunted" into the search and sure enough, there were hundreds of listings. I decided to refine my search, so I typed in,

- Haunted antiques
- Haunted clocks
- Haunted paintings
- Haunted mirrors
- Haunted dolls

I wondered if there was any truth in any of the seller's claims, so I placed bids on a number of items. That's how I ended up on eBay, and ultimately owning "Haunted Harold—eBay's Most Infamous Haunted Doll."

THE LISTING

When Greg relocated to New York City in 2001, he moved in with his older brother on the Upper East Side. Since he didn't have a full-time job, Greg and his brother agreed that he would help sell antiques on eBay. His brother collected anything and everything, searching local thrift stores for treasures that included Art Deco nudes, antique ivory dice, old textiles, and dolls. Lots of dolls.

Greg's brother was a highly rated seller on eBay, which, in Greg's opinion had become a place to sell weird things. In his opinion, the auction site was oversaturated with items that sellers described as "exceptional." In his eyes it was simply a case of people cleaning out their closets, attics, garages, etc. and realizing they could sell those items on eBay. There were also a number of sellers on eBay who closed their brick and mortar stores to sell their inventory on the web. Why pay rent for a store when you can pay a fraction of the cost for a storage space OR work out of your own house?

Greg also understood that the best way to sell items consisted of using keywords, nice photos, clever descriptions… and a good story. He wanted to sell a beat up composition doll on eBay. In an antique store, he thought this doll might sell for around $9.99. He thought that by putting it on eBay, along with a whopper of a story, however, he might be able to get $40-60. So he came up with the tale of "Haunted Harold."

Anthony Quinata

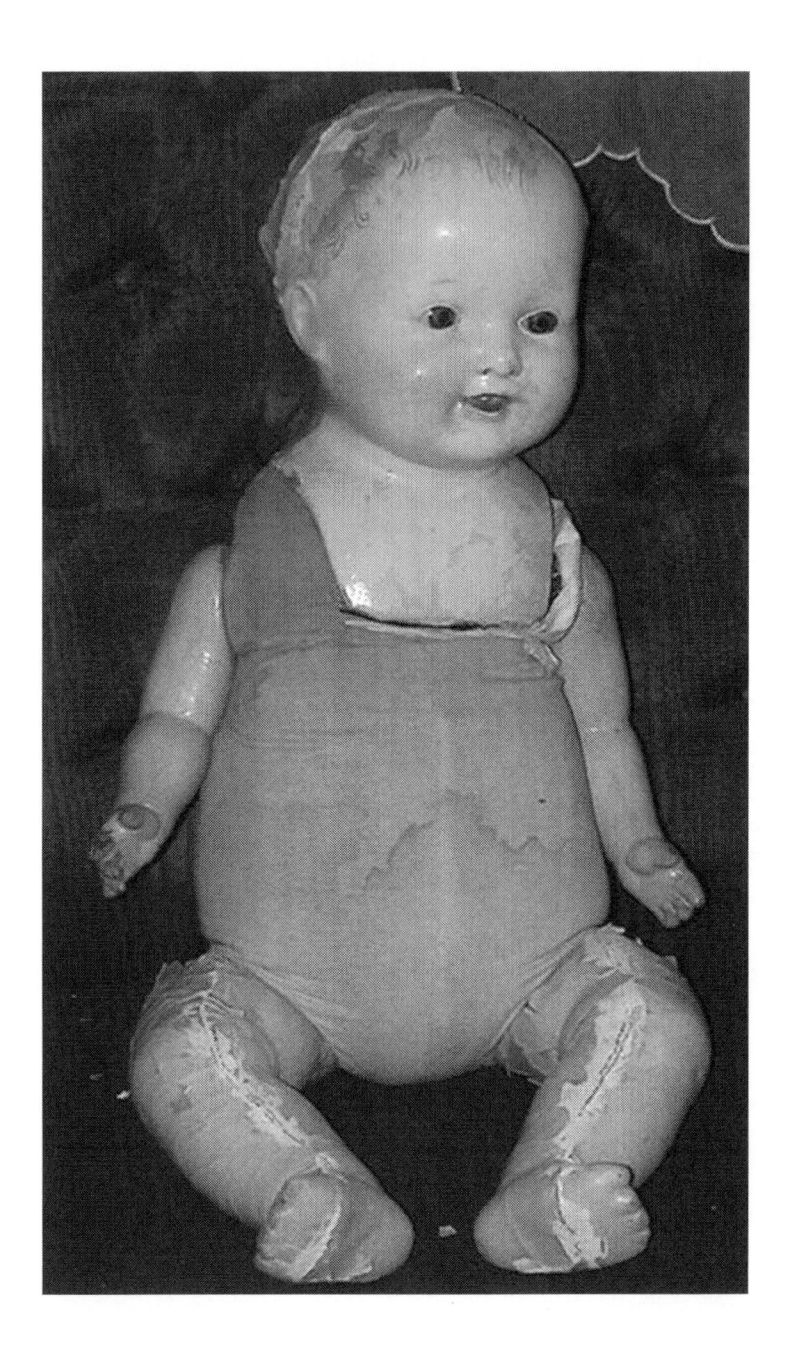

I'm sure it's happened to us all at least once or twice. You are walking around the flea market or antique mall looking for a treasure or two, and you come upon a beat up looking doll. You think to yourself, "oh that's charming", or "the child who owned that doll must have really loved this thing"... but what I thought after seeing the doll that is offered today, should never, ever, be repeated...

This doll was purchased in a small, dirt lot flea market in the quaint town of Webster, Florida. Webster is a very charming, industrious town about 60 miles south west of Gainesville. They have a weekly flea market offering treasures, bargains, and aisles of kernel corn...anyways I digress... I had arrived at the flea market fairly late in the day, when most people were packing up to go home. That is when I saw an elderly man placing the doll in a box. It looked interesting, so I asked the man if I could see it... the conversation went something like this...

Man: you don't want to see this doll

Me: sure I do, what do you want for it?

Man: well, that's a good question, because it's very old... (the man looked like he was going to begin to cry) ... it was my son's, I bought it for him when he was born, and he passed away a few years after...this doll has sat in my work shed for over 60 years. I wasn't going to bring it out today, but I figured I just needed to get it out of there... anyways, I want 20 bucks for it.

I gave the guy 20 bucks, put it in a bag, and walked away. When I was half way down the aisle, the man came running over, visibly out of breath....

Man: I have to warn you about something, I can't just let you take him like this... the reason it has been in my shed, is that the doll brought an eerie presence into our house after our son died... we would hear crying and singing from his bedroom...when we went to check it out, there was nothing, just the doll. Other things started to happen, and the priest told me I should burn the doll, I tried and tried, but it would barely burn, that's why his arms and head and legs are so worn. Anyways I just wanted to let you know...

I told him ok, and chuckled to myself as I walked away... that was until I got home, and my life has never been the same... Two days later my cat died, my (girlfriend) left me for the pool guy, I began to have chronic migraines, and this is only 2 days after purchasing the doll!

A week later, I began to hear children laughing and crying in my basement...Every time I would go to check it out, of course, nothing... This doll has been in an armadillo *coffin in my basement for the last year and half, and I need to get rid of it... I really do believe it's cursed, sometimes I touch it, and it seems like it has a pulse, maybe I'm just paranoid, maybe not...*

The cursed doll measures 21"tall. His / her / its head, arms, and legs are all composition. The eyes are closed when it's lying down. Please ask any and all questions before you bid on this doll. I have not had it out of the coffin for years, so if anything else happens this week I will be sure to let you know. This auction is sold as is! WITH NO RETURNS! PLEASE! Winner pays exact shipping and optional insurance.

Check out my other auctions for more vintage collectibles and other fine antiques. Ask all questions before you bid. Even if you think you are sure about condition, pictures, etc., please ask all SPECIFIC questions, BEFORE BIDDING. Thanks for looking and Good Luck!

—⚉—

Greg posted a video showing the doll moving and talking, saying the word, "here," or "Harold." It became a phenomenon, with over 100, 000 views. It was talked about on Art Bell's Coast to Coast radio show. Paranormal websites were discussing this doll around the world.

When the auction ended, the winning bid was $700, but the winning bidder never made good on the deal. So Greg put the doll up for auction a second time.

It's been over 2 weeks and I am still receiving emails daily about this cursed doll.

My life, needless to say, has been fairly hectic. I made an emergency trip to Florida after becoming violently ill after the auction ended. High fever, stomach pains, painful coughs, etc... I was interviewed by the Long Island Press. (Some people are actually taking this story serious, amiss all the skeptics).

I have also been doing research on ghosts, hauntings, cursed antiques, and other paranormal activity. Oddly enough there have been more supposedly "haunted" dolls on eBay...some convincing, and some completely absurd!

When in Florida this past week, I was able to make it to the Webster flea market to see if I could find any more information about the doll or the original owner.

I wasn't able to find the gentleman who sold me the doll, but I did find someone who had said he knew the man, and was a longtime friend of the family. (He was also sure to tell me that the man, had passed away some years before...?)

The man, his name was Walter, told me that gentleman whose name was Harry, did in fact have a son that had passed away only after a year or two of being born. He also told me that the son was severely disfigured. Walter wouldn't go much further than that, as he began to tremble and sweat profusely.

The winner of the original auction has an unrecognizable email, and the phone number I got through eBay is not a working number. I am guessing the winner was either too scared, or maybe even cursed by the doll. Either way they received negative feedback, since this doll has been tormenting me for too long. (If anyone thinks I am making this up can email me for more details.)

Before the last auction ended, I had set up my video camera in the middle of the night. I put the camera on a bench and used the built in "night vision" feature as my only light. I wasn't able to add the video footage that I took of the doll originally, since the auction had less than 12 hours left.

I want to thank everyone who has contacted me and offered me advice about the doll. I would really like to get this doll to someone who could research it, or contain it. It needs to be either locked away in a controlled environment, or destroyed. (Although so far, that seems to be impossible).

Again, the cursed doll measures 21" tall. His/her/its head, arms, and legs are all composition. The eyes are closed when it's lying down.

Please ask any and all questions before you bid on this doll. As you can see I am a very serious eBay power-seller, I sell high-end antiques and collectibles. This doll has affected my business tremendously, it has made me severely depressed and I haven't been physically able to list anything in the past two weeks because of my sickness, and how weak I have been. This auction is sold as is! WITH NO RETURNS! PLEASE!

Winner pays exact shipping and optional insurance. Check out my other auctions for more vintage collectibles and other fine antiques. Ask all questions before you bid. Even if you think you are sure about condition, pictures, etc., please ask all SPECIFIC questions, BEFORE BIDDING. Thanks and God bless!

The past few days have been pretty quiet actually. I know a lot of people have been checking in to see if any "strange" or "weird" things have been happening. It's not like the doll is running around and trying to kill me, you would just have to live with this thing, to really "get it". In case you are wondering, this is the doll that was discussed on 'Coast to Coast AM', with George Noory. I was not able to hear the show, but this is the doll.

I thought about bringing the doll to the local church, but I am scared to touch the doll or bring it into the presence of the most holy. I have thought about getting an iron ore safe to transport the baby doll I have named "Haunted Harold." A lot of people have been asking about the armadillo coffin that I had Harold in. After he leaves, I will be offering the coffin on eBay, so please keep looking. I warned people last time, but again, please do not look directly into the doll's eyes. Some have said, eyes are the window of the soul…well, some souls are very, very black indeed…

God Bless.

—⁂—

I am not sure how true this is, but someone emailed this to me. I guess when the first auction was up, the FBI (?) performed an X-Ray of the doll. Truth be told, I guess they found that a human baby was inside the doll!

Also, after awaking this morning to strange sounds outside of the window, I received a very disturbing email from an eBay user.

It looks like not only did I have the unfortunate luck of purchasing a haunted doll. I guess it has turned me into an "evil doer". In so much, that after the doll leaves my possession, I guess I am going to still have some very bad luck. Here is the email in its entirety: (the text of the email is in red)

"You will receive due punishment from the gods. I'll be there to judge you at cremation day. You are an evil doer. I can see it in your writing. Last night I talked to the lord of the lords. When you go to bed (your couch) look around you, look to the ceiling and you'll see what somebody is about to put on you. Something will come from a light bulb and will wrap around you. I see green and red. That might be the color of the thing coming to wrap you. Turn off the light, avoid looking at the guitar, and do not close your eyes or things will get very very bad for you. Sleep with a cross near you or you will not see daylight anymore.

Soon will start the dance of the spirits and you are the main sacrifice host. I know all about you because I feel you. I'm not a pizza girl, I'm the spirit of my god, the lord of the lords. I can read your words before you say them and I can see a dialogue between you and the lord of the lords about to happen soon. About to happen in your own bedroom right after you ship that doll Greg. I recommend you to keep it and bury it 5 feet underground or your evil ad talk will turn against you.

I see the following:

Lord:You have been evil and naughty Greg!

Greg: Please, please lord of the lords, please don't kill me... Please don't kill me lord (begging). I'm scared. Lord. I'm scared, please. (sick crying)

Lord: Silence picador (sic)!

Greg:Well, you better pull the trigger, because I don't give a f-! (now singing) I'm reeeeadyyy, ready for the big ride baaaaabyyyyy!!!

Lord: Silence picador (sic)!

Flesh burning..."

Any suggestions or comments about the eBay user's "vision" would be greatly appreciated.

People have been asking me why I canceled the bids and re-listed the auction:

THIS IS SIMPLE... this morning after getting that very weird email, I decided to post it, without realizing the F- word was in it. In fear of eBay canceling the auction, I had to re-list the auction so I could take the word out. The auction is exactly the same. It even ends the same day as the original auction. The first bidder, did not pay me, or even contact me. Obviously by canceling the bids, it gives people a chance to bid again. So... good luck, and keep the questions and suggestions coming.

OK... this is bizarre, (if everything else hasn't been weird enough) ... Someone pointed this to me earlier this afternoon, but hadn't been able to post about it now. Here is basically what someone emailed me...

"Hi, I have been watching your auction. Am I seeing things? In one of the pictures the baby's eye is white clouded and I see a face in it. Do you see it?"

I didn't see it, then... OMG!!! So... I zoomed into the photo, and here is what I saw... All I can say is wow, any ideas?

Well I think now that it's pretty obvious that the FBI X-raying the baby article is a fake. Whoever made the gif, has added their own little hidden message.

Thanks for all of the advice and suggestions. Someone recently emailed me saying that their daughter has seen the doll wink and laugh at her. Anyone with kids see anything like this? I know that they are supposed to be more in touch with the spirit world.

Wow. Well this whirlwind of an auction is finally coming to a close (well hopefully)! It looks like the curse of "Haunted Harold" has surpassed even the wildest of bizarre occurrences or dreams (but that is another story completely) I have been getting some very interesting emails from many people who are psychics, and have claimed to have studied the supernatural and occult phenomenon for a good part of their life. A few people have said they definitely feel a spirit attached to this doll. They say it's a "male" spirit and it is very angry. They have instructed me to bury the doll, or try to destroy the doll.

I still would rather get this doll into the hands of someone who can control it, or study it. I have had it for too long, and just want it out of my possession. At the same time, I feel that this doll is special, and needs to go to the right person. That is why the criticism about the price doesn't bother me. Who is to say the price of a tormented spirit? $100? $500? How much to finally put the soul to rest? If the right person is out there, they will pay almost any price, since their good deeds will come back to them many fold.

(YEP, ANOTHER UPDATE TO MAKE MY AUCTION EVEN MORE UNBELIEVABLE) Tell that to the people that swear they see the doll's eyes moving!

This time his auction was won by Kathy, a family friend, who made good on her winning bid.

KATHY'S STORY

Kathy lived in Dublin at the time she won the auction, but planned to be in New York to attend her aunt's upcoming wedding, and to go on a cruise to Bermuda with her fiancé, Rick. She met with Greg in Manhattan two weeks before the cruise to get the doll. Seeing it for the first time, she was surprised at how large it was. Greg handed the doll to her in a Duane Reade drugstore bag. Rick, her fiancé, wasn't happy about the whole thing. He let her know that he thought she had paid way too much on it. Kathy says that she didn't believe that the doll was cursed, but wanted to use it to learn how to do doll restoration. When Rick saw Harold he had to agree that it would be a doll that Kathy could learn a lot from.

Shortly after receiving the doll she began to experience some coincidences and "strange things" happening to her and her family. Kathy and Rick put the doll in the trunk of their rental car and left it there until her aunt asked if she could see the doll. The idea that it was supposedly haunted struck her as hysterical.

The next day her aunt called Kathy asking to be picked up at work. Her back had gone out and she couldn't walk. She was diagnosed with a herniated disc and put on bedrest until her wedding.

The very next day, the back of the groom-to-be went out. The chiropractor who diagnosed her aunt, made a diagnosis of a herniated disc with him as well.

Then, Kathy's back went out. The chiropractor probably wondered what was going on with this family, but no doubt enjoyed the income these strange coincidences brought him.

On the day of the wedding, the hairdresser for the bride and bridesmaids was a no show. The wedding cake fell apart and the groom made his vows in a wheelchair.

Kathy and her fiancé Rick had planned to go on their cruise with Kathy's aunt and her new husband a week after their wedding. Just days before they were supposed to go, Kathy received a phone call from her aunt. She and her new husband weren't going to be able to go on the cruise because they both developed bronchitis and strep throat. Kathy's aunt had also been stricken with shingles. According to Kathy, it never occurred to her that all of these things might have had anything to do with the doll.

Before she and Rick left on the voyage to Bermuda from New York it was suggested to her that it might be interesting to bring Harold with her as it's supposedly haunted and she was going into the notorious "Bermuda Triangle." She brought the doll with her in the same bag she received it in. They checked in and watched her three pieces of luggage go on board the ship. When they made it to their room, their luggage wasn't there. By noon that day, the crew were able to find two of the bags, which had Rick's clothes, but not his shoes. Kathy's luggage containing all of her clothes, and shoes (with the exception of the change of clothes she had in a carry on), were still missing. Her toiletries, toothbrush, clothes to change into, shoes (she boarded the ship wearing sandals that were uncomfortable to wear for long periods of time), bathing suit, formal wear, her camera, were nowhere to be found. Despite what the crew said was an "extensive" search for her luggage, they were unable to find it. She spent the entire cruise wearing two outfits. Sadly, she missed the formal events she was looking forward to attending on board the ship.

Ten minutes before they were getting off the ship when it returned to New York, Kathy was called by the Purser's desk. Her luggage was finally located. It was dropped off by a man who shared a small room with three friends and said the bag was in their room throughout the entire cruise. Rick was understandably upset, as was Kathy but, again, it never occurred to either of them that it might have had anything to do with the doll Kathy had with her.

When Kathy and Rick returned to Kathy's aunt's house with the doll in tow, her aunt had been pain free without any back issues for two weeks. Suddenly, her back went out again, causing her to end up having to go to the emergency room.

That night, Kathy decided that when the post office opened the next morning, she'd be there waiting. After the fiasco on the cruise, and her aunt ending up in agony shortly after seeing Harold again, she wasn't taking it back to Dublin on a plane. She was shipping him home. She wasn't going to chance luggage going missing again, or worse still, the plane going down in mid-flight. She began to wonder if there really was something to stories Greg told about the doll.

A year later, at Rick's insistence, she put Harold back up for auction, hoping that whomever did win it this time, would know what to do with it.

EBAY'S MOST INFAMOUS HAUNTED DOLL IS BACK

After the winning bidder failed to pay for her first auction, she had a second one for Harold. That's when I came across it. I knew nothing about the doll or its stories. What caught my eye was the listing's title described it as "eBay's Most Infamous Haunted Doll."

I didn't see her original listing, but a reposting of Greg's listing, and the two videos that Greg had up. It was obvious to me from the "stutter" in the video that what was supposed to be the doll's lips moving was really nothing more than a camera trick.

The second video was of the doll's right arm moving up. My first thought was "fishing line." I found out years later, that is supposedly what did make the doll's arm move.

Watching the videos made me laugh. What did catch my attention though was the auction's reserve.

A "reserve" is the least amount that the seller will accept. For me, "reserves" were like a gap in a fence with a sign over it saying, "Don't look through this hole." I just had to find out what the amount that she had to have for the doll was. I put in a bid of $300 thinking it would easily get the auction officially started and I was right. I was *shocked* to see I had an active bid of $295... for a doll I didn't even want! Based on the number of views from Greg's auction, and hers, which totaled over 500,000 at that point, I was hoping that *someone* would outbid me.

Almost immediately I received an email from Kathy asking why I wanted the doll. I wrote back telling her the truth... I really didn't want it. I was simply curious about how much the reserve was.

She sent me another e-mail —
I don't believe that this doll is haunted. I do believe it's cursed.

Well, I have to admit... that was an attention getter! She told me that she'd had the doll for a year before putting it up for auction. She described what happened at her aunt's wedding, and what happened on the cruise. What she wrote next though....

My fiancé and I knew a couple, John and Veronica, from work. We became friends. John and Veronica liked to travel, and they were going to Amsterdam. The night before they were to leave, they came to our home for dinner. I had just gotten the doll and since Veronica was a collector of antiques, she asked if she could see it. I showed it to her. She made a comment about the bad shape the doll was in, and laughed.

A few days later, John called us from Amsterdam. He told us that Veronica had died. She went out on the balcony to have a cigarette and fell down the stairs, hitting her head on the steps. She fractured her skull, had brain injuries, and died as a result. I couldn't believe it... Just three days before, John and Veronica were at our house eating dinner, and laughing.

After Veronica's death, John decided to move back to South Africa. They had a boarder named Stephen who was staying with them, but suddenly was without a home. We offered him the extra room we had at our house.

I used to keep the doll in a shed in our backyard. The night I showed it to Veronica, I put Harold in the closet of the extra room and forgot about it. That was the same room we would later offer to Stephen.

Stephen was originally from Wales and before he came to live with us, he went back there. While he was there, he had a physical and came back with a clean bill of health.

Three months after moving into the room in our home he began to have difficulty swallowing. Then he started losing his voice. He went back to Wales to see what was wrong. He was diagnosed with Stage 4 cancer of the larynx, and was given only a short time to live.

We continued to email each other, and I learned that even though Kathy was childhood friends with Greg's older brother, at the time she was bidding on the auction she lived in Dublin. After winning Greg's auction, she told Greg to hold onto it, instead of having Harold sent to her in Dublin. She had plans to go back to the Connecticut for two weeks to attend her aunt's wedding. While she was there, she'd go to Manhattan and pick up the doll.

STRANGE MAJIK

"Great stories," I thought, "but as soon as someone outbids me, I'm out." As sincere as Kathy sounded, I just couldn't get over Greg's listings and how preposterous they were.

Thank God, someone did outbid me—by $5. His eBay handle was "Strange Majik." Majik sent an email to me telling me not to bother bidding because the doll was his, and that he'd just continue to outbid me.

"It might end up being yours," I thought to myself, my testosterone levels quickly rising, "but it's going to cost you." I decided to run the auction up on him, continually bidding up the price before dumping it on him. With that thought in mind I put in another bid of $325. Once again, I was the high bidder. I hoped that this guy meant what he said, and that he'd outbid me again. He did.

I outbid him again. When he'd put in a higher bid than mine, I repeated the process. I knew that this was driving him crazy, and I was having a good time doing it. Kathy wrote me to say he was complaining about me upping the ante on him. He wanted her to pull the auction and sell the doll to him for $400. Kathy refused. When she told me this, I couldn't help but laugh.

Kathy and I continued emailing each other regularly. She wanted to hear about my experiences as a paranormal investigator. I wanted to hear more about her experiences with Harold.

Majik continued bidding. Every time he did, I'd have fun offering more money than him. No one else was making a move on the doll, just Majik and I. I was sure everyone else watching the auction was wondering who these two idiots were and why they were bidding so much on this ugly doll!

The day finally came when the auction was scheduled to end. I had a $680 bid on the doll. With four minutes to go, Majik put in a bid of $700. I put in a "proxy bid," authorizing eBay to bid for me up to a certain amount.

My new bid was $720. I waited for Majik to outbid me... and I waited. I watched the clock quickly count down the end of the auction, and waited some more. "He's going to try to snipe the auction by putting in a last minute bid for the doll," I reassured myself.

The auction ended and eBay announced, **"Congratulations! You Won!"**

"What?" I screamed out loud. "That's not what was supposed to happen! Majik was supposed to outbid me!"

Almost immediately I received an email from Kathy that said that if I still didn't want the doll (I didn't) I didn't have to pay for it.

"A deal is a deal," I wrote back. "I'll send you the money, and you can send me Harold."

"I'll tell you what," she wrote back. "I'll hold him for two weeks to let you decide if you really want to have it. If you don't, I'll send your money back to you. If you do still want it, I'll donate half of the money to a local children's hospital." She said she would donate the other half to another charity, but I don't remember what that charity was anymore.

Three weeks after the auction ended, Kathy wrote to tell me that she still hadn't sent the doll to me. "I've boxed him up and it's ready to be sent to you," she wrote to me in an email, "but I wanted to give you more time to change your mind."

"I haven't changed my mind," I wrote back to her. "Like I said, a deal is a deal. Go ahead and send it."

The next email I received from her told me that she took the box to the postal service near her home. Kathy watched to make sure that the man behind the counter took it and put it in a bin before she turned to leave. Ten minutes later, as she was driving home, she heard on the radio that the postal workers had gone on a strike. She was convinced Harold was responsible. "I should have thrown the damned thing in the ocean and given your money back to you."

A couple of weeks later, Kathy wrote me to tell me that the strike was over, and that I should be receiving Harold soon. She also said that she was worried for me.

"I HAVE A MONSTER FOR YOU."

I was actively bidding on, and winning, a number of things on eBay. After winning Harold, I turned my attention to mirrors that were supposedly haunted. I even bought one that had a newspaper article pasted on the back announcing President Lincoln's assassination. I was getting so many packages, for a while every other day was like Christmas.

One morning, I was standing on my porch when Gary, my postman, pulled up in his postal station wagon and said, "I have a monster for you, today." I assumed it was something I won… and it must be *huge*.

I decided to walk to his car in case he needed help carrying whatever it was he was talking about. Instead of a large package, he handed me a box around two feet high. I looked at the return address. It was from Dublin, Ireland. Harold, "eBay's most infamous haunted doll," had finally arrived. And after what Gary had just said, I wasn't sure how I felt about it.

I put the box on my dining table and just looked at it for several minutes. I didn't know if the stories Kathy told me about the doll were true, and I wasn't sure anymore that I wanted to find out.

Before opening the box, I re-read copies of the emails she sent to me. Taking a deep breath, I cut the box open. The doll was in a Duane Reade drug store bag; the same one Greg gave Kathy the doll in. I looked at it but didn't take it out. I didn't want to touch it.

I decided to use my Tri-Field EMF meter, which measures manmade, alternating, magnetic currents, to see if I could detect any anomalous electromagnetic fields coming from the doll. The theory is that these sorts of readings could indicate the presence of a ghost.

The meter's needle didn't budge. It didn't even quiver.

I did the same thing with my Natural EM meter, which measures natural, direct currents. Once again… nothing.

I sighed and thought, "It looks like I spent a whole lot of money on what is basically a very ugly doll, and nothing more. Kathy's stories about it will still make a great chapter in my book."

I decided to take the doll out of its bag, put it on my couch and take pictures of him. Before touching it though, I sprinkled it with holy water. "No sense in taking any chances," I thought to myself. Nothing showed up in the digital pictures either.

HAROLD SPEAKS!

Even though I didn't get anything on the meters, or on any of the digital images, I had other ideas in mind. I wanted to see what I could capture as far as EVPs go. EVP stands for, "Electronic Voice Phenomena," a mysterious event in which human-sounding voices from an unknown source are heard in white noise, digital voice recordings, and other electronic media. Most often, EVPs have been captured on audiotape.

The voices are not heard at the time they're recorded; it is only when the recording is played back that the voices are heard. Sometimes amplification and noise filtering is required to hear the voices.

Some EVPs are more easily heard and understood than others. And they vary in gender, age, tone, and emotion. They usually speak in single-words, phrases and short sentences. EVPs have been recorded speaking in various languages. Sometimes they are just grunts, groans, growling and other noises.

The quality of EVPs also varies. Some are hard to understand and are open to interpretation as to what they are saying. Some EVPs, however, are quite clear and easily understood. They often have an electronic or mechanical quality to it; but can also be natural sounding.

The quality of an EVP is categorized by researchers as:

Class A: Easily understood by almost anyone with little or no dispute. These are also usually the loudest EVPs.

Class B: Usually characterized by warping of the voice in certain syllables. Lower in volume or more distant sounding than Class A. Class B is the most common type of EVP.

Class C: Characterized by excessive distortion. They are the lowest in volume (often whispering) and are the hardest to understand.

The most fascinating aspect of EVP is that the voices sometimes respond directly to the person making the recording. The researcher will ask a question, for example, and the voice will answer or comment. Again, this response is not heard until later when the tape is played back.

Where do the voices come from? That, of course, is the mystery. No one knows. Some theories are:

They are voices of people who have died. This is why many researchers go to cemeteries seeking EVPs (and often with great success). In this context, the phenomenon is sometimes called instrumental trans-communication or ITC.

They are from another dimension. It is theorized that there may be many dimensions of existence, and somehow beings from some other dimension are able to speak and communicate with ours through this method. A good question is, however: How do they know English and other languages of our dimension?

It's been suggested that somehow the researchers' thoughts are projected onto the recording. In other words, they come from the researchers own subconscious.

Some people believe that these voices are angelic or demonic in origin.

Skeptics assert that there is nothing to EVP recordings whatsoever—that the "voices" are either hoaxed, random noise interpreted as voices, real voices already on the tape, or picked up from radio, cell phones, and other such sources.

I did an EVP session, and once again, I didn't get anything suggesting that the doll was haunted.

I decided to put Harold back in the bag, I included the bottle of holy water, and a crucifix as well. "Better safe than sorry," I thought to myself. Kathy may or may not have had an overactive imagination, but I wasn't taking any chances until I find out one way or another.

Whatever supposedly "haunted" object I won in an eBay auction, I wanted to see what a psychic might have to say about it. Harold was no exception, and I knew who I wanted to be the first one to do a reading on him.

April was someone whom I had known for a few years. She wanted to go on investigations of reported hauntings with me, and claimed to be a psychic, but I didn't know whether I believed her or not. I decided that having her do a reading on Harold would be the perfect way to find out.

I called her and told her that I had some objects I wanted her to read. She agreed and we decided to meet in the basement of the Tattered Cover, an independent bookstore, in Cherry Creek, Colorado. I didn't tell her about Harold, or that I was planning on bringing him.

April has an ability known as "psychometry." In other words, she can discern information about an object simply by touching it. I couldn't wait to hear what she would say about Harold. Before she did, I asked her to give me her impressions of other objects I won on eBay. I wanted to see if what she said matched what the sellers wrote about them. I decided to save Harold for last.

As soon as I pulled Harold out of the Duane Reade bag April asked, "Is that Harold?"

My heart sank. "How do you know about Harold?" I asked.

"He's been all over the Internet," she said.

"Great," I thought. I was hoping she would do this not knowing anything about the doll, just as she had with all of the other objects I'd given her that day. I considered calling it off, but decided to see what, if anything, she got that wasn't on the Internet. I put Harold on the table we were sitting at. I also pulled out the holy water and crucifix I had in the bag with the doll.

As I sprinkled Harold with the water April chuckled. "You're using holy water on him?" she asked. I didn't answer her. April took Harold in her hands. "Wow, he's in really bad shape." She kept turning him over in her hands. "He's a composition doll. I think he was made sometime in the '30s. I'm getting something about the spirit in the doll being a child molester, a molested child, or both."

Shortly after she said that she started trembling, and crying. "I'm sorry Anthony, but I can't hold do this."

"Why not?" I asked her.

"He's just told me he's going to kill me!" she said.

In all the time I'd known her, April had always had a flair for the dramatic, so I didn't take what she said too seriously. Disappointed I didn't get much more, I took the doll back from her and put it back in the bag. A total of about a minute and forty-five seconds had passed, according to the timer on the digital recorder I was using, to record the session with April.

"I'm really sorry," April said, "but I have a heart murmur, and I heard Harold say, 'I'm going to kill you.' Then it started to feel as though he was grabbing my heart."

"It's okay. Thanks for trying," I said, barely able to hide my disappointment. This was the first time I had ever heard of April's heart condition. To be honest, I wasn't sure I believed she had one.

When I got back home I decided to listen to the recording of the readings April did. I didn't hear any EVPs until we got to Harold. As I listened to April chuckling about the holy water, I also heard a male voice angrily say, "Shut up!"

Then, while I sprinkled holy water I heard an agonizing scream that sent chills up and down my spine. But that was nothing compared to what I heard next.

When she mentioned that she felt that the spirit within the doll was either molested as a child, a child molester, or both, I heard what I can only describe as an angry roar. Then I heard a male voice shouting, "I'm going to kill you, bitch!"

It was immediately after that that I heard April saying, "I'm sorry Anthony, but I can't do this."

"What the hell is going on?" I wondered, as I nervously glanced at "eBay's most infamous haunted doll" in the Duane Reade bag.

CRYSTAL CLEAR PROTECTION

One of my favorite things to do at that time was to go to the Tattered Cover bookstore, and sit down in their coffee shop with a cup of coffee, a number of books. One of the baristas, Rachel, who was also a friend of mine, asked what I was up to. "I want to write a book about haunted objects I won on eBay."

I told her about some of the things I was going to write about, including Harold. She asked me to bring the doll by the next time I was in the store so that she could see it.

When I returned a few days later I told Rachel I had Harold with me. Rachel and I agreed to meet when she her shift was over.

We decided to go down into the basement of the store to look at the doll. It was the part of the store that they sold bargain books, and where authors did book readings and signings. There usually weren't a lot of other people down there, so Rachel and I would be pretty much by ourselves. At least, that's what I thought would happen.

We were joined by five of Rachel's other friends, four girls and a guy, who wanted to see the doll as well. I was surprised, but suggested that we sit around a long table.

After I was introduced to everyone I turned on my digital recorder hoping to capture an EVP or two. I took Harold out of his bag without saying a word. As soon as I put the doll on the table, every single one of them pulled out a crystal and put it in front of them. "I guess she did tell them about the doll," I thought to myself.

They began asking me questions. "How did you get the doll?"

"Why do you have it?"

"Has anything happened to you personally since you've owned it?"

I answered their questions, and told them the stories about the doll, including some that Kathy told me. "I thought Rachel already told you all of this," I said.

"No," one of the girls replied. "She didn't tell us anything. Only that you were going to show her an 'interesting' doll you had."

"Then why did all of you pull out crystals as soon as you saw the doll?"

"For protection," she said. Rachel and all of her friends nodded in agreement.

The guy who was with them spoke up. "For me it was its energy. It's awful… dark… scary. That's why I pulled mine out." I had no idea what to make of what any of them just told me.

When I got back home that afternoon I listened to the recording of the time I spent with them at the bookstore. I was a little aggravated because I could hear what sounded like cursing, but the voice was drowned out by a loud buzzing sound. I tried to clean the recording up as best as I could on my computer. What I heard was even more disturbing than what they told me that they felt coming from the doll. "Goddammit! Stop it!" and what sounded like painful growling.

"Stop what?" I wondered. And *what* was causing that buzzing noise? Whatever it was really seemed to be bothering the spirit in the doll. It bothered me too. I didn't bother to listen to the entire recording, because I could barely hear the conversation Rachel's friends and I had over the humming.

It didn't occur to me until later, much later, where the sound came from. It was the energy of the crystals protecting their owners.

The next time I was in the bookstore, I told Rachel what I heard on the recording. "Whoever the spirit is, I think it's trapped in there," she said.

"Trapped?" I asked. She nodded.

"Why do you think that? "I asked. I'd never heard of such a thing. "And how does something like that happen?"

"I don't know. Some kind of gypsy magic, I think. It's just a feeling I had when I saw it."

A spirit imprisoned inside the doll by some kind of magic? I didn't know why, but as soon as she said it, it made sense to me. I wanted to find out more. I didn't know of any gypsies in Denver, Colorado, however, I did have an idea where I might be able to find a couple.

"I CAN'T HELP YOU"

Having two sisters, and a brother, who live in Southern California, I like to visit there as often as I can. Another reason is Venice Beach. I love its carnival like atmosphere complete with street performers, artists, tattoo shops, a freak show, stores selling souvenir t-shirts, and psychics. I decided to bring Harold with me the next time I go there.

I wanted to talk to a mother and daughter duo who did palm and tarot card readings on the sidewalk from their condominium. I wasn't sure, but to me they looked like they were from Romania, the birthplace of gypsies. My sister Meridith, her daughter, Jennifer, and I went to the beach. I brought Harold along in his Duane Reade bag. Seeing the daughter giving a palm reading to someone, I decided to see if she could get anything from my doll.

I approached the young woman who had gotten her palm read after it was over. "How was it?" I asked. "Was she any good?"

"It was good," she said smiling. "She told me things that she couldn't have known. Things that happened in my past. She also told me things that are supposed to happen in the future, but I guess I'll have to wait and see about that," she laughed.

"I'm thinking of getting a reading from her," I said. "What do you think?"

"Go for it," she said. "I don't think you'll be disappointed."

I looked over the board that listed the type of readings she did, and the prices for each one. "Object reading," wasn't one of them. I decided to ask for one anyway. "Hi. Do you do psychometry readings?"

She looked at me puzzled. "What do you mean?" Her accent reminded me of the gypsies I saw in the "Wolfman" movies I used to watch when I was a child.

"Can you tell me about an object just by touching it?" I asked. "If you can, I'd like you to do a reading like that with the doll I have," lifting the bag I had Harold in.

She shrugged her shoulders. "I can try."

I opened the bag. She looked inside, took three steps back, and held up her hands in front of her. "I'm sorry. I can't help you," she said. "Please go away."

"What do you mean you can't help me?" I asked. "You can't read the doll? Or you don't want to touch it?"

She shook her head. "I can't help you. Now… please… go away!"

I wasn't giving up so easily. "You obviously got something when you looked at it." She nodded. "Can you at least tell me what it was when you saw it?"

She shook her head. "I'm sorry. I can't help you. Please go away. Leave… now… please."

I saw her mother come out of their condo out of the corner of my eye. I was relieved. Maybe *she* would do a reading. "Perhaps your mother can help me."

"I'll ask her," she said, turning and hurrying off. They weren't close enough for me to hear what they were saying, but whatever it was, her daughter kept looking back at me, wide eyed, and arms waving.

Finally, her mother looked at me angrily, saying, "We can't help you! Now go!"

"Can she at least tell me what she saw?" I shouted back.

"No! I said we cannot help you! Go away!" They both turned, walked back into their condo, and closed the sliding glass door behind them.

My sister, niece and I walked away. "Wow, that was weird," I finally said.

"She had an attitude," Jennifer said.

"What do you mean?" Meridith asked.

"Did you see the look on her face?" she replied.

"That wasn't an attitude you saw," Meridith said. "She was afraid."

My first thought was to dismiss it as *pedophobia*, the fear of dolls, but I made it clear I wanted her to read *a doll*, and she agreed to try. "Whatever it was that she picked up on," I said, "and whatever it was she told her mother, scared the living shit out of both of them."

THE WHALEY HOUSE

Whenever I visit my family in L.A., one of the other things on my "must see, must do" list is a trip to the Whaley House, in Old San Diego. Built in 1857, it was started with the construction of a granary that later became the courtroom. The two-story house and store addition was designed by a man named Thomas Whaley. It was the first two-story house in San Diego, and was built from bricks made in Whaley's own brickyard. "My new house, when completed, will be the handsomest, most comfortable and convenient place in town or within 150 miles of here," he would boast.

Today, it is referred to as "The Most Haunted House in America." It's also the house where I caught my first EVP of a woman crying, "Oh… no! Please God… I can't!" I was walking up the stairs when I recorded it. Only the docent, Michele (the woman I was dating at the time) and I were in the museum, and I knew it wasn't either of them. I had my digital recorder on for about 30 seconds and didn't realize I had captured anything for a couple of weeks after I returned back to Denver.

Several months later I was upstairs in the museum again when I felt the chill in my body that signals the presence of a conscious spirit to me. I took a couple of pictures with my digital camera. The first one didn't show anything. In the second one there was a full bodied apparition of Whaley himself. It looked as though he were standing right next to me, looking over the banister and down the stairwell. Once again, I didn't realize what I had until after I returned home to Denver.

I decided to take Harold with me to the museum. I was a little worried that I wouldn't be allowed to bring the bag he was in with me but I'd been there so often that the docent recognized me and suggested I buy an annual pass to save myself "a little money."

I put Harold behind the door of the master bedroom. I also set my digital recorder in the same area. Even though I was fairly certain the doll and recorder were safe there, I decided to remain on the second floor.

I saw someone standing in the hall looking out the window facing the backyard. My curiosity got the better of me and I asked him what he was looking at. He told me that it was his second time visiting the home.

The first time was when he was ten years old with his parents. While they were upstairs he looked outside the same window, and only back then, he saw a little girl playing in the garden below. As he watched her skipping, she looked up at him, smiled, waved... and vanished.

Now, twenty years later, he was back hoping to see the same little girl again.

Shortly after we said our goodbyes I met two young women who told me that they were from the U.K. They were vacationing in San Diego, had heard about the Whaley House, and decided to visit hoping to see a ghost or two for themselves. I told them about the guy I had just met and about the girl he saw. All in all, we talked for about 20 minutes.

When they left I went behind the door, and retrieved the doll and recorder. I turned the recorder on and listened to see if I captured any EVPS. I had. When I was talking to the girls. It was a male voice. I could faintly hear the young ladies and me talking in the background.

Much louder, was a male voice saying, "Go for it!"

"You can get some!"

"They're whores, I'm telling you! They'll fuck you!"

On, and on, it went... for the entire time the girls and I spoke.

As I listened to them leaving in the background I heard the voice groan, "I... am... so... disappointed... with... you!"

THE PEAS WERE GOOD

Back in Denver, I decided to have another try at getting a reading from a psychic who didn't know anything about the doll, so I took it to "Celebrations," a semiannual psychic fair. It's a huge event that attracts metaphysical vendors, healers, speakers, authors and, of course, readers.

I walked past the readers' booths looking at what each one had to say about themselves, and decided to go with three that I seemed to resonate with. Two of them were tarot card readers, and one billed herself as a clairvoyant. All three said, "No," to my request for a reading of the doll.

I decided to do my own reading on the doll, but since I knew so much about it already, I thought it made sense to do a tarot card reading. The problem was, I didn't know how. So my first step was to buy a couple of books and a card deck from a vendor there. I didn't know if it would work or not but I wanted to give it a try. After all, I reasoned to myself, if the doll does have a spirit trapped inside of it, it makes sense that the cards would work on it too. The woman at the "store" gave me a strange look when I told her my plan, but recommended a couple of books, and suggested that I use a Ryder Wait card deck.

I didn't get around to trying to do a reading until a few days later. Every time I had Harold with me for a period of time, it drained my energy and took me a few days to recover. When I did finally get around to attempting the reading, I sat Harold on my kitchen table and opened one of my books. I didn't bother to read it, but skimmed until I found what I was looking for. I decided to do a "Celtic card spread," because it seemed to offer the most complete information, and started "reading" the cards.

As I was going through what each card meant, in each position, I wasn't sure if the reading was for the doll, or for me! For example, one of the cards suggested that a book would be written. I just couldn't imagine the doll writing a book. I didn't know enough about the doll to begin to even think about writing a book myself. I couldn't figure out how anything the cards were supposedly saying was helping me to understand the spirit in the doll, either.

I was in the middle of all of this when my phone rang. "Saved by the bell," I thought to myself.

"Hi, Anthony! It's Angie." Angie was a mutual friend of April, the woman who did the psychometry reading on Harold, and I. "What are you doing?"

I didn't want to tell her what I was really up to, so I said, "Nothing important. What did you have in mind?"

"I was wondering if you were free to join me for lunch."

"I'd love to!" I told her. The card reading was confusing, and being around the doll was exhausting. Besides, Angie was a good looking woman.

"Great! I'll be by in half an hour." I looked up at the clock on the walk. It was 11 o'clock. 11:30 came and went and Angie hadn't shown up. I wasn't surprised. She lived her life on "Angie time." By 11:45, I suddenly felt in need of a nap. I got up from the table, went to my bedroom, laid down, and promptly fell asleep.

I woke up to a terrified scream. "Anthony!"

Groggily, I called out, "Angie?"

"Where are you?" she cried.

That's when I remembered we were getting together for lunch. I looked at the time. It was one o'clock. I ran out of my room and saw Angie standing flat against the wall next to the front door, pointing at the entrance to my kitchen. Her eyes were wide with fear.

"I'm so sorry, Angie. I was tired and laid down to take a nap...."

"Is that Harold?" she screeched.

Oh shit... I didn't put the doll away. I ran to the kitchen table, grabbed Harold, put it in the Duane Reade bag, and a closet off of the dining room.

When I came back out to the living room I saw Angie standing where she was before. She hadn't moved. She just stood there crying. I walked up to her and put my arms around her. I could feel her trembling. "Are you okay?" I asked.

"No! When I parked in your driveway," she sobbed, "I felt as though I was in some kind of danger. I didn't know why though. When I got out of my car, it felt even worse. I walked up to your door and knocked, but you didn't answer, so I just came in. I kept calling for you. I looked around and when I walked into the kitchen I saw the doll sitting on your table. It looked at me like it was grinning, and saying to me, 'The carrots were good. Do you have any peas?' I was so scared I turned around and tried to run out the front door but I swear something stopped me! It was like someone was standing in front of the door and wouldn't let me out! That's when I screamed for you."

I couldn't apologize enough. I couldn't explain what happened to her either. I found out that she heard about the doll from April. "Anthony, Harold won't hurt my kids will it?"

"Why would it hurt your kids?" I wondered out loud.

"I don't know," she said, "but I swear it felt as though it was more interested in my kids than me."

HAROLD GETS PHYSICAL

I still wanted to get a card reading done on the doll, but after attempting to do it on my own, I decided to try again to find someone who knew what they were doing. When I asked my friend Diane if she knew anyone who did card readings, she answered, "I'll do it."

Diane was an original member of my ghost hunting group, and was even responsible for arranging our very first investigation. "I didn't know you read cards," I said.

"Well, It's been a while, but I'd be happy to give it a try if you want me to," she told me. We agreed to meet the next day where she worked during her lunch hour.

When I arrived with the doll we went to a conference room for privacy. I brought my digital recorder with me, not only to record the session, but to hopefully catch an EVP. When I took the doll out of the bag, Diane made a comment about a molested child. "Why do you say that?" I asked. April had said the same thing. Personally, I thought the reason was because the doll was the size of a two-year-old, and pretty beat up looking.

"I don't know," Diane said, gazing intently at the doll. "It's just a feeling I get."

She laid out the cards in a Celtic spread, and did her "reading." Afterwards, I said to her, "You really didn't know what you were doing, did you?"

"Give me a break," she snapped back. "I told you it's been a while since I did it! Hey, I gave it a try at least."

"Oh well," I thought. "Maybe we got an EVP or two."

I turned the recorder on, and Diane and I listened to it together. When it got to the part where she talked about feeling as though the doll harbored a child that had been molested, we heard a loud, roaring, adult male voice saying, "Fuck you!"

"Whoa!" I said. I looked at Diane. Her eyes were as large as dinner plates. I replayed what we just heard.

As we listened to it again, I noticed Diane scratching her left hand between her thumb and forefinger. She looked down and said, "What the fuck?"

"What?" I asked, stopping the recording.

"Does this look like a bite to you?"

I immediately became suspicious. "I just watched you scratching your hand," I thought to myself. "Let me see," I told her.

She held her hand out. I couldn't believe what I was seeing. There were two red indentations between her thumb and forefinger. I ran my finger over them to make sure. Then I tried to make the same sort of dimples on my hand by scratching it the way I saw Diane doing hers. It wasn't happening.

"Do you have a ruler?" I asked. I wanted to measure the marks.

"No, not in here. Not that I know of."

I looked around and saw a fine tip Sharpie pen on a table next to a white board. I saw stir sticks for coffee on the table as well. I got up and grabbed a stick and the pen. I held the rod up to her hand, and marked the edges of the "bite" on it, and a line where the gap was in the middle.

I then held the markings up to the *painted on teeth* in the doll's mouth. They matched *exactly*.

We were both freaked out and decided to stop there. Neither of us wanted to be alone with the doll in the conference room any more. We walked back to her office, and found that two of her co-workers were there, having returned from lunch. Diane told them what happened.

"Diane, what happened to your eye?" one of the ladies asked.

"What do you mean?" Diane responded, puzzled.

"It looks like someone hit you!"

I asked Diane to look at me and sure enough, the area under her left eye was red, and swelling. It obviously wasn't a bug bite. It did look like she was punched.

I took the doll out of the bag, and held its hand up to her face. The size of the hand matched the bump on Diane's cheek perfectly. It looked as though the doll had hit her.

The look on the ladies' faces turned from skepticism to fear. They didn't want to talk about the doll anymore, and I could tell they were relieved when I said I was leaving and taking Harold with me.

THE OUIJA BOARD SESSION

In between my attempts to learn more about what was going with the doll, I kept it in a locked cabinet, which was in a locked storage room. I had other items I won on eBay such as a haunted violin, a painting, airplane parts from the Flight 401 crash in the Everglades, a relic reportedly from the New England area during the Salem Witch trials, and more dolls… a lot of dolls. But Harold had a space all to himself.

I also had things given to me by people who bought them at antique stores, flea markets, and such, and ended up thinking that they were creepy as well. I even had a Ouija board I personally bought from a yard sale. Walking into that space, the energy was so thick, it was like trying to walk through water.

After I won her auction, Kathy told me that she had been writing posts in an online group. It was a member of that group who first suggested that she bring the doll with her and Rick on their cruise to the Bahamas. She also told me that they were hoping I'd stay in touch with them to let them know what was going on with the doll once I had it. I agreed.

After the incident with Diane, I asked an admin with the group to send me all of the posts which Kathy wrote. They were fascinating to read… starting before she even won the auction. She explained that she didn't really think that the doll was haunted, but wanted to learn how to restore dolls, and was told that Harold would be perfect to learn on. Her posts started from there, and talked about her experiences with the doll. She wrote about how everyone who was in her aunt's wedding party who saw the doll and laughed at it, ending up needing a chiropractor afterwards. She also wrote about her cruise ship experience, and Veronica's passing.

She wrote about feeling exhausted and suddenly needing to take a nap one day. When she woke, she found a poisonous spider crawling up her blouse. She screamed, brushed it off and killed it. She called her fiancé Rick, who told her he was coming home. He asked her to repeat what happened and what time it happened. He then showed her the back of his shirt. There was a stain on it. A friend of his saw that same type of poisonous spider on his back at the same time one was crawling up Kathy.

A year later after she talked about Stephen becoming sick. She said she was putting the doll up for auction, hoping that someone who knew what they were doing would buy it. She also said that she still didn't believe the doll was haunted, but cursed.

Her last post talked about me a little, and how she was worried for me.

Reading her posts increased my curiosity and desire to find out what was going on. That's when I decided to try using the Ouija board I had. I didn't want to do it alone, not because I was afraid of the board, being possessed, or anything like that. I wanted a witness to whatever, if anything, did happen.

I asked April but she wanted nothing more to do with the doll, even though she would call me occasionally to say that "H boy," as she called him (the "H" didn't stand for "Harold"), would come to her, especially in the middle of the night, to harass her. Her fiancé, Wyatt, had another idea. Rather than using a Ouija board, he thought I should take it on a cruise, just like Kathy did, and toss it into the ocean.

I asked Diane, but she had had enough of the doll during the 30 minutes she spent with it to last her a lifetime she told me. I asked other members of my ghost hunting team, who declined as well. Except for one, Heather, the newest member of my group. "I'd love to," she told me.

I didn't have a whole lot experience with a Ouija board, and neither did Heather. Because I had done an investigation alone with her once before, I wasn't worried about her making any crazy accusations afterwards.

We didn't do any "protection rituals" or say any prayers to safeguard ourselves. We didn't turn the lights off or light any candles either. We simply sat down, with Harold in between us, to her right, and to my left. I turned on my digital recorder, we put our fingers on the planchette, asked questions, and I hoped for the best.

Is there anyone here?"
Y-E-S
"Are you the one trapped in the doll?"
Y-E-S
"Is your name Harold?"
N-O
"What is your name?"
A – H – M – E – D.

"Ahmed?" I asked out loud. I looked at Heather. She only nodded. From that point on, the board didn't "answer" any more of our questions.

"Let's see if we got any EVPs," I suggested. We didn't hear anything other than ourselves until I asked for a name. A clear, strong, male voice came through, not saying "Ahmed," but "Adam." It was almost as though it was correcting what the board spelled out.

We looked at each other stunned. Heather was the first to speak. "I have to be honest with you, Anthony. I really don't think there's any spirit attached to the doll."

"Why?" I asked.

She shrugged her shoulders. "I just don't feel anything coming from it."

We sat there in silence. Suddenly, Heather grabbed her side and cried out. "What's wrong?" I asked her.

"I don't know! My side just started burning!" She looked at me with tears in her eyes. "Where's your bathroom?"

I told her. She got up and went to it, almost running.

She came back out a few moments later. "Would you look at this?" she asked me as she lifted up her blouse. I couldn't believe what I was seeing. There was a long, red, angry gash on her right side, the side Harold was sitting next to her. It started from the middle of her belly and curved around to the middle of her back.

She looked at me, scared. "How do you think it happened?"

"I don't know. You said that you didn't think that there was anything to the doll because you didn't feel any energy coming from it. Are you going to see a doctor about that?"

"I don't know. Do you think I should?" she asked.

"How would you explain it if you did?" wondered out loud. "A supposedly haunted doll did it after I said it *wasn't*?"

"I'm going to go," she said. Grabbing her purse, she gave one last scornful look at the doll.

That was the last time I ever saw her. Come to think of it, I never did hear from her again, either.

THE STANLEY HOTEL

The Stanley Hotel in Estes Park, Colorado is famous as being the setting for Stephen King's book, and movie, "The Shining." It's also known as being haunted. After several years of actively investigating reports of apparition, poltergeist, and haunting activity, I chose the hotel as the location for the last investigation of the Rocky Mountain Ghost Hunter's Alliance.

Christy was one of two assistant directors of my group at the time. She was with me when I did my initial investigation of the hotel to determine if there was anything to the stories told about it. It didn't take long before Christy and I experienced things we couldn't explain, such as smelling a woman's perfume in the Billiard Room, when only she and I were in it. It happened so often I asked one of the hotel staff if they perfumed the air for some reason.

We met a couple, Sarah and Eric, who asked us what we were up to. After we explained that we wanted to see if there was any truth to the stories about the hotel, they told us they were there celebrating their one-year wedding anniversary. They told us that they honeymooned there, and it was then that they heard that the hotel was haunted for the first time. They asked what we thought. It was too soon to make any sort of determination as far as that went, so I encouraged them to join us on the ghost tour we signed up for earlier. They signed up for it as well.

After the tour was over, Sarah walked up to me and asked if Christy and I would like to check out their room. They were on the third floor. Unfortunately, none of the stories told to us on the tour were from the third floor, but I agreed anyway. "If there is anything in our room, I don't want to know about it," Sarah warned me.

As soon as they opened the door to their room I sensed a presence. I immediately walked in and started taking pictures while Christy spoke with Sarah and Eric. After a few minutes I went back to the door and started taking more pictures of the room.

Sarah walked up to me and asked, "Well?"

I continued to take pictures as I answered, "Well… what?" After all, she did tell me *not* to say anything if I thought there was anything going on in their room.

"Is our room haunted?"

"I thought you didn't want to know if it was," I said to her teasingly.

"I do now," she said, matter-of-factly.

I looked at her, snapped another picture on my digital camera, and said, "There is a presence in here…." As soon as I said that, we heard a thud. Sarah turned around just in time to see the comforter fly off of the bed, hit the wall four feet away, and came to rest on the floor. She started screaming, and coming towards me, her hands up around her ears waving back and forth. "What do you want me to do?" I thought to myself.

I became aware of more screaming and looked around the corner of the doorway. I saw Eric, and behind him, Christy, who was also coming towards me, mouth wide open, screaming, her hands mimicking Sarah's. I thought, "A ghost hunter who's afraid of ghosts. That's kind of like a claustrophobic cave explorer."

Eric moved behind his wife, and stood there staring at me, wide eyed, but silent. "Is everyone okay?" I asked. Eric answered by picking up the comforter and throwing it back on the bed.

Later, when I looked at the pics I had taken, I saw that the remote control that was sitting on the comforter was moving towards the foot of the bed with each pic. The last one I took showed the remote at an angle on the foot of the bed. I caught it just as it was falling off. That was the sound we heard before watching the comforter fly towards the wall.

That incident was enough for me to come back several times to do an investigation of the hotel. I was there so often that when people asked if the hotel really was haunted, the staff would suggest, "Go ask Anthony Quinata."

"Who's Anthony Quinata?"

"He's a famous ghost hunter."

This explained the dozen or so people gathered in my room during my last scheduled investigation of the hotel. I was staying in room 418, which according to the hotel staff is the *most* haunted room in the hotel. Christy asked me if I would bring the doll with me, so when I arrived earlier in the day, I put it in the closet.

"I have Harold here," I told Christy, after answering a barrage of questions about whether or not the hotel was haunted. By this time, the crowd had thinned out from more than a dozen to about eight people.

"Where is he?" Christy asked.

"In the closet."

"Can I see him?" she was wide eyed. She had heard stories from other team members, but hadn't been around it herself.

I got the doll out of the closet, pulled it out of its bag, and put it on the bed. I put the wooden crucifix I kept with it next to the doll, and sprinkled it with holy water.

"What's with the holy water," a woman who was with the group of strangers in my room asked.

"I'll tell you what," I replied. "Why don't you wait 10 minutes, and you tell me."

A man standing next to her said, loudly, "I'm from Manhattan, New York, and we don't believe in that bullshit."

"I'll tell *you* what," I smiled at him, "why don't *you* wait 10 minutes, and you tell me what you think as well."

I turned back around and saw Christy leaning on the bed, staring at Harold. I walked around the bed to where she was and quietly said, "You're brave. Can you feel its energy?" She nodded. "It doesn't bother you?"

"It does," she said, without taking her eyes off of the doll. "I'm just not going to let it intimidate me."

I sat there looking at the doll with her, when I became aware that there wasn't anyone talking in my room anymore. They all moved outside into the hallway. "What happened?" I asked Christy. She shrugged her shoulders without taking her eyes off of the doll.

I got up, and walked out into the hallway. "Hi! Why is everyone out here?"

"We're talking about your doll," the woman who asked about the holy water answered quietly. She looked scared.

The cynic from New York pushed past her and walked up to me. He looked at me wild eyed. "What the hell is up with that doll?" he demanded.

"What do you think is going on with it?" I asked, genuinely curious. "Did something happen?"

"I swear that damned thing wanted to kill me," he said, loudly.

"Well, two people are supposed to have died after coming into its presence, but I thought you didn't believe in that sort of thing."

He looked at me for a moment, muttered, "You're crazy… having it." He shook his head, turned and walked away, followed by everyone else in the group.

Starting that very day, Christy's life began to unravel, going to hell in a handbasket, and would continue to do so for many years afterwards. Like so many other people, it was the last time I would see her. I didn't hear from her for another 8 years, when her life finally started turning around for the better again.

Later that night, Stephanie, who had been assigned by management to escort my team and me into parts of the hotel not normally accessible to the general public told the night auditor, Anna, "Go up to Anthony's room and check out his doll!"

"Why?" Anna asked.

"Just go and take a look at it. I'll cover the desk for you." So the auditor, a young woman from Indonesia went up to my room. Michelle, my other assistant director, was standing in the hallway.

"I'm here to see Anthony's doll," Anna informed Michelle, who opened the door for her. There, on the bed, where I left him earlier, was Harold.

I was in the hotel's concert hall at the time. When I came back into the lobby, Anna was visibly upset. "Why would you have a doll like that?" she demanded.

"Oh, you saw it?" I asked.

"Yes… Stephanie said I should see it. When I asked her why, she wouldn't tell me. She just kept insisting I should take a look at it. So I went up to your room and the moment I saw it I got a splitting headache, my stomach started to hurt, and I felt nauseous. None of it went away for two and a half hours! You need to get rid of that doll!"

I didn't know why she was so upset with me. *I* didn't tell her to take a look at the doll. Her suggestion that I get rid of it wasn't the first time I'd heard that. It wouldn't be the last time, either.

WHAT IS A MENISCUS ANYWAY?

As more and more people found out about the doll, the question, "Have you ever been hurt by it?" came up over and over again.

My typical answer was, "No. It knows better. Besides, I have a lifetime supply of holy water to keep it in line." The truth is that I had it for a few months, and nothing had happened to me… at least not physically. Then all of that changed one night.

I was sitting in a chair playing a UFC mixed martial arts game on my Xbox. When I had enough of not winning, I got up and started to move the chair back where it belonged when suddenly my right knee gave out and I fell to the floor. It didn't hurt, it just wouldn't support me. I couldn't for the life of me figure out what happened.

The next day I was going for a walk when my knee suddenly gave out on me again, and I fell to the sidewalk. No pain. No warning. I just collapsed. When I got back home I put a knee brace on, and made an appointment to see my doctor, who also happened to be an aspiring sports physician.

"What's going on?" he asked me.

"I tore my meniscus," I told him. I don't know how I knew that, I just did. Up until that moment, I had never even heard the word "meniscus," let alone say it.

"How did you do that?"

I told him about playing the game, getting up from the chair, collapsing to the floor when my leg wouldn't support me. I also told him about going for a walk the next day, falling down a couple of more times. I could tell by the look on his face that he didn't agree with my self-diagnosis. He told me I probably just sprained my knee somehow, and to keep wearing the brace. I wasn't happy, but I did what I was told.

A few weeks later I went back to see him, told him my knee wasn't getting any better, and asked for an MRI. He didn't think it was necessary even though he was surprised that my "sprain" hadn't healed yet. He asked me what I'd been doing. "I'm not out dancing every night, or doing gymnastics, if that's what you mean."

He sent me off and told me to come back if things didn't get any better. They didn't so I did. By this time, I couldn't straighten my leg. I insisted on an MRI again. He again insisted that I didn't need one. "I'm telling you, I tore my meniscus."

"Anthony," he said, patronizingly, "look… if you did tear your meniscus you wouldn't be able to walk without falling."

"I guess you missed it when I told you that the first time I saw you," I said angrily. He reluctantly agreed to schedule the MRI. After he received the results he called me and left a message saying he needed me to call him right away.

"I just got the results of your MRI about 30 minutes ago. You tore your meniscus.

"Wow, well there's a surprise," I thought angrily to myself.

"You're going to need surgery to correct it as soon as possible. I've already contacted an orthopedic surgeon who's waiting for you to call him."

I made an appointment with the surgeon who looked at my MRI and suggested that I receive the surgery a.s.a.p. Like, the next day! He was planning on going on vacation but was postponing it for a day, after seeing my test results. Most of my MDL was gone and arthritis had set in.

The surgeon told me afterwards that he removed the inflammation and felt the surgery, overall, was a success. He prescribed physical therapy, twice a week, for 6 weeks.

To this day, 10 years later, I still can't straighten my right leg completely. It serves as a constant reminder that it wasn't a good idea to taunt the spirit in the doll.

HAROLD HAS HAD ENOUGH

While I was recovering from my surgery, I came up with the idea of taking Harold to be read by renowned psychic, Peter James. According to James, his first encounter with ghosts was three young victims of an apartment fire that occurred in the apartment building he lived in. It happened when he was 8 years old. They became his playmates for three years after that.

It was his three friends who gave him the skills to link up to hundreds of other ghosts on what he called the "other side"—abilities that he would later use to communicate with dozens of spirits on the ocean liner, *The Queen Mary*.

James began researching the paranormal in the late 1970s or early 1980s. He moved to Southern California and settled in West Hollywood.

After going on a ghost tour aboard the Queen Mary, he claimed he encountered a ghost. This led to him conducting regular tours on the ship beginning in 1991.

One of the things that impressed me was how important his credibility was to him. I knew he was a straight shooter, and that was why I wanted him to read the doll. I had an ambitious plan at the time. I'd fly out to Los Angeles, do the Queen Mary tour with James, introduce myself, and ask him to do a reading on the doll.

The morning I was due to fly out to L.A., it was raining outside, so I wanted to allow myself extra time to get to the airport. I got the doll out of the cabinet in the storage room, and put it in my living room. I kept thinking about something I read in Katherine Ramsland's book, "Ghost," about an incident involving coins. In her book, she wrote about looking for something she thought might be in her purse. She emptied her bag onto her coffee table, dumping coins in the process.

Not finding what she was looking for, she sat there and took one more look around her apartment. When she looked back at the coffee table, all of the coins she dumped were stacked together.

I don't know why, but I couldn't stop thinking about that. I even grabbed her book, sat down, and re-read that part. "Okay," I thought to myself, "I read it. Now what?" It only made me later than I should have been if I were going to get to the airport on time to catch my flight. The thought occurred to me that missing my flight might have been the point.

I decided to get up and take one last look around to make sure I wasn't forgetting anything before I left. I walked into my bedroom and looked around. That's when something caught my eye on the window sill. Coins… quarters, dimes, nickels, and pennies, stacked together, one long row, in no particular order. I don't stack coins, but even if I did, I sure as hell didn't stack them the way I saw them. They weren't piled on top of each other. They were side by side, on their edges, at a slight angle.

My first reaction when I saw it was to laugh. I wondered which one of my friends was playing a joke on me and how they did it. Shaking my head, I looked closely at the coins. I thought that they were being held together by super glue, or pancake syrup. I even thought that perhaps the condensation from the water was keeping them in place somehow. I reached out and touched them expecting the coins to roll away from me. I literally jumped when they all came loose from one another, and scattered.

I went from being amused to feeling terrified in one fell swoop. I took a couple of steps back from the window. Suddenly, I felt the presence of a woman standing behind me. I spun around fully expecting to see someone standing there. What I saw instead was a crystal clear vision of a commercial airplane exploding, breaking in half, and falling down into the ocean. It was as though I were watching a movie playing in the middle of my bedroom. I can't begin to describe the fear and dread I felt as I watched this happening, feeling as though I was somehow responsible for the tragedy.

When the vision stopped I could see Harold, sitting in the middle of my living room, peeking out of the top of the bag. I would have sworn he was grinning at me. He was making it clear how he felt about being read by James.

"Alright," I said, "you win. You're not going with me to Los Angeles." I took the bag and put it back in its cabinet and locked the door.

That was in 2005, one year after I won the doll on eBay. It would be locked away, and kept out of the public eye, for the next 8 years.

HE'S BACK!

May 2013, I was in Erie, Pennsylvania. Harold was the furthest thing from my mind. Every once in a great while I'd see someone asking online if anyone knew what happened to the doll. He was in a storage unit in Denver, CO, and I didn't have any plans to take him out anytime soon. Then I saw a post on my Facebook wall, from my friend, La Shan.

"Hey Anthony! Look what I saw at a flea market today. A doll that reminded me of Harold!" I looked at the pic she posted. I was surprised she even remembered the doll.

Of course, people started asking, "Who's Harold?"

I explained how I won Harold in an auction on eBay, and that the doll was supposedly haunted. I was asked to post a picture, so I did.

Almost immediately people started commenting about the doll, and complaining, about getting headaches, feeling sick to their stomach, and fearful, from simply looking at the picture. Some people protested that I should have warned them that would happen.

One woman commented about how ugly she thought the doll was. The next day that same woman messaged me on Facebook. She told me that she fell asleep that night and woke up feeling as though Harold was staring at her from behind. "I was so scared," she wrote, "that I couldn't move for 10 minutes."

"How do you know it was Harold?" I wrote back. "Did you see the doll?"

"No, but I could feel it's hatred towards me."

"What did you do?" I asked.

"I finally forced myself to get out of bed, and I burned sage to cleanse my house. When I couldn't feel Harold's energy anymore, I poured sea salt outside the perimeter of my house. Anthony, I live alone, out in the middle of nowhere. I've never felt so afraid living here before. You don't think he'll come back, do you?"

I wrote her back saying I didn't know, but I didn't think so.

"You don't understand. Like I said, I live alone, and I don't ever want to feel that afraid ever again."

I started to write back that what happened may have been due to the remark she made about the doll. That's when I saw a notice telling me that I couldn't respond to her messages. She blocked me.

I deleted the post.

"Maybe it's time to restart my investigation as to what is going on with the doll," I thought to myself. But since I was in Erie for a couple more weeks, and the doll was in a storage unit in Denver, there was little I could do about it then.

I called my friend, Gina Marie, who is a "sensitive" herself, on the phone to ask her if she saw Harold. She told me she had, and that she didn't like the doll. "Its energy is extremely negative." I wanted the opinion of someone who hadn't seen the post, and comments, on Facebook. I asked her if she knew of someone who was credible who would look at a picture of the doll, and give me their impressions. Gina Marie told me that she did know someone, and would ask her to look at it later that day.

She called me later and said, "I asked my friend Anna to look at a picture of Harold and tell me what she thought. "Anna said it was the *darkest* energy she had ever encountered."

"What does that mean?" I asked.

"She said as soon as she looked at the picture her throat started to tighten. She said, 'The energy in the doll literally goes for the throat.'"

I decided that since I couldn't do anything about the doll, I'd just put Harold out of my mind... at least until I got back home to Denver.

I OWN THE DOLL

When I did get back to Denver, the doll was, one again, the furthest thing from my mind. Until I received another Facebook message from La Shan.

"Hey, Anthony! Did you see the video on YouTube about Harold?"

I wrote back and told her I hadn't, so she sent me the link. When I clicked on it, I was stunned to see that that the video had more than 33,000 views. I watched it and saw that the description was based on the original listing that Greg wrote about the doll.

I pulled up the video again two days later and was surprised to see it now had more than 36,000 views. I'd been keeping Harold locked away, out of the public eye, for the last 8 years hoping that interest in the doll would have died down. In June of 2013, the video La Shan told me about proved that wasn't the case.

I was also bothered that the information, through no fault of the person who posted it, was wrong. That's when I decided to break my silence about owning the doll. I wrote in the video's comment section that I've owned it since 2004.

"Can you prove that you own the doll?" she wrote back.

I told her, I could. I went to a local convenience store and bought a USA Today newspaper. I chose it because it had the current date in large print.

While I was there, I called my friend Camille and told her what I was planning on doing. "There's a lot of misinformation on the video," I told her. "I want to clear some of it up. I might even make my own YouTube video about the doll." Camille agreed it was a good idea. I bought a paper and went to a Wal-Mart before going to the storage unit containing the doll. While I was in the store I heard a voice in my head say, "She'd better stay away from me."

I got Harold out of the unit, went back to my hotel room, took a couple of pictures, and sent them to the person who posted the video. As far as I was concerned, that was going to be the end of it. I had no other plans, other than putting the doll back.

I went to a Starbucks to enjoy a coffee and a book. That's when I remembered the warning I heard earlier. I called Camille and immediately knew something was wrong. She didn't sound like herself. "Are you okay?" I asked.

"I'm really sick," she told me. "I go between feeling really hot, and really cold. I've been vomiting too."

"When did this start?"

"After I got off of the phone with you this morning."

"I'll call you back," I told her and stormed back to the hotel. I felt myself becoming angrier with every step. When I got back to my room, the doll was still where I left him. I thought about what Kathy said, "Harold doesn't move. He just sits there and hurts people."

I grabbed the bottle of holy water and started splashing the doll saying, "Don't you *ever* attack Camille, or anyone else I love, again! Do you understand me?"

A few minutes later, I heard the same voice I heard in Wal-Mart say, "Okay… she's okay now."

I called Camille back and this time she answered sounding like her usual self. "How are you feeling now?" I asked her.

"Much better! Thank you!" she answered cheerfully.

"When did you start feeling better?"

"Just a couple of minutes ago."

WHAT'S MY FAVORITE COLOR?

A couple of days later, Camille and I were eating lunch together. She asked me where Harold was and I told her I put him back in the storage unit. I was lifting my fork up to my mouth when she asked, "What did you do to your arm?"

"What do you mean?" I asked.

"Your right arm… it looks as though you scratched it on something," she said, wide-eyed and concerned.

I looked and was shocked at what I saw. The gash was about 6 inches long and bleeding. It looked as though it happened just moments before. The crazy thing is that I didn't feel it when it did. "I don't think Harold's happy about being back in the storage unit," I told her.

She visibly shuddered at that statement. "Are you going to leave it there?" she asked. "Maybe you should take it back out."

What I'm thinking of doing," I told her, "and this didn't occur to me until just now, is to see if I can get another psychic to do a reading on it."

She surprised me by asking me if she could come with me when I do. We made plans to meet at her house a few days later. I'd seen a sign at a store where psychics frequently showed up to do readings that said it was hosting a "metaphysical fair" that Saturday.

The night before we were going to go, I felt the presence of a spirit. It was definitely conscious and letting me know that I did not want to be read by a psychic. I wasn't about to let that stop me this time.

When I showed up at Camille's home, she asked if I would mind going with her to check out yard sales she had seen advertised before we went to the store. I told her I didn't so we stopped by a couple of different homes where Camille bought some "treasures" she had found. Harold was in the back of her car and she was moving him to make room when she said to me, "Harold's eyes just changed colors."

I looked, and sure enough, his normally light blue eyes were black. Black as coals. There wasn't even any sclera (white) in them. I was reminded of the eyes in the masked face that Phyllis sent me. I couldn't help but shudder when I saw it. "I don't think Harold's happy about us going to get him read after this," I told her.

When Camille and I pulled into the parking lot of the store there were only a couple of cars in the parking lot. "I'll bet the fair was last Saturday," I told her, "and no one's bothered to take the sign down." We walked into the store and found out I was right.

Rather than leaving we stayed in the store. One reason Camille wanted to come with me was the last time we were here, there was a glass box with a butterfly design that she wanted to buy for her daughter. She wanted to look around and see if it was still there.

A few minutes later I recognized someone walking in the door that I met a few years before. Maria was there to drop off slips of paper announcing that she would be doing a group medium session the following Saturday. I asked her if she did object readings, and she said no. I said, "You are able to read energy though."

"Yes."

I asked her if she be willing to try something for me. She agreed not knowing what I was going to ask her.

I went out to Camille's car and came back in with Harold in the Duane Reade bag. Maria, Camille, and I went into the conference room of the store. I handed the bag to Maria. She pulled Harold out, and closed her eyes.

"Anthony, what is your favorite color?" she asked me.

"What's my favorite color? What does that have to do with all the tea in China?" I wondered.

"Yellow," I told her.

"Yellow," she repeated softly. "First of all, I see a girl who owned this doll when she was around 10 years old. She's... I don't know how to say this she's naïve. It's like she's protected, or very spoiled. Maybe even developmentally behind her age. She has long hair, tied in the back with a bow. Her hair is greasy."

A few moments later she continued, "I see the girl as an old woman now. 75 years old, with short grey hair, wearing a white shawl. She had rheumatoid arthritis, and bony hands. She's lonely. She spent most of her life isolated. Her life was uneventful... content."

Maria became silent for a few moments, then repeated that she was getting feelings of loneliness, melancholy, and sadness. She paused again, opened her eyes and said, "Of course, I may be wrong."

She closed her eyes again. "The doll maker, the person who made this doll, wasn't happy ... she was crying when she made the doll. The doll maker's energy is in the doll."

Camille asked her if she knew where the woman who owned the doll was from. "The South," Maria answered. "She came from a family of means. They were comfortable. Like I said, the girl was either protected... not allowed to leave her home... or she was very spoiled. Of course, I could be wrong about that.

The doll was made earlier in the last century and the woman owned her until the 1960s – 70s when she died."

Camille asked, "Do you think that if the doll were repaired and wore nice clothes it would have a better energy?" I mentioned to Camille earlier that day that some people had suggested that perhaps the doll wouldn't be so negative if it were repaired, and clothed. She laughed and said she was thinking the same thing.

Maria looked at Camille as though she wondered if she were kidding. "The doll would still have the lonely energy attached to it even if it were repaired. Changing the energy would be complicated." She suggested I take the doll up into the mountains, into a forest, and release the energy of the doll there.

I shared with Maria that I felt the presence of a spirit in the doll the night before. She laughed and said, "I don't believe that spirits can be 'trapped' in an object. Maybe my skepticism kept me from sensing a spirit, but I don't believe it can happen."

She put Harold back in the bag. "Of course, I could be wrong."

HAROLD'S AFRAID

I decided that since I had the doll out anyway, I might as well see if I can get any answers for myself from it. My plan was to take the doll to a cemetery, along with my Tri-Field and Natural EM meters and a digital recorder to try to get some evidence, and possibly even some answers. I called my friend Debbie and asked her if she'd like to join me. She agreed.

When we picked a spot to do the experiments I set up the Tri Field recorder to see if it registered anything anomalous while I asked questions with my recorder on. I also turned my digital recorder on to try to catch an EVP or two. Nothing happened... at least not on the Tri Field.

At one point I felt uneasy. "Harold doesn't like it here," I said to Debbie, and turned the recorder off.

It was dusk, and starting to become dark. We listened to the recording when suddenly, the Tri Field started going crazy. I videoed the meter on my camera. When we heard my comment on the recorder of me saying that Harold wasn't comfortable in the cemetery, we both heard an EVP saying, "They're coming for me."

We decided to call it a day, and left... quickly.

THERE'S NO SUCH THING AS A HAUNTED OBJECT

I went back a couple of weeks later to the same store I got the reading from Maria. This time I went during the middle of the week. It was a crap shoot as to whether or not there would even be a reader there, but I wanted to get another reading on the doll. A young woman named Erica came in. I asked her if she'd try to do a reading on the doll. She agreed, so I handed the bag to her. She put it down on the floor next to her. She began by saying, "I don't want to touch it."

"Why not? Is there something about the doll that you don't like about it?" I asked.

Erica continued to look inside of the bag. "It's happy that it's not locked up anymore. Whatever that means."

"Wow," I thought to myself.

"I get the little girl who owned it died. Well, I'm sure did, because the doll's so old!" Erica said laughing. "She loved the doll. I don't like it though. I don't even want to touch it."

"How old would you say the girl was when she died?" I asked.

After pausing for a moment she said, "Six."

"Someone's done something to the doll," she continued. "It's seen periods of time where it was... loved."

I wanted to ask what she meant by 'someone did something to the doll,' but another woman who was in the same room, but who wasn't sitting with us, spoke up agreeing with Erica. She said that she could feel the energy coming from the doll as well. I asked her what her name was. "I'm Zanda." Erica told me that she and Zanda "tag teamed" with each other during readings.

"I'm feeling the energy over here," Zanda said. "It's kind of a dark gray, and when I get that it means that there's an energy attached to it that needs to be cleared…."

"It wants to be fixed," Erica said while Zanda was still speaking.

"Yeah," Zanda answered. "It's not necessarily haunted, but it can be cleared."

"They really do tag team with one another," I thought to myself.

"It sat somewhere for a long time," Erica chimed in. I kept trying to look at each one of them as they spoke. The way my head kept going from side to side made me feel as though I were watching a tennis match. "Like, either it sat in storage, or was forgotten somewhere, but it sat for a long time."

"I get more like it was packed away, and forgotten," Zanda said.

I was impressed by that since I did have Harold "packed away" in storage for a number of years.

"I get hurt from it."

I was looking at Zanda when I heard that. "I'm sorry?" That statement from Erica made me really take notice.

"I get hurt from it," she repeated.

"Do you mean actually, physical hurt, from the doll?" I asked.

"No, it was just like a feeling… there's hurt surrounding it."

"Oh, I see," I said, clarifying what I thought she meant. "Like there's hurt feelings surrounding the doll."

"Yes. After a while dolls tend to take on their owner's energy," she started to explain. "That's why people get so freaked out by them. There's a lot going on with its head."

"What do you mean?" I asked.

"There's a lot going on around its head. I don't know if it was dropped, or that's how the girl passed away… but I'm getting something with a fall."

I immediately thought of Veronica and how Kathy told me she died falling down a flight of stairs.

"But it wants to be fixed," Erica stated. "I don't want to touch it." That last statement seemed to come out of the blue.

"Is there a reason why?" I asked.

"There's something telling me not to touch it. Yeah, I just… I don't want to touch it." She kept looking at the doll. "I don't get anything… it's not that it's necessarily evil, or anything like that… there's a lot of… it almost feels as though the doll… in the condition it's in… it's like the doll, it wants to be fixed. It doesn't want anybody looking at it, or touching it, because it's not the shape that it used to be in. I don't know if that's necessarily the doll or someone else who's attached with it. But I get a creepy feeling from it. I get a lot of sadness. I can hear her mom holding it, and crying."

"Can you give me an idea as to where the girl who had the doll is from?" I asked.

"Somewhere in the South, like Georgia. I'm seeing a plantation house. She came from a wealthy family. I don't know if someone's called it 'possessed' before? It's like someone called the doll possessed, and it doesn't like it."

That evening, I gave a lot of thought to what the readers said about the doll. I was struck by the similarities between what they said. And the differences. Both Maria and Erica talked about the doll being owned by girls who came from wealthy families in the South. Both of them denied the idea that the doll might actually contain a spirit.

On the flip side of the coin, Maria said the girl who owned the doll lived to her 70s. Erica talked about the girl dying at the age of 6.

If these were the first two readings I had after acquiring Harold, I would have put him back in storage. But I had other experiences with him in which I had literally seen him hurt people in front of my eyes. I also had EVPs of a male voice, not a young girl or elderly woman.

The night before Mara's reading I felt an energy of a conscious spirit that didn't want me to take it to a psychic to be read. I thought, "Not only is there a spirit inhabiting this doll, but it's conscious, and a trickster."

"You might have fooled them," I said to the doll, out loud, "but you're not fooling me. I'm far from done trying to figure out what your story is."

HAROLD MAKES HIMSELF KNOWN

I was surprised when Erica called me about three weeks after doing the reading. She seemed just as surprised she was calling me. "I don't know why," she told me, "but I keep feeling as though I'm supposed to get together with you for some reason."

"Do you eat sushi?" I asked.

Erica laughed. "Actually, I love sushi! Why?"

"I'll tell you what. I've been thinking about asking you to do another reading of the doll. If you'll do that, I'll buy dinner. Deal?" We agreed to meet the next day.

I decided to video this reading with my camera. I took the doll out of the bag, and put in on the floor next to Erica, and a crucifix in front of the doll. Once again, Erica didn't actually hold the doll but simply looked at it. "I'm not getting anything different than I did before. I just keep feeling the energy of the girl who owned the doll."

"I want to try something to see if it makes a difference," I told her. I removed the crucifix. "Are you getting anything new from it now?"

Erica looked down at the doll and shook her head. "Wait a minute," she said, suddenly. She had a confused look on her face. "I'm picking up a male energy now."

She told me that the male, a young man, *was* a part of the doll. It was like he was *trapped* inside of the doll. The little girl she sensed before was his sister... his half-sister. They had the same father, but a different mother. Her mother was Caucasian. His mother was Black, and worked for the family. He was the product of an affair. They all lived on a plantation somewhere in the South.

Erica said that the girl was loved by her older brother, and tagged along with him everywhere he went. They were inseparable. She talked about seeing a river running through the plantation grounds. There was a "tire swing" that hung from a tree next to the water and one of the girl's favorite things to sit in it while her brother pushed her out over the water.

"The little girl fell out of a tree and died," Erica said quietly. "She fractured her skull. That's how she died. Her brother was blamed for it. That's why he's trapped in the doll. You can free him though."

"How am I supposed to do that?" I asked.

"The plantation still exists. It's still a working plantation. When you find it, I'm being told you'll know it. The people who live and work there will know the story of the boy and the girl, but to them, it's only a story that's been passed down. I'm being told that once you find the plantation you'll know what you need to do to free the boy from the doll."

"I keep hearing the number 3. I don't know if that means three months from now, three years from now, or the month of March, but somehow the number 3 is important to all of this." (Author's note – this is my third published book). "Are you thinking of opening a museum? The boy is saying something about you starting a museum."

I was stunned. Before Erica arrived that day I was looking at plans for a home that included a "children's room" in the basement. "I don't have any children," I thought to myself, "so I'd probably make that room into a museum of the haunted things I have, and make Harold the center piece." I *thought* it. I didn't say anything to Erica about it. How did she know about it?

More importantly, how did the spirit she was supposedly in touch with know about it?

AUDELLE SAYS HELLO

I'd been posting videos on YouTube which I recorded on my cell phone trying to communicate with whatever spirit was in the doll. I wasn't revealing a whole lot in them about the doll, or the stories connected with it.

After Erica did her second reading, I posted parts of it online, but left out the parts she talked about such as the plantation, the little girl, her brother, the river, the tree swing, etc. I did this was so that I could weed out the loonies who were constantly trying to claim a connection to the doll, such as a woman I'll call Julie.

Julie sent me a message on Facebook Messenger one morning telling me that she believed that she owned Harold when she was younger. I wrote back and asked her why she thought this and she said that she remembered a picture of her as a child holding onto the doll. I asked where the picture was taken and she said she believed it was in Gainesville, Florida.

That got my attention since Greg wrote in his first listing that he purchased the doll in Webster, Florida, approximately 60 miles south of Gainesville. I asked her to call me and gave her my number.

As we talked, I began to have my suspicions about her. She told me that her family lived in Gainesville… or was it Jacksonville? She couldn't remember.

The more we talked, the less I believed what she was saying. Especially after she told me that the reason she messaged in the first place was because, that morning, her sister visited a medium who told her that she (Julie's sister) was killed by Harold the Doll, while she was holding Annabelle, the Raggedy Ann doll now in the Warren Museum in Connecticut. "Well," I thought to myself, "that's quite the story…." I got off of the phone with her as quickly and politely as I could.

A few days after Erica's reading, however, a chain of events did happen that convinced me that what she told me in her reading was correct.

One of the things I edited out of the videos I posted of Erica's readings was when she told me the name of the little girl. "It sounds like 'Annabelle,' but it's not. It's a longer name. It starts with an 'A' …it sounds like 'Annabelle.'"

So when I received an e-mail from someone named Fiona that said, *the next time you talk to Harold, tell him Audelle says hello*, it got my attention. I immediately thought about what Erica said, "It sounds like 'Annabelle,' but it's not. It's a longer name. It starts with an 'A' …it sounds like 'Annabelle.'"

"Audelle" didn't quite fit the bill, but it was close enough for me. I wrote her back and asked her why she said that. *I've had dreams of owning the doll you call Harold since I was a child,* she answered back.

She told me that she was on YouTube searching for country songs to add to her collection when she saw a picture of Harold in the sidebar. *I knew immediately it was the doll I'd seen in my dreams for years.*

After talking to Julie, I wasn't so sure. After all, composition dolls such as Harold weren't all that uncommon. Still, the whole "Audelle" thing.... I had to make a phone call, so I asked if we could continue after I was done. She said that she'd be waiting for me.

By the time I was done with my call I forgot about writing Fiona. Then I saw her email again, about an hour and a half later. *The next time you talk to Harold, tell him Audelle says hello.*

I was hoping that she'd still be willing to talk to me. I wrote to her and asked her if she'd call me so we could talk. She agreed, so I sent her my number.

After thanking her for calling me, I got right to the point—"Did you see the video of the reading I did with Erica?"

"Yes."

"Well, she gave me a name that sounds like the one you gave me, but not quite," I told Fiona.

"Does the name 'Auralia Audelle' make sense?" Fiona asked.

I heard Erica's voice in my mind again - "It sounds like 'Annabelle,' but it's not. It's a longer name. It starts with an 'A' … but it sounds like 'Annabelle.'"

"Talk to me," I told her. "Who are you, and what is your story?"

She told me that she was 28 years old. As long as she could remember she dreamt of living on a plantation "somewhere in the South, carrying the doll you call Harold. I carried it everywhere with me. I had a brother. I followed him everywhere he went… until I'd hear my mother calling me, 'Auralia… Auralia Audelle!' That's when my dream would end and I'd wake up."

"Do you remember anything about the plantation you lived on in your dreams?" I asked.

"Not much… it was in the South… there was a river, and I loved to play on a tire swing. My brother would push me and I'd swing out over the water."

I couldn't believe it. She just told me details Erica told me in her reading but that I edited out of the video.

"What else can you tell me?" I asked, barely able to contain my excitement, or my skepticism.

"I think I was six years old when I died."

MASON

Before we hung up she told me that since her divorce a couple of years before, she was taking medication to cope with her anxiety and help her sleep. One of the side effects was that she couldn't remember her dreams. "I'll stop taking my pills," she told me. "I won't be able to sleep as well as when I do take them, but at least I'll be able to remember my dreams."

I tried to discourage her from doing this, but she insisted. She was as intrigued, and as curious, as I was to find out if she could learn anything more.

A few days later she contacted me on Skype. Instead of doing a video, we messaged back and forth.

I stopped taking my medication, and my dream came back. I had two brothers, not one. They were both older than me though. One brother's name was Michael. He was my real brother. He had blonde hair, like me. My other brother wasn't my real brother, but my half-brother. We had the same father, but different mothers. I think he was a mulatto. He had curly brown hair, and beautiful green eyes.

I immediately remembered what Erica told me about the spirit tethered to the doll. 'They had the same father but different mothers. The little girl's mother was white, but his mother was black.'

Even though he was only our half-brother," she continued, *"Michael and I followed him everywhere. I adored him. He loved me too.*

"Do you know his name?" I asked.

Mason... his name was Mason.

She paused waiting for my reaction. I was too busy writing notes to respond, so she continued.

Everywhere I went, I took the doll with me too. I was a tomboy and I loved climbing up trees. Even when I climbed trees I tried doing it with the doll in one hand. Mason was always worried about me. He kept worrying about me falling and hurting myself."

That was all she could remember. I thanked her and signed off. Before I did she promised that she would get back to me if she learned anything new in her dreams.

I sat there looking at her messages, and my notes from our phone conversation. "Was this woman for real?" I wondered out loud. Ever since Erica's reading in which she switched from saying that she didn't believe that an object could contain a spirit's energy, to saying that a soul was tethered to the doll, I wasn't sure what to think. Now, a woman was telling me things that she couldn't have possibly have known Erica told me in her reading… and she said it was all coming to her in dreams. My head was swimming. I didn't know what to think… or believe.

I didn't hear from Fiona again for almost two weeks after that. She messaged me through Skype again.

I'm at work, but I had another dream last night that I have to tell you about. I know how I died.

I wasn't there when her message came, but saw it a couple of minutes later. I wrote her back hoping that she was still there. "Did you see this in your dream?" I wrote back.

Yes.

"What happened? What did you dream?"

I was climbing a tree, and I fell. I was laying on the ground. My hair on the back of my head felt wet. It was soaked with blood. Mason was looking down at me with those beautiful eyes of his. He looked scared. He kept saying, 'I told you not to climb that tree! I told you that you were going to hurt yourself!'

I knew that I was badly hurt, but I wasn't afraid. Mason was there. 'Don't worry,' he told me. He picked me up and carried me to the house of a woman who was our nanny. She was also some kind of a witch doctor. She was black, and had an accent. I think she was from Barbados.

Mason kept begging her to help me. She said that she'd try. Then she laughed and said, 'If this girl lives or dies, her mother will blame you for it. You'll be blamed for what happened.'

I tried to tell her it wasn't his fault, but before I could, I woke up.

It wasn't until after she told me this that I remembered something else Erica told me in her reading – 'After the girl died, her mother blamed the boy. She accused him of murdering her daughter, even though that's not what happened. It was an accident. The mother didn't believe that. There was a woman who practiced Voodoo who worked for the family as a housekeeper. She told the woman to trap the boy's spirit in the doll to punish him for what happened.'

I started to think that Fiona may, in fact, be the little girl who died... reincarnated. I also began to believe that the spirit in the doll was her half-brother blamed for her death and trapped because of it.

I encouraged Fiona to keep in touch with me and tell me what else she saw in her dreams. As much as Fiona's dreams seemed to corroborate Erica's reading, I couldn't just take it at face value. I needed to validate what Fiona was telling me. To me that meant that what I had to do next was to try to find the plantation where all of this supposedly happened.

A BRIEF HISTORY OF COMPOSITION DOLLS

Harold is what is known as a "composition doll," so I decided to do some research into composition dolls and their history. I found out that composition dolls were manufactured from approximately 1909 through the early 1950s. The height of the market for composition dolls was the 1920s through the 1940s. Composition is generally a mixture of glue mixed with sawdust. Even though composition was used to make doll bodies from approximately the late 1870s, *only* dolls with heads made of these materials are referred to as "composition dolls."

Very large dolls, like Harold, were generally not made of all-composition because they would be far too heavy for a little girl to play with. They were known as "Mama Dolls," their head and lower limbs were made of composition, but they had a body made of cloth. Mama dolls are a young toddler doll with a voice mechanism that produces something sounding like "mama," usually when tipped, rocked or shaken. The legs were made to "swing" freely thanks to sewn, jointed cloth hips. These joints allowed the dolls to "walk." The dolls were chubby in appearance, and, thanks to their composition head and limbs, they were advertised as "unbreakable." The dolls were also advertised as "life like" by many companies.

Mama dolls started being produced as early as 1915; however, the dolls didn't become wildly popular until the early 1920s. By the mid-1920s, a large number American companies were manufacturing the dolls. By the late 1920s, demand for the dolls slowed down somewhat.

I tried to narrow it down even further by talking to a doll expert. I didn't have the doll with me at the time, but she told me to look for a manufacturers mark on the back of the doll's neck. I couldn't find one on Harold. That told me that the doll more than likely wasn't made by a company known for making quality dolls, such as Madame Alexander, Effanbee, American Character, Amberg, and others, but one of many companies that copied their designs and sold their dolls unmarked.

Bonnie May, a composition doll collector wrote to me saying, *He was most likely made in the 30s. The same man in New York owned all the molds that made composition and hard plastic dolls for a long time. If anybody knows Baby Genius by Madame Alexander who is made in the thirties, Horsman had a doll from the same mold.*

The man who owned these molds would make knock offs of all the popular dolls selling at the time. He would even sell them right outside the factories of the doll makers like Madame Alexander. He would make the dolls cheaper, with pretty outfits made out of cheaper material, and sell them out of a stand in the street. A lot of people couldn't afford these dolls that Madame Alexander, Horsman, Arranbee, etc., were making, so they'd buy them from this man. He basically ripped the doll makers off but produced a lot of dolls and made a lot of money that way.

Now that I now had an idea as to when the doll was made, this would have given me an indication of a time frame for when the girl supposedly died. So when Fiona continued to contact me, whatever she said had to fit within that era. Which is when things started to unravel.

—m—

I found the tree I fell from when I died, Fiona Skyped me.

I became excited. If she identified the tree, then that meant she found the plantation! I remember Erica saying that if I find that estate that all this happened on, then I'd know how to release the innocent spirit entombed in the doll. "Where is it?" I wrote back.

She sent me a map marked with the area where the tree supposedly was. It was near a river.

It was also in the middle of New Orleans, Louisiana. Now, I'm not an expert on New Orleans history, but I didn't think there were any plantations there in the middle of the 1930s.

I asked her how sure she was of this, and she said that she was certain. It was the same tree she saw in her dreams. I didn't know what to say, so I simply thanked her for letting me know.

She must have figured out what I was thinking, because she wrote back to me a couple of weeks later. *I found the plantation that I used to live on.*

"Do you know the name of the plantation?"

Destrehan, she wrote back. I immediately did a Google search. Found it. It even had a manor house. "Could this really be the place?" I wondered.

Located in Destrehan, Louisiana, it was built between the years 1787 – 1790. During the 19th century, the plantation was a major producer of indigo (a natural dye extracted from plants), and then sugar cane. While the plantation has a long, important, history, it was sold to the Mexican Oil Company in 1914, which built an oil refinery on the property. The company tore down the additional buildings around the manor house and built employee housing. The mansion itself was used in a variety of ways including as a clubhouse. In 1959, American Oil tore down the refinery, and abandoned the site.

Not only was it not a working plantation in the 1930s as Erica had suggested, but it is 25 miles *upriver* from New Orleans, where Fiona claims the tree that she fell from was. It occurred to me that Fiona wasn't seeing these things in her dreams.

When I heard from her again, she told me that she knew when she died—sometime in the early 1800s. How is that possible? When she first contacted me, she told me that in her dreams she saw herself carrying the doll everywhere she went. A doll that wasn't made until 1930s. And now she's claiming that she died in the early 1800s?

Despite all of that, I remained certain that she was the reincarnated soul of the young girl Erica told me about.

THE PHILIP EXPERIMENTS

I began to renew my own investigation, primarily EVP and Tri Field Meter experiments. The reason I'd resisted doing this before was because I wanted to avoid what is known as "The Philip Effect."

In the 1970s, a group of Canadian parapsychologists wondered if the human mind can produce "ghosts" by, imagining one, visualizing it, and expecting it to manifest. So they wanted to test their theory by attempting an experiment in which they would *create* an apparition. The investigation took place in Toronto, Canada, in 1972, headed up by world-renown expert on poltergeists, Dr. A. R. G. Owen.

The theory the experimenters were testing was that by using extreme and prolonged concentration, they could create their own ghost, by thinking it into reality. In order to produce this apparition and make it as 'real' as possible, they even came up with a life story; circumstances of the specter's history that it could 'relate' to.

They also gave the presence they were attempting to create a name, "Philip Aylesford." They concocted a heartbreaking story, explaining in full detail, his life and what led to his tragic death.

The next step was to try to contact Philip. In September of 1972, the group began their experiment. After some initial problems they attempted to duplicate the atmosphere of a spiritualist séance. Dimming the lights, they sat around a table and surrounded themselves with pictures of the type of castle they imagined Philip would have lived in, as well as objects from that time period. It worked.

Within a matter of weeks, Philip "broke through," and made contact. Not as an apparition or ghost, but through a knock on the group's table. "Philip" rapped answers to questions that were consistent with his fabricated history, but not beyond what the group had imagined. "Philip" was able to give historically accurate information about real events and people. The group theorized that this information came from their own combined knowledge of history.

Things started taking off from there, creating a wide range of occurrences that couldn't be explained scientifically. "Philip" was able to move the table, causing it to slide from side to side. More than once, the table even chased an experimenter across the room. No one was touching the table when this happened.

In the end, the experimenters were never able to explain how and why these things happened, beginning with Philip's arrival. Was Philip a direct result of the group's collective subconscious or perhaps did they conjure an actual entity that simply latched onto the story?

While some people would say that this experiment proved that spooks don't exist, except in our minds, others say that what was proved is that our unconscious could be responsible for these kinds of the occurrences, but only some of the time.

Still, others believe that even though Philip was completely made up, the Owen group really did contact the spirit world. A fun (or perhaps demonic) spirit saw an opening because of these séances to 'act' as Philip and produce the extraordinary psychokinetic phenomena recorded.

What caused the manifestation?

Why did it adapt itself to the expectations of the people conducting the experiments?

Was it an entity simply playing the role of the spirit they intended to contact?

Whatever the answer, I intended to avoid it by staying out of the investigation of the doll as much as possible. I began considering bringing in a paranormal investigation group to see if they could corroborate Erica's reading, and Fiona's dream, using electronic equipment beyond my EMF meters and digital recorder.

"I'M NOT A PSYCHIC"

I met a woman named Laurie on Facebook, and we became "friends." At the time, I was doing EVP experiments with the doll, and told her a little about it, but she really didn't want to know much. She did tell me that, after we talked about it, she looked up and watched one of the videos I posted on YouTube, of an EVP experiment I had done with the doll. She decided that she had seen enough.

Laurie and I were talking on the phone and she asked how things were going with the doll. I told her, "I'd tell you, but I'm not sure you'd believe it. Hell, I'm not sure I believe it myself. But apparently there's a spirit trapped in the doll." I didn't tell her about Fiona, and her dreams.

"I think you should contact a 'Strega,' to see what I can do to release the spirit trapped inside the doll," she suggested seriously.

"Let me guess," I said, "you know a strega."

"I do come from a bloodline of Stregas on one side and Santeria on the other."

"I didn't know that." I knew she was simply trying to be helpful, but past experience told me that what she was saying might have repercussions. "I appreciate the suggestion," I told her. She continued to insist that I contact a Strega. "I'm telling you as a friend, you need to stop."

"Please..." she said, teasingly, "you and the doll are in Denver. I'm in Long Island, New York. What's he going to do?" She started laughing. "Tell him to give it his best shot. I'm not scared."

"Well, all I can say at this point is that *if* something does happen to you, you cannot say I didn't warn you."

A couple of hours after we hung up I heard from someone who told me that she believed that Harold was upset about something she said. I was talking to her when I started receiving the messages from Laurie on Facebook. I didn't get back to her for a few minutes.

"Hi, been dealing with an incident that Harold might be responsible for," I wrote to her.

She wrote to me that I should tell Harold to behave, and then offered to help in any way she could.

"What do you think you can do to help?" I wondered.

I really don't know how I could help. The one thing that comes to mind is pray, she wrote.

"Prayer is always good," I wrote back.

A few minutes later she wrote back to me. *OMG Anthony. I had to step away from the PC as I was typing. My dog started yelping in terror… that is a first… WOW! He's okay now, but something has him shivering…. I mean REALLY SHAKING….WOW! I have never heard this dog yelp so loud! He's lying at my feet trembling. What's going on?*

"I don't know," I wrote back. The truth was though, I had a good idea.

Anthony, he has never done this before. He's so scared he won't even get up…. He's just curled up in a ball. He has his head down, his ears back and he's trembling. Now things are falling off of the walls. I was in the living room just a few minutes ago, and there's nothing there to make these things happen. I'm scared. What I've started to do is pray.

I didn't respond. I really didn't know *what* to say. I didn't hear from her for several minutes. I called her. "What's going on? Anything?"

"I don't know. I locked myself in the bathroom," she told me.

"Where's your dog?" I asked her.

"He's outside the door whimpering, and crying."

"Well, let him in for God's sakes!" I couldn't believe she actually locked him out.

"Do you think it's safe to do that?" she asked.

I could hear the fear in her voice. I could even understand why she did what she did. Her 160 lbs. Bull Mastiff was supposed to be *her* protector… not the other way around. I felt sorry for her dog, and hoped I could say something that would make her open the door, and let her dog in.

"Look, if it's who I think it is, he's in your home, and the doll is here with me. Do you really think your bathroom door is going to stop him?"

"Anthony… when will this stop?" She was crying.

"I don't know, I really don't. It might stop in a couple of minutes, a couple of hours. It might go on for a couple of days, even weeks..."

She interrupted me by moaning a prayer, "Oh God... please help me. Make it go away."

"... it will go on until his anger is spent, or he thinks he's made his point." I continued.

"I have to go," she said abruptly.

"Where are you going?" I asked.

"I don't know, but I'm taking my dog and we're getting the hell out of here." The phone went dead.

A little while later, she messaged me saying that she was going to try to get some sleep, but she wasn't sure she could. She also said that her dog was following her *everywhere* she went. As long as he was with her he was fine. The moment she was out of his sight, he started to cry, so she was going to do something she'd never done before—let him sleep with her.

We talked again the next morning. She told me that the night before was "the strangest night ever." First, the dog crying like someone was killing him. A fan turned itself upside down. Things were falling in her living room. She couldn't handle it so she went to bed. She woke up around 2 a.m. with a "screaming headache," and started violently vomiting. Then, as suddenly as her sickness came, it left.

"Sounds like Harold," I told her. "I'm sorry, but I tried to warn you."

"Yes, you did try to warn me. Anthony, is the worst over?"

"I don't know..." I started to respond, because the truth is, I didn't know.

"The dog is so big, he has never shown any type of fear like that, Anthony. He really was scared last night... he's sleeping right next to me. If I want to get out of bed for anything I have to jump over him, that's how big he is. We slept with the lights on...

I have a fancy plaque with my family name and history on it. That is where I have the candle underneath it for my dad. That fell off wall and just missed the candle, thank God. I wasn't in the room when it happened, but it looked like the stuff was thrown off the desk. And the fan being upside down... that didn't fall. It looks as though it was put that way...."

Then I have these thoughts going through my head and I know they're not my own. I don't know what to do. I don't know how to handle this. I'm not a church goer, but I do believe in God, and this is no time for me to have any distance from God or Jesus. I am going to church and speak to one the priests about what is going on here.

Like I said, there are thoughts running through my mind that are not my own, almost negotiating with me. They're telling me what the issues are, but warning me at the same time that I'm not supposed to tell anyone, or else... I don't know. This is why I don't know what to do or how to go on.

This is a problem I've never dealt with before, and I have absolutely no knowledge of what to do. I know it's because I offered to help you. Once again you were right, I shouldn't have.

What am I going to do? I've never seen anything like this, except in the movies. Now you can think I am crazy, or you can help me understand what I am dealing with and direct me from here....

I just hope you don't think I am crazy."

After a few moments I realized she had hung up.

I immediately tried calling her home phone, and her cell phone. She didn't answer either of them. I'll admit, I did wonder if her imagination was getting the best of her. I tried calling her home phone a second time and this time, she answered the phone. "Anthony," she said, "I don't have any 'abilities,' I'm not a psychic or anything, but last night I kept having these thoughts that I know were coming from Harold."

I asked her what she was referring to and she told me that she was afraid. "I was warned not to tell anyone, especially you, or I'd pay for it."

I could tell she was genuinely frightened. "Laurie," I told her, "if it is Harold, he's preying on your fears, and if you listen to him, then it's the first step in controlling you."

"That's what I was afraid of," she said.

"Tell me what he said, and I'll tell you what to do. I'll deal with him afterwards," I said.

When Laurie told me what she had heard, I asked her how much of Harold's story had she read, and what videos I had posted on YouTube she had watched.

She admitted that she had seen one of the videos in which there were "a lot of orbs," but insisted that she wasn't familiar with his story, and hadn't seen any other videos.

Even if she had, I wondered as she was telling me what she claimed Harold was telling her, how did she know details I've never shared with anyone? Details I edited out of the videos I've posted, and never written about except in my own private records of events and readings?

"I saw a shadow walking through my living room last night. My dog saw it too and ran under the table and laid next to me, whimpering." I asked her to describe the specter she saw to me. It sounded eerily similar to how Fiona described her "brother" in her dreams.

She went on to tell me, "He told me that he respects you and looks up to you like a father figure. He wants me to ask you for the doll. He wants to live with me because he's afraid of you. He says that you're 'mean.' He said to me, 'I get blamed for everything. Even Anthony blames me for everything that goes wrong. He thinks I'm trapped in the doll, but if that was true, how could I be here with you?'

He does have a good point, you know," she continued. "If he is trapped in the doll, like you think, then how was he able to come to me last night?"

"Laurie," I said, "what he said confirms to me that he's a trickster. He's a liar."

"What do you mean?" she asked.

"If he weren't bound to the doll, why would he ask you to take it away from me so he could come and live with you?"

"Good point," she said after a moment. "I didn't think of it that way."

"Umm... hmm," I responded.

Then she said, "When I told him no, that I didn't want the doll, and I wasn't going to ask you for it, he said that it was okay, that someone would be coming to get him from you soon, anyway."

Now, *that* bothered me, but I didn't say anything.

After a few minutes of silence between us, Laurie muttered, "Oh God... I know all of this happened because I offered to help him. The dog is pacing back and forth, on alert. It's barking at nothing, Anthony. I'm really scared. I don't know what to do. I should have listened to you… I shouldn't have teased Harold the way I did. I should have listened to you."

The next thing I heard was a click. "Laurie? Are you okay? Are you still there?" I looked at my phone. She had hung up on me… again.

After hearing from Laurie and what happened to her the night before I went for a walk and thought about what it all meant. Due to the growing interest about the doll, and all of the misinformation on the Internet about it, I thought that I might write a book or film a documentary about trying to discover the truth about the doll.

That afternoon, a couple of hours later, I received another phone call from Laurie. "Harold wants me to tell you that he likes the idea of you writing a book about him. He doesn't like you wanting to make a movie about him though. He said that he doesn't want you making him into a carnival sideshow."

I had no idea how to respond. I had a flashback to Erica telling me that the spirit in the doll *liked* the idea I had of opening up a museum in my home and making the doll the centerpiece. Suddenly it started to sink in that whoever, or whatever Harold was, he could read my mind.

HAROLD MEET CHANCE

I was living in a pet friendly, extended stay hotel, at the time. Not that I had a pet... but that was about to change. A young woman who also lived in the same hotel had a job going door to door for a pest extermination company. She came across one home in which the owner asked her if she was interested in one of the puppies he had. He was giving them away for free. She couldn't pass up the opportunity and snatched one up.

"If you know of anyone else who wants one, I'm giving them *all* away!" she was told. When she came home with her new puppy, she found out that several of the guests wanted one. For the next few days she'd come back to the hotel with another puppy in her arms.

One of the puppies went to a woman who named it "Justice." She decided, after a couple of weeks, she just didn't have the energy it took to properly take care of it. So she offered it to a couple who were also staying in the hotel. After a couple of weeks, they too decided it was more energetic than they cared for, and they offered the puppy to me. I took it.

I didn't like the name it had and someone suggested I name it "Chance," since I was giving the puppy its third chance at a forever home. I quickly discovered Chance had a lot of energy. I began referring to him as my "weapon of mass destruction." I took him for long walks to try to burn some of that energy off, and he still had plenty of puppy energy to spare. When we'd get back to our room, I noticed he hated coming back in. I'd either have to pull him by his leash, or physically pick him up in order to get him back in our room. This happened for two weeks. At first I thought it was because he wasn't tired enough. Then it occurred to me what really might be happening.

Harold was in my room, on an end table, and had been since the first day I moved in. It got to the point, I didn't even notice the doll. But Chance did. I wasn't sure if Chance was reacting to the doll, or Harold was reacting to Chance, but I knew I had to do something about it.

"Harold, I'm sorry I didn't do this before, but I want to introduce you to Chance. He's the newest member of our 'family.' He's already had two homes and this is going to be his last. He's going to live with us so I want you to make him feel welcome."

I knew the true test would be to see how Chance behaved the next time I walked him. When we came back, Chance pranced into our room on his own, without a care in the world.

A couple of weeks later I tried to take a picture of Chance, but there were so many light anomalies flashing on the LCD I said, "I'm glad you like Chance, Harold, but I'm trying to take a picture of him. Would you please let me do that?" The orbs stopped immediately.

THE "SCIENTIFIC" INVESTIGATION

After what happened to Laurie, I decided to have a team of investigators look at the doll and try to determine what was going on. Up until that time I had been conducting my own "investigation" using a Tri-Field EMF meter, a Natural EM, and a digital recorder. I wanted to bring more equipment into the equation, but I didn't want to spend the money to buy them.

Lockdown Paranormal was a group composed of Deputy Sheriffs who worked in a county jail. I was introduced to them by my friend Colleen who, at one time, was a Deputy Sheriff herself and worked with the founders of the group, Randy and John. She told me that she had mentioned Harold the Doll to them and that they'd be interested in doing an investigation.

Even though I wanted to have an investigation with equipment I didn't have, I was still hesitant to say yes because I didn't want to be responsible for what happened. I told her I'd consider it. Later on, she told me know that they were still very interested in doing an examination of the doll, and were aware of the "danger" involved. "They're Sheriff's Deputies," she told me. "They work in a jail, and deal with dangerous prisoners all of the time."

That made sense to me. I agreed.

I told Camille what I was going to do, and she asked if she could join us. We met Randy and John at a Starbucks near Camille's house. After a few minutes of small talk, I told them a bit about the doll. I was fully prepared to call the whole thing off if something didn't feel right about them, or I thought they weren't taking what I told them about the doll seriously. Erica, the clairvoyant, eventually joined us, but said very little.

We decided to go out into the parking lot and do some tests with their Ovilus 3 to see what happens. Personally, I was more interested in watching them in action and seeing if they knew what they were doing.

There are teams who do not consider an investigation "scientific" unless technology is used. The problem as I saw it is that "paranormal phenomena" is a human experience. Secondly, most of the devices these teams used weren't designed to detect ghosts, in the first place. The Ovilus is an exception to the rule as far as investigative tools go.

The idea behind the Ovilus is that spirits use electromagnetic energy to manipulate words in the devices 2,000 + word dictionary to communicate with the living. Invented by a man named Bill Chappell who founded Digital Dowsing, LLC. When he was 47, he was asked if he could build a device to communicate with the dead. He thought the idea was rather silly but he went ahead and gave it a try. If anyone had the capability to do it, he did. His background includes a career as an engineer in the robotics and semiconductor industries, and teaching college courses in microprocessor design and C programming.

On April 23, 2007, he tested his first prototype device at the haunted Waverly Hills Sanatorium in Louisville, Kentucky. What happened would forever alter his view of the supernatural. He has since dedicated his abilities to the search for concrete proof.

I was looking for answers as well. Was there really a spirit in the doll called "Harold" who was murdered and ritually trapped in the doll for a crime he didn't commit? If so, where did this happen? How did it happen? How can he be released? Is the spirit something that I want to release, or will doing so create more harm than good?

I was hoping that Lockdown Paranormal would provide some of those answers for me. While we were out in the parking lot, the words, "guilty," and "apple," kept coming up on the Ovilus screen, enunciated by a robotic voice.

"Guilty? What are you guilty of?" Randy asked.

"Apple."

"Apple? Are you hungry?"

I saw a problem with the Ovilus. It was easy to create meanings out of the words rather than allowing them to speak for themselves. This went on for several minutes. Erica announced she was leaving, wished us luck, got in her car, and drove away. I wanted to continue this at Camille's house a short distance away and asked her if she was okay with that. She agreed.

When we got to her home, I set the doll on the kitchen table and Randy and John continued their investigation. This time they were asking questions, hoping to capture answers on their digital recorder. Personally, I was hoping that they came prepared to do more, but they considered this a "preliminary examination" of the doll. While they were doing this, Camille busied herself around her house, and answered phone calls.

After a couple of hours, Randy said something about suddenly having a headache. I told him, I wasn't surprised. Many people have told me about getting headaches from being in the doll's presence, or simply looking at its picture. He asked if I would mind that they ended the session, and when I agreed, he and John left, promising to review the "evidence" they had gathered so far. "We'll let you know if we find anything that would justify a more thorough investigation of the doll."

I told them I was looking forward to hearing their findings. I didn't hear anything for a couple of weeks, and when I did, it wasn't from them. It was from Colleen.

"Something happened to Randy while he was reviewing the evidence of the investigation," Colleen told me.

"What do you mean something happened?" I asked her. "*What* happened?"

"I don't know. I called John to ask him how things were going with the investigation and he said that something happened to Randy. That's all he said." Colleen sounded worried. "He told me that he'd call me back in a few days and let me know. Whatever happened, it sounded bad. I think Randy had to go to the ER."

I made Colleen promise to call me as soon as she heard anything. She promised she would.

I called Camille and let her know that something, I don't know what, happened to Randy. She asked if he was okay. I told her I didn't know, but I'd let her know as soon as I heard anything.

"I've been wanting to ask you something about what happened during the investigation," Camille told me.

"What's that?"

"Do you remember how that machine kept saying the word, 'apple' over and over again?"

"Yes."

"Well," she continued, "they kept asking if the spirit was hungry. I was thinking that maybe it was trying to say that the girl fell out of an apple tree."

"Holy shit," I thought to myself. "That makes *complete* sense to me!" I told her.

My head started swimming. "Why didn't you say something then?" I asked.

"I don't know… I mean they were supposed to know what they're doing, and it was just a thought I had every time I heard the word, 'apple.'"

I asked Colleen if I could have John's number, and she told me she'd ask. A day later she told me that she talked to him, and he said it was okay to give his number to me. "Did you ask him what happened?"

"Yes," she responded. "Something happened, and Randy was hurt really bad. I'd rather that John tell you though."

I thanked Colleen, hung up with her, and immediately tried to call John. I left a message, and waited for his call. When he didn't call back right away, I called again, and left another message.

Two days later, John called me back. We exchanged pleasantries. John asked me if there was anything new with the doll. I told him, "No, nothing new. How about Randy? Is he okay?"

"He's okay now, but he missed work for a couple of days," John told me. I heard a trace of fear in his voice.

"What happened to him?"

"Well," John continued after a pause, and a sigh, sounding unsure how to tell me. "He was listening to the EVPs we recorded when he heard screaming. Lots of screaming. People screaming."

"Screaming?" I thought to myself. "People screaming?" That didn't make sense to me. There was only supposed to be one spirit in the doll.

John let that sink in before going on. "Then he heard demonic laughter."

Now, that made even less sense to me than the screaming did. "Demonic laughter?" I didn't believe demons exist. I usually stopped listening once claims of the demonic came up in investigations.

"What else happened?" I asked.

"Well...," John said, sounding reluctant to even say what he was about to say, "his back went out, and he fell to the floor unconscious."

"What the hell?" I asked myself.

I was able to get ahold of Randy on the phone a few days after that. I told him I heard what had happened to him.

"I do have a bad back," Randy told me. "So that might explain what happened there. But I was listening to the recording and I had headphones on. When I heard what sounded like women screaming, fear went through my entire body. Then I heard that demonic laugh and suddenly it felt as though I had been hit in my back, and the back of my head with a baseball bat. I've never actually been hit by a baseball bat, but I imagine that's what it would feel like. I fell to the floor and I think I was unconscious for at least 20 minutes. When I came to, I couldn't move. I laid on the floor for about 30 minutes before I could get up, and my head throbbed so much I had to take a few days off from work."

"How are you doing now?" I asked.

"I'm okay now, but I never want to be around that doll again," he told me. "You really need to get rid of that thing. There's something evil attached to it."

I thanked him for his concern. He promised that they'd bring me a CD of the recording they'd made.

I never did receive it. I haven't seen nor heard from them since, either.

Several months later, I stumbled upon their report on the internet. I listened to the EVPs that they included as part of their evidence. In one of the recordings the question, "Who are you?" was asked. It was followed by a chilling reply.

"None... of... your... business."

HAROLD'S ANGRY WITH ME

After Lockdown Paranormal's investigation of the doll, I was confused. I didn't know what to think of the supposed screams they recorded, or the idea that there was a "demon" somehow connected to the doll. Okay, I did know what to think. I didn't believe it. I decided to take another break from the doll, and not do anything with it for a while. Just how long "a while" was supposed to be, I wasn't sure. I just knew I needed a break.

Then I received a call from my friend, Donna. "Harold's pissed at you."

"He's pissed at me? Why?"

"He says that you should be doing more to help him but you're not. He's really angry." I was stunned to hear her say that, because Donna was as skeptical as they come when it came to the doll.

"How do you know this?" I asked.

"I was thinking of calling you, and these thoughts just came to me. I don't know how else to say it. I heard in my head, 'Tell Anthony I'm angry that he's not doing what he needs to do to help me.' You really need to do something."

"I didn't think that you believed in this," I told her.

"I don't know whether I do or not. I'm just telling you what I heard in my head."

When Donna told me she "heard" from Harold, I could tell she was shaken up, but the problem was I didn't know what I was supposed to do. I hadn't spoken to Fiona in months, and even if I had, I wasn't sure how reliable her information was after telling me she died in the early 1800s, holding a doll that wasn't made until the 1930s.

"I'm doing the best I can, but at this point I'm at a loss as to what to do next," I told her. "For one thing, how do I know he's as 'innocent' as Erica says he claims he is? Jails and prisons are full of people who are 'innocent.'"

"I don't know what to tell you," Donna said, "but you need to do something, otherwise he told me that your life will *never* be normal again."

After we hung up, I did the only thing I could think of. I had a heart to heart talk with Harold. "Donna said that you told her you're upset with me for not doing more to help you. I want to help… if you're as innocent as Erica says you are, I want to release you from you're the doll. If you want me to help you, you're going to have to help me. I have no clue where to start. You're supposed to have died in the South, but where? I don't have the time, money, or energy to go on a wild goose chase. If this is going to happen, you're going to have to help me from your end."

I didn't know it at the time, but what I asked for would be answered, and set in motion a chain of events that would change my life, forever.

THE DREAM

It was around two in the afternoon when I suddenly felt exhausted and decided to take a nap. While I was sleeping I had a dream that the doll and I were in a shack. The walls of the hovel were covered with old, dirty dolls. I could hear angry, agitated voices and when I looked to see where they were coming from, I saw three men looking at me and the doll. They were afraid, but I wasn't sure what they were frightened about. I did know that they were talking about the doll.

Suddenly they ran out of the shack. That's when I realized that they had set the structure on fire. The flames quickly consumed the building and I was barely able to grab Harold and run out before it burned to the ground. The men were standing outside shouting at me. I don't speak Spanish but I knew they were saying I should have left the doll inside to burn.

That's when I woke up.

I shared my dream with a few friends who asked me what I thought it meant. Some of them thought it was omen that the hotel I was in would catch fire. I didn't think so. I told them my thoughts.

"Something's going to happen… soon…, and my life will never be the same."

DARKNESS RADIO

I received a text from Kathy, the woman whose auction I won Harold from. We had been in contact on and off over the years after she returned to the United States with Rick, who was now her husband. She asked me if I'd be interested in doing a radio interview with Dave Schrader of Darkness Radio about Harold. In all of the time I've had the doll up to then, I could count how many interviews I've done about it on one hand.

I had never heard of Schrader or Darkness Radio, but I agreed to do the interview on two conditions. The first one was that she does the interview with me. I felt then, and still do now, that she is an important part of Harold's story. The second condition was that she admit to knowing that when Greg originally put the doll up for sale, the story he listed about the doll was bogus when he listed it.

A few years before, I saw a blog written by Greg admitting that he made up the story about Harold on eBay, hoping to make a few more dollars off of it by claiming it was "haunted." I wasn't surprised since I didn't believe the story to begin with. What did surprise me was reading that Kathy was aware of this and that she bought the doll hoping to capitalize on the doll's notoriety by flipping it for a profit. I believed what Kathy said when she told me that she bought it to learn doll restoration.

I responded to Greg's post saying that I'm the one who won Kathy's doll in 2004 and have had my own experiences with it. In Greg's post, he alluded to the idea that he was going to write more about the doll, but didn't.

I questioned Kathy about what Greg wrote and she admitted to knowing that Greg had made up the stories in his listing, but she insisted that she did buy it to learn how to restore it. At the same time, she admitted that when she bought it her plan was to hold the doll for three months before relisting it on eBay.

I told her that the *only* way I would consent to doing the interview was if she admitted everything she had just told me on the air. The truth is that I was more interested in her admitting this than I was in doing the interview. "If you don't admit to this, and it comes out later," I told her, "not only is your credibility about the doll gone, but so is mine."

She agreed, so I agreed to do the interview. Kathy kept her part of her agreement, and I couldn't have been prouder of her. Dave was an excellent interviewer, and overall I was happy I agreed to do the interview although I thought we'd have more time than we did.

A couple of weeks later, I received a message on Facebook, then a text on my phone, followed by a voice mail. By the time I'd gotten all of them, a day had gone by. They weren't from Kathy this time, but from Dave. I called him and he told me he had been trying to get a hold of me but wasn't sure he had the right telephone number. He said he was associated with the television show, "Ghost Adventures," and that Zak Bagans and Aaron Goodwin were planning to film an episode at the Island of the Dolls in Mexico.

Zak told Dave that he thought it would be a great thing if they could bring "Robert the Doll" with them. Dave said, "I told him… 'The museum isn't going to let Robert out of its sight, but I do know the guy who owns Harold the Haunted Doll. I'll ask him if he'll let you take the doll with you.' So what do you think? Are you interested?"

I told Dave I'd consider it but only on the condition that it's treated with respect. "If they treat it as a doll or a prop, there will be hell to pay." Dave assured me that Zak has a great deal of respect for these sorts of things, so I agreed to talk to someone from Tupelo Productions.

I didn't hear from them for several days so I assumed that they found another doll they wanted to go with, which was okay with me. The only reason I agreed to even talk to them was so I might have another chance at an investigation, since the one done on the doll several months before by Lockdown Paranormal had ended rather abruptly. Not only that, but Zak, Aaron, and the Ghost Adventures crew often used more sophisticated equipment invented by Bill Chappell and I was hoping that they'd use some of the equipment on Harold.

When I did finally hear from Cory, a producer with Tupelo, I told him the same thing that I told Dave. "This is the real deal. It may have started as a hoax, but Zak and Aaron need to treat it seriously. If it's just going to be a prop on the show, or made fun of, I won't agree to this because someone will pay a price." Cory assured me that Zak was aware of the doll's reputation and would treat it with respect.

"There is one more thing," I continued. "The doll needs to be handled with kid's gloves. Its left arm is falling off, and I'm concerned about that. Not only that, but I think that the spirit in the doll is too. There's a woman in Australia who's been helping me research composition dolls and the other night she told me that she was on her computer looking them up when her husband said to her, 'Why don't you get off the computer and have a smoke with me.' They were in their garage and they were startled when they saw a shadow figure standing in front of them. The lights in the garage were behind what they were seeing.

'Do you see that?' the man said to his wife.

'I do,' she told him.

She told me that they could see the head, broad shoulders, and arms of a man standing on the other side of their car. She also said that the figure stood 3 meters (a little over 9 feet, 8 inches) high."

"Wow," was all Cory could say after a moment of silence taking it all in.

"Her husband pulled out his cell phone to take a picture of it. Just before he snapped a picture off, it moved very quickly to their left, its right. She told me he took another picture, and screamed in agony. She asked him what was wrong. He told her that his left arm felt as though it were being ripped out of its socket."

"I have no doubt that Harold was letting me know that it's concerned about losing its arm," I told Cory.

After another moment of silence, all Cory could say was, "Wow."

GHOST ADVENTURES CALLS

After speaking with Cory I made a few phone calls of my own asking if anyone was aware of anything I should be concerned about. I had heard from the staff of Stanley Hotel that members of another ghost hunting television show pretty much left a mess when they were done shooting. Harold was in such a fragile condition that I didn't want it coming back even worse.

No one I talked to had anything bad to say about the Ghost Adventures crew, so I decided to go ahead and let them use the doll. One of the people I talked to was author, and a director of a New Orleans ghost tour, Kalila Smith.

"I think it's something you should consider," Kalila told me. "It'd be good exposure for the doll."

I told Kalila that I wasn't so much interested in the exposure as in finding out the nature of the spirit in the doll. And seeing the results of their investigation on the doll.

She and I had spoken before about me coming to New Orleans, which I planned to do because I wanted to find out more about how a spirit could be trapped in the doll. She asked if I was still planning to come visit.

"I think I'll wait under after the Ghost Adventures episode airs," I told her. "I'm hoping that once I learn more about what's going on with the doll, I'll know what I'm supposed to do next."

Since I didn't hear anything negative about GAC, I called Cory back and told him I'd be willing to lend them the doll so they could take it to the Island of the Dolls, in Mexico. At that time, all I knew about "Isla de las Munecas" was that it was a small islet that had creepy looking dolls hanging in trees. I shipped the doll to New York, where My Tupelo is based, the day after deciding to allow GAC to take it there hoping it wouldn't be a waste of their time. After all, I'd never known the spirit in the doll to perform on command.

A little over a week later I received a phone call from Cory. "Harold's a star!" he told me laughing.

"So, it went well?" I asked.

"Very well. Zak couldn't be more pleased. I wanted you to know that we're shipping Harold back to you. You should have him sometime tomorrow. Thanks for letting us use your doll."

The next day I was doing laundry while I waited for Harold to arrive back at the hotel. I was transferring clothes from the washer to the dryer when suddenly my legs flew out from under me. I grabbed a hold of the table that was there to fold laundry on. That's all that kept me from cracking my skull on the floor.

I laid there for a few minutes. I heard someone come into the laundry room a couple of times and leave. Neither time was I asked, "Are you okay?" which I thought was odd. When I finally got up off of the floor, I saw a puddle of water halfway between the washers and dryer. "How in the hell did that get there?" I wondered. The clothes were damp, not dripping wet.

Cameron, the general manager of the hotel, and Jennifer, the young lady who worked at the front desk came rushing into the laundry after they saw me laying on the floor on the hotel's monitor. "What happened?" they wanted to know. I explained how I slipped on a puddle of water, but when I went to point it out, it was no longer there.

"I was signing for a package for you when I looked at the monitor and saw you laying on the floor," Jennifer said.

"That explains what happened," I thought to myself. "Harold's back. And he was letting me know he's not happy at having left in the first place."

CELEBRATIONS

I decided to take the doll back to the Celebrations psychic fair to see if I could find someone willing to do a reading. I was a little apprehensive thinking I might be stopped for carrying the bag it's in and having to explain the doll at the registration desk, but I paid my entrance fee and went in without so much as a questioning look.

Most of the readers sit at tables lined up against the wall with signs explaining their particular services. I walked around looking at them thinking I'd like to get a Tarot card reading, but everyone I asked said it wasn't possible. A couple of the readers asked to see the doll, and when I opened the bag I could literally see the blood drain from their face before they told me they couldn't do it.

Then I saw Shirley's sign. It said she was a psychometrist. Perfect. The only psychometrist to do a reading on the doll was April, and that was 10 years before. Erica had done three readings of the doll since, but refused to touch the doll.

I found out Shirley wasn't a full-time psychic. She wasn't even signed up to work at the fair but was filling in for a friend of hers who had to cancel at the last minute. She asked me to show her Harold, but when she did her reading, she closed the lid to the bag and put her hand on that, not touching the doll directly. I was careful not to tell her anything about the doll. I just sat there and took notes while she spoke.

"There's more than one spirit in the doll. There's a little girl. Her family is from Europe... Asia?" She looked at me for confirmation. I simply shrugged my shoulders, not saying a word.

"There's a Haitian nanny. The girl called her, 'Nanna.' I'm hearing a J sound… as in 'Jane?'" She looked at me again for confirmation of what she was saying. I glanced up from taking notes and again, simply shrugged my shoulders.

"The girl was afraid of her father. He was abusive. Physically abusive. He abused her and the nanny," she continued. This was the first time I'd heard this. "She had polio. She had trouble walking and she went into the doll when she died. She had a high fever, and was unable to move the left side of her body."

None of this matched what little April told me, and very little of what Erica and Fiona told me. I waited for her to continue her reading. "The nanny helped the girl enter the doll when she died. The nanny is still around but not in the doll. She does have access to the girl in the doll though." Shirley looked at me and smiled. "She likes you."

"Can you give me an idea as to what she looks like?" I asked, thinking of what Erica and Fiona told me.

"She has blondish… brownish hair. She was extremely stubborn… willful. I'm feeling a pain in the side of my head." Hearing that made me sit up and pay attention. "She never got the love she wanted, especially from her father. Her mother was oppressed by the father. They lived somewhere that was ruled by Puritans."

She was beginning to lose me again. The Puritans were a group of English Protestants in the 16th and 17th centuries. How could this little girl, who supposedly lived during that time period have a doll that wasn't made until the early 20th century? Unless she was suggesting that the girl lived in one of the New England states. But didn't Erica and Fiona say the boy accused of killing the girl, and the girl herself were from one the Southern states? Now, I was starting to feel a pain in *my* head.

"I think the father was from the East Coast, and that the mother was from Britain."

Hmmm… according to Erica and Fiona, the girl and her brother lived in the South….

"She didn't have any sisters *or brothers*," Shirley continued. The pain in my head became a little more intense.

"Her father had money, but he made it dishonestly. He was a bit of a shyster. He didn't like the girl, so he ignored her most of the time. She acted out to get attention. Julianna… Julia."

"Who's that?" I asked.

"I think it's the girl's name. Julianna… or Julia. Definitely hearing a 'J' sound."

Once again, what Shirley was saying didn't match up with what Erica was saying about the girl's name starting with an "A" and sounding like "Annabelle." And it didn't come close to what Fiona said she heard herself being called in her dream, "Auralia Audelle." I put my hands on both of my temples and looked at Shirley wishing I had a couple of aspirins.

"How old do you think she is?" I asked.

"About 7," Shirley answered.

"Well," I thought to myself. "*That* fit with what Erica and Fiona said. Not only that but, come to think of it, the hair color and the idea that she was willfully stubborn fit as well."

"The girl has a slight accent when she speaks. The nanny put her spirit in the doll because the house she grew up in was emotionally cold. Like the father. Julianna wanted to feel beautiful, and celebrated. When people look at the doll, that's how she feels."

I couldn't help but wonder if Shirley had somehow forgotten *what* the doll looked like. It's hardly the vessel I would want to be in if I wanted to feel beautiful and celebrated.

Shirley interrupted my thoughts. "You may think you chose to own the doll, but the truth is that the doll chose you. She chose you to own it." Shirley was looking at me and smiling.

"Thanks Shirley. How much do I owe you?"

After I left the Fair that afternoon I called Camille and told her about Shirley and her reading of the doll. Camille hadn't heard of Celebrations before. She thought it sounded like fun and wanted to get a reading herself. I offered to go with her. I wanted to see if I could get another reading, like a Tarot card reading on the doll while we were there. We agreed to go the next day.

When we got there, the first thing we both did was see an aura photographer. I was hoping that I'd be able to get a picture of Harold but it didn't work that way. When we sat down we put our hands on a metal box that had a metallic outline of a hand on top of it, which supposedly measured our energy and that's what the picture showed. It wouldn't work on the doll I was told.

Afterwards, I introduced Camille to Shirley who was even more amped up than she was the day before. "I'm glad you're here!" she told me. "I was getting more impressions from the little girl in the doll. I was going to text you and share them with you.

"Well, since I'm here..." I said, asking Camille if she'd mind if I got a reading about Harold before she got hers. "Not at all," she said. She wanted to see what Shirley had to say as well.

"I was getting something about the year 1915," Shirley began, but didn't bother to explain what the year was supposed to mean. She put her hand on the bag Harold was in again. "I'm seeing a rocking chair. The father sent the nanny home, or off to run an errand when he killed the little girl."

"Was this in 1915?" I had to ask. After all, the doll wasn't made until sometime in the 1930s. I looked skeptically at Camille who smiled back at me with a look that said, "Don't say anything."

Shirley was too involved in what she was doing to see the looks between Camille and me. Or if she did see them, she didn't let on she had. She kept going. "He... the father... hit her when she was on her side. The first blow didn't do it, so he picked her up and smacked her up against the corner of a dresser. Then he threw her on the floor like a rag doll."

Whether this really happened or not, I stopped smiling and flinched at what I heard.

"The nanny was let go after the child died. She didn't know about it until the next day. The father told her it was an accident. The nanny demanded she be allowed to see the girl. She could see the girl's spirit. She kept asking to see the girl's body.

The nanny took the doll with her. She asked the father for it to remember the girl by. The nanny and Julianne were close, and she put the spirit of the girl in the doll so that she could still be close to her.

Do you keep the doll in front of a television?"

I was stunned when she asked me that because the truth is, I did. I'd been doing so for almost a year at that point. One day it just came to me to put the doll in front of the television while it was on so it could watch the "redneck" shows that were gaining popularity at the time. I thought that since Harold was supposedly from the South, he might enjoy watching shows filmed there.

"Julia says that you let her watch television. She likes Disney movies, and she also likes comedies."

"Okay, I'll start leaving the television on the Disney channel, as silly as it sounds," I thought to myself.

What Shirley said next not only snapped me out of my thoughts about having the Disney channel on continuously, but really got my attention. "I think they killed the uncle together."

"Who's they?" I asked.

"Julia and the nanny. They used something to hit him over the head with."

The new wife had nothing but trouble. Her pregnancies ended in miscarriages, and she eventually became barren. When she found this out she started drinking and made her husband's life a living hell!

He (the father) trafficked children through the West Indies. Also forced young women into prostitution servicing the troops. He was from a British owned or occupied country.

Yes. She was seven years old.

Her father told her no one would ever marry her because of her polio.

He had a half-brother who was mean. The uncle would stand Julia up and watch her fall down. He'd then leave her on the floor crying.

The doll was given to her by her nanny to comfort her.

She wants her story to be known. Wants to help other children. Wants to be celebrated. Does not want to be released at this time. You'll need to go through the nanny to do it. "

"How am I supposed to do that?" I asked Shirley.

"You'll need to contact her directly."

When she said that, I decided to let the reading end.

For more than a year now I thought I was dealing with the spirit of a young man. Now, Shirley is telling me it's the spirit of a young girl. Of course, Erica did, at first, pick up on the spirit of a young girl during her first two readings of the doll. She also said that I'd have to find the plantation in which this *boy's* spirit was trapped. Once I do, I'll know what to do to release him.

I decided that if that's the case, then I'm going to put off finding the plantation until *after* Harold's appearance on Ghost Adventures. Hopefully, I'd have a better idea of what I'm dealing with then.

THE FLASHLIGHT TESTS

I'm not a big fan of the ghost hunting shows on television but I started to watch them on occasion to get an idea as to what was going on as far as the equipment being used to investigate supposed haunting activity. On one show I saw something that made me laugh. They were using a flashlight to "communicate" with the spirits supposedly haunting the building. The flashlight would turn on or off in answer to their questions. "On" meant "yes," and "off" meant "no." I wasn't sure how they were doing it, but I immediately thought that the flashlight had to be manipulated remotely somehow. I turned the show off, shaking my head.

Several months later I had the same show on. I was about to turn it off when I heard an explanation on how the flashlight was set up. I decided to give it a try. I took a Mag-Lite flashlight and slowly turned the top until the bulb turned on. I then carefully unscrewed the top until the bulb turned off. I tapped the body of the flashlight and the light turned on. Another tap and the light turned back off.

I put the flashlight on the nightstand in front of the doll and asked a question. "Is there someone in the doll who is willing to answer my questions? Turn the light on for yes."

The flashlight came on. "No way," I thought to myself. I said, "Whoever turned the flashlight on, can you turn it off again so I can ask you some more questions?" The flashlight turned off. I almost had to change my underwear at that point. I took my camera and started recording a video of what was happening.

I didn't know what to ask so I started making questions up off of the top of my head.

"Harold, if you're willing to communicate with me, would you please turn the flashlight on?"

Nothing.

"Okay… would you turn the flashlight on if you *do not* like being called Harold?"

The flashlight came on.

"Are the stories that Shirley told me about you true? If they are, please turn the flashlight on."

Nothing happened. I took that as a "no."

"Is what Erica told me about you true?"

Once again, the flashlight remained turned off.

"Am I completely on the wrong track as far as finding out the truth about you?" I asked.

A few moments later, the flashlight turned itself on.

"Do you want to hurt me?"

The flashlight came on again. I began to freak out, and had to remind myself that I wasn't sure that the spirit in the doll really was communicating with me using the flashlight.

I decided to ask one more question that night. "Harold, some people think that you're a demon." I carefully worded my next statement. "If you're *not* a demon, please turn the flashlight on." After several seconds the flashlight remained unlit.

"So does this mean that you *are* a demon? If it does, please turn the flashlight on."

The flashlight came on for a couple of seconds, and then turned off. I thought to myself, "Does this really mean that Harold is a demon?"

The flashlight turned on again. This time, it stayed on.

"I WILL NEVER FORGET THAT NIGHT"

I created a website for the doll that people could go to if they had any questions. I created a group on Facebook for anyone who wanted to discuss the doll with me. I also reactivated my blog about Harold. Visitors soon started telling me about feeling ill while reading about the doll. I was told about telephones and computers crashing after logging on to the website, my blog, even the Facebook group I created.

Perhaps the most disturbing, and confusing thing I heard, happened in the week leading up to the show. My friend Marianne was following Harold with a great deal of interest. She read everything she could on the doll. She even invited a few friends over for a "Harold party" the night he was to make his television debut on Ghost Adventures.

The Wednesday before the show aired, Marianne and I were talking on the phone and she told me how excited she was that people were coming over to her apartment to watch the show with her. She fell asleep shortly after we talked. At 3 a.m. she was awakened by what sounded to her like a young boy, around 5 years old, calling out her name. Since she lived alone and didn't have any of her grandchildren with her that night, she got out of bed and walked around her apartment, wondering who could have possibly called her name. When she didn't see anyone, she sat down on her couch, feeling confused and unsettled. The voice kept echoing in her mind. She had never heard that voice before, and didn't know where it had come from.

Twenty minutes passed and she told herself it was nothing more than a dream. She went back to bed. Lying there she realized that she didn't want to go back to sleep. She was afraid she might hear the voice again.

The next night she went to bed and said her nightly prayers thanking God for protecting her from evil in this world and the "other world." No matter how hard she tried she couldn't fall asleep. She could still hear the child's voice ringing in her ears. After a while she closed her eyes, and hoped nothing like that would happen again.

Later that night, around 3:30 a.m. she was awakened again by her name being *screamed* this time. "It sounded like a woman," Marianne told me later that day. "I'd say that she was in her late 40s, early 50s."

When Marianne heard her name she felt what she described to me as a "raw, wild energy." She sat up in bed so violently her bed literally shook. Her heart pounding, her entire body shaking, she jumped out of bed and turned on every light in her apartment. "I was pacing around in circles. I was too jumpy to want to sit down. I felt like I couldn't breathe so I went out onto my balcony to get some air."

Several minutes passed before she went back into her apartment, still shaking. Her mind was reeling. Feeling afraid, she wished she wasn't alone, but was glad at the same time that none of her grandchildren were there either night this happened. She kept repeating to herself, "Anthony... Anthony... Anthony... I've got to call Anthony. This is something he needs to know about!"

She calmed herself down with a glass of water. Not wanting to go back into her bedroom, she sat on her couch until daybreak. Feeling safe, and reassured by the morning sun she found the courage to go back to bed. Unable to stay awake, she fell asleep not feeling safe in her own home.

She called me later that day, telling me about what happened the two previous nights, asking me if I thought it might have anything to do with Harold. "I don't think so," I told her. "From what I've heard, there's only the spirit of a young man in the doll, not a child. I've never heard of a woman. I don't know what to tell you. Are you okay?"

"Anthony, I will *never* forget this night as long as I live."

THE LAUGHING DOLL

When the day finally arrived for the first airing of the episode, I was both excited and uneasy at the same time. I wanted to find out what Bagans, Goodwin, and the Ghost Adventures crew uncovered in their investigation, but I really wasn't crazy about all of the exposure the doll would get from being on the show.

Camille and I had lunch together that afternoon. Before she left to go home to watch the show with Steve, her husband, I asked her to take a picture of me holding Harold in front of my hotel to commemorate the day. After she took a few photos I suggested we go grab a cup of coffee. She agreed.

"Let me put the doll back in my room, and we'll leave," I suggested. I put the doll back and was walking towards Camille who was waiting for me at the inner set of doors in the lobby. When she saw me she began to open the door. As she did, I heard what sounded like a laugh, but more like a cackle. Even though it was close to Halloween, I was still surprised by what I heard.

"Did you hear that?" I asked Camille.

"Yes." She answered.

"What did it sound like to you?"

"Like a witch's cackle. It sounded like it came from a doll."

"That's what I heard," I told her. I turned around and saw two young girls sitting in the lobby. As far as I could see, neither of them had a doll, but I walked up to them anyway. "Hi! Do either one of you have a doll with you?"

Both of them looked at me blankly. I repeated myself. "Do either of you have a doll?"

"No," the older of the two girls answered. Looking at them, I assumed that they were sisters.

"Huh… I just heard what I thought sounded like a doll's laugh, and I was just wondering if one of you had a doll," I explained.

"I heard it too," the older girl said.

"I didn't hear anything," the other girl said, looking puzzled.

Both the older girl and I looked at her surprised. "You didn't hear the laugh? It sounded like a witch's laugh. Since it's almost Halloween, I thought one of you had a doll that did it. You really didn't hear the laughing?" I asked. The little girl shook her head.

I walked into the hallway and saw two boys playing at one end. I didn't think it was one of them. I walked up to the front desk where three guests were being checked in. Neither they nor the woman at the front desk heard anything. I was stunned because it was so loud.

Camille and I didn't sit down to drink our coffees but got them to go. She was anxious to get back home to watch the show on television. So was I. Still, I wasn't prepared for what I saw.

GHOST ADVENTURES, THE ISLAND OF THE DOLLS, AND HAROLD

My entire reason for going public about owning the doll was to make known that yes, there really is something "paranormal" going on with the doll. No, it's not what is circulating on the Internet and YouTube videos. Most of what people thought they knew about the doll was based on Greg's original listings on eBay which he later admitted were a hoax.

In my wildest dreams I never thought the doll would end up being featured on a popular show, let alone be investigated at the "Island of the Dolls" in the process. The reason I decided to go ahead with it was that I was hoping to learn more about what was going on with the doll, and I thought that the Ghost Adventures Crew would be the team to help me with that.

Because all of the negotiations were done last minute, I sent the doll by overnight delivery the day before it had to be in New York in order to be packed and ready to go to the island. I wasn't invited to be a part of the filming, so I was as much in the dark about what happened with the doll at the island as anyone else, outside of the stars of the show, and the production crew.

Located just south of Mexico City, between the canals of Xochimico, is the tiny island known as, "Isla de las Munecas (Island of the Dolls)." Home to hundreds of dolls, severed doll limbs, decapitated heads, which decorate the island's trees, it was never meant to be a tourist attraction.

It is known for being dedicated by Don Julian Santana Barrera to the lost soul of a poor girl who drowned there in strange circumstances. Barrera was the caretaker of the island. According to legend, shortly after finding the little girl,

Barrera saw a floating doll near the canals. He thought that the doll probably belonged to the girl. He picked up the doll and hung it to a tree, as a way of showing respect and support the spirit of the girl. According to those who were close to him, Barrera was tormented by the idea that he was not able to save the little girl's life.

Fifty years after he began collecting dolls and hanging them on the island, Julian was found dead, drowned in the same spot he claimed the girl died.

I didn't know *any* of that the night the show aired for the first time. I also didn't know what happened while Harold was there. I read a quote from Zak Bagans describing his experience with the doll as the "most terrifying" he'd had in the 10 seasons he'd done the show. What that meant exactly, I didn't know but I'd be finding out, along with everyone else who watched the show.

The episode had a dramatic start, which only increased my expectation of what was to come. I had to hand it to Zak for even wanting to do this considering he admitted to having a phobia of dolls to begin with. Nick Groff wasn't on the episode. He was home with his newborn baby girl.

It soon became clear to me that Harold was not be going to be the focus of the investigation, but the island was, which made sense. I was never told that Harold would be the focus of the investigation. I was told that Zak wanted an authentically haunted doll to see what would happen if they brought it to the island. So when Harold was introduced 10 minutes into the show as a "guest investigator," I was disappointed, but I got over it quickly.

I was surprised to see the suitcase he was in. I'd never seen that suitcase before. After I made it known in 2013 that I owned the doll, Camille thought that the doll needed to be in a better bag, and found one at a thrift store. A black Samsonite, soft shell bag, with brown handles, and a shoulder strap. I didn't see the need for it at first, but when I put the doll in it, I agreed with Camille it would better protect it in its fragile state than the Duane Reade bag did. That was the bag I shipped Harold to them in.

"Guys, I want to introduce you to our guest investigator," Zak told Aaron and Jay, "one of the most haunted dolls in the world… Harold the Doll." He warned them not to touch it or look into the doll's eyes. He then began relating stories directly from Greg's original listing on eBay. He talked about Kathy as being a woman who owned the doll, and whose friend looked into the doll's eyes, dying a month later from a brain tumor. A story I had never heard before. Ironically, as he was telling this story, the camera did a close up on Harold's face almost forcing you to look into its eyes.

"What if we take one of the most haunted dolls in the world… to the Island of the Dolls," Zak continued, "to see if the energy inside of this doll has some kind of reaction to the dolls on the island.

This isn't Barbie's boyfriend. This is for real."

They took Harold to a psychic medium in Mexico City, who, according to Zak, knew *nothing* about the doll. I couldn't wait to hear what she had to say.

According to Sabrinah, the psychic they took the doll to, there were 5 spirits inside of the doll. "What?" I said out loud. "I'm only aware of one." My skepticism meter about the authenticity about this medium immediately went to red.

"One of the owners of this doll was a woman… she was crazy… like she was in a psychiatric hospital," the woman said, according to her interpreter. "… and she's telling me that it's dangerous to be carrying this doll around, because you can get sick because of the manifestations of this doll."

"Well, I totally agree with *that*," I thought to myself, having experienced the same thing. "At least she got that right."

Bagans looked as though he were having second thoughts about this doll. Goodwin didn't look all that excited about being around it either.

Sabrinah began speaking again, and the translator said, "She just told me that you should treat well that doll because the spirits could manifest and it could get pissed off, and it could attack…," echoing what I told Cory. Except, I said "spirit," not "spirits."

Leaving the interview with the psychic, Zak says he felt a pain in his left arm and showed three small bruises to the camera. It was then he remembered that I asked them to be careful of the doll's left arm because it was falling off.

A couple of things happened in the show that were eerily similar to my own personal experience. At one point, while Zak, Aaron and Jay were "exploring" the island at night, a fire mysteriously started, reminding me of my dream. The second incident happened in the shack on the island—the shack filled with dolls. Zak was carrying the doll in the bag I'd sent him in. I felt chills when I heard

Aaron say that according to the psychic, it was a "good island" that they were bringing a "bad doll" too. For me, it was further confirmation of my suspicions about the nature of the doll.

Bagans decided to take the doll out of the bag. Before he could, what sounded like a cat fight broke out, and a doll began laughing. Much like the laughter I heard earlier that day in the hotel lobby.

Goodwin described what happened as being in a real life "horror movie." "Welcome to my world, Aaron," I thought to myself as I heard him say that.

After the episode ended, I felt that I still didn't know much more, if anything at all, than I did before the show started. I didn't believe what the psychic medium said about there being five spirits in the doll.

I had said to people before the show aired that I'd know what I needed to do after the show aired. It seemed to me that what I needed to do was my own investigation of the doll.

GHOST ADVENTURES AFTERMATH

I expected to be attacked after the show aired, and I was. People were accusing me on the Internet of fraud and trying to make money off of Harold's appearance on the television show. I did receive offers from people who wanted to buy the doll, and I thought that some of them might actually be serious, but I turned them all down.

I began to seriously consider doing my own documentary film on the doll. I thought it was the best way to get the truth about the doll out there. The problem was I didn't really know what the truth was. I began to feel as though I were trying to solve a 1,000-piece puzzle with 600 pieces missing and no picture to work with. So I started buying new equipment to conduct my own investigation on the doll. I already had a Tri-Filed EMF meter, and a Natural EM meter. I had an expensive digital recorder but I didn't have much luck recording EVPs on it, so I bought another one.

I also purchased:

- An SB7 spirit box.
- A REM POD that emitted an EMF field that set off alarms when that field was disturbed, theoretically by spirits.
- Full spectrum video camera which filmed in all ranges of light.
- Two new Mag Lite flashlights—one for yes answers, one for no.
- An Ovilus 4 which was an upgrade from the Ovilus used by Lockdown Paranormal.

I wasn't trying to prove the doll was haunted… to anyone. As far as I was concerned, there was no doubt whatsoever that it was. What I was hoping for was meaningful communication with the spirit in the doll. I also wanted to know how this could happen.

Was Erica correct? Was there a spirit of a young man in the doll who was wrongly accused of a crime he didn't commit, who was then murdered and trapped within the doll? Fiona contacted me telling me of dreams that she had been having since she was a child that seemed to validate what Erica told me. If that was the case then I wanted to know, "How do I help free him?"

If that really wasn't the case, and I found out that the little girl was murdered, and he did do it, then as far as I was concerned, the case was closed, and he could remain trapped in the doll.

Of course, I also had to remain open to the idea that none of it was true. If that were the case, I was okay with that, too.

I didn't have a lot of hope of finding anything out using the equipment, but at the time it was all I could think of doing. I had come to the conclusion after Shirley's reading that if there was a spirit in the doll, it was cunning, manipulative, devious, and simply didn't want me to know the truth.

For that reason alone, I didn't want to take the doll to another "psychic" who would want me to take what they said at face value. I wanted to be able to validate what I was told. At least Fiona seemed to validate what Erica told me and so that's the theory I was working on. This is why I didn't believe the psychic in Mexico City that Bagan and Goodwin featured on the show. But that was about to change.

THE BABY IS SAD

I did get results with the equipment. The SB7 spirit box scans AM and FM radio frequencies, and as the theory goes, is used by spirits to communicate with the living. One night, I recorded a session on video in which you can clearly hear, "My name is Harold."

Did I believe it? No. As I said, I'd already come to the conclusion that the spirit was a liar, and didn't want me to know the truth. Whatever the spirit's name really was, I didn't think it was Harold. I'd just about given up hope of ever finding out what was truly happening when I received a message on Facebook from Jane (I've changed her name to protect her privacy).

Jane hadn't seen the Ghost Adventures episode and didn't have the slightest bit of interest in seeing it either. She was on YouTube hoping to learn how to make stuffed toys to sell in order to raise funds to pay for a service dog for her oldest son, Vincent, who was diagnosed as being moderately to severely autistic. (I've changed his name to protect his privacy at his mother's request.)

She doesn't remember why, but somehow she ended up watching a short video about Annabelle the Doll. The doll, which served as the inspiration for the movies, "Annabelle," and "The Conjuring" (neither of which Jane has seen either), first gained public attention when it was written about in Gerald Brittle's biography, "The Demonologists" about Ed and Lorraine Warren.

Here's a brief summary of the story of Annabelle the Doll—

Annabelle is a vintage Raggedy Ann doll purchased in 1970 by a mother for her daughter Donna's 28th birthday. The doll supposedly began moving around Donna's apartment and would leave messages for her on parchment. There wasn't any parchment paper in Donna's home.

After Donna and her roommate began experiencing even more unexplainable phenomena, Donna contacted a medium. The psychic told her the doll was inhabited by the spirit of a seven-year-old girl named Annabelle Higgins, who was supposedly murdered in the girl's apartment. According to the medium, the spirit of Annabelle was in the doll.

Donna's friend Lou, was skeptical about what the psychic told the girls. Apparently Annabelle wasn't pleased. One day while he was taking a nap, he claimed that the doll attacked, and tried to strangle him. That's when Donna turned to the Warrens for help.

The Warrens informed Donna that Annabelle was actually not inhabited by a little girl as the medium said, but an inhuman spirit. A demon. The Warrens removed the doll from her home.

On their drive home, according to the Warrens', their power steering and brakes failed with the doll in the car.

The Warrens had a special case built for the doll in their Occult Museum. They believe it is responsible for at least the death of one visitor to the museum who taunted the doll and was told to leave by Ed Warren for doing so.

After watching the video about Annabelle, she saw a picture of Harold in the sidebar. Curious about the doll, she clicked on it, and briefly watched a video talking about the doll, based primarily on the stories in Greg's original listing.

She doesn't remember why, but she paused the video before it was over. Whatever it was, she promptly forgot about it, until Vincent asked her if he could play a game on her iPad. When she refreshed the screen, there was Harold. Vincent looked at it, looked away, and immediately looked at it again. His reaction to the doll unnerved her to the point that she did some research, and found out that I was its owner. She sent me a message on Facebook Messenger.

I'm a little disturbed. My autistic son, Vincent, just happened to, by accident, look at a picture of Harold on my iPad. Bad mother left it open on your page. He looked at it and said the baby hurts ... Baby is sad... he needs help.

Don't take it the wrong way ... it was my fault. Just thought would like to know. He tends to see people's auroras [sic] *colours.*

"Thank you for sharing," I wrote back. "How old is your son?"

He is only 6. We are in Australia. He seems very drawn to Harold.

"I hope you don't mind me asking, but why do you think that is? Children seem to have the same reaction as your son, saying that the "baby" is sad. I'm trying to understand, because I trust their instincts."

I really don't know. When we first moved to this house, he kept telling me about the sad man. He has paint… we are on aboriginal land!!! I have walked around our house many times catching him talking to someone/thing. Due to his autism he doesn't say much… to anyone. But talks to ease with whatever is in our house. He really was so taken with Harold. I tried to just dismiss it… telling him it is just an old doll, but he kept on with the baby is sad… 'He hurts.'

"Thank you. I started saying, just last night, that Harold is a thousand piece puzzle with 600 pieces missing. Your son may be providing a piece to the puzzle."

Happy to help if can. He really is a sensitive soul. I am drawn to Harold too for some reason. If Vincent can help I will let him, but his safety will always come first. If can be honest, do you think Vincent could get hurt by Harold?

"I don't think so. The spirit in the doll *typically* goes after those who disrespect it."

BE CAREFUL WHAT YOU WISH FOR

Larry, who is a fan of the television show, Ghost Adventures, was watching the episode about the Island of the Dolls the night it first aired. He, too, found himself strangely drawn to Harold when the doll was introduced as a "guest investigator." When the fire inexplicably started on the island, he knew he had to find out more about the doll. Immediately after the show ended, Larry googled the doll, found a video, and several websites talking about it. After a bit more searching he found Harold's website, and Facebook group page.

He began reading the posts and wanted to help me understand what was going on. He read where I wrote that the reason I created the group and posted on it was so that people could help with the investigation by providing input about the posts, but he wanted to do more. He wanted to be more hands on. "I wish there was something more I can do to help," he thought.

He would soon learn that there's a lot of truth in the adage, "Be careful what you wish for."

The next night, Larry was having trouble getting to sleep, a problem he'd had for years. He turned off the television, all of the lights, and went to lie down in bed with his wife and 3-year-old son. He still couldn't stop thinking about how much he wished he could help me solve the mystery of the doll. He closed his eyes and clearly saw in front of him the face of a woman looking back at him.

He immediately opened his eyes and found himself back in his bedroom. He closed his eyes and saw her again. He couldn't see her body, only her face. She was surrounded by a fog, and the only light seemed to be coming directly from him.

Suddenly, the face of a young child appeared next to her. Because of the child's haircut, he assumed it was a boy. The feeling of sadness and fear coming from them was almost too much for Larry to bear. He saw the woman's arm reaching out to him out of the fog. Even though she didn't say anything, he knew that she was asking him to help her and the child.

Without warning, another face appeared in front of the woman and child. It was gaunt, and badly burned. Larry couldn't help but notice how thin the man's eyebrows were, and that his scorches seemed to be more severe on the right side of his face. He was completely without any hair, as though it had all been singed off. He made a noise, like a snarling growl, aggravated with woman and child for asking for help. Larry was terrified by the anger and hatred he felt coming from this figure.

A large, muscular, veiny arm appeared out of the fog. Larry could only see it from the shoulder down. The hand had long fingers, and nails so long they looked like claws.

Terrified and overwhelmed by all of the sadness and fear he sensed, he opened his eyes and recited the Lord's Prayer. Closing his eyes again, he became aware of two more figures in the background, one taller than the other. They seemed to be afraid of angering the burned man even more than he already was.

The arm made a sweeping motion and the woman and child were suddenly gone from Larry's view. When he saw this he recited the Lord's Prayer a second time. He opened his eyes and recited the Lord's Prayer a third time.

He closed his eyes and the vision was gone. "What the hell did I just see?" he asked himself as he lay there, his heart beating like a drum inside his chest.

As he tried to process everything the thought came to him, "I have to tell Anthony about this," followed immediately by a second thought, "What if he thinks I'm crazy?"

He contacted me on Facebook Messenger, and we discussed what he saw. *I'm no artist,* he wrote to me, *but I'll try to draw what I saw.*

After sending me a picture of his sketch on Facebook Messenger he told me he was going to have someone he knows who *is* an artist draw a sketch of the three faces he saw. "I want you to see what I saw," he told me. "I'll never forget the smirk on his face as long as I live."

Anthony Quinata

THE JAILER

I was talking with my friend Melanie, who *is* an artist, and owns "Dutch Girl in New Mexico," a custom greeting card making company. I was telling her about a woman who drew a sketch of Harold and asked me for $70 for drawing it. Melanie offered to draw a sketch of the doll for me – for free.

No matter how hard she tried though, she just couldn't bring herself to do. It took her several weeks, from early November to late December to finally getting around to drawing an image of the doll. What she drew was a horned figure standing behind four other people, its arm holding them close. In her drawing there was a woman, and two children. There was also a shadowy figure she couldn't see well enough to make out any details. She tried to draw the doll itself, but was unable to do so.

She was putting the drawing in an envelope to send to me, when she felt inspired to do another one. She wasn't sure why, but she knew she had to do another one for me.

A few days later she was driving home from work when an image popped into her head. A woman holding onto the bars of a cage, her mouth wide open in a silent scream. Standing with her in the cage was what appeared to be a little boy around 5 years old, whose mouth was open in a scream as well. An older boy stood next to them. He didn't appear to be screaming, but looked terrified.

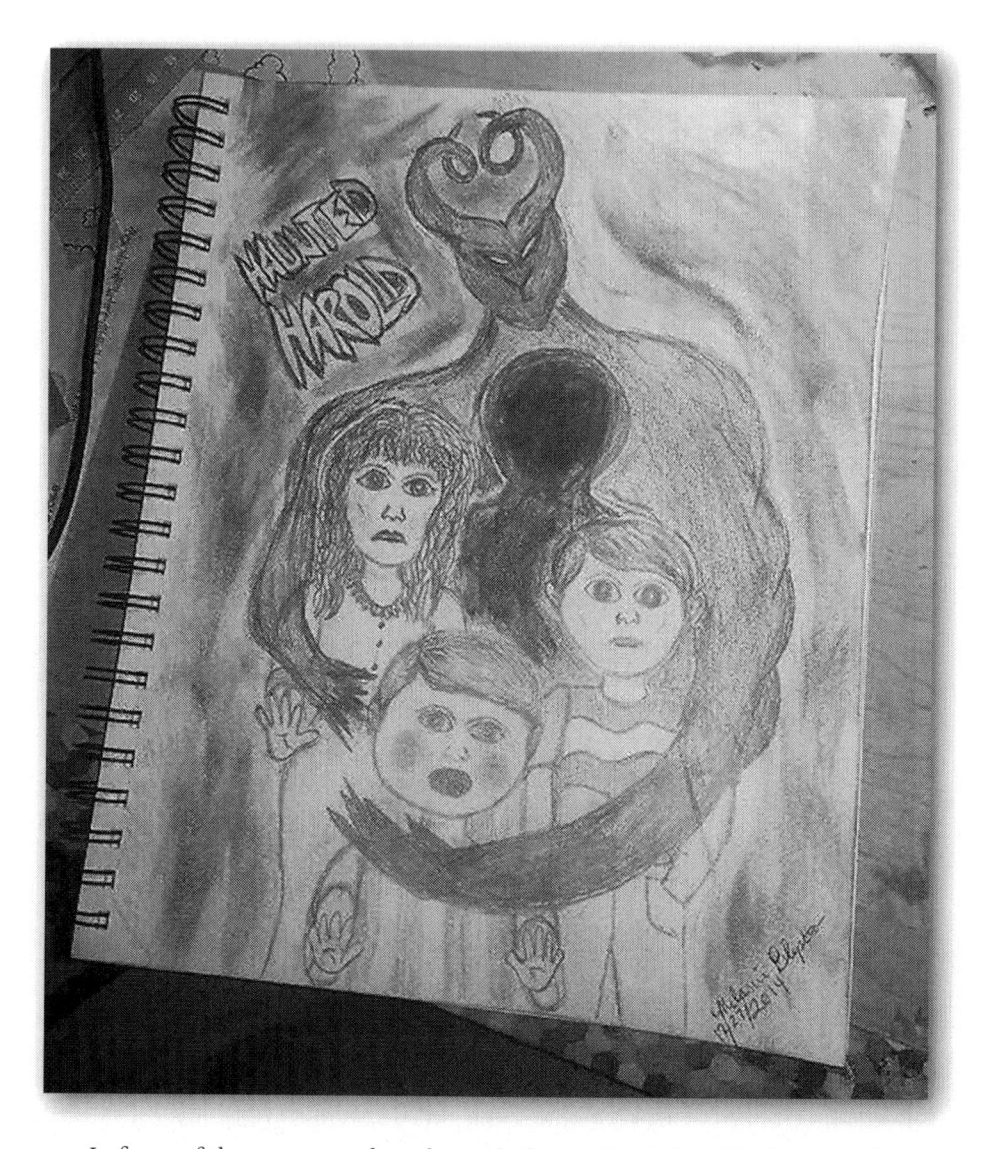

In front of the cage, one the other side from where the older boy stood was a dark figure whose face she couldn't see. He was manacled to the bars with what looked to her like a chain. Even though he was shackled, she told me, he appeared to her to be able to go wherever he, or the horned figure behind him, wanted him to go. "Whatever he is," she thought to herself, "isn't good. He's bad... really sinister."

The horned figure was enormous, with huge powerful muscles, long fingers, and nails. He had red, glowing eyes, and his arm was wrapped tightly around the outside of the bars. It was obvious to Melanie that he was the one in control. His presence felt even more malevolent to her than the shackled figure. The impression lasted a few seconds and disappeared.

A few days later she started cutting out what she saw for me with cardboard paper. She decided to start with the woman she saw. As she was doing so, she developed an intense headache which forced her to stop. A week later she felt able to work on it again. "I tried to put the doll in with the others, but I just couldn't do it. He wasn't meant to be in the picture. I just knew that they had to do with Harold. I didn't know how, but I knew that they did."

When I asked Melanie questions about what she saw, she told me that she assumed the younger child was a little boy "because of its haircut. It wasn't a razor cut, but it was cut short, like a boy's." I sent her a picture of the child in Larry's sketch. "Yep. That's what it looked like."

The next thing she told me about her artwork really stunned me. "I put clothes on the woman and the children because it didn't feel complete without them, but really all I saw were their faces. Except for the woman. I saw her hands gripping the bars tightly."

"All she saw were their faces," I thought to myself. "Just like Larry. All he saw were faces as well."

That same day, I received another message from Jane - *Not sure if this means anything to you or not... I showed Vincent two of your YouTube clips. He didn't say much but went into a trance. After about 3 minutes he looked at me and said, "Mummy you know the lady and the children are scared. That black blob won't let them go to the sunshine...."*

Anthony Quinata

THE CHILDREN ARE SCARED

"Do you think he can say how old the children are, or how many?" I wrote back.

I will have to ask in a roundabout way. I don't want him to think I am pushing Harold on him. Its 9 30 pm here so will ask him over weekend if I can catch him in the right zone (autism is a hard journey... but I do believe they are very in tune with many things). He was very sure about there being more than one child. He said children on more than one occasion.

He is a beautiful boy (I am biased lol), but one thing I know is he can't lie. Autism makes you see things very black and white. He has no imagination.

"Did *you* happen to see the Ghost Adventures television episode with the doll in it?" I messaged her.

No not yet. Will watch that one when my boys are not around. I just hope what Vincent says is making some sense. Would hate to be leading you in wrong direction.

I didn't care that she hadn't watched the show. I just wanted to make sure she wasn't being influenced by the show, and somehow prompting her son by what she'd seen.

The next night, Jane messaged me again.

Can I tell you something? I went to check on Vincent early hours of the morning (something I don't always do). He moved around in his bed so his face was facing me... and he spoke. I am not sure if he said, "Be free" or "Be careful". It shocked me a little.

"Was he awake?" I messaged back.

No and it didn't sound like him. I will be honest... I'm beginning to think this might not be a good idea.

UNCLE ANT

Hey, tried to get Vincent to look at Harold and ask him about lady and children.... He didn't look comfortable. All I could get from him was, 'It won't let me look. He doesn't like me.'

Vincent did art therapy today. The image he painted is at therapy still so I can't take a picture of it..., but he did say to David (art therapist), 'It's what he wants... the doll on iPad.' Now that might be nothing but just seemed strange!

I asked Jane if she saw what Vincent drew.

Yes, I was watching him through the two way viewing mirror. David was talking about emotions to Vincent and how they make him feel, what color those emotions make him feel/ see. He's been doing art therapy for 6 months now....

I didn't hear from Jane for a couple of days.

Vincent was home today as he was unwell. We watched your clip on which you mention us in a roundabout way. Vincent said, "That's me mummy, but the doll doesn't like me. The blob won't let me help them. The little boy is scared. He wants his mummy. Mummy wants him. She told me to tell him to go to the sunshine. But he can't.'

A few minutes later, I received this message.

I'm beginning to think Vincent and I should step back from you. I am so sorry, obviously. A couple of people have worked out who I am. I was told to stay away from you and to keep my retarded son away from this page as we don't belong. I am sorry if we caused you any trouble.

I was angry. Not because Jane was protecting her son and herself. I understood that, but the idea that someone would call Vincent "retarded." I wanted to know who it was. Instead, what I wrote back to her was, "I understand. Both you and your son have been a very important part in helping me understand what's going on with the doll. I'm grateful. You are both celebrated in my prayers. Blessings."

With that, I thought that I'd never hear from her again. About 10 minutes later, she wrote,

Do you want us to stay in touch or just stay back? Either way we/I will help. Just not happy when people call my son retarded.

"Personally, speaking," I wrote back, "I think you should stay away from anyone who would refer to Vincent as 'retarded.'"

Autism is an amazing journey. I would have no other tour guide. I love him... I love the fact he can't lie.... Life is black and white, no in between. When in between does happen, it hurts him to the point he sobs as he doesn't understand. His swimming teacher told him he was on fire (good at swimming). He jumped out the water as he thought he was on fire. Breaks my heart but makes me proud as that's the way he sees everyone.

Hey can I send you the painting he did? You need to see it I think. I think it needs to be with you.

"Thank you!" I wrote back. "I would love the painting. It might go a long way in helping me understand what's going on with the doll."

I will help you, as will Vincent, as long as he is willing. But Vincent comes first. As soon as he is in danger, I will stop. Vincent calls you Uncle Ant.

I knew next to nothing about autism, but I couldn't stop thinking about what Jane told me about Vincent's inability to lie because of it. I began wondering if what Vincent was revealing about the doll not only answered my questions, but was so close to the truth, that "the black blob" as he called it, wanted Vincent and his mother to stop talking to me. "If that's the case," I thought to myself, "I think I need to take what Jane is telling me more seriously than I have been."

How many spirits is 'the black blob' keeping from the Light, and who are they?

How did such a thing happen?

Who, or what, is the 'black blob?' Vincent was talking about?

These questions started keeping me up at night. I found myself hoping that Vincent could help me understand what the hell was going on. But in light of Jane's fears, I messaged her saying, "I'll leave it up to you as to whether you want to share with me anything more Vincent reveals about the blob in the doll. Please stay in touch, if you're okay with that."

We will.

I didn't hear from Jane for another four days. I was just checking into a hotel in Virginia Beach, Virginia, Harold in tow, when she messaged me.

Here is a picture of the painting Vincent did.

From what I could tell, there was a black spiny figure that reminded me of a sea urchin, with red eyes. It was surrounded by four, what looked like stars, with gold painted in three of them. "What did he say about this painting?" I asked.

He didn't say much to me really... just it is what he sees when he looks at Harold. He did say it makes him sad!

The painting seemed to confirm what the psychic medium in Mexico City said. "Are there five spirits in the doll?" I wondered. If that's the case, what am I supposed to make of Erica's reading, and Fiona's dreams?

Really, he keeps on to me that you must have it. He won't even pick it up. It is sitting on the table at the other end of house, which is where he put it the other day when we got home from art therapy.

"I'd love to have it," I reminded her. To me it was another piece of invaluable evidence helping me to understand the nature of what was going on with the doll; and right at that moment, I was so confused, I didn't know what to think.

I didn't hear from Jane for another week. Then I received these messages—

He really goes into a deep trance-like condition, and a real dull voice. I really want to record him doing this so you can see... it's really quite freaky.

I don't want to lead you on a wild goose chase but I want to be honest with what he is saying.

He has had a real awful week at school—swearing, and lashing out at people. Just thought you would like to know.

I was sorry to hear about what was going on with her son, but I didn't know if swearing and lashing out was common or uncommon with autistic children, or at least Vincent. What I *wasn't* thinking was that it had anything to do with the doll.

Another week passed before I heard from Jane again.

Tried to talk to Vincent but with not much luck. He says the blob is shouting and very mad.... he said it's telling lies. That was the last thing he said.

"I've had an idea for a while now that it's a liar. Vincent seems to be confirming that," I wrote back. What I found reassuring is that Jane told me that, due to his autism, Vincent isn't capable of doing the same.

It's almost as if he thinks it's mad at him.

"I think that whatever it is, it's angry that the truth is slowly but surely coming out." I thought about what I could suggest she do to help her son. "Are you Catholic?"

No Hun, I'm not.

"Okay... no problem. I just want to suggest that you buy a Saint Benedict crucifix to hang in your home and a Saint Benedict medal for yourself, and one for Vincent. Get them blessed by a priest, if you're comfortable with that, or bless it yourself with holy water. It'll help with the black blob.

The idea that the black blob became upset and, according to Vincent, is starting to tell lies, suggests to me that Vincent is telling something I wasn't supposed to know. But I think that whatever this black blob is, it's being prevented by God from hurting Vincent."

Vincent sends a big hug to Uncle Ant, and so does mummy.

THE CROW

I didn't hear from Jane again for a few more days. I was a little worried about Vincent since she told me that the way he was acting was out of character for him. I decided to touch base with her and find out how they were doing.

We are both good. I would tell you if anything was going on, I promise. I have sort of kept him away from the topic of Harold the last few days.

I laughed to myself and wrote back, "I can understand why!"

I was surprised to hear back from her the next day after reassuring me that Vincent was okay, and she wasn't bringing up the doll.

Hey Hun, can I ask you a question.

"Absolutely."

Does a crow (the bird) mean anything? It's been at Vincent's window for the last 4 hrs. More than likely just me having a panic over nothing.

Anthony Quinata

I did a quick Google search on the subject and sent this back to her—

The crow is a spirit animal associated with life mysteries and magic. The power of this bird as totem and spirit guide is provide insight and means of supporting intentions. Sign of luck, it is also associated with the archetype of the trickster; be aware of deceiving appearances. If the crow has chosen you as your spirit or totem animal, it supports you in developing the power of sight, transformation, and connection with life's magic.

"That's what I found regarding the bird in a paranormal context. There's no doubt more.... Of course, it could have just landed on Vincent's window sill."

Yes.

"Are the crows still there?"

Yes, and there is only one. Just keeps pecking at the window. Sorry to disturb you.

"No, not at all. You're not disturbing me, and NEVER have." I wrote back, continuing to see what I could find out about what might be going on. "Hang on a sec. From what I've just read, it's probably because it sees it's reflection in the window, and is looking for a fight."

Wow, that's good! Never seen them here before. The Kookaburras usually chase them away. Now I feel stupid!!

"No, don't feel stupid. Don't ever be afraid to ask me a question, especially when you're worried about Vincent... or yourself! Keep in mind, it's also the archetype of the "trickster," which I believe the "black blob" to be. However, we have to consider "non-paranormal" explanations first. Having just said that, I say, 'better safe than sorry.' I'll sprinkle holy water on the doll and tell the entity that if it is responsible for the crows to knock it off! Let's see what happens after I do that."

Just was a little freaked as I don't see them here and it was at Vincent's window.

I didn't see her message about being freaked out, and I didn't tell her what I was doing. I was splashing holy water on the doll. "I command you, in the name of Jesus Christ, our Lord, that if you, whoever or whatever you are, have sent the crow to Vincent's window to scare him or his mother, that you send it away *now!*"

"Is it still there?" I asked Jane.

It has moved away. It's sitting on the fence about 600m away.

"Are you okay with that?" I asked, stunned that using the holy water actually seemed to work. Did something or someone in the doll really send the crow?

Yes. That's fine as long as it's away from the window. I must look like a nut case to you. Lol

"No.... okay, maybe a little bit," I wrote back, hoping that teasing her would relieve her anxiety.

Later that night, she wrote to me. *"The crow is gone as far as I can see. It was on the fence early this morning, but I've not seen it since. Thank you."*

A CLUE

I received Vincent's painting. It was even more disturbing to look at in person. A few days later I was talking to Larry about his vision. I was asking him questions about what he saw. He was trying to explain to me the feeling he felt when he saw the man with the charred face, and his smirk. That's when I noticed something I hadn't noticed before, on Vincent's painting, even though it was right in front of my eyes. Three of the stars had gold in it. One of them had black instead. Was this the burned man Larry saw?

I was so excited, I messaged Jane right away with my discovery, and what I thought it might mean.

"Vincent's painting may have the clue I've been looking for! I just noticed it last night!" I hadn't told her about Larry's vision, and the burned man.

Now you have me intrigued. What is it?

"I just noticed one of the smaller 'lights' has black in it. Which might explain a lot. If the 'black blob' is keeping the woman and the children (the stars with gold) trapped… the smaller light with the black may be the one appearing to, and attacking, people! I'm now thinking that instead of one malevolent spirit and four 'victims,' there are two malevolent spirits, and three victims!"

Really? Wow! That doll likes to keep you on your toes. Makes me sad to think about the poor spirits trapped.

WHAT IS THAT SOUND?

*V*incent just woke up crying... saying, "The doll (I assume Harold) comes to me in my dreams. He is very angry... he hurts my eyes. Vincent also said his name is..." but I couldn't understand as he was sobbing. I tried to record it but wasn't quick enough... sorry.

First time he has talked about Harold in weeks. He is a mess at the moment. I have him here with me. He is watching the bubble lamp. When he regresses like this it really gets me down. He is usually such a happy little boy. It was just strange since this is the first time he has mentioned Harold in weeks. Breaks my heart.

A few days later I messaged Jane to ask how Vincent was. I didn't hear back. A couple of days after that, I finally heard from her again.

Vincent was talking about you. Something about you traveling.

I didn't have any plans to go anywhere any time soon, so I asked, "Anywhere specific?"

No, he just said you were going a long way to a place you had never been to, but people would be cross.

"Cross, as in angry with me?"

He just said yes. He's still being all strange Hun, so could be nothing.

Once again, several days passed before I heard from Jane again. When I did, she seemed to be panicked.

Omg Anthony... Vincent has gone very strange. He keeps asking me if I hear that noise... 'It's here, it's coming.'

I'm scared I have never seen him do this. He's been rocking in his corner. He keeps mentioning you.

"What's he saying?"

Just can I hear it? It's here. I need to tell Uncle Ant.

I grabbed my digital recorder and turned it on, thinking it might be worth a try to get an EVP that might explain what Vincent is hearing. I let the recorder run for a couple of minutes. When I listened, all I could hear was a *loud* buzzing that made me think of a swarm of insects, like wasps, or locusts. "Is that what Vincent is hearing?" I wondered.

He just vomited ... Gotta go.

I decided to *soak* the doll with holy water. I was surprised to see a message from Jane a few minutes later.

He's asleep now. I'm going to watch him, just in case. PLEASE take care of yourself.

When I saw Jane was back on Facebook about 6 hours later, I sent her a message not knowing if she'd even see it.

We are fine thank you. Vincent can't remember any of it. He can't even remember being sick.

"Wow... I have to admit, I'm happy to hear he doesn't remember anything."

I am just happy he is ok. I will be honest it really scared me. So do you have any idea what it was about?

"I wish I did. If I had to guess, I'd say it was what Vincent calls the black blob."

Well, pardon my language, but the black blob can fuck off!

Anthony?

"Yes?"

Why do you think this is happening to Vincent?

It was a good question. I only wished I had a good answer. But I didn't. "I don't know," was the only answer I could give her.

THE DOLL IS ANGRY

The next time I heard from Jane she told me that she stopped "following" what I was writing about the doll.

The less I know, the better.

It wasn't unusual for people who've had a personal experience with the doll to feel that way. At one point I felt the same way. It was *one* of the reasons I put the doll away. "That's a great idea. Especially considering everything that's been going on with Vincent."

I don't even know what drew me to it in the first place. I don't usually follow any of that sort of stuff.

"It might not have been your idea to begin with," I wrote back. "I've come to the conclusion that I didn't choose to own the doll…it chose me." I told Jane about the eBay auction, and how I planned to dump it on Majik, but in the last few minutes, he didn't bid on it. No one did, leaving me stuck with a doll I didn't even want to begin with. "I don't know how to explain it. I just know that I was meant to have it."

It really is powerful, isn't it?

"Seems to be. Especially when you consider that Vincent is being harassed by a spirit tethered to a doll in Denver, and you live in Australia! It would help if I had a name. That way I could address whoever is harassing Vincent directly. Do you remember what name he told you when he had that dream?"

I don't know for sure, but it sounded like Eve or Evelyn.

"That sounds like it might be the woman Vincent talked about!" I wrote.

He is sure was it a lady. I will ask though, to make sure.

"… and he said she was angry with him?"

He was saying it / she hurt his eyes. Can it be something it's not?

I wasn't sure how to answer Jane. I still wasn't even sure how I felt about the idea of one of the spirits, *if* there really was more than one, being a woman. Marianne talked about a woman screaming her name. Larry saw a woman in his vision. Melanie saw one in hers.

But Larry and Melanie saw their visions *after* watching the Ghost Adventures television show. I often wondered if what the medium on the show said had any influence on what Larry and Melanie saw. Even if it had though, Marianne heard the woman scream her name *before* the show aired. Now Vincent, whom I was almost certain didn't see the show, is talking about seeing a woman. I decided I had to ask Jane again, "Did you see the Ghost Adventures television show with Harold in it?"

Not yet. Why?

"Because the psychic medium they used to them that there was a woman who should be in an insane asylum."

Really?

"I didn't believe it, but now I'm starting to wonder. He said that *she* was angry with him?"

Yes, he woke up saying it is angry, the doll, it is hurting my eyes.

I didn't respond right away. When I did, I said, "I'm just trying to figure out who, or what, we're dealing with here."

I don't want to give you false information. That's why I want to get him to talk to me before I tell you too much. Vincent can be complicated at times, and I don't want to lead you astray.

A few days passed before I heard from Jane again. It was obvious to me that she was struggling to understand what was happening to her son.

It scared the living day lights out of me Anthony. I'm afraid it will happen again… I can't let it. Vincent is my child and I am supposed to protect him.

"I know it's hard, but try not to be afraid. This is like a vicious dog. If it smells fear, it'll attack you using what you're terrified of. Fear is what it wants you to feel. That way you'll stop talking to me, and *that* is *exactly* what it wants."

I'm not letting you go anywhere. You're the only one who seems to be able to control it! I'm so sorry to do this to you.

"Don't worry about it. Sooner or later… we will win this thing. I'll help you stop it from bothering your son. I promise." As soon as I said it, I found myself hoping that it was a promise I could keep.

"THERE'S SOMETHING IN OUR HOUSE."

A week later, I messaged Jane to wish her a happy birthday. We chatted for a bit about her plans with her family that day. Something didn't seem right. "Are you okay?"

I guess so.

"You don't seem like it. What's going on?"

Just a strange night. I think I'm going mad.

"Do you want to talk about it?"

You wouldn't believe me if told you. I will be ok. How are you, young man?

"I want to hear what happened," I wrote back. I could feel myself becoming angry and impatient.

I think that there's something in our house.

My first impulse was to write, "AND YOU DIDN'T WANT TO TELL ME ABOUT THAT?" Instead, I wrote, "Tell me about it."

Look, I'm just going to sound stupid or like a real fruit cake.

"Try me."

It's ok; let's not worry about it.

If it were just her, I'd have dropped it with that. But it wasn't just about her. There was a child involved, and she was making it about her. I could feel the heat rising in my face. "So you don't trust me. Is that it? Okay…" I was going to say, "Fine," and drop it, but I stopped. There was a child involved.

I do trust you. Please don't say that.

I didn't respond. So she continued.

I went to check Vincent last night as he was talking or mumbling in his sleep. Nothing unusual... he does that a lot, but I like to make sure he is ok. As I walked towards his room (which is at the other end of the house from the main bedroom) it felt weird. I can't really put my finger on it, but it just felt DIFFERENT. As I got to his door I went to open the gate (he has a safety gate) but I couldn't open it. It was if it was glued shut or someone was holding it shut so I couldn't lift the catch. I tried, and tried, for what seemed to me, forever. Then it was as if something went past me. It didn't touch me, but I just felt a slight breeze as if someone walks close to you, if you know what I mean. During this, I opened the catch on the gate with no problem.

See, now I sound like a fruit loop.

"Not to me," I tried to reassure her. If anything like this happened again, I wanted her to feel she could trust me enough to tell me. "I'm just surprised you were so reluctant to tell me."

Sorry, but it scares me.

"I'm sure it does. If it happened to me, I'm sure I'd have to change my underwear after it happened!"

Not for myself, but for Vincent and Edward (her younger son). I'm afraid of what it could or might do to them. When it happened, I was more than scared. I hated not being able to get to Vincent. I just wish it would leave him alone.

"I think that there's something that the black blob doesn't want known. I'm just not sure what it is yet. Personally, I think that what happened is because, thanks to you and Vincent, I'm getting closer and closer to the truth, and the black blob is panicking. It wants to stop Vincent, and you, from talking to me. The thing is, it almost worked."

I'm sorry.

"Don't get me wrong. I'm not upset with you. I understand completely. There *are* times I want to give up, but then I remember what Vincent said about the mother wanting the children to 'come into the sunlight' but they can't; and she's in the dark with them. That's why I can't... I won't... give up. Not until I know what the truth is, and I'm depending on you and Vincent to help me find out what that is."

I just hope that we... I mean Vincent, can help you end this quickly.

"I do too," I wrote back. "For all of our sakes... I do too."

"HELP THEM."

The next afternoon, morning in Australia, I sent Jane a message asking her how she slept that night.
Okay.
"Not good?" I asked.
Whatever it is doesn't seem to want me going near Vincent.
"What do you mean?"
Whatever it is doesn't like me going in Vincent's room when he's sleeping.
"What happened?"
I think it scratched me ... so I got Vincent the hell out of there.

"Do you have a picture?" I was relieved when she wrote that she did, and sent it to me. There were three distinct scratches on her left forearm. "I'm glad you had the presence of mind to take a picture."

I'm just glad it was me and not Vincent.

"I'm sorry," was the only thing I could think to write to her at that moment.

I felt helpless to stop what was going on. I didn't know how to stop it. Even if I did, if I were honest, there was so much I felt I needed to know first. So much I wanted to know, like, how the hell did all of these spirits end up in the doll? I didn't think they were attached to the doll. Ever since Erica's reading, I thought of at least the one spirit being "tethered" to the doll. But now there were five? Are they all "stuck?" Is that's what's going on?

What are you sorry for?

"That all of this is happening to you and Vincent," I answered. I didn't want to tell her I wasn't sure how to stop it just yet.

It's not your fault. Please don't ever think that.

"I just wish I could end this sooner than later."

It was weird as it didn't really hurt. It was more like a burning sensation. Always seems around Vincent's room.

"It's an important clue as to the nature of this entity." Some people believe that scratches, such as the ones Jane had, suggests the presence of a demon. Then there's the "black blob" Vincent painted with its red eyes, and Melanie's vision of a demonic looking entity with red eyes; many people who call themselves "demonologists" will tell you that red eyes are a characteristic of a demonic entity. Not that I told her any of this. She was scared enough without hearing that.

It's not going to hurt Vincent is it?

"No, if it was, it would have by now. I think it's coming after you because you're talking to me, and letting me know what Vincent is saying. When did the scratches happen?"

Early hours of the morning. Edward had woken up so I went and changed him as he was wet. Went in to check on Vincent (rooms are next door to each other at end of hall way). It all seemed ok. He was sleeping, so I pulled his cover over him as air conditioner was on and was quite cool. That's when I felt the burning feeling. Wasn't until I walked back into our room I noticed the marks. They aren't that big. All four of us ended up sleeping on the lounge floor together. Looks like it's the lounge floor for us again tonight. And my babies will be with me.

I suggested to Jane that she buy smoky quartz crystal. According to people who are "experts" in this sort of thing, it is a very protective and grounding stone. It brings physical and psychic protection.

It is also supposed to be an excellent stone for protection from negative energy, as it removes negativity and negative energy of any kind and transforms it into positive energy.

If it weren't 11 p.m., I'd be out buying some right now.

"Then do it tomorrow," I suggested. "Put it in Vincent's room. Let's see if it helps him to feel more comfortable in his room."

Is there anything else I can do tonight?

"There is one more thing," I wrote and then took a deep breath. "Until this is over, *unless* something happens, like you being scratched, bruised, etc., or Vincent says something about the doll… *do not* contact me."

Is that what you want? I would rather stay in touch... but will do whatever you want or think is best. Is this your way of saying goodbye?

"NO, this is NOT my way of saying 'goodbye.' This is my way of protecting you. If you're not talking to me, the entity has no reason to bother you. The female spirit may still contact Vincent, and the entity may bother him because of that, in that case, let me know...

Please don't misunderstand, I AM STILL HERE for you and Vincent. I just know from past experience what the "black blob" will do to those I care about. I'm not abandoning either of you. I'm doing this to protect you. This entity knows I care about you and Vincent more than even you know, and it's going to use that against me. It's going to use it as a reason to hurt you. I've come to realize that is its favorite way of attacking me personally. It's taken me years to grasp it, and to be honest with you... I didn't understand it until today. That's why I'm saying this."

I knew that Jane was afraid I was leaving her and Vincent to face this alone. But I honestly hoped that if she stopped talking to me, then the entity would leave her alone. It was the only way I could think of to protect her, and her son.

That night, the next morning in Australia, I sent Jane another message. "While you are out today, please buy sea salt and take a salt bath... both you and Vincent. It'll help cleanse your energy field (aura). Be sure to wash your hair with it, as well as Vincent's. Don't forget to buy smoky quartz, or black obsidian. Put them on the window sills of the rooms you're sleeping in, and leave them there. That should calm things down."

—⚞—

My decision to not talk to Jane and Vincent seemed to have had an unintended consequence. I received a chilling Facebook Message from Larry, who had the vision of the woman, child, and the smirking man.

I had another vision/dream of Harold as the doll. He was sitting by himself in this endless emptiness with 4 jars of light (they just glowed bright). Three were really bright, the 4th seemed dimmed. The 4 jars were in a big jar full of black smoke like substance. As I was thinking about the one dimmed light inside the jar, I got the overwhelming feeling that the black smoke was slowly leaking into that jar dimming its light. I get the feeling it's taking a good thing and turning it into a dark thing. I have no clue what it means.

Harold the doll said "help them" then it was gone. I, then, was wide awake and at attention. I have the feeling of 'I had to tell you this.'

"By shutting down one line of communication, was someone trying to reach out to me through another one?" I wondered. As I read, and reread Larry's message, what stuck out for me was the request for help. It wasn't, "Help us," but "Help *them*."

Was it a plea for help from someone *not* trapped in the doll?

Who was the "them" it wanted me to help? Was it the three trapped souls in the doll, or Jane and Vincent?

Had I done the wrong thing telling her I wanted to discontinue all communication with her and Vincent? Perhaps by doing that, I wasn't protecting them at all, but putting them in even more danger. I decided right then and there to change my mind about the whole "silence" thing.

THE HELL HOUND

I decided to let Jane know I changed my mind about *not* talking to her. I wanted to know, before I did, if my plan worked though. "Have you two been left alone since we stopped talking?"

Yes. I'm trying to project a strong and positive attitude. Trying not to project any fear. Although the house feels fine, I'm a little jumpy. The only weird feeling is around Vincent's room. Nothing has happened, it just feels "different" in there. Hence, why I won't let him sleep in there after the scratches.

Here is a picture he drew in his diary.

Due to his autism, his school required Vincent to keep a journal to help him process his feelings and emotions. Jane sent me a picture of what Vincent drew. It had some kind of animal, and the word, **DIE**, written next to it.

"What is that animal looking thing?" I asked.

Oh, and he said, 'The black dog you must not go near.'

"That's a dog?" I asked. It looked mangy, its hair was bristly.

Not sure if he means me, you, or him with that. He said black dog?

Just asked him again. He still says, 'Black dog… but you can't go near it. It stays in the shadow.'

I was a little freaked out by this because I adopted a puppy less than a year before, and it's black! Was I supposed to worry about *my* dog? I wanted to be sure before I jumped to any conclusions, such as, "I'm supposed to get rid of my puppy."

"Would you ask him if the figure in the drawing is a dog?"

Showed him the picture he drew again… still saying the black dog, that's in the shadows. I asked him if he had seen it. He just said it was here the other night… 'The night you slept on my floor.' That was the night he was sick.

I did a quick check of "black dogs and the paranormal" online.

The first thing that struck me is that these apparitions are typically spoken about in folklore from the British Isles. They appear at night and are generally associated with the Devil, or Hellhounds. Its appearance was regarded as a warning that someone is going to die. Black dogs are supposed to be larger than a normal dog, and often has large, glowing, red eyes.

In the meantime, Jane sent me three more pictures of drawings that Vincent had done.

I asked him why he drew all of that in his new school book. 'He is angry.'

THE GREEN DOOR

A young girl named Anna, someone I didn't know, sent me an email through the website I created for Harold. She told me that she had a dream about the doll. She said in her dream there were five spirits along with the demon. She told me it confused her because in her dream she thought there were only four spirits.

She kept asking who the fifth spirit was. The demon roared at her and slammed the green door shut in her face. From behind the door she heard a little boy say, "His name is Anthony."

Then she heard a woman say, "Be careful."

After that she said that the demon roared for Anna to go away and stay away.

I took this dream very seriously. The door of my hotel room is green.

WHAT'S IN A NAME?

I had this idea, based on what little I knew about exorcisms, if I could find out the name of one of the souls involved, I'd be better able to understand what was going on. So I kept using the Ovilus, and SB7 Spirit Box, hoping to get something meaningful, and helpful.

The Ovilus has a 2,000+ word dictionary, and the idea is that spirits are able to manipulate electromagnetic fields to pick and choose words to communicate. It also has a "phonetic" mode which spirits can supposedly manipulate to create words as well. Using the device, I'd ask, "What is your name?" Some names did appear on the screen, but to me, they were just names amidst a random order of words.

The SB7 spirit box, like most "spirit boxes" scans radio frequencies and it's believed that the spirits use the white noise to communicate with the living. The first spirit box I ever had was a radio I bought from Radio Shack, and hacked. The first time I used it I said, "If there are any spirits here who want to talk to me, say 'hi.'" I immediately heard four voices say, "Hi!" Another one said, "Hello." And one of the four was a woman. I was stunned. I used the hacked radio in enough investigations to convince me it was a viable means of communicating with spirits.

I turned on the SB7 after I gave up on the Ovilus, and asked, "What is your name?" I heard, "My name is Harold." I immediately thought to myself, "I don't believe you." What I did believe was that whoever the spirit in the doll was, it was a liar.

I decided to try one last time with my digital recorder. I was hoping to get one of the other spirits that were supposedly in the doll to communicate with me. "What is your name?" I asked. I caught an EVP. "Why are you doing this to me?"

When I heard this it made me think of a message that Jane sent to me a few weeks before, after she showed me the drawings Vincent did in his diary.

I sat down with Vincent just casually talking. I showed him the drawings in the school notebook, and asked him as subtly as I could about what he drew and what it was all about. I didn't get any names from him, Hun. Sorry. But he did say a little about the black cloud looking thing. I pointed to it and asked him who or what it is.... He looked at me and said, "Oh mummy that is cheeky and really not nice." He told me that "he" likes to be naughty and dress up.

I asked him what he meant. He said, "He can be really nice to you but he's really nasty, he likes to trick you into doing naughty things."

That was it, Hun. He then moved on to playing with his Legos. Sorry, was hoping to find out more for you. Vincent is still very strange; wish he would snap out of it.

I messaged Jane and told her about the EVP.

I would have chucked it and ran.

"LOL. To me it confirms that whoever this is sees itself as a victim."

What does it want you to do?

"Leave him alone."

Are you?

"Hell to the NO! Now I know why he doesn't talk to me, but picks on people like Vincent. I think he's afraid of me for some reason."

The EVP, asking, "Why are you doing this to me?" along with Vincent's description of "Harold," confirmed for me that there was something I wasn't supposed to know. That made me even more suspicious of anything it had to say.

On the other hand, as I told Jane, "If Vincent told me that the black blob is a man who wears an orange dress, garters, and high heels, I'd believe him." I had a feeling though, that the secret I wasn't supposed to know was worse than that... much... much worse.

LOTTIE

I told Jane about my efforts to get a name, and how I believed it would help me to understand what was going on, and why her son was being affected the way he was.

Here you go... talking to Vincent I decided to show him a YouTube clip of Harold (against my better judgement). We sat in play room with his bubble lamp. He was very relaxed and calm. I asked him about what the doll is and who or what he feels when he sees him. He didn't have much reaction at first but after a few minutes he said... now I'm not sure what this really means, he said, "You know, her name is Charlotte, but she hates that. You have to call her Lottie. She is looking...."

He was so engrossed with the YouTube clip.... He wanted to watch more but I said no... sorry. Sorry Hun, not sure if that really means anything or not.

Asked him who Charlotte / Lottie is? He just said, "Oh mummy she likes to sing. She is the nice one, she helps me sleep." It may be nothing, Hun. He's gone all strange again. He is here sitting in the corner... won't go to sleep.

I cannot begin to tell you how frustrated I was feeling at this point. It seemed to me that for every step I took forward, I took two or three steps back. Every answer only led to more questions.

I had a name, but I had no idea who it was, or how she was involved. Even worse, Vincent seemed to be paying the price for sharing it with his mother and me. I *hated* what Vincent was going through, but by this time, he was the only one I trusted to help me find out what was going on with the doll.

On top of that, there was the email I received from Anna, who said that in her dream I was one of the souls in the doll. Her dream told me that my very soul depended on me understanding what was going on. It made me question, "Do I have the doll? Or does the doll have me?"

A WARNING

I had to leave it up to Jane as to whether or not Vincent would keep helping me. For me, however, quitting was not an option. I decided to use my Ovilus to try to find out what the name of the black blob is. As soon as I asked, two words came up—

Beg

Find

If the spirits do use electromagnetic fields to manipulate words in order to communicate, it seemed to me that Harold was taunting me… "If you want to know my name, beg me… and maybe you'll find out."

That wasn't going to happen.

I decided to turn my attention back to the one name I did have, "Lottie." I looked back at my notes and found where Jane told me that Vincent said, "…mummy you know the lady and the children are scared. That black blob won't let them go to the sunshine…."

Was Lottie the woman Vincent was speaking of?

That was my first thought, but then he said that she sings him to sleep. Something didn't make sense, unless… Lottie wasn't the woman in the doll, but somehow a part of what is going on in the doll.

As I was going over these questions in my mind a message from Jane came in.

I walked into Vincent's room earlier to grab his school bag and, lo and behold, my friend is back just sitting on Vincent's bedroom window ledge. The crow has been hanging around since Saturday, but in the tree, not on the window ledge. Just thought it was me overreacting so I didn't mention it and carried on getting ready for school.

Came back from school drop off and doing the horses. I walked into Vincent's room to put his clean washing away (stupid crow still sitting on window ledge). The crow flew away once I got close to Vincent's bed. I carry on, put his clothes away. I then went to pull his bed out from against the wall so I could pick up his toys and dirty socks that always fall down the side, and then, as soon as I start to move his bed, my arm starts to burn....

What came next was a photo of her upper arm. There were three nasty scratches.

As far as I know I never scraped against anything when moving the bed. I hate that room.

"I can understand why," I wrote back. I then told her I wanted to take my dog, Chance, for a walk and that I'd message her as soon as I got back. Chance was still a puppy at that point, full of energy so he loved long walks. I was lost in thought, thinking about what happened to Jane. Chance and I were on the last leg of our walk, going past some low cut bushes. I heard what sounded like the clacking of three rocks hitting the ground, but didn't pay much attention. I thought it was Chance digging up something in the ground next to me.

Suddenly, something hit me in the side. Since it was a chilly night, I had a heavy coat on, so whatever it was didn't hurt… it just snapped me out of my reverie. I turned around and looked down just in time to see a rock fall to the ground.

"What the hell?" I said out loud, but to myself. I walked back and looked behind the bushes but couldn't see any kids. The shrubs were low enough, and spread out far enough, that if there was someone hiding behind them, I would have seen who it was who threw the rock at me.

I took Chance back to our hotel room, and I went back to where I was hit by the rock to try to figure out what happened. "Was it a warning?" I thought to myself. It wasn't thrown with enough force to hurt me. It was almost like a child threw it. A very young child.

When I got back to my room again, I messaged Jane telling her what had happened. "I don't think it was a coincidence that the crow showed up, and you ended up being scratched."

My friend is still at the window.

"Are you okay?" I wrote back.

Yeah, I'm okay. I took the safety gate off and shut Vincent's door. The crow I can kinda cope with. The scratches I can't. Makes me wonder what it'll do to Vincent... or Edward. Nothing bad is going to happen is it? I will be honest, I am scared. For Vincent more than myself.

I tried to think of a response that would calm her fears, but I couldn't. At this point, I wasn't sure what the hell was happening either. I decided to message her the only answer I could come up with. "I understand."

CLOSE, BUT NO CIGAR

"Who was Lottie?"
"How does she fit into this?"
"Why was she 'appearing' to Vincent?"

These were the questions I was wrestling with at this point, and I told Jane I was. I could tell she was wishing the whole thing would go away, and that she was wondering if the attention we were giving it was making things worse. What she messaged next, confirmed the perhaps it was.

Stupid thing back at Vincent's window now. I'm sure this thing knows when you start talking about it.

"Has it been hanging around your home the whole time?"

No... just showed up after you started talking about Lottie.

"Crap."

I decided to splash the doll with holy water, to see if it had any effect like it did the last time, but I didn't want Jane to know what I was going to do. "I have to get ready for an appointment by taking a quick shower. I'll be back shortly."

Okay.

I splashed holy water on the doll. "I don't know your name, but whoever you are, I command you in the name of our Lord Jesus Christ to make the crow leave Vincent's window sill!"

After that, I really did take a quick shower hoping it would relax me and help me think more clearly. I got back to Jane about 15 minutes later after my last message to her. "Is it still there?"

It's in the tree.

Better, but not well enough. Without saying anything to Jane, I splashed the doll again. Once again, I commanded whoever the entity was to make the crow leave. It took less than a minute to do this. "What's it doing? Where is it now?"

I can't see it. I can still hear it, but it sounds farther away.

DANCING WITH THE DEVIL

I heard from Larry again. He told me he was falling asleep when he heard a dog howling next to him. He woke up wondering what his dog was so upset about.

He opened his eyes to see what was wrong. That's when he remembered… he doesn't have a dog.

—⁂—

Hi

"Good morning!"

Hope you are okay?

I am. Why do you ask?

Long story. A mother who I know from school, not really friends, but we always talk.… She was saying how Vincent was a sensitive soul, so I decided to tell her how I thought Vincent had a kinda connection and sees people's colours.… She gets out her iPhone and says, "Let's try this.…" It was some stupid app (not sure of the name). I was like, yeah right this is going to work. "Well, see for yourself" are the words that appeared on her screen. Might just be coincidence but scared the shit out of me.…

She sent me a photo. It was a picture of the woman's cell phone screen with the words—

327- Anthony
479- family
641- free
396- must
067- dog

I thought it was a stupid app. It just did make me stop when it came up with that.... this was just a close up of her phone screen... taken on my phone.

My immediate thought was that it looked to be an iPhone Ovilus app. My second thought was that there was another reference to a dog, and I didn't think the message was about me saving a family's dog. First Vincent, then Larry, and now this woman's phone....

"What was this dog about?" I wondered. Some people suggested it was protecting me. Because of Vincent's drawing of a dog with the word **DIE** next to it, I seriously had my doubts that was the case.

Later that day, while school was in session, Vincent climbed a 6-foot fence trying to get away from something no one could see. Jane told me that he was very upset, and emotional... *asking a lot of questions about death.*

A couple of days later I messaged Jane to ask her how Vincent was doing.

Yeah being very loud and rude.

"Oh boy... what about?"

I have no idea. It's very unlike him. He called me a 'bitch.'

"Are you okay?"

Yeah, just a little shocked by his behavior.

I was stunned. The idea that Vincent was using a word I've heard the entity in the doll used several times during EVP sessions, starting with April when she did her reading shortly after I received the doll... I wondered if something more sinister than I was aware of was happening.

Concerned, I messaged Jane back about six hours later. "How's Vincent?"

Yeah, still very anxious. He has stopped the swearing and shouting thankfully. He spent most of the night sleeping on top of me as he was convinced there was someone walking around inside the house. He told me that the cheeky man showed up with a dog. The dog's eyes turned red, and it started growling at Vincent. The man said to the dog, "Not yet," and the dog stopped growling.

I was becoming more, and more, frustrated at this point. I wanted to do a "binding ritual," hoping that it would contain the spirit of whomever was tormenting Vincent within the doll. I was afraid if I did it on the wrong person, it wouldn't work. I was really afraid it would backfire, and I wasn't sure what the repercussions of that would be on either Vincent, Jane, or me, for that matter.

I'd find people who I thought might be the "trapped" souls in the doll. I'd be, in fact, convinced of it. Then the next day, I'd discover something else that would tell me I was wrong. "One step forward, three steps back. Cha… cha… cha." I honestly started feeling as though I was dancing with the Devil himself… and he was leading. I messaged Jane about how I was feeling.

Wish I had answers to give you. I am very glad I met you, but to be honest, I curse the day I stumbled onto the clip of Harold on YouTube. I hate that Vincent got to see Harold and that he had the reaction he did to it. If only I had logged off properly.

I didn't tell her what I was thinking… that I had my doubts any of this was an accident.

"GO VISIT ANTHONY."

I was discussing the doll with Donna, a friend and brilliant internet researcher, who'd been helping me research the clues Vincent was giving me regarding the identities of the spirits in the doll, when Jane messaged:

Are you doing anything with Harold?

"Just had a huge discussion with Donna about him. Why do you ask?"

My clock fell of the wall at 10 minutes to 10. Now this thing is going nuts at the glass door.

A picture of a large crow came up.

I'm sure it just nearly knocked itself out by hitting against the glass.

Without saying anything to her, I grabbed the holy water and started soaking the doll. "Is it still there?"

No, it left.

I really liked that clock. I don't think it likes being talked about, I'm beginning to think. I'm scared.

"Because of what happened with the clock?"

Not so much the clock, although it's been on that wall for over 3 years and never moved. This crow does freak me out. And my day gets better, just got a phone call from school to say Vincent has passed out. Couldn't find anything wrong. So watching him is all they can do.

I told Jane to put sea salt in Vincent's room in a place that was out of the way to absorb more of the negative energy that might be in there. That afternoon (Denver time) I sent her a message to see how he was doing.

"Good morning!"

Hey Hun.

"How's Vincent?"

Seems to be ok, thankfully. He was weird last night though, pacing back and forth outside his bedroom. He made me take out the sea salt. He said it doesn't like it. I had it in his window by his bed.

"Did you know why it bothered him?"

No idea. He seems much happier though this morning. Nothing else, I hope, can go wrong. Scared me yesterday when I got to school and he was in the ambulance.

"I can imagine."

He can't even remember it. He said everything just went black.

"What did his teachers say happened?"

This is what they said… after morning tea they (his class) were going back to the class room. Vincent stopped and started to walk towards the oval (opposite way to class room). They let him go as some times this is his way to self-calm if stressed. Teacher aid followed him, he didn't get too far down the path and just collapsed.

He doesn't even remember going that way. When he came to, he asked why he was there and where was his class.

I was worried about Vincent, but I didn't know what to say. The only thing I could think of was, "That's weird."

I know… scares me as Autism often comes with seizures but he had the test at hospital and there was nothing. Even the paramedics said they could find nothing wrong. They checked everything from blood sugar to fits.

The next day, I received another message from Jane.

Can I ask what are you doing right now? I was just asking as my friend was back at window. Nearly part of the family now.

"Oh brother. Tell it, 'Go visit Anthony,'" I wrote back jokingly, splattering the doll with holy water. A moment later I wrote to her, "You know, if you tell it that, and a crow shows up at my window, I'm going to crap my pants!"

I poured some more holy water on the doll and then asked, "Is the bird still around?"

Back in the tree now.

"Well, that's a little better. Probably checking out a map to see where the hell Denver is."

LOL, you're welcome to it if you want it.

"No… thanks. But I'd better go buy some adult diapers just in case."

Maybe I shouldn't have told it to come annoy you... it's now got a mate. Alfred Hitchcock's "The Birds" springs to mind.

"The Birds" was a 1963 horror thriller film directed by Alfred Hitchcock. Based, loosely, on the 1952 story "The Birds" by Daphne du Maurier, the movie was about a town in California that suddenly and for unexplained reasons, was attacked by ferocious birds over the course of a few days.

A few minutes later she wrote: *I went out to the bin which is over by the shed and they both came swooping... neighbour was outside her house. She must have thought I was mad. I dropped the rubbish and ran. Stupid bloody birds*

"I'm trying not to laugh as I'm picturing this. Not that it's funny... but imagining what your neighbor must have been thinking...."

I spoke too soon. After we signed off I took my dog Chance for a walk. As we were crossing the street, I heard cawing. I looked up in time to see a crow flying straight for my head. If I hadn't ducked at the last possible moment, I'm sure it would have flown into me, possibly knocking me out as fast as it was going. I had to change my underwear when Chance and I got back to our hotel room.

A WARNING FOR ME

Good morning.
"Hi!"
Hey Hun. Are you okay? Vincent is worried about you.
"What did he say?"
It was a strange conversation. Vincent & I were laying down watching Power Puff Girls, eating Maltesers. Out of nowhere he suddenly says, "Does Uncle Ant like Maltesers?" I said, "I really don't know mate." He then turns and says, "It doesn't want me to tell you, it said it would hurt Uncle Ant" I tried to ask him what he meant, and who would hurt uncle Ant and how, but he didn't say a word after that... just laid next to me staring.
The crow is back. It showed up as soon as I started talking to you.
Later that evening, Australia time, I thought I'd check in to see how things were going. "How's my friend?"
Been hiding under the teacher's desk. Told them he can't sleep at night because of the bad thing in his bedroom. Now they think I'm twice as weird as before.
"How long has he been doing this?"
Teacher told me yesterday when I picked him up. Just this week, I think.
"Let's see if it continues."

"How he did do today?"
Don't even ask. My life sucks!
"What happened?"
Everything that could.

"What does that mean?"

It's ok... it's not your problem.

I hated it when she started up with these self-pity parties. "WHAT HAPPENED?"

Sorry Hun. Vincent had the worst day. He swore, he kicked, and he cut his head open... tripped a teacher aid over. I picked him up and he called me a bitch. He told everyone he hates me.

"Did he say what was wrong?"

I can't get anything from him. He is screaming... rocking back and forth... I suck at this Mum thing.

It was early morning when we were messaging; just after 4 a.m. Mountain Standard Time. "What day is it there?"

Thursday night.

"Is Vincent going to school tomorrow?"

I have to go in with him tomorrow to meet with the principle and Special Ed teacher. They will decide what they are going to do with him then... I try so hard, I give up.

"Has he taken a bath yet?"

Can't get him near water at the moment.

"Then I need you to do what I ask... step by step. Okay?"

Yes. I'm sorry Hun. Not your problem. I am so sorry.

"First of all, I need *you* to knock that off." I knew Jane was tired, and scared, but now I needed her full attention if I was going to help her son. "Secondly, I need you to tell me *exactly* what he's doing at this moment."

When she didn't respond, I asked again. "What is Vincent doing at THIS moment?"

He is sitting in the walk in robe in the dark.

"What else?"

Swearing his head off... calling me motherfucker. He doesn't do this Anthony.

Personally, I didn't think it was Vincent who was doing this, but I didn't want to open up that can of worms. "Are you able to talk to him?"

I need help.

"I'm trying to help you, Jane."

I know Hun. But why should you?

"Either you want my help or you don't. Which one is it?"

Please... I am sorry.

"Okay... the FIRST thing YOU need to do is to STOP being a 'victim' and start helping me, so I can help you. And you do that by answering my questions. Do you understand?"

Yes.

"Thank you. Do you have any ground up basil?" Basil has been used in folk magic for centuries to soothe people's emotions and anxieties.

I have basil growing in the herb garden.

"Get some from your garden and after you do, let me know. It doesn't have to be a lot. The same amount you'd typically get to use in a meal."

Ok.

"Go and get some NOW." I used the break while she went to get some of the plant to take a few deep breaths of my own. I'd grown fond of Vincent and didn't like the idea he was going through what he was, and that the entity in the doll might be responsible for it.

Ok got it.... Ground it.

"Do you still have sea salt available?"

Yes.

"Yes!" I said out loud to myself. I may have even done a fist pump. "We're going to have Vincent do a bath with the basil and sea salt. It should help him feel better."

Ok, how much?

"Will he take a bath now, or do we need to wait a bit?"

Give me a minute I will try. I will run a bath. How much water?

"Whatever amount you normally do. Let me know when you're back."

Just running bath.

"Okay... what is he doing now?"

Still in robe. But he is talking. Which is something.

"He's calming down?"

Yes. Ok, bath ready how much salt, basil do I put in it?

"A cup of the salt. Put half of the basil in. If he has bath toys, put those in, so he's comfortable."

Ok.

"Is he still calling you names?"

Just trying to get him out of robe. Give me a second.

"Is he still calling you names?"

Ok he's in the bath. Still shouting.

"The sea salt and basil should help him calm down."

I just want my boy back.

"I understand. That's what I'm trying to do here. I need you to record all of these events. Video it, write it down in a journal.... Something. In case we do have to bring in outside help, it'll go to your credibility."

I don't care if people believe me or not.... I live this!

"I understand, but since I'm not there, we may have to bring someone else in to help Vincent. Is he calming down at all?"

Yes.

"Good... make sure you wash his hair and head as well with this solution of water."

I will try.

"Don't try... do it... before he gets out of the tub. I know this is scary for you. But I need you to trust me."

Washed from head to toe. Dried him... back in the walk in robe.

"How is he behaving?"

He is a lot calmer. He looks tired. At least he isn't calling me motherfucker any more.

"Good... it worked. The bath seems to have cleansed his energy."

Thank you.

"Is that word ever said in your house?"

No, it's not, thank God. Not until Vincent starting screaming it at me.

I could understand why she was upset. But I needed her to appreciate that what's been happening *was not* because of her, or anything she did, or didn't do. "Here's the deal—IF you keep this victim attitude going, the entity wins. Do you understand? Tell me what's going on."

Sorry... He is in robe still but calm. Has asked for milk.

"Excellent... what time is your appointment with the school tomorrow?"

Appointment at 9.

"Whatever happens, try your best not to let it get to you, because this is not about you, or Vincent. The entity is pissed. It's about him. But they don't understand that. Do *you* understand what I'm saying?"

Yes I get it. But it's hard, that is my child, my baby, my world. I hate this! But yes, I understand.

"That's what the entity is preying on... those feelings. It wants you to stop talking to me, but that's the WORST thing that can happen.

Let me know what happens after the appointment BEFORE you go home. Okay? Especially if Vincent is still with you for some reason." I was hoping that the school wouldn't make Vincent leave.

Ok, and thank you. Sorry for being a babbling mess.

"Jane, the entity's goal here is to isolate Vincent. Perhaps you too. We can stop it, because it's early in the game. But I need you to do EVERYTHING I ask. No excuses. When darkness and light are in the same room, light ALWAYS wins." I knew I was asking a lot of her, especially considering that we'd never met, and she knew nothing about me.

I can tell you now if it thinks it's going to get its hands on my baby boy it has another thing coming. I will fight it all the way back to the hellish hole it came from... with your help. God... sat here with tears running down my cheeks.

"Jane, I know you're scared. You have every right to be. I don't know anyone who wouldn't be in your position. But that's exactly what I need from you. I need you to turn that fear into anger, and use that fury to fight with me for your son. So, from this moment on... I need you to help me by doing what I ask, and being completely honest with me."

Not that I thought she was *lying* to me, but I didn't want her holding anything back about what was going on. "Do we have an agreement?"

Yes.

"Thank you. What is Vincent doing now?" I felt relieved, but I knew from past experience that people tend to go into denial and minimize things for the sake of their own sanity. It's a natural, human reaction. It's why I was being so tough on Jane, even though I felt badly about it.

Sleeping in the robe.

"Then the bath worked. Let him sleep and you do your own bath. Same solution, but do not use the same water he was in!" I didn't think she would, but I wasn't taking any chances. The water she bathed Vincent in contained the energy he was struggling with, and needed to go down the drain. "Make your own bath. Then get back to me."

One word comes to mind... failure... my life.

"And that's EXACTLY what it wants you to think. Keep thinking that, it wins, and you lose your son. Do you understand me?" I didn't hear back from her, and couldn't help but wonder why I hadn't. Then about an hour later, she finally messaged me.

Did the bath.

"How do you feel?"

Ok.

"Not better? I mean, energetically."

Yes I feel ok... tired. I do feel calmer.

"Good... excellent, actually. You and Vincent need to get a good night's sleep. You have a hard day ahead of you with having to deal with the school admin. Try to get some rest. We will stop this thing from harassing Vincent! I promise."

Not knowing who or what I was up against, I wasn't sure how I was going to keep my promise, but I knew I wouldn't give up until I figured it out. I said a prayer, asking God to help me do just that.

WHO YOU GONNA CALL?

I tried to find a group in Jane's area that might be able to help her, and me, figure out what was going on, but without any success. I found out about one group that belonged to the "family" of a group featured on a television show here in the U.S., but I didn't think that qualified them to deal with what Vincent was going through. I was pretty sure she was growing tired of me and whatever was attacking her son. Unfortunately for Jane and Vincent, all they had was me to help them.

On top of everything she was dealing with at home, now she had to face the school administration about Vincent's recent behavior. If I could, *I* would have gone and explained to the school administrators what I believed was going on. Not that they were going to believe *me*... "I have this doll that I won on an eBay auction, and it seems to be cursed.... Not only that, but I believe that there are five spirits trapped inside of it somehow."

"That would go over like a brick," I thought to myself. All I could do was let Jane fend for herself as best she could with the school administrators. I had no idea what to suggest as to how she could even begin to explain what was going on without *her* being carted off.

"Are you okay?"

Yes.

"Are you sure?"

Yes.

I didn't believe her, but I wrote, "Good, I'm really happy to hear that! Let me know what happens at the school. We're going to fight this entity together."

Thank you.

"You're welcome. I've been trying to find an Aussie group to help you. No luck so far. I did learn that this sort of thing is much bigger here in the U.S. than it is there in Oz. A lot more groups... not that most of them know what the hell they're doing. So you're stuck with me, which is why I'm going to ask you to do a thing or two after the meeting at school."

Ok.

Her one word responses told me that she was as tired of all of this as I thought she was. "How is Vincent?"

Sleeping.

"I'm glad he's able to sleep!"

Sorry for being such a pain.

"You're not. It's just that this would be a lot easier if I were closer to you and could talk to Vincent directly, as well as document some of the things he's going through. I don't mean to be repetitious but since I can't I need you to tell me *everything*... even if it doesn't seem all that important. You never know what might be the key to solving this whole thing. But until that happens, I'm here for you and Vincent."

You don't have to if you don't want to.

"Do I have a choice? At this point I feel like I'm riding a monster that I can't stay on, but I'm too scared to get off of. I don't know that I would, even if I thought I could. I couldn't do that to you and Vincent. Speaking of Vincent, when do you go to his school?"

I have to leave now. Wish me luck.

"Good luck! Let me know before you go home how it goes. Don't forget to bring a jar with a lid by the way!"

I don't have Facebook on my phone.

"Okay, then as soon as you get home. How far away is the school?"

Five minutes up the road. What am I doing with a jar and lid?

"Is there a Roman Catholic Church nearby you?"

I have no idea.

I wasn't surprised. I didn't think Jane and her family were Catholic, but she and her husband hadn't struck me as being particularly religious to begin with.

"I think you should bring the jar with you to the meeting just in case you need to bash someone on the head! Just kidding!"

LOL

"You'll go to a Catholic church and fill the jar with a good amount of holy water. After that, go to the store you bought the crystals and get some sage. Then get back to me."

I was on pins and needles while she was gone hoping that everything went as smoothly as it could and that Vincent wasn't asked to leave the school. Despite everything that happened there, Jane told me he liked the school, and he really connected with his teacher.

Home.

"How did it go?"

Ok, I guess, they are going to give him more time in the special ed unit, rather than the classroom. He has psychologist coming to see him at school next week.

"Well, let's see what we can do from this end. How far away is the church from you?"

About a 30 minute drive.

"Is that the same town where the store is that you bought the crystals?"

Yes.

"Okay, I'd like you to get a good amount of holy water from the Catholic Church there, and some sage from the store. Okay?"

Ok.

"You're going to bless and cleanse Vincent's room. There should be either a metal tank or a fountain for the holy water. The more you get the better. Don't get a small amount. You want A LOT. If there's a gift shop at the church, see if they have a small St. Benedict medal or crucifix. If there isn't one, it's okay."

Saint Benedict's crucifixes are often used during exorcisms, and medals are used to ward off and keep demonic spirits away. Not that I believed there was a demon involved but, I thought, whatever was bothering Vincent seemed "demonic" to me.

Ok

"You're going to cleanse the energy in Vincent's room after you bless it with the holy water. That's why I want you to go to the store you bought the crystals from and buy some sage. If the store has sweet grass, get that instead."

Sage and sweet grass are from the American plains and is traditionally burned by American Indians for cleansing, purifying, or creating sacred space. Native Americans have burned sage, sometimes called smudging, in their ceremonies to purify themselves, protect physical and spiritual well-being. The rising smoke from burning sweet grass symbolizes the purification of the people's hopes and needs.

I had a feeling she was reading all of this and thinking, "Holy water? Sage? Sweet grass?" cursing the day she first laid eyes on the doll. I needed to make sure that she was still with me.

"Are you okay?"

Yes Hun. I am ok. Just waiting for the last phone call from school and then I will go.

"Last phone call?"

Had to get the occupational therapist to go to the school to observe Vincent. Now waiting for school to call back to confirm it's all good to go.

I was happy to hear that Vincent was being allowed to stay in school and that things were being done there to "help" him… not that I thought that they would.

Ok so I'm off. I need Holly Water, sage/sweet grass. Is that right?

"Holy water. LOL"

Yup… that too.

"If you ask for 'holly water' they'll know you're not…. ROFL @ 'Yup, that too!'"

Maybe I need wine.

"I'm thinking I could use some myself right now! LOL"

Stupid question, but do I just go into church and ask? Never done this before. LOL

"Yes… there'll be an office on the grounds. Tell them you want holy water for your home. They'll tell you, or show you, where it is."

Ok, just looking up what the church looks like—they always look like normal houses here. I'm used to English churches!

"There might even be a literal fountain of holy water within the church. LOL You Brits love to brag!"

LOL. Just what I'm used to seeing, they look like toilet blocks here. They hide. Ok, catch you later.

I wasn't sure, but it seemed to me that being proactive about what was going on was helping her to feel better. It was about three hours before I heard back from Jane.

"How are you?"

Good thank you. Didn't realize that holy water was a rare commodity.

"Well, you think that's bad... can you imagine what their reaction would have been if you asked for 'holly water?'" I couldn't resist.

LOL. It's kept under lock and key. People were stealing it all the time.

"No way!"

Yes... I had to wait for the lady who had the key to come back from a meeting. They keep it behind a locked door in another locked room.

I'm a Catholic and this was the first time I'd ever heard of this, but I wasn't going to make a big deal out of it. The important thing was that she was able to get some holy water. "Did you get sweet grass or sage?"

Both... and a feather?

"You're going to use the feather to disperse the smoke," I told her. Normally, it's done with an eagle feather, but here in the United States, unless you're a Native American, having an eagle feather is illegal. That might not be the case in Australia. Once again, I decided not to make a big deal out of it.

He put salt in the water. What was that for?

"Who did... the priest?"

Yes.

"'That's a rite of minor exorcism. Making water "holy" is actually a two-step process. The priest separately exorcises and then blesses the salt, and then the water. Finally, a mixture of the two is made and blessed, 'in the name of the Father, Son, and Holy Spirit.' Then a prayer is said 'that, through the invocation of [God's] holy name, wherever this water and salt is sprinkled, it may turn aside every attack of the unclean spirit and dispel the terror of the poisonous serpent.' I'm glad you met with him."

I'm now designing a poster and a leaflet for him for upcoming events.

That made me laugh. I loved how things worked out.

"Here's what I want you to do… dip your finger in the water and trace a cross on the walls, windows, and door of Vincent's room. As you trace the cross, say a prayer asking God to seal and protect the room, and Vincent, from whatever is bothering him."

Ok… do I need to do it in any particular order?

"No. Just keep repeating the prayer each time you trace the sign of the cross."

What prayer should I be saying?

I thought about having her say the St. Michael prayer, but I wanted her to pray from the anguish she was feeling. "Make one up."

Really?

"Yes… it's your intent and your love for Vincent that God responds to, more than the words themselves. Tell me if you feel any bodily sensations as you're doing it."

Ok… I will go do it. Be back in minute.

Ok… done.

"Did you feel anything while you were doing it?"

Not really, apart from it feeling colder in his room.

Red flags immediately started going up in my head. I didn't want to let Jane know that I was starting to become even more concerned by what she had just told me. This might be worse than I imagined. It certainly wasn't something I wanted her dealing with on her own.

"Okay… that's what I wanted to know. Thank you. Did the store tell you how to use the sweet grass or sage?"

No.

"Okay… well, put it away for now. Let's see how Vincent is with his room."

Ok. Where do I keep the holy water?

"Put it away until Vincent gets home."

What? Anywhere? It doesn't need to be in fridge or anything? Sorry if that sounds stupid….

"No, it's a great question. Putting it in a cabinet will work. How cold was Vincent's room?"

It was just cooler. You can feel the change in temp as soon as you walk in. Kinda gives you goose bumps.

Suddenly, *I* got goosebumps, and chills. "How long have you noticed that?"

Just before Christmas, but it doesn't get as much sun as there are trees outside. But today the air con is on... still feels cooler in there. We have ducted air con so each room is set at the same temp.

Guess who is now sitting at Vincent's window... just sitting there.

IT'S TIME TO CALL IN THE CALVARY

"It's time to call your new friend, Jane… the priest. Ask him to come and bless your home." I knew that this wouldn't go over well. She was afraid of what this priest would think, since she had just met him and he had even asked her to do a job. When she didn't respond, I wrote to her, "Just do it."

Ok.

"NOW."

I have to go pick boys up.

"When?"

At 3.

It was 2:45. Plenty of time for her to call, but as tired as she was fighting something she couldn't see, I was just as tired fighting her. "Okay… then wait until you get home."

I'm tired, I'm scared and want whatever it is to leave Vincent alone.

"It's time to call the priest, Jane. Ask him to come and bless your home. Let me know when you make the call."

I'm on the phone now.

"With the church?"

Yes.

"This is beyond sage and sweet grass. When you told me what you've been feeling in Vincent's room, I knew what we were doing wasn't enough." I was relieved that she reached out and asked for a priest to come to their home. I knew she didn't want another person thinking she was crazy.

Someone is coming tomorrow.

"Okay… good. Thank you."

Not the one I met from the church today, but another local priest. He's through the same church. The other guy gave me his number. The other guy also wants to talk to Vincent and bless my car. Do they normally bless cars?

HOUSE BLESSING

The next morning, I messaged Jane. "How's Vincent? How are you? What time does the priest come over?" It was late there, probably after midnight Australia time, so I really didn't expect to hear back from her, and I didn't until several hours later.

Vincent is good, thank you. 11am priest comes. How are you?

"Ask him to bless Vincent, Edward, you, and your husband as well. I'm good, thanks."

Yes, he was very adamant he was going to bless the car too, when speaking on the phone.

"Probably to keep you safe. Whatever we're dealing with seems to be intelligent. He's not taking any chances of blessing your home, and it taking refuge in your car. Did you explain to him what's going on?"

Yes.

"Please do me a HUGE favor."

What?

"Start keeping a journal beginning with the priest's visit. A detailed journal of what happens while he's there. Vincent's reaction and actions. Your reaction and actions. Any changes in behaviors, feelings, emotions… even changes in the temperature of the rooms, etc. Does that make sense? You can do it after he leaves. This will help me help you afterwards, if necessary."

Yes I will.

"The temperature change in Vincent's room was and is SIGNIFICANT. When you told me about the temp change in Vincent's room, it explained his behaviors to me. I'll explain later."

Ok... so write everything that is different or unusual?

"Yes. Write an account of the priest's visit too. Start with that."

Right, here we go.

I waited a while, then sent her a message. "How did it go?"

Good..., very good.

"Does Vincent's room feel differently from before?"

Yes... lighter if that makes sense!

"Absolutely! How is Vincent?"

Smiling. How he did last year.

"How are you?"

I'm good. Feel tired but good.

"I can only imagine. Yesterday, when you described the temperature change in his room, it told me that there was an entity in his room feeding off of your energy. If it was feeding off of yours, it was also feeding off of Vincent's."

Ok...What do I do exactly?

"You did it. The priest blessing the room should have removed whatever was in there. Now, light the sage, and as the smoke rises, use the feather to disperse it around the room. Make sure the smoke gets into the corners of the room up in the ceiling. You may have to relight the sage several times. Does Vincent have a radio or television in his room?"

No.... Only thing he has electrical is his bubble lamp.

"Okay then, after the sage clears, spend some "happy time" in there with him. Play a game, read him a story, sing songs, encourage him to play and have fun in there. That sort of thing. The entity and its energy is what kept bringing the crow back. We want to replace that entity's energy with new happy energy. Smudging the room will cleanse it of whatever old residual energy remains. Then we get Vincent's, Edward's, and your happy energy back in there."

The guy today gave Vincent a St. Benedict medal attached to some beads. He told Vincent to keep it on him in his pocket.

"It's a chaplet," I explained. A chaplet is a string of beads that are used by Catholics to pray variations of the Our Father and Hail Mary and to count the prayers as they go. "He, no doubt, blessed the chaplet. It'll protect Vincent."

I think he blessed everything, even my husband and Vincent's fish.

"What's Vincent doing?"

Playing trains with Edward.

"The next step is to see if Vincent sleeps in his room. That's why you want to spend "happy time" in there with him. Not now, necessarily, but sometime today.

Oh, I didn't tell you, but I did a binding ritual on the doll, without realizing that there was an entity in Vincent's room. It pissed it off. That's why Vincent acted out. I 'locked the entity in' but locked that one in his room out. I broke the binding here, and will redo it. That'll keep it from coming back. Vincent should go back to his old self. Let me know if he says anymore about the black blob, but I doubt he will. It should be done."

Thank you so much... for everything.

"You're welcome," I wrote back, "but honestly, it's God and the priest you should be thanking. Not me."

"It's over," I said to myself as I redid the binding ritual over the doll, with prayers, holy water, and sea salt. I didn't know it at the time, but I was wrong.

IT'S OVER... OR IS IT?

I heard from Jane on occasion over the next two weeks. When I did she told me that Vincent was back to his old self, and even started sleeping in his room again. She was happy that things were back to normal, and that she had her son back.

Personally speaking, I was still trying to put all of the pieces together. I was happy things were over for the family, but for me, it was just beginning. I'd learned a lot since the doll appeared on the Ghost Adventures show... just not the way I expected to.

Then one night I woke up from a *sound* sleep. I felt as though something was wrong, but I didn't know what. Then my phone dinged telling me I had a Facebook message.

So sorry... have just had the craziest day.

"How are you? What's wrong?"

Everything.

"What do you mean?"

Didn't mean to wake you. Sorry.

"You didn't... I've been awake."

Has anything happened on your end?

"No. Why, what is going on there?"

I went into Vincent's room... all was normal, put clothes away and picked up a few toys. Ended up with stinging on back of my neck... now I have scratches. This was twenty minutes before I left to pick up Vincent. Get to school, hop out of car... hear Vincent screaming at the top of his lungs. His teacher says he's been screaming for the last thirty minutes. He asked for you....

"What did he say when he asked for me?"

I wasn't there when he asked, the teacher aid just told me he was asking for uncle Ant.

"Crap... okay...." I tried to think of what might be happening to cause this, but I couldn't come up with anything.

He has been so happy... I was hoping he'd stay that way.

"So was I."

It took three of us to carry him to a safe spot in school...I have never seen him like that.

"Did he say anything to give you an idea as to what is going on?"

I tried to talk to him but it was hard to talk at school. When we came home he was exhausted. He has had a shower, now lying in my bed watching 101 Dalmatians.

"Well, that's positive! Has he drawn anything? Painted anything?" I'd learned over the past couple of months that Vincent communicates best, at least with this sort of thing, by drawing or painting what he's seeing that's making him upset.

Not at home. He painted a turtle looking thing at school when he was supposed to be painting a picture of family.

"Can you send me a pic of it, and one of your scratches?"

Picture is at school still. Art teacher just showed me and let it go.

Jane sent me a picture of the scratches on her neck. "I'm so sorry, I was hoping that this was over for Vincent and you."

Please don't say sorry... I am sorry for causing so much trouble.

"You're not." For the life of me, I couldn't understand why she always seemed to feel that way.

"I see three scratches. Am I correct?"

Sorry... it's not the best. One long and two little ones. Is that bad?

"Well... some people would say it's a sign of something 'demonic.' Now, I'm *not* suggesting that it is. As far as I'm concerned it's another clue, letting us know what we need to do in order to stop it. I'm just not sure what 'it' is at this point. *Do not* worry. We will win this one too."

Thank you.

"You're welcome. I'm going to try to find a group out there, again, that has dealt with this sort of thing. We probably need to start documenting what's going on from an outside source."

I got a couple of hours of sleep, then messaged her back. "How's things?"

Ok.

"How did it go last night?"

Yeah all was quiet. Vincent slept in bed with me.

"Was he afraid to sleep alone?"

He just wanted cuddles from Mummy. He never said he was afraid.

"Let's just keep a close eye on him."

Yes... Thank you so much and I am sorry.

"For what?"

Getting in the way not being strong enough to deal with this on my own.

"Don't be silly. I've been dealing with this sort of thing since 1990. How long has it been for you?"

Too long. LOL

"I know what you mean! I'm trying to find someone in Australia to help me assess what's going on."

Thank you.

"I've got to tell you, finding someone I trust to help you won't be easy. But don't give up!"

I won't.

"One way or another... we ARE going to stop this thing!"

—⚋—

I messaged her later that day. It was late evening in Australia, and she and Vincent had just gotten back from going for a walk. I asked her if she had any idea what was behind Vincent's outburst.

I have no idea. Hence the walk we did. It was strange as he was screaming and carrying on, and then as if a switch was flicked he stopped and acted as if nothing happened, I don't think he even knows he was doing it.

"Are you journaling all of this?"

Yes Hun, as you asked. And for me too.

"Good. Thank you."

Things continued to go from bad to worse. The school suggested that Jane take Vincent to a hospital for observation.

Wasn't good to send him as the way he was Friday. Still waiting to hear from school now.

"The school didn't want him to attend?"

No... If you had seen him Friday you would know why. He was just screaming I could hear him as soon as I got out of the car at school pick up. He was on the floor outside his class room. Took three of us to carry him to a safe spot. He just went stiff when you tried to pick him up. Lasted about 30 minutes. It was before this he was asking for you.

I found myself wishing, again, that I was closer to the family so I could see for myself what was going on, and perhaps be of more help. I thought this was over. Now I didn't know what to think and felt completely helpless to do anything about it.

He's been fine since.

"Thank God for that! If you need to talk, message me!"

I messaged her back the next day. "Are things quiet there?"

Seem to be, although I did notice the crow was back at Vincent's window.

When was this?

Early this morning.

It seemed more holy water was in order. Without saying anything to Jane, I wet the doll. "Is it still there?"

No it went away.

"Good... Let me know if it comes back."

Ok Hun.

"Be sure to make a note of it in your journal," I instructed her.

Yes Hun... already have.

Good. We will probably have to use it later.

Ok.

She was exhausted, and wondering if this was ever going to end. I felt the same way, and I wasn't on the receiving end the way her family was. "If this doesn't end soon," I thought, "the entity might end up claiming both of them."

How is it going with Harold?

"I've been taking a break from it," I told her honestly. She and her family weren't the only ones tired of dealing with whatever was going on.

Good to hear.

"Jane...."

Yes?

"I'm sorry. I thought it was over. I really did."

ANOTHER QUESTION ANSWERED

I started to withdraw from people, especially those wanting to "help" me with the doll. I was tired of so-called "intuitives" telling me what the "truth" was about the doll, and others who were saying I was making all of this up. Even people with whom I confided about what was going on seemed to think either I was nuts, or Jane was lying, and I was crazy for believing her. I didn't think she was, but still, I also found myself pulling away from Jane as well.

What are you up to?

"Trying to unwind. You?"

Not much. LOL

"You're feeling better?"

Yes Hun, I'm fine. Thank you.

"I'm sorry I'm not very communicative lately, but I haven't been with anyone. How are you?"

All good Hun. Was checking in.

A couple of days later, I came up with an idea I wanted to run by Jane. It was almost midnight Mountain Standard Time when I messaged her. "Are you there?"

Yes Hun.

"How are you?"

Ok, thank you. How are you?

"I'm good." I was lying. I was frustrated as hell. "Would you mind doing a HUGE favor for me? Would you ask Vincent to paint a picture of me? However he normally does it. I'm trying to understand what is going on with you and Vincent. It might help if I know how Vincent sees me in all of this." I wanted to know what my role in all of this was.

Ok Hun, of course I can.

"Thank you! By the way, if Vincent does paint it, it might answer a question I have; which in turn, will answer another question I have—about you and Vincent."

Oh, ok... I think.

"LOL, I'm not sure I know what the hell I just said either."

Jane said that Vincent saw people in terms of their "auras." I wanted to see how Vincent saw me. I was hoping it might tell me why it was coming after Vincent and Jane, and not me, since the doll was often only a couple of feet away from me on my nightstand, in my hotel room.

"Has the crow come back?"

Haven't seen it today.

"How is Vincent?"

Yeah good. First day back at school today so will see how we go.

"Fingers crossed."

Jane messaged me again about two days later. *Hope all is good.*

"Hi, I'm good. Tired. But good. How are you?"

Good Hun, thank you.

"How are Vincent and Edward?"

Good... both are good.

"Is Vincent back to being himself?"

Yes... he had two amazing days at school.

"How were they amazing?"

Calm, relaxed, and listened.

I was so relieved to hear this. "Did you ask him to paint a picture of me?"

It wasn't unusual for Jane to promise to do something and then forget in the daily roller coaster of trying to deal with her son's autism, and now, this entity.

Yes.

Another reason to feel relieved! "And?"

"Sorry he hasn't done it yet. Will get him to do it over the weekend."

And... disappointment sets in once again. "Okay... I'm just trying to confirm an idea I have. Of course, I could be wrong, but..., the painting will help me figure it out."

Ok Hun. Will do ASAP. Just have to catch him in the right mood.

Even though I was upset, I didn't want to let Jane know that. She had enough to deal with.

"I know what you mean." She did tell me once that she couldn't *force* Vincent to paint. He does it when he wants to. Still, I suddenly began feeling even more emotionally drained, and wanting to withdraw even further. If it weren't for the fact that Vincent is a child, I more than likely would have. I was tired of it all.

Vincent will only paint if, when and what he wants.

"I understand."

I decided to check in a few days later to see how things were going there. I was hoping for the best. "How are Vincent and Edward?"

Vincent is unsettled. Edward seems ok.

"Unsettled?"

Doesn't want to play or sleep in his room.

"How long has this been going on?"

Only since Friday.

"It's Sunday evening there?"

Yes.

"What's Vincent doing?"

He's next to me here in bed almost asleep.

I was happy to hear that Vincent was able to sleep despite what was going on. His life was hard enough, without having this entity preying on him. I only wished I knew how to stop it.

Edward is on the pull out next to me on the other side. Been asleep for a few hours. I'm off to sleep still not feeling 100%.

I could only imagine. With everything that was going on, I thought she was much stronger than she gave herself credit for being. I knew she was afraid, but was carrying on as best she could.

"Good night."

I messaged Jane again, that afternoon - morning in Australia. I was worried about her. "How are you feeling?"

Yeah getting there, thank you. How are you?

"I'm good. Thank you. How's Vincent?"

He was awake from around 3 am.

"Why? Do you know?"

He didn't really say... he got up, looked out the bedroom door (this is when I woke), slammed the door shut, ran back to bed and then nearly climbed on top of me.

"What did he say?"

He didn't say anything. He just snuggled into me. He could have just had a bad dream... I don't know. This is what he drew on Saturday when I was at the market. My husband showed it to me yesterday.

The painting appeared to be a single eye with tentacles emanating from it. It was disconcerting to look at. Even more unsettling was the thought that Vincent probably saw it *before* he painted it.

"Please save the painting for me. The painting, the names on the drawing, etc., its ALL evidence; although I'm starting to think I know what needs to be done."

Yes, of course I will save it for you.

"It's important to me that Vincent's life goes back to being as carefree as possible."

Yes, please I would love that too.

"I really think that this will be over soon. It's just a matter of time. We need to take this one step at a time, and you need to share with me *every* unusual behavior, as you have been.

By the way, thank you for showing the painting to me. Is there a reason you waited?"

I didn't know about it till late yesterday. It was on the breakfast bar in the granny flat. Alan just mentioned to me if I had seen what Vincent drew Saturday.

Vincent has finished your painting.

The painting had a blue background with a white figure in the lower left, holding up what looked like arms, warding off a black mass of energy coming down on it from the upper right hand corner of the painting. The white form had a great deal of gold in it, as well as purple and green.

You are the gold thing apparently.

"It answers a lot of questions for me," I messaged Jane.

Really?

"For one thing, I'm frequently asked if I'm ever attacked by the entity in the doll. This tells me that the answer is, 'yes,' and it looks as though it's on a constant basis. It also says to me that one of the reasons it's coming after Vincent is that it's an attack on me. It confirms what I've thought for a long time, regarding my own life."

I went on to explain to her that over the years I'd been plagued with misfortunes, bad luck, lost opportunities and friends, as well as potential relationships. I refused to blame Harold but what I saw in the painting was that none of this was an "accident." It was an assault on my life from whomever, or whatever, the entity trapped in the doll was. I'd often wondered if that was the case. As far as I was concerned, this was proof. I wasn't just helping Vincent, I was fighting for my own life, while I was fighting for his.

PISS ON HIM

It would be several more days before I'd hear from Jane again. When I finally did, she seemed to be at her wit's end.

Everything was so good after the blessing. It was like it used to be. The house and Vincent's room felt so different. Vincent was happier and back to his old self.

The last week or so I'm not so sure, and I don't know if it's just me reading too much into normal everyday things that just happen, or something is going on again. I keep trying to look at things logically and find an answer.

"Is there something going on in Vincent's room that you haven't told me about?"

We don't go in there to be honest. Vincent has stopped going in since last week. He either sleeps with me or he climbs into bed with Edward... they sleep holding each other.

"Is there a reason you don't go in there?"

It doesn't feel any different if that's what you mean and nothing has happened to any of us in there since the blessing.

"Then why don't you go into his room?"

I don't really know to be honest. It's as if a sixth sense keeps you out... if that makes sense.

"Well, from this point on, it's *imperative* you tell me *everything*... no matter how silly, trivial or whatever, happens. Do you understand?"

Yes Anthony, I promise.

"It's the ONLY way I can protect you and your family. I fully expect the entity's attention to be turned towards me, but it may be pissed enough to strike out at you and Vincent."

You must be physically and mentally exhausted.

"I am. Not to mention emotionally as well; but I'm sure you are too."
I am. I just wish this were over... once and for all.

—⚏—

"Good morning! How are you?"
I'm good thank you, all is quiet and good here. How are you?
I'm not sure why, but I suddenly began to sense something was wrong on her end. "Are you okay?"
Yes... stupid crow is back.
"When did it show up?"
About 15 minutes ago as far as I know, or that's when it started going loopy pecking and scratching at the glass door.
"Okay... do you still have holy water?"
Yes.
"Go through the room and sprinkle the same way you saw the priest do it." I wanted Jane to start taking control of the situation thinking it might help her deal with her anxieties about the bird.
Ok. Done.
"Is it still there?"
It's moved to the fence.
"Good! It responds to religious provocation. Take some sea salt and sprinkle it outside of the window sill the crow comes to. Then pour some holy water on top of the sea salt."
Ok... done.
"Awesome! Let's see what happens. Okay?"
Ok. Umm... it now has its mate.
I wasn't expecting that to happen.
It's freaking poor Edward out.
"What are they doing?"
They just sit there. At least it's not scratching the glass. It was doing the scratching at the door this morning. Maybe I should just chuck the bottle of holy water at it.
"I'm going to do something here."

Ok.

I plastered the doll with holy water. "Any difference?"

They are now sitting on top of the garage roof squawking very, very loudly.

"They're trying to scare you... and Edward."

Well they have succeeded with Edward.

I poured more water on the doll, commanding the entity to make them leave. "What about now?"

They are still on the roof of garage, but quiet.

Close but no cigar, as far as I was concerned. If they were going to be stubborn, so would I. I knew the holy water was painful to the entity. The first time I splashed it during the first reading I had done on it I heard it scream on an EVP. I imagined it writhing in agony as I emptied the bottle on the doll.

"Now?"

They have flown off/away. Thank you... thank you.

"It's not my doing. I commanded him in the name of Jesus to tell the crows to leave... then I got pissed."

All I can say is thank you.

"The entity is an asshole. He's a bully who likes to scare women and children."

Well he's quite good at it.

"At least he responds to religious provocation. Piss on him (I think that's an Aussie expression). LOL"

Sort of. LOL

I was relieved that the crows left, and that I was able to make Jane laugh. "How do Aussies say it then?"

LOL... I don't know!!!

"Ask Edward. He's Aussie... you're such a Brit!" I was happy for the light moment.

I think it's something like, "I wouldn't piss on him if he was on fire."

"We say that here!"

Well then I don't know.

"I think the holy water feels like fire to the entity to be honest with you."

I wanted to see how the rest of her day went, so I messaged Jane the next afternoon.

"Good morning!"

Hey Hun.

"How did things go overall yesterday? Any more problems with the crow(s)?"

Have not seen the crows since.

"Are the boys awake?"

Vincent is. How are you?

"I'm good. Just wanted to check in. How's Alan by the way?" Alan is Jane's husband.

Yeah he's good.

Even though her husband declared he was skeptical about the doll, and anything "paranormal," even he began to wonder about what was going on with his son. He was even talking about the possibility of selling their home.

I don't want to move. We've lived here a long time. It will be hard on the boys... and if there is something here it will more than likely follow us where ever we go. Sucks hey.

"I didn't think he believed in this sort of thing."

I didn't think he did, either. But after everything that's happened, I guess he's changed his mind.

—⋙—

Night time in Denver is afternoon in Australia where Jane and Vincent lived, so I would occasionally message her before I went to sleep. "How's everything?"

Good Hun.

"No crow(s)?"

Nope.

"Thank God for small favors! Vincent is okay?"

Hope so, he's at school... no phone calls so I would say he's ok.

"Okay, just wanted to check in before I go to sleep. Good night/day."

Ok Hun, thank you. Sweet dreams.

I woke up a couple of hours later, around 1:30a.m., unable to breathe. I'm asthmatic, and this could have been an attack, but I felt as though it was more than just that. I had a nagging feeling that something was wrong with Vincent. I decided to check in and find out.

"Hey you."

Hey Hun.

"Is everything okay?"

Vincent has lost the plot.

"Shit… here we go again," I thought to myself becoming fully awake, noticing I was having an even harder time trying to breathe.

Author's note—What Jane thought were crows were apparently ravens. Crows tend to gather in large groups while ravens typically travel in pairs. According to my friend Kim Steffey, a pagan, in the "Old Ways," ravens were often signs of black magic at work.

Harold the Haunted Doll

"IT HAS A BLACK HEART"

"What's going on?"
He keeps saying, "It's in there..." pointing to his bedroom
"Bless his room with holy water."
Yes ok.

Several minutes passed, and I hadn't heard anything from Jane. "What's going on over there?"

Vincent has calmed down. I did his room with holy water and salt, was that right?

"Yes. Ask him to draw or paint what was in his room."

Ok. Did anything happen on your end? Vincent said your name!

Nothing, other than the fact it was 2 a.m., and I was freaking out, wondering who could have possibly been in Vincent's room after I bound all of the spirits in the doll. I thought that would have kept this sort of thing from happening until I figured out my next step. "What did he say about me?"

This is how it went.... he went towards his room; I think he was actually going to the laundry. He called me, "Mummy, mummy!" I came to where he was standing. He just stood there saying it's in there pointing into his room. He then looked at me and said, "It wants uncle Ant." He said something after but I didn't catch it as Alan came running in too. He's now in walk in robe playing iPad.

"I *was* attacked. That's how I knew something was going on there."

Omg... Are you ok?

"Getting there. That's why I asked you to have him draw or paint what he saw."

Ok. I will let him have tea and get him to do it. Are you sure you are ok?

"Starting to feel better... just now." I was hoping that Vincent would be willing to do the drawing fairly quickly. Jane said that he wouldn't do it just because she asked. He did it when he wanted to. I had the feeling though that if *she* didn't think he was ready, she wouldn't ask; and then forget to later.

Ok Hun. Vincent is being very strange

"What is going on now?"

No... false alarm. He has calmed down. Just had to move his bedding and pillow into walk in robe. Looks like he's sleeping in there tonight. May shut myself in there with him....

"I don't blame either of you. Hell, if I were there, I think I'd have to lock myself in the closet too!

I'd lock myself in one here... if I had one. The bed here is too low to hide under... just tried. LOL

By the way, what time is it there?" I just looked at my clock. It was 4 a.m. in Denver.

8 p.m.

"Well, keep me informed if anything happens. Did he do the drawing? Painting?" Like I said before, I was afraid that Jane would forget once things calmed down, and she was feeling grateful it was over.

No... Still eating tea, taking a long time.... I will try in a minute.

"When you say 'tea,' I think 'drink.' But you just said he's 'eating tea.' Does that mean "tea and snack?"

Sorry Hun... English thing. Dinner meal at night.

A photograph of Vincent's bedroom came up on my screen. It was a picture of what was obviously a little boy's room complete with a Spiderman doll on the bed, and plenty of toys on the floor.

Here's his picture.

The next pic that came up was of his drawing. It showed the same bed, and *something* with black tentacles coming out of the ceiling above the headboard. The Spiderman doll was missing from the bed. What looked to me like a little truck was on the floor at the foot of the bed. Near the head of the bed a figure that looked like a girl wearing a dress was on the floor.

"It looks like the *same* entity he painted in the picture of me. Is there a doll on his floor?"

No there is only Lego car and trucks on floor.

"Would you please ask him about it?"

His answer was, 'They come together.' I said, 'What do you mean?' He said, 'That,' and pointed to the dark squiggle, 'and that...' pointed to the doll thing.... 'They come together.'

My cell phone alarm went off. It was 5 a.m., the time I'm usually waking up. I was anything *but* tired at this point. "This could be IMPORTANT!"

I asked if it was Lottie. He looked sad and said, "I miss her."

"Wow... one last thing... ask if it has a name. The 'doll thing.'"

Was just going to say sorry, not being much help. He is getting tired. But I will ask. Hang on. He just looked at me when I asked, and said it has lots of names. He's tired Hun ... Do you want me to ask any more?

"I'm sorry... I'm just afraid he won't remember anything tomorrow."

It's ok Hun, what do you want to ask him?

"Would you ask him to give you one or two of the names? Then that'll be all. Or ask him if it is a doll. That'll help."

Hmm.... asked if it was a doll.... this was his answer... 'It's not a girl's doll mummy... It likes you to think it's a doll, but it's not, its heart is black.' He didn't give me any names. Sorry. Will this ever end?

"It will."

Sorry Hun.

"Don't be.... I'm not at all sure why you are."

Just been a long day. All good... still here and fighting.

"Every time this sort of thing happens, the entity tips its hand, and brings us closer to the truth.

Just glad you are here with us through this. Sorry not much help.

You BOTH have been a HUGE help!"

Hmm... Bed in the walk in robe. He's not coming out. Wish me luck. Thank you Hun, for everything.

I wasn't sure what Jane was thanking me for. I thought that the binding ritual would have ended all of this. That Vincent wouldn't be bothered anymore. It didn't seem to work, and I didn't know why. *I* was the one who wasn't being much help.

"It just occurred to me," I messaged Jane, "that what Vincent said about the doll IS important! I think I know what's going on!"

THE DEVIL'S DOLL

"I was sitting here wondering why, if I bound the entity to the doll, this just happened. What did Vincent see in his room? Then I remembered what Vincent said, 'They come together.' That is HUGE!"

Ok.

I knew Jane had *no idea* what I was talking about, but I admired her for at least trying to keep up. "It confirms that the entity IS trapped inside of the doll! It also explains how the entity could go from here to there! Which is why, even after the binding ritual, it's still showing up."

I don't understand.

"What Vincent saw isn't the same spirit that was in the doll. This is DIFFERENT ONE altogether. It's the entity Vincent painted attacking me in his picture of me. Do you remember Melanie's artwork?"

I sent her a picture to remind her of what I was talking about.

"I think that the spirit that was attacking Vincent before, the one that left his room when the priest blessed your home, is the one shackled to the cage. He's the one who calls himself, 'Harold.' I think that what Vincent saw in his room was the horned figure that is keeping the spirits trapped. I don't think it's in the doll though. I think it actually OWNS the doll."

Ok.

I couldn't help but laugh out loud when I read Jane's response. I was sure that at this point she was thinking, "Anthony's lost the plot." Maybe I had, but as far as I was concerned, another *huge* piece of the puzzle just fell into place. Vincent was right. This wasn't some "ordinary" girl's doll. Not only that, but I didn't own the doll either. I had custody of it—that was all. *The real owner of the doll was the Devil himself.*

IT'S NOT A REAL DOG

The next day Jane found her horses out running free. She didn't know how it happened. She said whoever set them loose had to be strong because the gate was so heavy. While she was out trying to gather her horses back into their stable, Vincent was having problems of his own.

You there?

I wasn't. I was walking my dogs. I had a new puppy Bentley, who was from the same litter as Chance. He came into my life after my friend Tereva passed away. When I got back I saw her message, and wrote back, "I'm here now. Good morning!"

Hi.

"Hi." I could sense something was wrong. "What's going on?"

It's ok Hun. It all calmed down. Vincent just went into his room to get a book and he freaked out.

"What happened? Did he say?"

To be honest I don't really know exactly what happened as I wasn't here, but Alan said Vincent was hysterical. He had to carry him out of the room....

"Did you ask Vincent?"

Alan had settled him by the time I got home so I didn't push it. Alan said he kept saying, "It touched me."

"Would you please ask him to make a picture of what happened?"

I have to go take Edward to the doctor, so will be back later Hun. I will talk to Vincent tonight and see if I can find something out. The reason I was not here last night was some idiot let my horses out of the paddock (Australian term for corral).

213

"The reason why I'm asking you to do this is because it'll help me figure out what happened. If I can understand that, I might know what we can do about it."

Ok Hun. Thank you.

The next afternoon I saw that Jane was on Facebook, so I decided to message her. "Hello!"

Hi x 2 back!

"How are you?"

Good thank you. A good night's sleep did wonders. How are you?

"I'm happy to hear that *you* are feeling better. How's Vincent?"

Yeah still not his normal self. Refuses to go anywhere near that end of the house. He's following me everywhere I go. Even jumped in the shower with me. He's like my little shadow.

"Did you ask Vincent what happened that night?"

To be honest Hun, I felt like shit last night. I left boys to Alan and went to bed… sorry. I did ask him to draw what had happened to him and he said he would.

I didn't hear again from Jane until the next day.

He came home from school with this!

The picture Jane sent was a drawing of what looked like a snarling dog, or wolf. It also looked like something that was way beyond Vincent's ability to draw at such a young age. Although I didn't really believe in such a thing, I couldn't help but wonder if the drawing was somehow "channeled" through him… much like the spirit paintings that were so popular in the early days of the Spiritualist Church.

"Holy shit!"

Yeah… exactly.

"Did he say what it was?"

He told the Special Ed teacher it's what's in his bedroom. I then had a thirty-minute grilling about letting him watch horror films.

"Did you ask him about the other night?"

He said that's what's in his room. It likes to stay high. It grabbed his arm… that's why he dropped the books. I asked him if what grabbed him is what he drew. He said yes. He is currently sitting under the table. I don't know who cried more on pick up, him or me.

"Please ask him if it's a 'dog.'"

Ok.

I normally check to see if there are any messages from Jane early on in the evening, and then before I go to sleep, but that night, I was dealing with another issue. I was glad that I took the time to look before going back to sleep.

I'm sorry Hun. I feel I rely on you too much. I hope I didn't interrupt anything. His answer to, 'Is it a dog?' was, 'It growls like a dog and looks like a dog, but mummy, I don't think it is a real dog.'

"DON'T EVER think you're bothering me again! I was talking with the security guard here at the hotel, after walking my dogs about a concern I had. Vincent is much more important to me. I can catch up on my sleep."

Thank you.

"I have more questions but I don't want to upset him, or you, than either of you are already. The questions are because I'm trying to figure out what to do to stop this shit from happening A.S.A.P."

I'm sorry.

"For what?"

For causing so much trouble, waking you up... not being able to help Vincent.

"You are helping him... by telling me what's going on." I was lying in bed, in the dark, messaging Jane when, "Holy shit... I just felt what I thought was one of the boys jumping onto my bed... but Bentley is lying next to me and Chance is sleeping a little farther away. OMG... just felt it walking next to me."

Are you ok? It's not attacking you is it?

"I'm okay. It probably just wants to let me know it's here."

Are you sure? Vincent is talking about you... right now.

"What is he saying?"

He's in the bath saying, "Its mad... he shouldn't have told me. It knows... uncle Ant is in trouble." Now I can't get him out the bath.

"Put sea salt in the water. Ask him what he shouldn't have said. Wash his hair with the sea salt water."

Will this ever end, Anthony? What am I doing wrong? Sorry, trying to be honest and tell you everything! The picture—Vincent said it's mad about his picture. It doesn't want you to know. Appolon... what the hell does that mean?

"Appolon? Where did 'appolon' come from?"

Vincent just said it.

"Ask him to write it down, and if he knows what it means."

Ok. I am sorry I am trying, I promise.

"Ask him to WRITE IT DOWN. NOT TOMORROW... not next week... TODAY.... TONIGHT. Then send me a pic of it."

Ok.

"Jane, I know you're afraid. I know that's why you resist what I ask you to do on occasion. But it only makes things worse when you do."

An hour went by, and I didn't hear from Jane. "What is going on?"

I have got Vincent out of the bath. I have heated up some chicken soup, I will then get him to do whatever you want.

"How is he?"

I washed him in salt and his hair.

"Did it help make him feel better?"

He has calmed down a little, thank you. He is sitting in our bed watching Horrid Henry.

"I know you think you're protecting Vincent but getting him to talk is the BEST thing you can do. That's why I keep pressing it. Threatening me in order to keep him quiet is a tactic. Ask him to write, draw, or both, "appolon." Now, before he forgets. Before *you* forget."

She sent me four pictures altogether. Two of them showed Vincent drawing the "black blob." The other two had the words, "Abadon," and "Apollyon" written next to the blob.

Does that mean anything??

"I think the first word is 'Abandon.' The second word Vincent wrote was 'Apollyon' not 'appolon.' I'm glad I asked you to ask him to write it out. Didn't want to research the wrong name or word. Did he finish the drawing?"

That's it, sorry. He's sitting here with me, now.

"Please ask him what 'Apollyon' is. I'm wondering if the first word is, 'A bad one.'" Hoping against all hope, I decided to do an internet search of the two words that Vincent wrote.

They turned out to be names. As soon as I got over the shock of what I was seeing, I wrote to Jane, "I know what the words are! They're actually names! The spirit we've been fighting with appears to have been into some BAD stuff. I believe that's why he is trapped in the doll! Now that he's been bound to the doll, he's been replaced, probably by the one who's will he's been carrying out.

I don't know how Vincent did it, but he found out the name of the one keeping the souls imprisoned! This is HUGE! I CANNOT tell you how important it was you had him write down what he was saying."

Is Vincent going to be ok?

"It's not over yet, but we have what we need to fight this thing and win! When this is over I PROMISE I will tell you everything. For now, please trust me."

I do trust you... 100%. Just keep Vincent safe...please. Omg... look at your time over there I am so sorry.

"Don't be... I'd gladly do it ALL OVER AGAIN to protect Vincent. Thank you so much for doing what I asked right away! This thing was counting on you NOT to... it was counting on your fear in order to win."

Vincent just said he loves you.... Just before he fell asleep. He just snuggled down in the bed... said I love you mummy. I love uncle Ant and Spider-Man too.

I laughed... Vincent saying he loved me *and* Spider-Man in the same sentence. "I'm in good company," I thought.

Then I remembered what I found out earlier, and it occurred to me that I'm not in such a great group after all. I looked at the doll and said to the entity that I'd been fighting with, and trying to protect Vincent from, "You son of a bitch... I know what you didn't want me to know! You lose!"

THERE'S THAT "B" WORD AGAIN!

Now that I knew what the demon's name was, I knew I'd have to hurry and find out how to deal with it because it wouldn't be long before it unleashed its fury on Vincent. In my mind, I pictured a cornered animal, ready to fight.

Got this for Vincent.

Jane sent me a picture. It was a Saint Michael the Arc Angel pendant, along with a Saint Benedict medal.

"Perfect! Did you sprinkle them with holy water?"

No should I? How are you feeling Hun?

"Shower the necklaces with holy water... say a prayer asking that St. Benedict and St. Michael keep Vincent safe, then put them in his room."

Knowing that Jane and Alan not only weren't Catholic, but *not* religious to begin with, I knew I was asking a bit much from her. Still, I hoped that she would take what I was saying seriously enough to do what I was suggesting.

Yes I will... Ok it is a necklace.... I can hang it above his bed.

"Don't tell him. Let's just see his reaction. Keep an eye on it. If he removes it, please let me know."

So make him wear the necklace?

"No, it might make him crazy. Putting it in his room works."

Oh ok, thank you. I will do the holy water and hang it in his room.

"Did you do it already?"

Yes, done in his room.

I was hoping that they were going to have a quiet night, until Jane messaged me a frowning emoticon. "Uh oh... what's going on?"

Yes, he was asleep... I was talking to my mum, could hear a noise. Now he's taken up residence in robe again. He is being very strange....

"Did you ask him what happened?"

He's not talking... staring and grunting.

She sent me a picture.

That picture freaks me out, it doesn't even look like him.

Looking at the picture she sent to me I had to agree... it didn't look like him... at all. "Where was he sleeping?"

In playroom, on a mattress.

"Okay... give me a few minutes. In the meantime, will he let you come near him?"

Yes, sort of.... OMG... he just called me bitch... 'Go away bitch.'

"Okay... just a moment." I did the only thing I could think to do at that moment. After dousing the doll with holy water I suggested that she try to approach him again.

He has vomited... I have him on the mattress on the floor... he seems a lot better.

"Get some holy water, and trace a cross on his forehead saying, 'May Almighty God bless you in the name of the Father, and of the Son, and of the Holy Spirit. Amen.' Then tell me his reaction."

Ok done... He is just laying down... seems ok.

She sent me a picture of Vincent. It looked to me as though he were laying down, but it was hard to tell, it was so dark.

Sorry bad picture.

"I can't see anything."

Sorry it's dark. He's just laying down, but at least is talking. Has asked for chocolate milk.

"You blessed him with holy water?"

Yes.

"And he didn't fight it?"

No just stayed still.

"That's a good sign. NOW, I need you to ask him to draw, or paint, what made him upset. I thought I knew who the woman is in the doll, but I was wrong. I do know the identity of the black blob. The reason this is important is because it's helping me understand why the binding wasn't completely effective. The good news is that Vincent didn't rebel against being blessed, and the blessing on my end stopped what was going on. I'm SURE the idea is to get you to the point where you don't want to tell me anything anymore. He's my only reliable source of information and what he calls the black blob wants to stop him. But Vincent isn't the target. Does that make sense?"

I don't understand... if Vincent isn't the target, then why is he acting this way? What does it want?

"Keep in mind, Vincent will survive this. It's you who it's trying to scare, so that you'll start to think that by ignoring it, it'll stop. Which you've already done a couple of times."

Ok.

"He wants to scare *you* to the point that you'll want to stop. The reason the ferocity is increasing is because we are getting close to stopping it. That's why I believe its intent is to scare you. This has NOTHING to do with you as a mother. Do you understand?"

To be honest, no, not really... but I trust you.

"That's all I'm asking. Once I found out its name from Vincent, it's been fighting a losing battle and it knows it. I was picked to release the three in the "cage." I don't know why, but it's what I'm going to do. I need your help, and Vincent's help to do it. The ONLY way it'll win is if you stop talking to me. That's exactly what it wants."

Ok.

"God WILL NOT allow any lasting harm to come to Vincent. You and I, on the other hand, will have to live with the memories of all of this."

As long as Vincent is ok.

"It's NOTHING you did wrong that brought this about. You need to know that. Now, *please*, ask him to paint, or draw, what happened. It's the way he communicates best about this. Apollyon can scare him, terrify him even, but it CANNOT touch his soul. Do you understand what I'm saying?"

Yes.

"Is he sleeping?"

Yes... do you want me to wake him?

"No, I'm happy he's sleeping. It proves my point that Apollyon is doing this to him to scare *you*. It's a tactic."

So who is Apollyon? I'm confused.

I sent her a copy of the pic of the artwork Melanie created.

"The horned figure in the back holding the cage closed and the three spirits in captivity."

Yes, I see that but who or what is it.

I sent her a copy of Revelations 9:11— **They had as king over them the angel of the Abyss, whose name in Hebrew is Abaddon and in Greek is Apollyon (that is, Destroyer).**

There was a long silence on her end. "Are you okay?"

Yes I think so. You have to understand he is my baby boy I love him.... I love both my boys and will fight till the end of the earth for them. He asked me to make it go away.

"We will. Did you ask him to draw what upset him? Or do you know what upset him?"

I tried last night to get him to draw, but he didn't want to... it was about 2:45am. I asked him why he was in the robe he didn't say much really he did say it likes to watch and he keeps looking up all the time like in the corner of the rooms.

"Okay... please ask him to draw it one more time. If he doesn't want to, tell me. By the way, the corners of what room?"

Mainly the playroom.

"He sees it in the playroom?"

I don't know if he sees it in there but he says it likes to watch and that's where he kind of applied it to. The playroom backs on/shares a wall with his bedroom.

"I'm trying to figure out how to explain the next step... Apollyon changes the game a bit. This involved somebody skilled. REALLY skilled in Magick. Unless Apollyon himself made it happen, but from what I know, that isn't possible. I'm trying to make sense of this in light of Vincent's painting... then we can take steps to end this right away."

As I said I will try again... he wasn't really very willing yesterday. He is usually more cooperative in the evenings after a bath and a bit more relaxed. I will try again Hun. I promise. Just need to catch him at the right time.

I went to a Catholic gift store the next day to look for a St. Benedict's crucifix to put in the bag with Harold. I was hoping that by doing so it would help contain Apollyon. While I was there I wandered to the back of the store where I saw a large statue of St. Michael the Archangel. In Christian tradition, St. Michael is "one of the chief princes," and leader of the forces of heaven in their triumph over the powers of hell. The name Michael means, "Who is like to God?" and was the war cry of the good angels in the battle fought in heaven against Satan and his followers.

The statue was large, heavy, beautiful, and *expensive*. I decided to buy a smaller inexpensive image of Michael instead.

A week went by. I would occasionally, but clearly, see the statue of Michael in front of the bag that Harold was in. After seeing it for the third time I took it as a sign that I was supposed to put the statue in front of the bag. So I went back to the store and bought it.

"Just purchased this St. Michael the Archangel." I messaged Jane, sending her a picture as well. "I saw the statue at a Catholic gift shop, and kept going back and forth between buying it, or a St. Benedict crucifix. Both were expensive. I kept seeing the statue though, in front of the doll, so I bought it. I'm calling in the Calvary to help us help Vincent."

I like that.

That evening I blessed the statue with holy water, saying a modified version of the St. Michael prayer— **"St. Michael, the Archangel, defend Vincent,** and protect him against the wickedness and snares of the one trying to harm him.

May God protect Vincent I humbly pray, and do you, oh Prince of the Heavenly hosts, by the divine power of God, cast aside Apollyon, and any spirit associated with him who seek the ruin of Vincent's soul."

I then sent Jane a message asking how everything was going in their home.

Vincent just had a massive shouting duo with Alan.

"How did it begin?"

Alan asked Vincent to move his toy taxi set and Vincent just lost it.

"How long ago did this happen?"

About 30 minutes or so.

"Is that when it started?"

Yes, why?

"That's when I blessed the statue."

Oh....

"It's probably just a coincidence. Let's see."

The next morning, I woke up to see this message on my phone.

Vincent just trashed his bedroom, not sure if important or not but thought would let you know.

"It might be. What's going on?"

Her response was to send pictures of Vincent sitting in front of his bedroom, throwing toys into it. His floor was covered but it didn't appear as though he were throwing them into his room as much as he was throwing them at someone, or something.

"Did you ask him what's going on?"

I did. He was just sat there throwing things into his room, shouting 'Get out!'

"Can you talk to him and ask him who he's talking to, or is he too amped up?"

I have him in the bath now.

"Don't forget... put sea salt in the water. It sounds as though he's getting fed up with the presence in his room and starting to fight back. In other words, he may be losing his fear of it."

Ok that's good yes?

"Yes, he's fighting back... taking control back."

Yay...

Her halfhearted cheer made me smile. "I keep seeing that we need to put an image of Jesus in his room. Do you have one?"

No... I have a Bible, and a children's Bible in the office.

"Put the children's Bible in there for now."

Suddenly, I saw a vision of St. Michael. His presence was incredibly powerful as he hovered over Vincent. I heard Vincent, unafraid, asking, "Who are you?"

"My name is Michael."

I could see "Michael" standing over Vincent with his sword drawn, much like in the statue I had in front of Harold, and he looked angry. Looking back down at Vincent he smiled, and said, "I'm here to help you. I'm here to protect you."

I felt hot tears rolling down my cheeks as I watched this. I thought what I had done earlier by blessing the statue and saying the prayer I did, it only angered Apollyon, and he was taking his wrath out on Vincent. Seeing this told me I did the right thing.

Michael's voice was deep and soothing. "Do not be afraid, Vincent. God loves you. I love you. God sent me to protect you. Don't be scared. I'm with you now. Don't be scared."

My vision of St. Michael comforting Vincent ended when my phone dinged, signaling a Facebook message.

I put the children's Bible in Vincent's room. He's still in the bath... singing.

KEEP THE WATER WARM!

I told Jane about my vision of Saint Michael watching over Vincent. "I saw the statue a couple of days ago, and envisioned putting it in front of the bag. I didn't buy it then, but kept feeling I needed to go back and get it. So I did."

I ...We are so lucky to have you, I mean that. I would have gone insane by now. You keep me grounded. LOL, I can't get him from the bath, he is singing so loud and so well LOL

"Just keep the bath water warm! LOL

LOL, yes.

I was happy that Jane was in high spirits seeing and hearing her son singing. I wanted to say something that would continue to keep her that way. "Seeing Saint

Michael watching over Vincent, protecting him, telling him not to be afraid, makes me think that ALL of this will be over soon."

Oh, I hope so for everyone's sake! Sometimes I feel as if I'm standing watching what's going on...Almost as if it's some weird TV programme. I can't even imagine how you feel.

"Believe me, I know! I'm often saying that if it weren't happening with me involved I don't know that I believe it myself! I have to tell you though, you're much stronger than I gave you credit for. Not only that, but you've risen to the occasion when Vincent and I needed you to do so. Thank you."

Thank you! Because you believe in Vincent and me, you gave me strength, and because he's my son and I need to fight for him! Neither of us would be able to do without you and your compassion. Still scares the crap out of me. And I don't really understand it, how or why.... But I/we trust you, and Vincent loves you!

"Honestly, there's a lot I still don't understand yet. My biggest question is, 'Are the children in the doll, really children?' From what I've been able to find out in my research, one of the most common disguises demonic entities employ is to pretend they're children when they're not."

I will sit down with Vincent and ask him again.

"Show him a picture of the painting he made in art therapy and ask which one of them is a child. That'll help. I just don't want to do anything that'll cause bigger problems for Vincent, your family, me, or even the world, by doing the wrong thing and releasing what should remain bound. But if what Vincent is saying is correct, and there are innocent souls trapped inside of the doll, I need to help them.

Like I said, I'm at a point in which I TRUST Vincent completely. I just need to know so I can do the right thing, and only you and Vincent can help me with that.

I think that what's pissing Abaddon off is that Lottie is apparently telling Vincent what is going on, and Vincent is telling me what he sees and hears. Silence makes this thing powerful. Vincent sharing what he's hearing and seeing is taking its power away"

Ok... but please tell me if I'm doing the wrong thing or asking Vincent the wrong thing.

"Right now, my BIG question is, 'Are the children really children?' My inclination is to believe that they are because of Vincent's painting. But I need to know for sure, and ONLY Vincent can answer that. That's why I believe that Abaddon has stepped in and is stepping up his attacks on your son.

Perhaps you can show Vincent his painting and ask, 'Uncle Ant is wondering which one of these are children?' And leave it at that. Anything else will come when he's ready."

TRUST ME... I'M A PSYCHIC

I often wondered why "Abaddon" didn't just come after me directly. I didn't have a good answer. I *hated* the idea that a young child like Vincent was in the middle of all of this, but I didn't know what to do to stop it. I thought that if I stopped communicating with him through his mother the attacks on him would stop too. But they didn't.

While all of this was going on I was hearing from various psychics, and even non-psychic types, telling me their opinion of what the truth was as far as what was going on. Only Vincent gave me information that I could verify as being correct. When I asked one woman who claimed to be "intuitive" why I should believe what she was telling me about the nature of the spirits in the doll, her response was, "Well, you're just going to have to trust me that I'm right."

I trusted Vincent. He was right on so many things, including clues that I've chosen not to share here. Whether I liked it or not, as long as he was willing to talk to me, I was going to have to listen.

Jane did what I asked of her and made a video asking Vincent who were the children in the doll. I had a hard time understanding Vincent, not because he was autistic, but because of his Aussie accent. I did feel better when Jane laughingly told me that she didn't always understand him either. That's why I asked her to send me a transcript with one of the videos she had made.

Jane: Vincent, Uncle Ant wants to know are any of these in your painting children?

Vincent: These two are and they're scared. This one is, is… he pretends to be a kid, but is very nasty!

Jane: Do you know who this one over here is?

Vincent: She's the lady who helps and watch. (Pointing to the black blob) I don't like him.

Jane: Okay. Thank you.

"OMG! 'This one is, is (pointing to the 'star' with black inside of it) pretends to be a kid, but is very nasty!' THAT puts a whole new spin on this! I'm wondering if that's the one who calls himself, 'Harold!' Harold visited a woman in Long Island, New York... a friend of mine at the time. He pretended to be a young man. Since talking to you, this confused me. Vincent may have clarified it. I think that what he's done is confirm that he is manipulative and a liar!

It appears that along with the two children, there is a woman who is helping them. That makes three of them who need to be released. Now Melanie's image of one of the spirits in the doll being shackled is starting to make sense. Vincent says that she's right... he's NOT supposed to be set free!"

I just asked Vincent about the lady. He said she's like their mummy, but she's not. She watches them to be safe.

"That is huge! I'm excited and thinking out loud. I may have to take Nyquil to get to sleep tonight and I don't have a cold!"

LOL ... all good Hun.

A MUCH NEEDED LAUGH

I wanted to understand how all this happened, and why. How do souls become, and remain, stuck inside of a doll against their will?

Secondly, how do I release the three, and bind the two?

The second question, to me, was *more* important to me than the first.

I'd had a tremendous amount of angst regarding the three "children." Should I release them or not?

The female according to Vincent wasn't a child, or a young girl… but a mother figure, watching over the two children.

"I believe," I said to myself, "that the next step is to release them. God help us all if I'm wrong!"

The next morning, which would have been nighttime in Australia I sent a message to Jane. I was wondering how Vincent's been since I put the St. Michael statue in front of the doll.

"I was wondering what you think about Vincent and how's he doing?"

In what way?

"Do he think he's doing better the last couple of days?"

Yes… but then there are so many factors, like now is Easter holidays, Alan and I fighting upsets him. We can go some days with no issues then all of a sudden they are back. That's why I find it hard sometimes on what I should tell you, what is just life, what is just autism and what is connected what to is going on. Does that make sense?

"Has Alan become more irritable lately? More argumentative?"

Yes.

"Recently?"

The last two weeks EVERY little thing upsets him, me, the kids, work. Just seems more on edge.

"Hmmm… that MIGHT be important." It was right in line with what I'd been reading about diabolical oppression. I asked because the same sort of thing had happened to me with other people, for years, and I didn't put it together until later. Good friends would turn on me suddenly… and tell me it was because *I* was being different. At first I thought that perhaps I was. But I realized in many cases I was being unjustly accused of doing things I wasn't doing.

"Jane, I believe that the reason it's happening is that you're acting as a go between Vincent and me. That may be the reason. It wants you to give up thinking that it'll bring peace to your home. I'm going to do something and see if it helps. I'll let you know what I do later. Like later today/tonight your time. Is that okay with you?"

Ok Hun.

"I need you to let me know if you see a difference in Alan's mood for the better."

Ok.

"*We* have to learn how to contain it. This thing will not give up without a fight, though."

Ok.

After dousing the doll with holy water, I got back to Jane. "Is everything okay? Are things starting to calm down a bit?"

Yes… why?

"Why am I asking if things are calming down?" I thought that was a strangely suspicious question.

Yes, as is weird… Edward has suddenly led down and going to sleep. Vincent is calmer? May be a coincidence but I like it.

"What about Alan? What is he doing?"

Sat here checking his schedule for tomorrow.

"Is he calmer than he was before?"

God yes…

"Do you remember when I asked you to give me a few minutes?"

Yes.

"I blessed the bag with holy water and commanded Abaddon and whomever is there to leave your family alone IMMEDIATELY. It may be confirmation that Abaddon IS who we're dealing with."

235

Yes... yes... yes!

"I want to ask if there's any way you and the kids can visit your mum and dad for a bit." Jane's parents live in England and I was thinking it might help if they went there while I figured out how to deal with the entity. There was, of course, the possibility it would simply follow them there.

I would love to... just not sure we can.

The next morning, I asked Jane how the rest of their night was after I blessed the doll's bag with holy water. Since the binding ritual I did *after* the priest came to bless their home, I had the bag zipped closed.

Pretty uneventful.

"Pretty uneventful? Does that mean not completely uneventful?"

Sorry, no it was good apart from the possum in the laundry.

"Oh... LMAO!"

Frightened the living daylights out of me at 1:30 am.

On my end, I literally belly laughed and told her so. "Sorry but that is not at all what I was expecting you to say! How did you get it out?"

With a long handled brush and a dustbin lid.

"That'll do it!" I was so grateful it wasn't something worse, although finding an opossum in your ceiling....

Vincent just says he loves you uncle Ant.

"NO! NOT AGAIN!"

I knew that Jane was trying to think about what was going on with her son as little as possible in order to create some sort of normalcy in their family, but more importantly, in Vincent's life. I however, didn't feel I had that luxury. I thought about it all the time and was constantly reviewing the messages between Jane and me.

"I want to talk to you about something. Vincent said, 'They always come together.' Do you remember that?"

Not really, sorry.

"Just a second… I was trying to find the message when Messenger stopped! Anyway, you told me he said the black blob and the doll always come together."

Wow, I just asked Vincent what comes together as he is here next to me, while looking at that picture he drew of what was in his bedroom. He didn't say anything but pointed to the black mass and then to the figure on the floor.

'That's what I'm talking about. I was thinking, if that's the case, then whatever the black thing is, it's NOT in the doll. It doesn't belong to the doll. The doll belongs to it."

—⚉—

I woke up to see that Jane had sent me a video with a message.

Please watch this. Not going good here. Are you there Hun?

"I'm here now."

I watched the video. What I saw broke my heart. Vincent was running from something I couldn't see, holding the remote to his PlayStation in his hand. He kept screaming over, and over again, at the top of his lungs, 'No… not again!

Not again!' I was glad she recorded it because no written description could have come close to describing the terror I was seeing from this little boy.

"This is IMPORTANT," I messaged Jane not sure how long before this had happened. "Ask him to draw, or paint, whatever upset him. IF POSSIBLE, record it, and EVERYTHING he says while he's doing it."

A couple of hours later Jane messaged me again. *I have got him asleep. I gave him a bath with salt, and then just held him until he fell asleep.*

"What started it? Did he say?"

Really don't know. Alan and I were sitting down having our evening meal when it started. That was just a small bit of it, believe me.

'What else happened?'

Not too much more than you have already seen. It just lasted for a long time.

"This video is really important. It shows what Vincent, you, Alan, and Edward are going through. The only missing piece now is what provoked it. In the video, Vincent was holding a video game remote. Do you know what he was watching? Or playing, I should say...."

Yes, Lego movie. He only has Minecraft, Lego movie, and a farm game.

I had to ask because when I was actively investigating things like this, the rule of thumb is, *eliminate the obvious before considering the paranormal*. "I hate to say this, but one of the 'obvious' things that needs to be considered is the idea that some people make crazy claims because they want attention."

Believe me having a child with autism is more than enough. The last thing I or anyone in this family want is attention. Off to bed.

"I'm sorry if I offended you, Jane. I just had to know he wasn't watching some 'creature feature' sort of thing."

No worries. I wasn't offended. I wasn't being sarcastic either.

"Okay... just wanted to make sure and clear the air if necessary. Try to sleep. Message me if anything new happens."

For me, sleep was harder and harder to come by. I spent a great deal of time researching and trying to understand what I was dealing with, but I wasn't able to find any case that came anywhere close to what I was dealing with.

Stories about "haunted objects," especially dolls were common enough. But this wasn't your run of the mill haunting. I found stories of cursed objects, but I couldn't find any that might help me understand what I was up against, and how to deal with it. I was still reluctant to accept, or even consider the idea that something "demonic" was at work here.

I took Vincent to the Catholic Church this afternoon.

"What happened there?"

He drew a picture of a dark thing with horns... he said it is mad with you ... with him....You will need to see.

She sent me a picture of what she was talking about. It was a building with several "stars." The "black blob" was outside the building.

Church was really good. The priest took Vincent for a walk and an ice cream, and gave him a special medal thing. Vincent was so happy and calm we are going back tomorrow.

Suddenly things started falling into place for me. I couldn't wait to share with Jane what I thought was going on. "Figured something out that should help us... there are FOUR spirits in the doll... not five as I was thinking. The one that is scaring Vincent has to be dealt with differently. Which is why the binding I did isn't stopping it.

Then there is the one shackled to the cell. He was the one originally scaring Vincent BEFORE the priest blessed your home. Afterwards, the binding ritual calmed everything down because he *was* bound to the doll.

NOW the 'keeper,' Abaddon, the figure in this image with the horns is the one attacking and scaring Vincent. I just put all of this together this afternoon."

There was *no* reaction whatsoever from Jane. That's when it occurred to me that I didn't even look to see if she was online when I began messaging her, I was so excited to share my thoughts. Knowing that she'd read it sooner or later, I sent another message... "I know it's confusing, but I was born confused, so it's easy for me to keep it together."

Later in the day I sent her another message asking about Vincent.

He's ok. Seems very tired and lethargic, but ok... a little quiet. We went back to church this morning.

"How did that go?"

Church was ok... didn't stay long. Vincent didn't like it inside. He wanted to leave.

I thought to myself, "When I was his age the last place I wanted to be was in a church. It was so quiet and somber. But we were talking about Vincent, and I didn't want to make any assumptions. "Did he say why he didn't like it in there?"

No... just he didn't like it and wanted to go! Was a lot better once we were back outside.

Because of my new theory regarding Apollyon being the "jailer" in Melanie's artwork, I wanted to try something with Vincent. "How is he with jewelry?"

In what way, for Vincent and jewelry... well, he is a chewer.

"I'll tell you what. Better still... I'd like you to try something for me."

Yes ok.

"I was going to ask you to put the necklace with Saints Michael and Benedict on him... just for a minute. Do you think he'd tolerate that? If not, just hold both in the palm of your hand and give him a hug for me. Either way, I'd like to know his reaction."

Ok... he should be fine with either for a little while.

"That's all I'm asking for... even if it's just a minute.

Just got it out of his bedroom. I will go try.

She messaged me again a few minutes later.

Ok, that went well… not. I put it on him he screams at me to take it off. He ended up breaking the chain pulling it off.

His reaction wasn't what I expected, but it still wasn't enough. "Hold the medal in your hand and give him a hug with it from Uncle Ant. Both medals."

Ok I will try.

"That's ALL I'm asking," I messaged back hoping to reassure her.

Ok, that was a little better. He let me put my arms around him for at least 30 secs no screaming. Then pushed me away saying, "Enough!"

I didn't know what to make of his reaction. Did he allow her to hug him because it came from me? "Does he normally let you hug him for longer periods?"

Only on his terms; part of the autism. Sometimes he loves hugs, a lot of the time he won't.

"Okay… can you take a picture of the necklace and chain for me?"

After seeing the last video, and hearing about the necklace, I decided to start saying a prayer for Vincent. **"In the name of the Lord Jesus Christ of Nazareth, I rebuke all spells, hexes, curses, voodoo practices, witchcraft, satanic rituals, incantations and evil wishes that have been sent Vincent's way, or have passed down the generational bloodline. I take authority over all of them and command that they go back where they came from and be replaced with a blessing.**

In the name of the Lord Jesus Christ, and powerful in the holy authority of His Precious and Wondrous Name, I ask, O Lord God, that you break and dissolve any and all curses, hexes, spells, seals, satanic vows and pacts, spiritual bindings and soul ties with satanic forces, evil wishes, evil desires, hereditary seals, snares, traps, lies, obstacles, deceptions, diversions, spiritual influences, and every dysfunction and disease from any source. Amen."

Hey, I can't find the pendent.

"Do you think Vincent hid it?"

No, I left it here in granny flat while I was cleaning up Edward.

What about the pendant? Was Vincent anywhere near it?

Still looking. Yes, he's down here playing with Legos. Perhaps he's hiding it.

"Ask him if he put it somewhere."

Little bugger isn't talking now. All I'm getting is shrugs.

"He hid it," I thought to myself. I was sure of it. I just wondered if he was instructed to hide it.

I still have the other Saint Benedict medal from the catholic priest....

I sent her the prayer I just said for Vincent, and suggested, "Let's try this. While you're bathing him, bless him by tracing the cross on his forehead with holy water. While you're doing that, say the prayer I just sent to you."

Ok...Anything else I need to do or say?

"Tell me his reaction. I'm going to try to get in about 4 hours of sleep in the meantime. I'll get back in touch as soon as I wake up."

Sweet dreams.

When I woke up this message was waiting for me—

Vincent had his bath. He was ok with salt in water. I said the blessing prayer thing and he then slid under the water. I tried to pull him to sit up, but he didn't want any of that. I managed to do the holy cross on him but he wasn't happy about it. He is hiding in our robe at moment.

I was stunned by what she wrote, but I had to be sure before I made any kind of conclusion about his reaction to what I asked Jane to do. "Ask him, ONE MORE TIME, to draw what is going on. Ask him to draw what happened when you two were in the church, when he wore the necklace... that sort of thing. Say to him, 'Vincent... what happened when we went into the church and when I put the necklace on you? Can you draw what you saw or felt?'

By the way, were you able to finish saying the prayer before he slid under the water?"

Yes I said the prayer.

"You finished it *before* he slid under the water?"

Yes... I just finished.

"What is he doing now?"

She didn't respond anytime soon, and I didn't think it was because she walked away. I couldn't put my finger on it at the time, but I knew *something* was wrong with Jane. She'd resisted what I asked her to do before, but somehow this felt different. "If your house is NOT on fire right now, Vincent needs you to stay with me."

I am.

"Unless your house is on fire...."

Funny you should say that...Alan lit a fire outside to burn the palm tree throngs and he had to catch it with the hose as it was going towards the house. This was about an hour ago.

She might have found this funny, but I sure as hell didn't. Something was going on, and she wasn't telling me. "WHAT IS VINCENT DOING RIGHT NOW?"

Sleeping.

"Speaking of which, when I woke up, I heard a woman say, 'Okay, I'm giving up now. I quit.'"

You know Friday night I had a dream....

I was quickly getting tired of what I perceived to be a game Jane was playing with me. "Okay, I'll play along... what was your dream?"

Confused....

"WHAT WAS YOUR DREAM?"

I guess the 'I quit' is me.

"Oh my God... I'm going to ask you one last time. WHAT WAS YOUR DREAM?"

Sorry... it's just I was not to tell you.

"WHAT WAS YOUR DREAM?"

I need to break away from you. That was my dream!

"Fine... do that." I was over Jane and this game.

I don't want to.

"I swear to God, if it weren't for Vincent....Tell me about your dream."

That was my dream!!

"What did you dream?"

I was told not to tell you, I needed to break away. It was a male voice, but in a fog like I didn't see anyone.

Reading that the voice came from within a fog reminded me of the vision Larry had in which he saw the woman and child appear in a fog, then the man with the burned face appeared out of the same fog before the other two were swept away.

It was like don't tell him. You need to break away.

"I know you're tired. I know you're scared. I know you love your sons. The 'black blob' is using your love for your sons, especially Vincent, against you. It's preying on it. Do not listen to the voice telling you that you're a lousy mother. It's the voice of what's coming after Vincent. It NEEDS you to think that in order to win. This has NOTHING to do with you. No one, NO MOTHER, is equipped to deal with what you're dealing with.

That's why I was sent to help. Because a child is involved, I won't give up until the fight is over.

That's why I had you say that prayer over Vincent, by the way. It confirmed for me what we need to do next."

TIME TO GET YOUR SON BACK

"Okay, this has gone on way too long. It's time to start bringing it to an end. Time to get your son back. I'm sorry it's taken so long, but I had to be sure. Did you find the pendant?"

No, Alan found the chain this morning before work.

"Do you have it? The broken chain?"

Yes. I think Alan put it in granny flat. Why?

"DO NOT throw it away."

Ok.

"Put it someplace safe. Keep an eye out for the medals too. Hopefully, you can find them."

Yes I will have another search today. It will be easier in daylight.

"If, and when, you find them, please put them in a SAFE place. If you don't, at least you have the necklace."

Yes.

"Okay, the next step is to call your priest friend and tell him what happened at the church, with the necklace (that's why I said that at least you have the chain—you can show it to him), and what happened when he was taking a bath and you said the prayer and blessed him.

It sounds like what is going on is, at the very least, something referred to as 'diabolical oppression.' In other words, Vincent is being attacked by a demon from the outside.

I also think that Vincent is being told not to talk about it, and he's scared to. That's the reason for the drawings. There was another clue in the drawing

Vincent made of the church you two went to. Did you notice that the demon was outside of the church?"

Not until you just mentioned it.

"That's huge, and that is what I believe will stop all of this from happening anymore. It was probably calling Vincent to come outside. When you and Vincent were inside the church, it was helpless, and couldn't control Vincent.

Tell me, based on all of that, what are you going to do?"

Go to the church and talk to the priest. What will happen?

"What do you mean?"

...to Vincent... what will the priest do?

"There is a ritual in the Church referred to as "The Rite of Deliverance." If he's familiar with it, that's most likely what will happen. It involves prayers, and blessings that will force the entity to stop harassing your son."

Ok.

"Of course, you do have another option."

What?

"Do nothing at all and hope it'll stop."

No, I will talk to the priest. I just want it all to stop.

A few minutes later she messaged me... *All sorted to see priest.*

"When?"

Tomorrow.

NO GREEN PEA SOUP PLEASE

Jane had contacted the priest who came out to bless their home before, so he had an idea as to what was going on, but not what had happened recently. "When you talk to him," I told her, "I want you to use these *exact words,* "Vincent may be diabolically oppressed by whatever is now in our home."

Of course, saying that could easily have backfired but since he was out to their home before, I was hoping that he'd take her seriously. Apparently it worked.

I messaged Jane the next morning at 5 a.m. my time, which would have been 9 p.m. their time, to check in. "How is everything?"

All ok.

"Are YOU feeling better?"

I'm fine, but it's not about me.

That made me smile because I sometimes wondered if she forgot that. When you're up to your ass in alligators it's easy to forget you're there to drain the swamp. "Vincent is okay?"

He's fine... happy... playing with Edward.

"Good... but *do not* let yourself be fooled into thinking, 'Oh, we don't need the priest anymore.' Speaking of whom, what time does he get there?"

2 p.m.

"I'd like to talk to you BEFORE the priest gets there so we can go over what he needs to hear to best help Vincent."

Alan is staying home too.

"Good. I was hoping he would."

Me too. He's afraid, and doesn't understand what's going on.

I wasn't sure I understood what was going on either. I could only hope that what I was about to suggest would make the priest take Jane seriously.

"Well, make sure you start off by telling the priest Vincent's reaction to being in the church, the necklace, which, granted could be an autism thing, but he's apparently hidden the medals, and submerging himself under water AFTER the prayer.

Then, if he doesn't know already, explain to him what is going on with the doll, the pictures Vincent's drawn, and show him the videos."

Ok… thank you.

"EVERYTHING I've been asking you to do… ALL of it… was for a reason. Just in case it came down to having to do this. Bringing in the Catholic Church."

Okay.

"Vincent needs you to be strong. I was JUST thinking of you and Vincent and how, thank God, this will be over SOON. If the priest needs to talk to me, you know how to reach me! One more thing, do me a favor, and let me know when he leaves what happened while he was there."

Of course Hun.

"By the way, Vincent's head won't be doing 360° turns, and he won't be vomiting green pea soup."

I bloody hope not. LOL

ABADDON SAYS, "KISS MY ASS!"

As the time grew closer for the priest to arrive at Vincent's, I decided to do a video blog talking, just briefly, about what was going to happen. I did four takes before I decided to remove the Saint Michael statue from the front of the bag, and put it off to the side. My plan was to introduce the statue back into the video, talking about why I bought it in the first place. I placed it on my bed, a good 14 or more inches away from the edge of the mattress so that, in case it fell over, it wouldn't become damaged.

I was filming the vlog with my camera phone when I heard a noise. I looked over and saw that the statue wasn't where I left it, but wedged in the tight space between the mattress and nightstand, upside down! I tried not to show it on film, but I was panicking inside.

I wondered how the statue could have possibly fallen over and ended up upside down. I pulled the statue out from where it was and saw that one of the wings was broken off. It didn't just fall over, that much I knew. I put it on the nightstand in front of the bag the doll was in, and took pictures for the record.

That night, I lay in bed trying to sleep, but I couldn't stop thinking... wondering how the statue ended up the way it did. I got out of bed, took the figure off of the nightstand and placed it where I thought I had earlier. I then measured the distance from where the icon was, to the edge of the mattress. "Hmmm...," I thought to myself, "the *only* way I can think of is if it was lifted up, turned over, and *shoved* down into this space with such force that it broke the wing off. It had to be angled in such a way that it would go between the bed and nightstand, and only one of the wings would be broken... not both."

That suggested to me that whoever, or whatever did this, was *intelligent*. I also realized that as easily as it shoved the statue into that space, it could have just as easily hit me in the head with it while I was filming the vlog, but that would have revealed what it didn't want people to know... that it's real. That it's pissed. That it's time of terrorizing Vincent was over.

I took the statue into my bathroom. I wrapped it in a towel, put it in the sink, and closed the door behind me as I left. I was genuinely afraid, and I wasn't taking any chances.

It was in that moment I had to admit to myself what I didn't want to acknowledge even while it was happening. The "black blob" *really* was a demon.

IT'S OVER... AT LEAST FOR VINCENT

"Is the priest gone?"
Just left about 15 minutes ago.
"I'd like to hear what happened. What did he do?"
He did a lot of praying with the other guy but the other guy seemed to be in charge. Lots of candles which Vincent wasn't too keen on. He doesn't like fire too much.
"The other guy? What other guy?" I wondered. I decided to let it go for now. "What's Vincent doing now?"
He's playing with the little boy from next door at the moment.
"Wow! That's great! Yes?"
Yes... amazing, it's been a long time since he's played with his friend next door. Just hope it stays this way, and I hope you get the answers too.

It felt to me as though Jane didn't really want to talk about what happened. It's been my experience, in the past, that once I help someone deal with an issue involving something like this, they typically want to sever ties with me. I can understand why. Seeing me reminds them of something they'd rather forget. But I'm usually a part of the resolution. I wasn't in this case, and wanted to know for sure it was over for this family.

"Jane, before you kick me to the curb, I'd really appreciate hearing what happened yesterday."
Why would I kick you to the curb Hun? What do you want to know?
"I want to know what happened when the priest came over today."
Two of them came to the house. I didn't know the one who came here before was bringing the other one. The second one, he had a long name, but told Vincent to call him

"Dez." I'm still not sure about him, but he seemed to know what he was on about. I think he was above the other guy.

We all sat down and went through everything that has happened right from the start. Vincent was not with us in the room at this point. He and Edward were playing. They asked about what we felt, our feelings, and our beliefs.

They then spoke to Vincent with some of the sketches he had done... just Vincent.

They then came back to Alan and me. I think Dez was a psychologist but not sure. He was on about if we had ever thought about medicating him, and how Vincent's mental health was. This was hard as what do you say, "He has autism."

"That's standard procedure, Jane. They were trying to determine the source of what was going on. It's also not unusual to bring a priest in who is a psychologist or even a psychiatrist."

Was ok. The one that came first stuck up for Vincent. Then we had cake... LOL, or they had cake. LOL, they ate nearly two cakes... is this normal?

"LOL... for me it is."

They then spoke between themselves for a little while outside, came back in, and sat with Vincent. They started to talk to Vincent about his beliefs, the Lord Jesus Christ and the Bible. I had to laugh and I really didn't think he would remember so much as he did from his short time at the Christian college... but he sat down with quite an in depth little chat with them. He then proceeded to recite scriptures he had learned in that time.

I had to laugh too, picturing this in my head.

I'm sure that Vincent impressed them! It was cute. They then gave Vincent a little break. In this time, they went to their car and got a lot of candles and the rest of the things they needed.

They then went through with us what they were going to do. First was to bless the whole house again. He gave us a laminated sheet of paper with a prayer on it that we had to repeat with him. One stayed in front leading the prayer. The other had Vincent's hand and led him. We went to every room. It took a long time.

Edward was getting unsettled at this point. Yeah hard to keep a four-year-old quiet. "Mummy why are you saying that?" Edward even told the priest off for spilling his water!

That made me belly laugh, and I told Jane I did.

Yes, I could have died. Anyway, house was blessed from top to bottom. They then let Vincent have a rest. Alan took Edward into our room to have a sleep. They sat down with

Alan and me and set the rules of what was going to happen next. So they got us all together. Edward was asleep at this point so he wasn't a part of it.

The priests did a lot of praying in Latin, I'm guessing. The candles were lit all around the room. Both held the cross and holy water. We were all told to recite a prayer together.

Then Alan and I were asked to step back... not out of the room... but just back. Vincent was still standing with them. There was more praying, and a lot of, "In the name of the Lord Jesus Christ." I take it this was them communicating with the black blob. I did miss a bit of it here as Edward was calling out so I had to go settle him.

When I came back they were still doing a lot of, "In the name of the Lord Jesus Christ we ask you...." Vincent did reply a couple of times or more but didn't say much. I know there were a few other things in there that they said but I can't clearly remember exactly what.

"That's fine." I was stunned she remembered as much as she did, actually.

I know towards the end it was something along the lines of "In the name of the Lord Jesus Christ do you still hold any of Vincent that would keep you from leaving him upon command?"

"Then what happened?"

More talking in Latin or whatever it is.

"I'm sure it was Latin they were praying in."

Vincent was blessed, I take it, although it seemed to be a longer process than the first time. Then Vincent had to recite a prayer with them.

Alan and I were also blessed again, and Edward was too, before they left.

"What did they say before they left? 'May we have more cake?'" LOL

LOL... yes. And a cup of tea. They also went back into Vincent's room before they left but I didn't see what it was they did or said.

"Jane, it's over. It's finally *over*."

Thank you so much for everything. Vincent is outside singing.

—⚏—

At little while later I received another message.

Look at what came back!

On Vincent's window sill was a bird... a Kookaburra.

Harold the Haunted Doll

EPILOGUE

Because Jane did *everything* I asked, albeit, reluctantly at times, we were able to show that Vincent was being what is referred to in the Church as "diabolically oppressed." For my own peace of mind, I *needed* to know that they did a Rite of Deliverance, in order to stop the harassment.

Now that it was finally *over* and Vincent was out of the picture, I thought to myself, it's just him (Abaddon) and me, and that's exactly what I wanted. I don't scare as easily as a seven-year-old child and his mother, although I knew for it to be truly over, I'd probably have to bring the Church in again…, and here in the United States, that might not be so easy.

"My next step," I thought to myself, "is to figure out the names of the three people trapped in the doll and release them." I also want to find out what happened, and why. Once that is done, I'll see what I can do about getting a priest to help me.

I asked Jane to ask Vincent to draw a picture of his room for me.

One thing the priest did say was to let Vincent have no contact with any of it so I have put it all in parcel to you. Vincent has done your picture will upload for you tomorrow.

When I received the picture, my first thought was that it wasn't exactly what I was hoping for. The "black thing" wasn't in his room anymore, but seemed to be watching him from outside his window. "Hmmm…," I wrote, "he painted that 'eye' once before."

I asked him about that… out the window?

"Yes. What did he say?"

He said, "That's the sun Mummy."

The next day I received another message from Jane— *He had a really good day, went to school with no drama. When I picked him up the teacher said he was like a different child. She said he was more engaged with the other kids and even spoke a full sentence in class. He won an award for making right choices and being a good role model.*

I have my boy back; I don't want to lose him again EVER to anything like that.

I received another message from Jane, only a few hours later.

I was talking to Vincent after his bath about school and out of the blue he said, "Mummy, you know as the old super hero dudes got rid of the black mean thing, it came to me, and it told me it wants Uncle Ant." I reassured him you are ok, but he was certain you were not! What that means I have no idea.

It meant what I already knew. It was over for Vincent, but not for me. Still, I had no idea what to say to her, so I didn't say anything.

What I did was pull out my rosary beads and I began to pray.

AFTERWORD

What *started* out as a "hoax listing" on eBay turned out to be a real life nightmare, not just for me, but for a family in Australia, and many other people as well. And the story is continuing to this day.

As I write this, Chris Baricko and his team is investigating the doll in Connecticut. He told me that he's experiencing good luck happening in his life since he's had the doll.

When he told me that, I remembered what Vincent said, *"Oh mummy that is cheeky and really not nice... he can be really nice to you but he's really nasty...."* Chris thought it was because the energy of the doll was "misunderstood," and if you respected it, it respected you.

To me, it confirmed what I already knew. The entity in the doll, the one who calls himself "Harold," is a trickster, a liar... manipulating people for its own purposes. I told Chris that the entity was treating him like a mushroom – keeping him in the dark, and feeding him full of shit.

I'm not currently planning any more investigations being done on the doll.

Having spent all of this time with the doll has changed my life in innumerable ways. Sometimes I can't help but wonder if it's even marked my very soul. I am aware of the reality of evil and how it can touch our lives in a way I was blissfully unaware of before and most people are now. That's one of the reasons I chose to write this book.

I was asked by my friend, Barb, "If you had to do it all over again, would you?"

I gave it a great deal of thought before I answered her. "I don't think I chose to be a part of this."

Looking back on all of this now, I think that the woman named "Lottie" (whom I've since been able to verify her identity, and even have pictures of her) chose me. I've also been able to identify three of the four souls trapped inside the doll by the demon. But telling that story would fill up another book altogether. One, I'm not ready to write just yet.

QUESTIONS AND ANSWERS

Question: Is the doll for sale?

Answer: No, it's not, and it *never* will be sold, or simply given away. I've received *multiple offers* from people who want to buy it. The offers have ranged from $100 to $50,000, and my answer has always been, "no." Especially now that I know the true nature of what is going on with the doll. How do you put a price tag on evil?

Recently a woman saw a series on television which, I will admit, did look eerily like Harold's story. It was centered on a doll that even resembled Harold. She became absolutely convinced it meant that Harold wanted me to give the doll to her.

I quickly became convinced that she's mentally unstable. No, I did not give the doll to her, nor do I plan to give it away to anyone else either.

Question: What do you plan to do with the doll?

Answer: My investigation into the background of the spirits in the doll is still on-going. I do believe, now, that there are *four* spirits in the doll, and one inhuman entity that "owns" the doll. I also believe that there are two other souls that are guiding me, through Vincent, and helping me to solve the mystery of the doll, how this happened, and eventually what I need to do to release them.

There is also one more spirit, a boy, whom Vincent hasn't been able to help me identify because he can't "see" who it is. I believe that spirit to be the one Erica and Fiona spoke about.

So my plan is to release them… period. Will I ever know how they've been trapped and why Abaddon is involved? I don't know. At this point, I'm too tired to even care.

Question: Is it true that the doll won't burn, and that if you look into its eyes, you'll die?

Answer: I don't know if the doll won't burn, I've never tried, and don't plan to. There are better ways of disposing an object such as this. Burning it may actually be the worst thing I can do. I believe that "Harold" is shackled to the doll, and burning it might release that spirit, and I don't know what the repercussions of releasing him would be.

Vincent has said that "Harold" and "Abaddon" are *not* to be released from the doll, however.

Question: How can you stand to be with a haunted doll?

Answer: Since this doll isn't just haunted, but cursed, and possessed, it's a pain the ass. I wouldn't wish it on my worst enemy. If it was simply "haunted" I might have gotten rid of it, or left it in my storage unit where I have a lot of other objects. But there are three spirits needing to be released. And that is no easy task because they aren't "attached," but "stuck" in the doll, held there by what is apparently a demon.

To answer your question as to how I can stand to be with this doll, in all honesty, if it weren't for protection and help from God… I would have crumbled a long time ago.

Question: How do you do this? I mean take care of that doll? As a person who believes in the paranormal, I wouldn't be near the doll. Anthony, aren't you scared that the doll will harm you? I hope that doll doesn't hurt you… you sound like really nice person. Maybe you could try to find out who haunts the doll, and then maybe you could help them move on.

Answer: I've been attacked and harmed by the entity in the doll more than once, as recently as early this week. I wouldn't wish my life on my worst enemy, to be honest, and I've lost several friends due to the doll's influence on them. I believe that there are three spirits *imprisoned* within the doll, and I've resolved to release them… that's how I do it.

Question: Isn't that God's job? To release the spirits in the doll?

Answer: I believe that what happened was becoming of something a human did – trapping the souls inside the doll. For that reason, it seems it's God's will that a human undo what happened.

I also believe that if God could have found a bigger, more tenacious bone headed fool to do it, other than me, that person would have the doll. I'm not a "hero." Just the biggest idiot God could find on the face of the earth.

MADCAP
Serenade

DAN KOPCOW

Black Rose Writing | Texas

©2024 by Dan Kopcow
All rights reserved. No part of this book may be reproduced, stored in a retrieval system or transmitted in any form or by any means without the prior written permission of the publishers, except by a reviewer who may quote brief passages in a review to be printed in a newspaper, magazine or journal.

The author grants the final approval for this literary material.

First printing

This is a work of fiction. Names, characters, businesses, places, events, and incidents are either the products of the author's imagination or used in a fictitious manner. Any resemblance to actual persons, living or dead, or actual events is purely coincidental.

ISBN: 978-1-68513-443-3
LIBRARY OF CONGRESS CONTROL NUMBER: 2024932094
PUBLISHED BY BLACK ROSE WRITING
www.blackrosewriting.com

Printed in the United States of America
Suggested Retail Price (SRP) $22.95

Madcap Serenade is printed in Garamond Premier Pro

*As a planet-friendly publisher, Black Rose Writing does its best to eliminate unnecessary waste to reduce paper usage and energy costs, while never compromising the reading experience. As a result, the final word count vs. page count may not meet common expectations.

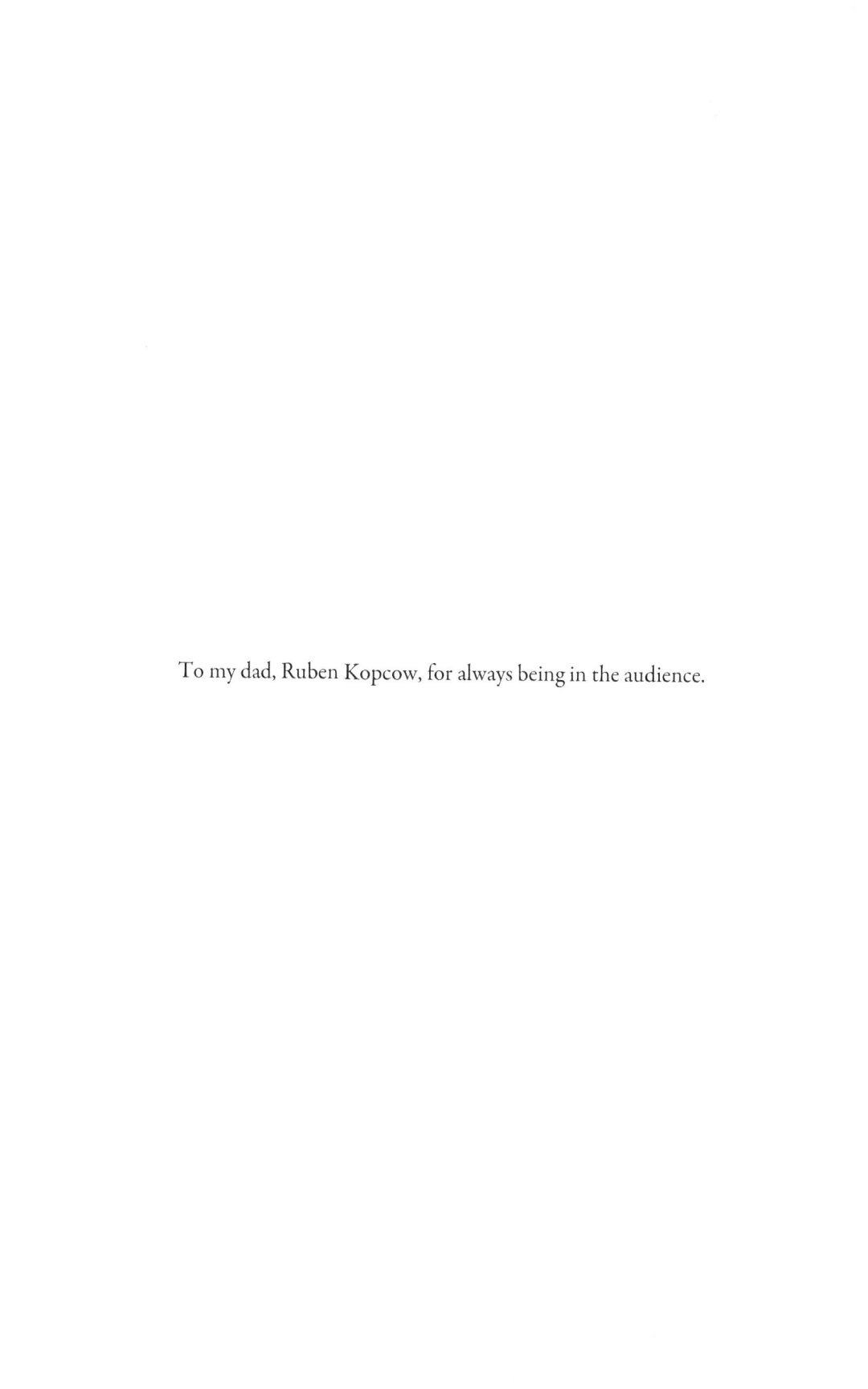

To my dad, Ruben Kopcow, for always being in the audience.

Praise for
Madcap Serenade

"Sex, drugs, Mozart, murder, mystery, and teens in love - what more could you want in a rom-com? Kopcow delivers a hilarious page-turner."
–Brian Fitzpatrick, author of the *Mechcraft* trilogy

"If you're looking for a riotously goofy tale filled with intrigue, drugs, murder, and young love, *Madcap Serenade* is right on pitch. Irreverent, mischievous, recommended. Kopcow's passion for music, food, and silliness serve him well in this love story."
–Fredrick Soukup, author of *Bliss*

"Dan Kopcow's *Madcap Serenade* is a perfect romantic comedy about a boys' choir, set in 1979. Eli, Jane, and a cheerfully libidinous crew of teenagers and their chaperones tour Italy, their plans complicated by the search for a mysterious drug and a slight case of murder. The sun never sets on this gorgeous book of love and seduction in all its forms. I was charmed and moved to tears, both by the story and Kopcow's masterful telling."
–Jon Frankel, author of *Isle of Dogs*

"*Madcap Serenade* has well developed characters, a very unique story line, and a great ending. Kopcow is a master of plotting and character flaws, intermingled with wit."
–Tabatha Waybright, award-winning author of *On Mystic Mountain*

"A glorious rom-com caper delivered with genuine wit and panache. It's one laugh out loud moment after another with mayhem and intrigue that will keep you laughing and guessing until the very end. With two mysteries, two murders, and one romance set against a backdrop of a seemingly innocent choral tour of Italy, this madcap musical adventure is a *Roman Holiday* for our times. You won't read a funnier book all year."

–F.M.A. Dixon, author of *The Little House on Everywhere Street*

"Dan Kopcow's *Madcap Serenade* offers up a plot twisty as an Italian countryside road—and as much fun. Along the way are adventures, mysteries, revelations, and romance. Music plays a large part, literally and thematically, while alternating narratives give us two unique protagonists with distinct voices but similar needs. Dan Kopcow is a superbly inventive writer, his prose crisp and funny yet poignant where it matters. Under the novel's zaniness, there's real heart. *Madcap Serenade* is a delightful performance sure to be applauded by YA readers and adults alike."
–Joanna Higgins, author of *Waiting for the Queen* and other works

"Dan Kopcow's storytelling is detailed and full of humor that is at times droll and other times irreverent. His descriptive style, attention to detail, and playful brand of humor kept me engaged across two continents and plot lines that intersect in a fun and satisfying way."
–Stacey Murphy, author of *Old Stones Understand*

"*Madcap Serenade* is a wild romp, with shocking twists, delicious laughs, and the promise of love just around the corner."
–Jenn Bouchard, author of *First Course*

"Eli and Jane are ordinary teenagers from Long Island who find themselves in Italy in August 1979. In this fun, twisty mystery, they are tracked by a government agent, get caught up in a narcotics scheme, uncover a murder mystery, learn secrets about their families, and meet Pope John Paul II until they meet each other. *Madcap Serenade* is filled with relatable, enjoyable characters and rich depictions of the Italian countryside, A great combination of humor, nostalgia, music, and mystery, *Madcap Serenade* is a boisterous and engaging adventure. Bravissimo!"
–Matthew Arnold Stern, author of *The Remainders* and *Amiga*

"We're off on a romp that takes the reader from Long Island, circa 1979, to St. Peter's Basilica in Rome. *Madcap Serenade* is, indeed, madcap, following Eli and Jane as they separately rush, stumble, and chase each other toward a climactic rendezvous outside the Vatican. Witty and fun, *Madcap Serenade* recalls the thrill and angst of first love amidst a decades old secret that is, at last, revealed."

–Steven Mayfield, award-winning author of *Treasure of the Blue Whale* and *Delphic Oracle U.S.A.*

"With his new book *MADCAP SERENADE*, Dan Kopcow weaves a twisty, adventurous story, full of mystery, murder, and music, all wrapped up in an endlessly funny rom-com. Despite the consistent laughs, Kopcow never sacrifices heart; he pulls you in with humor, but you stay for his detailed descriptions, colorful characters and the winding, wildly zany plot. Capturing the spirit of first love in all its excitement and torment, *MADCAP SERENADE* is both nostalgic and hopeful, a relatable but joyously over-the-top romance – with several thrilling, layered mysteries to boot – for fans of both genres."

–*IndieReader Discovery*

MADCAP Serenade

PRELUDE

***Prelude**—A short piece usually proceeded by a more substantial work; however, not lengthy enough to be considered an overture.*

With a subtle flick of his wrist, the choir director lifted his baton, indicating it was time for my solo. The wrist move was imperceptible to the untrained eye, but as a seasoned tenor, the baton's upward movement meant the start of everything. My mouth opened. My body was in perfect harmony, ready to breathe from the diaphragm and sing from the back of the head. It was late August 1979 and eighty-thousand people momentarily checked out of their lives, put aside their troubles, and focused on the sixteen-year-old American boy in his white dinner jacket and plaid bowtie singing in front of sixteen other American choir boys in their white dinner jackets and plaid bow ties. Half the world's Cardinals, sitting in St. Peter's Basilica, inched closer in their plush velvet chairs to hear better. This was a respite from their Sunday morning routine as well. Even the Pope, smiling and sitting attentively on his white throne just twenty feet from me, leaned in a little.

While that moment demanded utter concentration and focus, I became distracted and nervously scanned the vast crowd. Through a combination of hard work and an absurd amount of scamming, I had arrived at this point in my life, and I thought it was all I ever wanted. But at this actual moment, I was looking for a particular girl. This Italian singing tour had been filled with murder, death by natural causes, disturbing revelations about my late dad, drug traffickers, and government officials giving chase, general calamity, and wonder. But this girl, who I barely knew, had been the highlight. And I needed to find her. I knew she would be out there somewhere among the tens of thousands of tourists and locals clamoring for a sight of the Pope during this Sunday morning mass at St. Peters.

I just knew she and I belonged together. And then my life could truly begin. I hadn't really thought much beyond finding her. That had been trouble enough.

My choir director glared at me, knowing my mind wasn't one hundred percent on making him and the choir look and sound their best. I finished my solo, a contemplative seventeenth-century ballad in praise of God, and couldn't wait to step down off that stage and go in earnest search for my American girl. There was deafening applause, which I should have soaked in. But the last few weeks had given me some perspective that, up until I boarded the plane to Italy, I didn't even know I lacked.

After the concert, our choir was rushed off stage and escorted to a room for some refreshments. There was some press gathered, but the choir director fielded most of the questions. My cheek was pinched by our traveling band of nuns more times than I cared for. I still hadn't gotten used to the idea of Roman nun groupies.

When the coast was clear, some of the choir boys and I snuck out. We ran until the mid-day sun welcomed us into St. Peter's Square, where tens of thousands of people were still gathered to watch the Pope drive by in his Popemobile. Several corridors were blocked off with low, metal barricades to allow the Popemobile the ability to scoot among the crowd. Since we were still in our white dinner jackets, people allowed us through until we made it to the barricades. I supposed jacketed people had authority over non-jacketed types. I tried to spot the girl, but it was impossible despite being tall for my age. Soon, we were met by a few other members of our choir who either snuck out or were dismissed. I remained standing near the barricade with my fellow choir members for a half-hour, our number growing as more boys found us and were allowed passage through the crowds. Maybe everyone thought we would start an impromptu concert.

Through the din of the assemblage, I heard my name. I turned around and spotted her on the other side of the corridor, behind an exact set of barricades. She was maybe thirty feet away. She waved and I just about melted, and not from the midday sun. I was yelling, hoping she could hear me. I wanted to tell her I loved her. I screamed toward her and asked where she was staying so I could actually see her again. From the expression on her face, I could tell she didn't understand a word I was saying. We were so close, but separated by this chasm.

As I was waving frantically at her, something descended in front of me and blocked my view. A large hand grasped mine. I looked up to discover the Pope shaking my hand as he leaned out of his passing Popemobile. He smiled at me, suddenly realizing I had just sung to him less than an hour ago. There was a rush from the crowd, and I found myself pressed up against the barricade. The Pope's security detail saw the American choir was in danger of getting trampled and opened the barricades to let us through. I thought this was my big chance to run across the corridor and finally see her. However, I was prevented from doing so by the Pope, who still clung to my hand. He was effectively dragging me alongside his vehicle, advancing at a stately two miles per hour, all the while waving to the throng with his other hand. My choir ran behind me, chasing the Pope and me like the bulls at Pamplona. When I glanced back, Jane was gone.

PART ONE
LONG ISLAND, NEW YORK
JUNE 1979

CHAPTER ONE

Capriccio*—A quick, improvisational, spirited piece of music.*

The balding guy from Station Five was singing off-key this morning. His grizzled voice, a veteran of years of smoking and yellow coughing, strained to stay in tune and rhythm with the rest of the waiters. The Maître d', a distinguished elderly gentleman who was at least forty years old, sang louder to make up for Station Five's dissonance. Their voices were drowned out by the roiling pop of simmering tomato sauce and pancetta, which vaguely sounded like applause.

There were six waiters in all and one busboy. The busboy, rather than collecting dirty dishes, was busy conducting this ragtag bunch of food service industry-cum-impromptu choir. The waiters were not pleased at all. I'm embarrassed to admit the busboy was me. The waiters wanted to get back to their jobs, in which they had carved out a modicum of dignity before I arrived. They didn't want to rehearse being singing waiters, and they really didn't want to be taking orders from the owner's nephew. Mostly though, they didn't want to waste a perfectly good smoking break indulging a sixteen-year-old.

The waiters turned their backs to me and whispered to each other. I imagined I overheard the usual conversation.

"*That boy needs a father. Did you hear what happened to him?*"
"*That kid has no talent.*"
"*That boy needs a girlfriend.*"
"*The last thing we need is that boy.*"

I had heard it all before. Nothing destroys the promise of esprit de youth in a teenage boy quicker than the prospect of mandatory summer employment. It was the time in my life when I should have been outdoors, enjoying my young vivacity and expanding my mind. Instead, I withered in the grease-filled air of my uncle's restaurant's kitchen. To make it bearable, my uncle allowed me to organize the wait staff into a singing waiters choir to entertain the customers. Mostly, I believe my uncle allowed this nonsense since his restaurant was dying and he was willing to try anything at this point to stay in business. He had a head for food, but certainly not for numbers. I had been working at his restaurant as a busboy for two weeks and the singing waiters were yet to make their world premiere. I was waiting for this group to ripen before serving them.

The waiters turned back to face me. Two of the waiters peeked at their watches, hoping their mandatory rehearsal would end soon so they could duck out into the alley for a quick smoke. The others went through the motions, but were mostly focused on the black-and-white television behind me. The TV in the restaurant kitchen was perpetually on and the screen was always covered with a thick layer of steam and sauce splatters. The sound was always muted since it would have interfered with the clanging of the pots, yelling, and cursing from the cooks. Luckily, the cooks weren't due into the kitchen for another hour. I turned around to see what TV show was so captivating my tenor section. The news was reporting a brief story from Rome on the thirty-day Pope who had died almost a year ago in August 1978. The news story then went on to report the accomplishments of the current Pope, John Paul II.

I envied the Pope. At least he didn't have to spend the summer between his junior and senior year in high school stuck in the sweaty kitchen of a failing restaurant juggling filthy dishes and not having a girlfriend. I felt enslaved by the fiendish designs of my mother's brother, Uncle Jacob.

Things were not getting any easier. The singing waters disbanded before I could dismiss them. Now I knew what George Martin felt like when the Beatles broke up. I was essentially powerless at this point. I folded napkins in a quiet corner of the kitchen, hating my life.

During the lunch hour, my corner of the kitchen was filled with sous chefs and food preparers who managed to bump me into the sink filled with hot water whenever they walked by. I was the only one who was underage, didn't smoke, and had citizenship.

True, if I had any hope of filling my coffers with college savings or my pockets with spending money, I needed to work this summer. I had no intention of wasting my senior year on anything but fun. Plus, my mom had been on my case about me getting a job since the summer had begun.

But never in a million years did I think I would be a busboy at Tijuana Meatball. If nothing else, I knew I was meant for greater things. My uncle was a Romanian Jew. What did he know from Mexican-Italian cuisine? What exact niche did he hope to capture in the Long Island suburbs? One didn't need to access my uncle's therapy chart to note he was stark raving mad.

I was usually pretty good at scheming how to get out of these things, but for the last two weeks, I had labored in this hell hole, resigned to the fact that this would be my summer life. If nothing else, I was motivated daily to never return after this summer. My worst fear was to end up like my uncle and have to work in this restaurant. I was meant for so much more. I just hadn't figured out what yet.

Despite slogging trays piled with dirty plates of uneaten tamales parmigiana, I knew today would become brighter. I had received a note on my bike yesterday which I hoped would overturn this unpleasant screw. The note, taped to my handlebars, was from my friend Charley who said he would meet me here during my afternoon break today.

Through the small window that looked into the front of the house, I saw Charley enter the restaurant and take a seat. I slipped off my apron and found my uncle in his small office, going over invoices. His balding head sweated like a recently boiled egg and the sweat occasionally dripped onto his ledgers.

"What, Eli?" asked my uncle in his exasperated tone. I suspected he thought I would have been more compliant at this point.

"I need a break," I said.

"From what are you taking a break?"

"I'm worried about unnatural exposure to hot sauce," I said. I had just seen a documentary about OSHA on PBS.

"Oy vey," said my uncle, returning his attention and sweat to his books.

I tried to clean myself off as best I could and entered the half-empty restaurant. Charley was seated in the middle of the room at a two-topper, immaculately dressed. His pale face, blond hair, slight build, and clear skin spoke of a sixteen-year-old who had not experienced manual outdoor labor but rather a facial and massage in his home. Charley didn't need to work this summer nor any summer. Charley had had the good foresight to be born into an obscenely wealthy family. And he was my best friend.

"Eli, you don't want to work as a busboy all summer and end up like that stoner friend of yours, Eddie, do you?" asked Charley, getting straight to the point, as I sat across from him.

"My mother says as long as I'm broke, I should keep my nose to the grindstone," I said, trying to sound courageous. "She and my uncle are keeping me prisoner in this culinary labor camp. It sucks."

"I think it would be fun to work," said Charley.

"Spoken like a rich kid."

"Come on, Eli, let me lend you some money so you can get out of here and we can get into some adventure and trouble."

One of the waiters arrived to take Charley's order. This particular waiter hated being conscripted into the busboy's choir. Rather than serving me his revenge on a cold dish, he completely ignored me.

Charley made a compelling case about offering to spring me from the Big House. And it hadn't been the first time Charley had offered to throw a pittance of his vast wealth in my direction to provide him with a friend to play with. Sometimes I accepted. But this felt different. My mom had been working so hard and I felt some allegiance to try and earn my keep as best I could. I was hoping this feeling would pass.

"Thanks, Charley, but I can't accept. Tijuana Meatball needs me. If my plan succeeds, we'll be the only Mexican-Italian joint with singing waiters within a three-block radius."

"Well," said Charley, sipping some water. "I'm sure you'll get a wonderful review from the Acapulco-Milan Gazette."

I knew Charley was lonely despite his casual, insouciant nature. His parents were always traveling in a foreign country and leaving him to fend for himself. Well, fend as best one could with house staff. His parents had gone to Tahiti for a few months. Or maybe it was Taiwan. Or Tibet. Definitely something with a T. It was hard to keep up. I know if my family was off traveling the world, I would remember where they were. I desperately needed to see the world but the furthest I had traveled was a forty-five-minute train ride into Times Square.

Without sounding crass or vulgar, let me provide additional illumination to make one fully appreciate the scope of Charley's family's fiduciary capabilities. Someone once noted that there was an easy method to distinguish the economic classes in the American workplace: the poor wear their names on their shirts, the middle class have their names on their desks, and the rich have theirs on buildings. Charley's family's moniker graced seventeen buildings nationwide.

"Is that why you came here today?" I asked.

The ambient music in the restaurant switched abruptly from "O Solo Mio" to "La Cucaracha." I made a mental note to speak to my uncle later regarding his musical choices.

Lunch arrived but Charley continued to look at me curiously. His lasagna tacos looked no less appetizing in the soft dining room light than they did in the harsh florescent glare of the kitchen.

"I have a favor to ask," said Charley, smiling. I had known him since kindergarten. His parents, wanting him to experience some notion of normality, had decided to send him to public school. Even during those heady days, he was a consummate salesman. Once, when he was ten, he convinced our chorus teacher to give him an extra chocolate milk during a break because he claimed to be suffering from a rare form of cocoa osteoporosis.

"You want to join my choir?" I asked, indicating the wait staff.

"Way better," said Charley. "I want you to join mine."

If I had been sipping milk, it would have shot forth out of my nostrils. The Long Island Boys Choir was a professional choir I had longed to be a part of for years. It was expensive to join and there was a lengthy waiting list to get in. Charley had started off as a soprano when he was eight and was currently a tenor. I drooled over his stories about the choir, their New York City concerts, and European summer tours. They had even recorded an album. I had asked Charley for plenty of favors in my time. But I never had the nerve to ask him to get me into the Long Island Boys Choir. I was too intimidated to have that dream come true.

"You better not be kidding," I said.

"Calm down, I just need a small favor. It's a temporary thing. I need you to step in for me for one week this Christmas season. It's three or four concerts at most."

Christmas was one of the two busiest concert seasons for the choir. They had recently come off their other busy season—spring. The choir's big holiday finale was thirty angelic voices, ranging from eight to eighteen, singing "Silent Night" in front of a giant Christmas tree that was lit by real candles. That was also the album cover. No Jew had ever wanted anything so bad in his whole life.

"Wait," I said. "You've never missed a concert before. Rasper would never allow it." Douglas Rasper was the choir founder and choral director. I knew the members of the choir the way my classmates knew the lineup of the 1978 Mets.

"Rasper and I have an understanding," said Charley.

"And December?" I said. "It's only June."

"You'd have to rehearse during the summer. They are professional, you know. I'll pay you for your time," he said, counting off the benefits on his fingers. "You'd be busy with a great cultural effort, and you'd be helping out a pal. What's better than that?"

Charley wasn't used to people telling him no. But this sounded like a scheme. Not that I opposed that. I just liked knowing what angle he was working.

I was a tenor. I knew that. The Long Island Boys Choir had a long waiting list for tenors since all the soprano and alto voices kept changing. Puberty was really my enemy. It kept turning these sopranos and altos into boys taking my spot. It would be impossible to join the choir at this point without Charley's help. It seemed too good to be true. Even if it was for just one week of performances in December, I was enticed. But then I thought about my mom and my uncle. On the other hand, Charley did say he would pay me to rehearse this summer, and I guessed it paid a lot better than being a busboy.

"What's this one week off? Where are you going?" I asked. Charley's parents practically tobogganed on their piles of money in the winter, but left Charley with a strict allowance. They wanted him to understand the meaning of sacrifice, to build humility and character in their son. Of course, their definition of sacrifice meant a yacht that only slept four.

Charley didn't solely rely on their contributions. The procurement and/or sale of certain drugs were suspected. I made no judgments. After all, he was able to get by this summer without having to juggle baked burrito ziti.

"I can't say," said Charley. Being deprived of his schemes became intriguing. Then I realized what Charley was doing. He was laying out a chum line for me to follow. A bit thick, I thought.

"Then *yo trabajo en* Tijuana Meatball," I said. "*Molto bene.*"

"Alright, alright. I have plans for a romantic getaway. Everything's arranged."

"Charley, you're only sixteen. Don't you have to be, like, twenty-three to have romantic getaways?"

"My girlfriend wants to be in London for the holidays," he said.

"Who's this girlfriend?" I asked. "You've never mentioned her." But I knew better than to press the point.

"Rasper will never let me out of rehearsals," said Charley, picking at his food. "Missing a concert during the peak Christmas season will kill him unless I can supply a replacement." He put down his fork, finally surrendering to the food's inedibility.

"How are you going to get me into the choir to replace you?"

"I got you an audition with Rasper in a week. You just leap-frogged over thirty or forty other applicants. I explained to Rasper that you are a self-taught singer, and he trusts my judgment. He knows I'm serious about this."

"Yeah, but Charley…"

"Rasper almost always accepts boys he auditions."

"I know you say that but..."

"But what? You've been wanting this ever since the third grade," said Charley.

"What if I'm not good enough?" I said.

The waiter approached our table and took Charley's plate, sneering at me the whole time. Having the waiter overhear my admission of insecurity was the lowest part of my summer so far.

"Of course you're good enough or I wouldn't recommend you. I just need this favor. What do you say?"

Charley believed in the sort of redemption that only membership in a non-denominational boys' choir could provide. Something about Charley's value system, his possible illicit drug trade, his made-up romantic tryst, his conviction to absolve himself of his sins by being in this choir, and his attempt to reconcile my summer, all moved me.

"I don't know," I said. "Who's this girlfriend?"

Charley smiled mischievously, dabbing his mouth with his napkin.

"What is it?" I asked.

"There's one more thing. But I don't know if you'd be interested." He was laying it on with a trowel now.

"What?" I asked.

"The choir? We're going on tour this summer. To Italy. Milan, Florence, Venice, Rome. Three weeks in August. The whole thing."

I stared at the bad oil paintings of gondoliers and mariachi bands on the restaurant walls. Italy was my dream country. The one place I had to visit. For my father. I knew I would eventually visit there when I was an adult and could afford it.

"Join the choir for rehearsals now," said Charley. "And there's a chance Rasper will let you join us for Italy."

"Italy," I said, allowing the word to be spoken. Somehow, that made it real.

"Otherwise, it'll be too late," said Charley.

The waiter brought the check and Charley slid it over to me. "Tell you what," said Charley. "You pick up lunch and I get you an audition into the choir where an Italian trip possibly awaits."

"Now you sound like a game show host."

"Think of the Italian girls that will swoon at our singing," said Charley.

I had to admit he painted a pretty picture. The prospect held great promise. I would figure out how to pay for the choir tuition and Italy trip later. I never wanted anything more than to join the choir and get out of this summer job. Well, other than to have a girlfriend, but I hadn't managed to conquer that particular feat yet. Girls at my school just didn't seem interested in me. They usually went for the jocks or the loud, obnoxious kids. Right now, I had a much better chance at joining the choir.

Then reality hit me. I had as much chance of joining the choir and going to Italy as I did getting a prom date. Did Charley think I could be swayed so easily by such a blunt assault on my teenage hormones?

"I'll do it."

CHAPTER TWO

***Key signature**—The flats and sharps at the beginning of each staff line indicating the key of music in which the piece is to be played.*

"Don't be such a wanker, April," I said. "Take a drag."

"Jane," responded April. "You're not British."

If peer pressure was an event, I was training for the Summer 1979 Olympic Gold. Smoking pot was a well-practiced hobby of mine. In fact, there was a fine line between hobby and habit. But, as most girls my age will tell you, moderating your hightitude is the key when there are cute boys around.

We were at the Wall. It was where we spent every summer night. The group was made up of twelve regulars, mostly girls, along with varying hangers-on, cousins, and friends who were staying with family for a week or two.

One of the new boys to the Wall was Eddie. He was seventeen and killer cute. No "Saturday Night Fever" disco haircut for the manly Eddie. A shock of slicked-back, black hair graced his heavenly head. He smoked and strutted with the assurance and confidence that only comes with complete acceptance of one's place in life. And I wanted his place to be with me.

I knew he liked me as soon as we met. I leaned against the Wall next to him partially to be near him and partially to support myself in my half-drunk, half-high, and full-on-love splendor. Eddie sat on the Wall with his muscular legs dangling, swinging, and occasionally brushing my bare arms.

April hadn't told me much about him. She didn't have to. I was at the age when a boy's cuteness was sure to land him the job during the interview.

I took stock of these visiting tourists. I couldn't imagine coming here for a family vacation. How bad was home to voluntarily come here? Plainview was in the middle of Long Island; a one-hour train ride into the city. At least we weren't saddled with the name Hicksville, the town next to ours. Overall, my town was working class, dreadfully dull, and devoid of adventure. Admittedly, I was biased. I lived with an adopted family who didn't care much for me and my ways.

Later, I found out April had told Eddie a bit about me. She told him I was sixteen, had been smoking for eight years, had enjoyed smoking for seven of those years, was still a virgin, grew up in this small town, had a tight circle of friends, came from a small family, and was adopted. April also told him that if he hurt me, my friends would kill him.

Truth is that my friends wouldn't hurt a fly, let alone bash the brain of some horny, pot-smoking, Mott-the-Hoople-listening, vacationing molester. But Eddie didn't know that. He just came to the Wall because he heard he could get high and maybe get lucky.

That's why we all came to the Wall. It was a rite of passage in the eight-block radius of my neighborhood. Kids had been coming to the Wall for years to take this adolescent Sacrament. Even calling it the Wall was indicative of our desire to make our lives more exaggerated and decadent than they really were.

The Wall was built by Mr. Dietrich years ago. Mr. Dietrich had lived at 82 Wrightsborough Street all his life. He was a farmer who only grew debt. He came into some money through an inheritance from some distant relative. He sold the farm at a loss and disappeared into his house, a bitter and ailing male spinster at sixty-three. His house was eventually joined by other houses as his fields were bought and subdivided by developers.

Throughout these times, people only saw or heard from old Farmer Dietrich once a year when he'd walk to the bank for some presumably important transaction. Maybe he was gone for months at a time. No one knew or much cared.

Dietrich's house was set back from the street. In front of the house stood a crudely made wall of old stones turned up by Dietrich's till. Dietrich had gathered the stones years ago and built a single wall three feet high and about thirty feet long. It served no purpose other than to forewarn all passersby that here lived a hostile and slightly irrational coot.

Dietrich had been a terrible farmer but when he planted his Wall, he finally grew something that flourished perennially: teenagers.

When it got dark, we knew instinctively to collect at the Wall. It acted as a silent beacon for our restless souls. It was where our night plans were made and where our evenings ended. Drinks were poured, cigarettes smoked, pot inhaled, kisses traded, dreams shared, music played, and lives planned. In short, it was the coolest spot in the world.

When things got dull, we dared each other to sneak up to the dark house behind us and look into the front window. Whoever discovered Dietrich's clearly decaying body, probably on the kitchen floor with a broken bottle of rye in hand, would become a Wall legend for the rest of his or her life. No one had been brave enough or relished that kind of fame, however. We feared we would peak at sixteen and the rest of our lives would be a depressing downhill sprint.

Eddie's leg, still dangling from the Wall, brushed up against my bare shoulder again. I hadn't decided yet whether he would be the First One. It was an important decision. Since last Tuesday, it was all I could think about.

I had woken up at a sleepover at Suzie's house and we had a long talk about boys. Specifically, Suzie told me about how she was going out with Billy Dylan. Listening to Suzie's graphic details about Billy, I decided then and there I wanted to try sex. And be really good at it.

Looking back, it was just to remain popular. I was pretty and intelligent enough to fit into most of the crowds in my school. But it was like sitting down in the school lunchroom day after day, and the whole table was eating macaroni and cheese. And you've never had macaroni and cheese. You've heard about it. Your friends are always talking about how good it is. How comforting and easy it is. Now, I wanted to try it. And I wanted to try the instant kind—devoid of nutrition, probably forgettable, and not as good as homemade.

So, I was at the Wall, smoking a cigarette, debating with myself whether this Wall visitor, this Eddie, would be my first mac-and-cheese. I dragged deeply from my cigarette while the minutes loudly clicked by in my head.

By ten o'clock, quite a crowd had gathered. Some of the older kids were making plans to go into Manhattan to hit some nightspots.

Suddenly, a police car turned down the street. We all ducked behind the Wall. That, after all, was the purpose and prime benefit of the Wall. The neighboring houses were far enough away that we never bothered them with our noise. Some of the neighbors knew our parents and either decided to look the other way, possibly remembering when they were our age hanging out at their own Wall, or simply couldn't make us out through the haze of smoke and long hair that encapsulated us.

Eye-level with the gravel behind the Wall, I heard some giggling as we listened for the police car to drive by. Somebody whimpered as a lit cigarette burned their hand. I craned my head up, my body still pressed flat on the ground, and saw the back of Eddie, high and oblivious, still perched on the Wall.

"Eddie," I whispered. No response. I whispered his name several more times, wondering if that was really his name or if I had heard it wrong.

Okay, I thought, *no mac-and-cheese for Eddie, thank you very much.*

What if we were enjoying some spirited bonking and Eddie was just as clueless as to where he was and what he was doing? I couldn't let my First One be some oblivious-to-the-cops Wall-sitter. No way.

April reached up beside me, grabbed the back of Eddie's shirt, and pulled him backward off the Wall like a ventriloquist putting away his dummy. Eddie fell with a thud and a startled look.

As we bunkered down behind the Wall, a light flickered on and shone down on us. It didn't come from the direction of the street or the cops. It came from behind us. The light came from Dietrich's porch light. To say we were utterly shocked and surprised would be to underplay the moment.

We were trapped between that unexpected light and the Wall. I imagined the police on the other side setting up like a well-organized SWAT team.

I was a teenage deer caught in Dietrich's porch light. I envisioned that the police had been conspiring with Dietrich for years, advising him to keep his porch light off to better monitor us, record our actions, avoid movement in the house, to schedule public appearances only once a year to avoid suspicion and to lull these marauding kids into a false sense of security until this very moment.

The cops had been waiting years for the moment when Operation Bag-the-Wall-Stoners would commence and we would all be caught in a carefully constructed sting. We would be put behind bars, our parents and guardians humiliated, parole denied, our young futures ruined. Forget mac-and-cheese. No high school graduation or college for me. No marrying Shawn Cassidy and having three kids. No living in London like they showed in that documentary I saw on PBS last week. No, instead, I'd be one of those short-haired prison ladies who dressed only in gray, wore no makeup, and shuffled along with an empty tray to the cafeteria for the rest of my life.

I should caution I was a bit of a worrier when I was high.

Maybe the situation was exaggerated in my head. I took stock of my surroundings as objectively as I could. There was the police car driving toward our general direction in a slow and deliberate manner. Old Farmer Dietrich's porch light shone for the first time since pterodactyls had flown over these lands. Eddie was lying next to me. I took a good look at him.

He was concealing a badge pinned under his shirt.

Shit.

And a gun in his holster.

Double-shit.

"He's a narc," I yelled. "Eddie's a goddamn narc!"

All the kids ran for their lives, scattering in every direction. This attracted the attention of the police car which, as it turned out, had simply been passing by. The police car sped off down the street to pursue the running kids.

Eddie was gone. April and I took the moment to get out of there before Dietrich and his sting operation could ensnare us.

April and I walked around a little, occasionally looking over our shoulders to make sure we weren't being followed. We plodded around our neighborhood without talking. I felt horrible, but then April would burst into laughter and get me giggling. Inside the houses, TVs glowed with sitcom rerun warmth, but we preferred to be out and about.

Eventually, we got bored. The only place to go at this hour was the diner for some fries and vanilla ice cream.

April and I took our usual booth at the end of the diner with my back to the other customers. April was always pretty and composed, even after almost getting arrested. She tapped me on the hand and I turned around.

I was too shocked to speak. Eddie sat at the counter on the other side of the diner. He must have ducked in here, hoping to elude the police. Not a bad plan, since it was our plan as well. He picked at a plate of onion rings. He spotted us and nodded.

"Tell me this isn't fate?" said April.

"Should I?" I asked.

"You don't mess with fate," said April.

I got up and walked across the diner, sitting down next to Eddie.

"Hi."

"Hi."

"So, the badge..." I said.

"It's a fake, you moron," said Eddie.

"What?"

"It's a fake," whispered Eddie. "I'm not a narc."

"Then what the hell is that?" I whispered, pointing at his shirt. I didn't appreciate being whisper-yelled at in a public space by a potential boyfriend.

"Keep quiet," said Eddie. By this time, the other diners were listening intently to Eddie. "It's embarrassing," he said.

"This whole night is embarrassing," I said.

A quiet minute passed. "The Lone Ranger," said Eddie, running his hand through his hair. "It's a Lone Ranger badge and gun."

April laughed from across the diner.

A boy I didn't know came into the diner and walked toward us. He looked to be about my age but was taller than the other boys in my classes. He was also incredibly cute with his brown, feathered hair, and sensitive face.

"Freakin' embarrassing," said Eddie.

"Like from the TV show?" I asked, turning my attention back to Eddie.

"Just leave me alone," said Eddie. "I got business to tend to."

I stood up and walked back toward April.

"Hey Eli," said Eddie to the tall boy who had interrupted my conversation.

So, Eddie was really just a nerd with a thing for pot and the Lone Ranger? He went out to get high wearing a fake Texas badge and toy pistol? What an idiot. I breathed a sigh of relief.

April started talking to me, but I hushed her to see if I could overhear Eddie's conversation with this Eli boy. Eddie slid the plate of onion rings to Eli, offering him some. Eli picked up one of the onion rings and placed it on his index finger, unconsciously, while he talked to Eddie. I had the most sudden and fleeting thought that I wanted Eli to place that onion ring on my ring finger.

I leaned in but all I could make out was something about Eddie needing to go to Italy. Then, a car horn honked. I peered out the diner window and saw a large Cadillac in the parking lot. Eli and Eddie left the diner together but only Eddie got in the Cadillac. The parking lot was poorly lit, but I swore the driver was old Mrs. Querrel. She always wore a large fur coat. People are so weird.

I watched Eli walk alone down the street and desperately wanted to meet him.

The evening had been highly educational. For starters, I was most definitely not interested in being Eddie's Kemosabe. Nor did I ever wish to hear him utter "Heigh-Ho, Silver" within any context.

And for finishers, I knew I would be banned from the Wall for the rest of the summer. It was the social end of my teenage years.

CHAPTER THREE

***Maestro**—Any great composer, conductor, or teacher of music.*

"Eli, stop fidgeting and sit up straight," said my mom.

We sat sticking to the plastic chairs in the waiting room of Douglas Rasper's private audition space on a Saturday morning. At least, that's what Rasper liked to call it. During normal business hours, the waiting room doubled as a hallway at my old junior high school outside the chorus classroom. Since the school had no air conditioning, the hallway was sweltering. Rasper taught the boys' chorus class at the junior high before founding and directing the Long Island Boys Choir. Apparently, the choir made him enough money that he could leave the relative security of a public school teaching job last year.

Through the thick wooden door that kept us out of the chorus room, I could hear an eight-year-old male soprano singing with great exuberance about how, were he to come by possession of a hammer, he would put it to practical use in the morning. And in the evening. All over this land. Faintly, the boy's mother could be heard cooing at her son's high notes.

"Mom, you promise not to kvetch, right? I mean, I really want to make a good impression."

My mom did not want to be there. She needed to be back at work. Ever since my dad had passed away, she was the sole breadwinner in our house. She worked at a beauty parlor and helped my uncle run Tijuana Meatball. She had been to her beauty parlor in the morning so her hair was shiny black, like a polished ebony statue, and poofed up to vertical heights that defied physics. She wore her cat's eye glasses with the librarian necklace attached to them and was told by her beauty parlor co-workers she was the pinnacle of chic. She told me she never trusted their opinion.

"I don't like this," my mom said, continuing the conversation we'd had for the past few days. "And I don't like the idea of you traveling into the city. Who is this man to require parents to escort their children to auditions? The nerve."

"Kvetch-free, mom."

I was anxious enough without all this maternal negativity and second-guessing. My plan was to evade manual toil this summer and possibly be Italy-bound. Now all I needed to seal the deal was to have Rasper hear me sing and interview my mom. Rasper insisted on interviewing all parents to assess their level of dedication to the good cause.

It had not been an easy task to convince my mom to bring me here and give freely of her parental permission to join this professional boys' choir.

My father died when I was three. My mom was one of those widows who never bounced back. I always thought she was beautiful and cultured, but she didn't value those things. Plenty of available, age-appropriate men in the community had asked her out but she never seemed interested. Maybe she was just going through a dry spell. This particular rough patch happened to be going on its thirteenth year.

While searching for pizza money last month, my overriding concern for her loneliness came to bear when I found a dog-eared pornographic paperback in her nightstand. I'd always been worried about my mom but in a non-specific way. At least until that moment. It shocked me to learn that "The Farmer in the Belle" was the grand prize winner in the What-My-Mother-Chose-to-Read Sweepstakes. But, I rationalized, reading and sex were fundamental.

"It's time to put yourself out there again," I explained to her in the waiting room.

She had told me many times she felt no one on Long Island met her standards. Everyone was too snooty, too street smart. I had trouble understanding her and took the insult personally.

"You know, Eli," she said, "Just because we live in Hicksville doesn't mean the place is filled with upstanding hicks."

My mom said that a lot. I never knew what she meant.

"I'll be at choir rehearsals most of the summer, which will free you up. Think about it," I said, laying it on with an industrial-sized trowel. "You can have your Summer of Love. Your life could be like a Captain and Tennille song. Here's your chance to be Muskrat Susie."

"Eli," she said. "That's very sweet of you but I'm just not ready. You're growing up so fast. I'll worry about being alone when you go to college. In the meantime, I have you."

The chorus room door burst open and the eight-year-old boy filed out with his mother. The woman beamed, another obliging convert.

"Next," came a thundering boom from within.

"My God," said my mom. "The Great and Powerful Oz."

I had spent the past week doing deep research into Rasper and the choir. I asked Charley a million questions as I tried to prepare an audition strategy. Through persistent interrogation, I was also able to get Charley to divulge one of Rasper's lesser-known weaknesses and obsessions: Charlton Heston.

"Now remember, Mom, follow my lead if things aren't going great."

"Eli, I know this is important to you but there are a lot of boys who want to join. You might not get in."

"Summer of Love."

"You're just like your father," said my mom, smiling.

"Next!" the voice rumbled again. I sniffed the air for the aroma of a burning bush.

We entered the chorus room with the apprehensive caution of a Kansas farm girl, her dog, and three road trip buddies. It was a large open room with painted cinder block walls and no windows. There were three tiered plateaus arranged with chairs in the back half of the room which created a stadium feel. The walls were angled so the entire room was focused on the baby grand piano.

I had chorus class here a few years ago but the room felt different now, as if it had taken on a new look for this summer. It smelled of serious, professional purpose.

At the piano sat Douglas Rasper.

He was an imposing man, even with only the top third of him visible. He had thick, black, polished hair that was slicked back. It appeared to be dyed but that just added to the overall confidence of the man. He looked to be in his forties but may have been older. His eyes were set wide apart and accentuated his eagle's nose. His overall expression was one of deep concentration and scholarly rigor.

"Eli Mitchell," said Rasper in a mellifluous baritone. "Hello again, Mrs. Mitchell." He stood and shook her hand, then led us to the first row of chairs.

"Nice to meet you," said my mom.

"I believe we've met before," said Rasper. "Two years ago. Parent-teacher conference?"

"Eli has so many teachers," she said, not appearing to remember him. "I hope he was a joy in class."

We sat down as Rasper returned to his piano. He kept stealing glances at my mom. I tried to recall if I forged her signature on a report card and he was finally going to confront my mom about it.

"I apologize that Hubert Breggleman, my accompanist, isn't here," said Rasper. "He always attends choir selection. But he received news recently of his aunt's death in Italy. Shame, really. So, it's just us."

My mom shrugged. "I hear you have a fine choir," she said, sounding polite.

"Thank you," said Rasper, standing up and bowing. "I'll accompany myself today." He sat back down and waved me over.

I walked obediently to the piano with my sheet music. My mom looked around the room, then at her watch.

"Well, Mr. Mitchell," said Rasper, "your colleague, Charles Welsham, speaks very highly of you and your musical gifts. What are you gracing our ears with this morning?"

I handed over my sheet music. He opened it and I swear he did a double-take. His face attempted with great difficulty not to condescend, but it failed miserably.

"What is this?" he said incredulously.

"Billy Joel's 'The Piano Man.' He's from Hicksville, you know. Went to this school."

"Yes. Well, if we must," he said.

I sang the first three bars when Rasper's fingers crashed down upon the ivory keys discordantly.

"Mr. Mitchell," said Rasper. "Perhaps you envision me as a has-been playing some dive bar aside my empty tip jar. If so, I am not amused. Rather, I recommend a simple song that will let me truly assess the full range of your instrument."

"By all means," said my mom. "I never liked that Billy Joel."

"Happy Birthday," announced Rasper.

"My birthday's in December," said my mom.

"I'll have to remember that," said Rasper to my mom. He turned to me and said, "You know the birthday song? Although perhaps you can skip the 'How old are you now?' part."

My research told me the best way to get to Rasper was to make him feel superior. He loved believing he was changing lives and molding young people's destinies.

"That's brilliant," I said. "I never thought of my voice as an instrument before. And the simplicity of the arrangement should…"

"Eli, just sing happy birthday for the man. We have to go soon," said my mom.

I scowled at her, then sang a rousing version of the birthday song that would have put any five-year-old to shame.

"Excellent," said Rasper, never taking his eyes off my mom. "Your son is an excellent candidate for the choir. He comes highly recommended by one of my tenors, Charles Welsham."

"Great," she said. My mom didn't seem that interested.

"Of the Welsham Corporation," he added for effect.

"Eli and Charley are good friends," she responded.

"Soon, I will have Eli sight-reading music."

"I can already sight-read," I said.

He played a dramatic F-minor cord and let it pervade the air.

"I don't even know what that means," she said. "But I suppose if he must."

"Oh, he must."

"As long as he can keep his part-time job," said my mom. "He needs to earn money, you know."

I decided to increase my chances. "I can speak Italian, Mr. Rasper. I learned it from the waitstaff at my uncle's restaurant. For when we sing Italian songs in concerts and in case I go on tour with you." Actually, all I had picked up were Spanish curse words from one of the disgruntled waiters my uncle fired last week.

"A helpful skill," said Rasper. "I appreciate the initiative."

"And as I was telling my mom, who's a single parent, I look forward to your wisdom and tutelage on the subject of music."

Rasper arched his impressive right eyebrow, also dyed jet-black. "Mrs. Mitchell, this choir..." he said, staring at my mom, as if summing up his life's great wisdom. "Joining this choir requires the utmost dedication. Not every boy is ready for such demands. Are you fully committed, Mrs. Mitchell?"

I couldn't tell if he was laying it on thick or was genuinely interested in my mom. I hoped the latter if it helped me get into the choir.

"I can appreciate that," said my mom, playing with the handle of her purse. "And your commitment. But you play a lot of your concerts in the city, right?"

"We do. Every Christmas season," said Rasper proudly. "Right around your birthday."

"It's just that I don't like the idea of Eli going into the city."

"Mom, don't start."

"Oh, it's not you, Eli. I just don't like the city. You see, Mr. Rasper, I'm a country girl at heart but I stayed here for Eli."

My mom had often made me feel guilty about her big sacrifice to live near the big bad city until I graduated high school.

"Mom, it's just some rehearsals this summer. I'm only substituting for Charley for one week. It's no big deal."

"Mrs. Mitchell," said Rasper. "I can appreciate that. But joining the Long Island Boys Choir requires the deepest devotion. One doesn't just sign up for a few weeks. This is a long-term commitment for the sake of high art. It's not volunteering for a week of community service to wax the lanes at the local bowling alley. No. If Eli is in for a penny, he's in for a pound."

"I just don't know," said my mom.

"I understand," said Rasper. "Then it saddens me to say…"

"Charlton Heston!" I said.

"Pardon?" asked Rasper, intrigued.

"Eli, don't," said my mom.

It was interesting to consider the peccadilloes of this highly-educated, well-traveled, and cultured man sitting before us at the piano. Even Charley was puzzled by the enthralled obsession Rasper, an otherwise successful, heterosexual man, had with this big cheese-headed actor.

"What about Charlton Heston?" said Rasper.

"My mom's cousin knows him," I said.

"Cousin by marriage," said my mom, shrugging her shoulders.

"Really?" said Rasper. We had his undivided attention.

"She lives in England, my mom's cousin," I said. "Isn't that right, mom?"

My mom nodded, not sure where the conversation was going. "She was just telling me that Mr. Heston is filming somewhere in Europe this summer," said my mom.

"Europe," said Rasper, transfixed. "Why, we may be touring Italy this summer." Rasper played the opening credits theme from "*The Ten Commandments*" as he pondered this fortuitous turn.

"Although we're not really speaking with that side of the family," my mom said.

"Those damned dirty apes," I added.

"Eli!" shouted my mom. "Language." She turned to Rasper. "My cousin in Devonshire. That's the life. A quiet cottage in the country. Or a farmhouse. Away from the city. But I wouldn't expect you to understand."

Rasper stood up and considered my mom as if he had never seen her before. "On the contrary, Mrs. Mitchell, you might find it hard to believe but before all this education, I was a country boy." He spoke softly, even tenderly to her.

My mom sat up. "Really?" She matched his tone. I saw a window open in her eyes.

"Born and raised in rural South Carolina. And ask the parent of any choirboy. Eli will be in very safe hands. I've been an educator my whole life and this will be a rich experience for your son."

"Aren't there other boys waiting for this opportunity?" she asked.

"But then I wouldn't have the pleasure of your company, Mrs. Mitchell..."

"Phyllis."

"Phyllis. And perhaps Mr. Heston could be persuaded to attend one of our Christmas concerts?" said Rasper.

"Well, of course, I can ask," she said.

"And there's always the chance he might attend one of our concerts in Italy this summer. I mean, Mr. Heston is already there filming," said Rasper, momentarily on his own private Isla El Cid.

"He might even fly his plane there like in that airport movie from 1975. What was that called?" asked my mom.

"Airport 75," said Rasper. He looked my mom in the eyes. "Phyllis," he said, "remember, us country folks need to stick together."

Silence overtook the room.

"I think this would be a rich experience for you, Eli," said my mom, never taking her eyes off Rasper.

I sighed with relief.

My mom drew a deep breath. "Mr. Rasper, I think Eli needs this chorus. He needs to be around an educated male figure who's salt of the earth. You have my word that I will drop him off and pick him up from every rehearsal."

"Douglas," said Rasper, shaking my mom's hand. My mom smiled. He reviewed his clipboard, "Then it seems that Eli is my new alto."

"Wonderful," said my mom.

"Wait, alto?" I said. "Aren't altos usually junior high kids whose voices haven't changed yet? Charley's a tenor."

"I am sorry, Mr. Mitchell, but I have all the tenors I need. An alto, however," said Rasper, turning to my mom who had seated herself again and was in the process of re-applying makeup. "An alto is a noble voice. A boy who can sing from the lower registers as well as utilize his head voice is a force to be reckoned with."

"I always told him he was a force to be reckoned with," said my mom. "Eli will be the best altar boy you've ever had." She checked herself again in her compact mirror.

"Alto!" I cried.

"I am sure," Rasper said. "And by the time he's seventeen or eighteen, he'll be a tenor or a baritone. Now, as for the matter of the choir tuition…"

"Oh my," remarked my mom. "I didn't realize." I had neglected to tell her about the tuition, hoping that when she saw how happy I would be, she'd figure out a way to find the money.

"The tuition is one-hundred dollars, annually," said Rasper. "You understand that, although this is a professional choir paid to perform, the tuition covers my tutelage, all the basic music rentals, transportation in the choir Maxivan, and Mr. Breggleman's salary."

"It's just that we're getting by without a lot of extravagances as it is," said my mom in a low, broken voice.

Regarding our finances, my mom was being kind. Church mice routinely left us food and clothing at our doorstep while shaking their heads and pursing their lips. My mom just didn't have the money, Summer of Love or not. I didn't know what I was thinking. I could have asked Charley for the money, but I always felt strange talking about that with him. I always thought it would get in the way of our friendship. And I didn't have a lot of friends.

"I request the parents make this financial commitment to show their pledge to the arts," said Rasper. "Of course, we have benefactors as well. Mrs. Dolores Querrel and Mr. and Mrs. Clancy to name but three patrons."

"The Clancys?" said my mom.

"I mean Mr. and Mrs. Bartholomew Rollins. Everyone still calls them the Clancys," said Rasper. "Old habit."

I saw my dreams disappearing. I desperately wanted to join but there was no way we could afford the tuition. I suddenly felt guilty about adding more stress to her life. Charley was my best friend, but I couldn't do this to my mom. It was time to end the audition and go back to being a busboy. Defeated at such a young age.

"Well, Mr. Rasper, I mean, Douglas, unfortunately, we can't afford...," said my mom.

"Wait," I said. "Mr. Rasper, I'm here to substitute for Charley, right?"

"At first. But I suspect you will find a home here."

"Right. But for this season, Charley's tuition is already paid for. If I'm subbing for him, charging me tuition would be like double-dipping, right? I'm sure that's not what you mean to do. Maybe I could get a discount?"

"Well, I don't know..." said Rasper, smiling at my mom.

"He's very pushy, this one," said my mom.

I turned to her. "Hey mom, didn't Charlton Heston owe your cousin money for renting a horse or something? Maybe we can ask him for the money."

"Alright, Mr. Mitchell. Let's make your tuition twenty-five dollars this year," said Rasper, bowing deeply towards my mom. "We can't be expected to bother Mr. Heston with such minute problems."

"Mom, can I get an advance on my birthday gift?"

"Do I have a choice?" she said to me while looking at Rasper.

"Thank you!" I said.

My mom took Rasper's hand in hers and they shook for an uncomfortable period of time. I didn't quite understand what had transpired but couldn't believe my luck. I'd worry about how my mother was going to produce Charlton Heston some other time.

It was hard to imagine I'd be going to Italy this summer. My secret wish, ever since I was five or six, was to go to Italy and visit the town where my dad grew up. I knew in my heart he was special. I wanted to learn from the people he grew up with what kind of man he was and how he got out of his town and came to America. I felt if I understood him better, I would understand why it was okay that I didn't fit in my own life and was destined for great things.

My mom and Rasper were still shaking hands. I cleared my throat. Decorum settled in again as they let in some air between them.

"Oh my," said my mom. "This is so exciting. And travel to Italy!"

"Phyllis?" said Rasper.

"I'm sure you take on chaperones for these kinds of trips," said my mom.

"Of course, our European tours are chaperoned. Our patrons accompany us. But I think you misunderstand…"

"Misunderstand?" said my mom.

"Eli cannot accompany us to Italy. Only a select group of the overall choir tours in the summer and we have enough altos for our tour as it is."

"Well goodbye, then, Douglas. I look forward to seeing you again."

My mom grinned, grabbed her purse, and headed out the door.

"But I'm a tenor," I said.

"I am sorry, Eli. I look forward to your attendance at rehearsals this summer as we prepare for the Christmas season."

I suddenly understood why Soylent Green was people.

CHAPTER FOUR

Deceptive cadence—*A chord progression that seems to lead to resolving itself on the final chord; but does not.*

Being banned from the Wall had put me in a desperate panic. I was smoking my second cigarette of the morning, enjoying my Lucky Charms, watching H.R. Pufnstuf, and trying to come up with some way to get back into the good graces of the Wall-folk. No plan came to mind. Pufnstuf always made my mind wander.

My parents were both out. Despite the lush houses and manicured lawns in my neighborhood, my parents were not rich. But they somehow managed to put on the appearance they could keep up with the neighbors. They had adopted me when I was an infant. My real parents had died in a car accident. My adoptive father was a lawyer. My adoptive mom stayed at home, took care of herself, her house, her husband, and me. In that order.

After a few hours, I got dressed and walked over to April's house. I had heard a rumor at the Wall a few weeks earlier, before I was most injudiciously thrown out of the club, about a shopping bag full of heavy breathers. These were considered gold among our age set. These slight, poorly worded pornographic paperbacks with titles like, "Swedish Odyssey 1976," "Mindy and Mona: Cocktail Waitresses A-Go-Go," and, "The Trouble with Conjoined Twin Nymphomaniacs," all written by the same author with the trashy pseudonym "Gina Puttanesca," had gotten us through many an afternoon's dry patch. I can't say I understood everything that was going on in these strange, bouncy, sexual adventures. But this window into a forbidden adult world seemed a harmless pastime. I knew it was all bullshit but at sixteen, cheap, provocative, forbidden entertainment was fascinating.

It all ended up being Mrs. Eunice Clancy's fault.

Mrs. Clancy, who lived down the street from me, had been born again. Again. Apparently, the first time she was born again, it didn't take. She was fifty-seven and looked fairly sexless with her short brown bob, high-collar starched shirts, beige trousers, and mannish features. She had grown up in this area. In fact, aside from a few unexplained absences, she had been here longer than anyone else in the neighborhood. She might have been one of the prototype Wall members when she was a teenager.

Rumor had it that Mrs. Clancy had sown quite the wild oat in her day. Unbelievably, at least to me, she had been credited with setting fire to the old public school. On my first day there, I was told that I had old lady Clancy to thank for the shiny new school. Even the auditorium was nicknamed Clancy Hall. This all seemed quite odd when I considered she was a rich, genderless frump who nevertheless shuffled along the sidewalk with her privately owned shopping cart on her way to save thirty cents on a dozen cans of cat food across town.

Then, a few years ago, Mrs. Clancy disappeared for six months. Rumors sprang up like weeds. When she returned, religion had overcome her like a wave of piety and self-righteousness crashing upon the shores of her rabble-rousing. Maybe she saw the weeping face of Mary in her cat's hairballs. Clearly, it had not turned out to be the good kind of religion. All I knew was that one morning, she started dressing in a way that made the local catholic girls' school's dress code look positively alluring and raucous. She'd walk around town blessing people. Sometimes, while standing in line at the checkout, she'd start preaching the Good Word. I'd stand there and pray for an announcement about a cleanup in Aisle Five just to drown her out.

The kids on the block were generally indifferent to her. She was simply the rigid and zealous kook down the street. At best, her fanaticism was a drop of Holy Water in our neighborhood's sunshine. We didn't give Mrs. Clancy much thought.

A year or two later, I saw her smoking and wearing lipstick, whenever she got together with that awful Mrs. Querrel. Mrs. Clancy tried to hide it from me as she walked past my house. Unbeknownst to her, two of my passions were smoking and lipstick, so I absolutely noticed.

It turned out Mrs. Clancy had landed a man. Mr. Clancy was gregarious, a bit younger than she, a little plump, and had a weird sense of humor. But, generally, he was an agreeable sort. No one knew where they met. All we knew was that one day we woke up and there was a Mr. Clancy in our neighborhood. He, of course, had another name. I think it might have been Bart Rollins. I believe she took his name when they married but we, as did the whole neighborhood, continued to address her as Mrs. Clancy and him, naturally, as Mr. Clancy. After all, she had squatter's rights on the name in our memories.

The new Mr. Clancy also came with a grandson they were raising. It was strange to think of a kid being raised in that kind of wealth, privilege, and repression.

About a year ago, religion clobbered poor Mrs. Clancy over the head again. Maybe this time she'd work out the bugs in the system. She reverted back to the buttoned-up sweaters, long, prim skirts, Frankenstein-like orthopedic shoes, thick glasses, and man-hair. In fact, she looked more like a man than most men. Mr. Clancy didn't seem to mind. He was well-off and they moved into a much bigger house in the neighborhood.

April's mom, to earn a little spending money, offered her services to the community as a house cleaner. There was no shame in it, and everyone agreed she was quite industrious. Mrs. Clancy was one of the women in our neighborhood who regularly took advantage of April's mom's hygienic help. This seemed odd considering old lady Clancy was home all day. One day, we concluded that Mrs. Clancy was taking care of the godliness while April's mom worked on the cleanliness.

I arrived at April's house. As always, April was pretty, skinny, and smart. It was enough to make you hate her except April was also so nice. She was the only friend who hadn't abandoned me during the Wall Incident. We went up to her room and put on some music.

"You'll never believe what I overheard my mom telling my dad," said April, laying on her bed. "She's cleaning old lady Clancy's house and found a huge stash of Clit Lit!" April continued, barely able to contain herself. Our pubescent eyes lit up at the prospect of the pornographic paperbacks. The pot we had just smoked helped too. This was the equivalent of being in prison and hearing about a hidden carton of cigarettes. Clit Lit was used as barter and fetched quite a handsome price on our black market. It also did wonders for our standing in the teenage community.

"Jesus," I remarked, sitting up on the floor. "Old lady Clancy? I can't believe it."

"Obviously, they belong to her pervert husband," April said.

There was a silent hum of agreement between us. It all made sense.

"I mean, wouldn't you be reading with one hand if you were married to that repressed old battle-axe?" continued April.

"Coming home, thinking that this lady is going to snap out of her perpetual Sermon on the Mount and getting a lecture on the horrors of sex instead," I added.

We walked down to April's kitchen for a snack and felt sorry for Mrs. Clancy. And Mr. Clancy.

"How do we get at these books?" I asked, crystallizing what was dancing eagerly across both our minds at that moment. It was decided, with little disagreement from April, that she would steal her mother's copy of Mrs. Clancy's house key, make a duplicate at the hardware store, and return the original to her mother's collection.

That afternoon, April succeeded without detection.

The next day, after we watched Mrs. Clancy shuffle off with her shopping cart to buy her week's groceries and perform God's will in aisle three, April and I crept stealthily through her backyard.

"This has to be double-quick," I reminded April. She nodded in an equally nervous fashion. The back door opened easily. We stepped into Mrs. Clancy's sunroom and paused.

"How do we know no one else is home?" I asked April, kicking myself for not recognizing this obvious question before we began our burglarizing.

"Because no one is. He's away doing whatever he does. When was the last time they had a visitor besides old lady Querrel and she's off playing bridge or christening a boat with champagne," said April, who could always be counted on to drown out my panic with cold reason. It was great to have her around when I was high.

We proceeded into the den. The den and adjoining living room were exactly as we had imagined. The décor represented the many catholic lives of Mrs. Clancy. Portraits of Jesus and Mary flanked a lava lamp. Posters of bullfighters outlined a small, candled shrine to St. Francis de Assisi. Mr. Clancy wasn't well represented in the house except for framed photos of their angelic little grandson. He looked to be about eight years old. In fact, aside from the occasional framed picture of the happy couple taken at a church picnic, you'd never know Mr. Clancy lived there. As we crept up the stairs, I realized we were about to steal one of the precious few possessions he had in this house.

We came upon their bedroom. It was positively austere. A monk's room, by comparison, would look deliriously wild and wooly. It was hard to distinguish his side of the room from hers. Each side was decorated with the same dark, boxy furniture. There was a small closet on each side of the room as well.

April went to one side of the room and opened the closet. It was filled with Mr. Clancy's suits, assorted weekend and holiday clothes, and some souvenirs and knickknacks from Italy. Two small boxes were stacked on a shelf.

"Bingo," said April. As she lowered the boxes carefully from the closet shelf, I decided to have a poke around Mrs. Clancy's side of things.

The top drawer of her nightstand contained a Bible. It sat there alone looking pious and smug as if wondering why anyone but her mistress was exposing it to daylight. I closed the drawer while my other hand went to the bottom drawer.

"They're not here," whispered April. "This is old tax shit." She closed the box and carefully maneuvered her way back into his closet.

The bottom drawer of Mrs. Clancy's nightstand opened almost without me thinking about it. It contained a box of tissues, an autographed wallet photo of Jesus, an atomizer bottle marked "Holy Water," a nightgown, a Clit Lit, and the biggest goddamn vibrator I had ever seen.

"Holy crap," I uttered. Apparently, my surprise was loud enough to attract April's attention. I continued to stare at the sordid assortment of personnel belongings as April rushed over to my side. I picked up the Clit Lit.

"The Farmer in the Belle," I read aloud. It was very dog-eared.

"My God, what the fuck is that?" inquired April with stark incredulity, pointing at the monster-sized, cylindrical, red, ribbed vibrator. It looked like a sleeping fire hydrant.

"That, my dear, is an officially sanctioned, living and breathing vibrator," I said.

"That thing moves?"

We didn't really have time to find out. We were on a schedule. The Great Fire Hydrant seemed to have transfixed April as much as, I imagined, it had Mrs. Clancy. I thought of Mrs. Clancy in the context of this latest revelation and I came to a conclusion: The old lady was getting more interesting by the inch.

I opened Mrs. Clancy's closet door. Hidden behind the depressing black and brown robe-like dresses sat twelve large shopping bags brimming with paperbacks. I stepped out of the closet and tapped April on the shoulder. She was kneeling in front of the nightstand ready to light candles and pray at the altar of the Holy Vibrator Shrine. I foresaw years of therapy in her future.

"Let's go. Found 'em," I said.

We decided to take only what we could carry: about twenty paperbacks each. It didn't make a dent in Mrs. Clancy's huge inventory. We got rid of any evidence we had been there, straightening out the bed quilt carefully and closing all the open doors and drawers. We crept out of the house and raced across the street, giggling louder with each step.

"There had to be a thousand of them in there," said April as we reached her backyard.

"Maybe she's in a book club," I conjectured, breathing a bit heavy from our brisk escape.

I noticed April's purse was bulging.

"April, what's that?" I said.

"Oh shit, Jane."

She opened her purse to reveal the Vibrating Fire Hydrant.

"I must have taken it without realizing," said April, still transfixed by the object.

"Please tell me you're not planning on using that thing. You'd need to take some kind of class first."

"Like driver's ed?"

"April, you have to throw that away. Promise me."

"Promise," said April reluctantly.

We split our booty down the middle. April said goodbye in a dreamy state and went inside. I walked home and stashed mine away in my garage under the artificial Christmas tree. It was June so they were safe there. My mother cleaned my room a few times a week, so I had learned never to keep any contraband there.

As I put the books away, a small piece of paper flitted out of one of the books, twirling in the air before landing near my foot. I picked it up. It was a ticket stub.

Teatro dell'Opera
La Forza del Destino
Giuseppe Verdi
13 Giugno 1978
Roma, Italia

I pocketed it as a good luck souvenir from the afternoon's adventures.

Once everything was secure, I went for a walk. I thought about the Clancys and how I was very wrong and very right about them. It was one of my first insights into the complexities of adult life. I also learned how devious I was capable of being. I now had something to trade to get back to the Wall. Since Mrs. Clancy was hiding these books from Mr. Clancy, she clearly couldn't report to him they were missing. Nor could she report us if she ever suspected us. It might even work out that she suspected Mr. Clancy took the books and was reading them himself which might rekindle their relationship in the bedroom. I might have saved their marriage! It was the perfect crime.

"Get in, Jane."

I spun around and stared in horror. A familiar car pulled up beside me. The driver was April's mom. April sat sheepishly in the backseat. I quietly got in next to April. The car pulled away. April looked at me sadly.

"We're busted," she whispered.

We drove to my house. My mother's car was in the driveway. This was not good news.

"How did my mother find out?" I asked April. My mother had the entire day set aside for a hair appointment. And she would never give up her hair appointment.

"I called her at the salon," answered April's mom. "I told her I'd pick you up."

She looked at us suspiciously in her rear-view mirror. I couldn't speak out loud in the presence of April's mom without fear my words might be used against me in a court of law. Without giving away my actions to the driver, I quietly mouthed, "How bad?"

April pointed to the front passenger seat.

I glanced over. There, riding shotgun, was Mrs. Clancy's giant flaming-red vibrator, wrapped in a blue-and-white towel. It shone patriotically in the midday sun.

We pulled into my driveway, got out of the car, and started the long walk home. April's mom tapped us on the shoulder and pointed us around toward the back of the house. April and I held hands like convicts about to be sentenced. I knew April had not ratted us out. She was much cooler-headed than that.

On the other hand, I never should have let her back into the world with that faraway look in her eyes. April was trapped in some strange, euphoric vibrator haze. It had addled her brain, preventing any rational thought or precaution.

As we shuffled along the side of the house, I smelled something burning. April looked at me, then at her mom. April's mom kept calmly walking behind us. She didn't seem alarmed about the burning smell, so I ruled out my house was on fire. We weren't that lucky.

We rounded the corner. My mother stood next to the barbecue grill, burning one of our paperbacks. A small pile of books stood at her feet. They had found April's stash.

"Missy," my mother cried out, calling me by my kindergarten nickname. She threw another Clit Lit into the fire, then marched towards me. This wasn't looking good.

My mother took me by the arm and escorted me aside. She spoke quietly, almost peacefully, as if, in her mind, this was already resolved.

"This was your doing, right?" said my mother as she pointed towards the stack of April's Clit Lits. I stared in silence. "You had a hand in this, I can tell," she stated matter-of-factly.

The burning book made small wisps of gray smoke that drifted over the sunny, mid-day roofs. April stared at the fire like an Eskimo watching her igloo melting.

I finally nodded and suddenly felt ashamed.

"But why are you burning those?" I said in a voice weaker than I expected. "I mean, won't Mrs. Clancy want them back?"

My mother smiled at me in a way that suggested my stance on the matter was both futile and naïve.

"Come with me," she said simply. She guided me towards our garage. April and her mom followed us. "I know you hide stuff in here."

Our two mothers looked at each other. Then, they gave careful glances to make sure no neighbors were within earshot.

"Show me your half of the books," my mother demanded.

I heard the distant twinkle of an ice cream truck and mourned my childhood.

April's mom smiled softly as if suppressing something. It looked like relief and joy. She was about to speak when I pushed the artificial Christmas tree out of the way.

"Well?" said my mother.

I couldn't speak.

My books were missing. Someone had stolen my stash of Clit Lits.

CHAPTER FIVE

Vivace*—Direction to play a composition in a brisk, lively, and spirited manner.*

"Boys," said Rasper. He commanded the full and rapt attention of his choir. We were gathered in the same room where I had auditioned a week earlier. "This is Eli Mitchell. He will be joining our illustrious ranks as an alto." I stood there and smiled, feeling nervous and a bit too eager to please. "Take your seat over there, Mr. Mitchell," said Rasper, pointing me toward the alto section.

And with that quick and rather unceremonious introduction, I was a Long Island Boys Choir member. There were thirty choir members in total. I only recognized Charley and one or two others. The rest were from different parts of Long Island. I took my seat next to boys who were at least two years younger than me and whose voices were only just beginning to change. Some smiled back at me, but others watched me with suspicion. Usually, it took years of training in the preparatory choir before you joined the Big Show.

Charley waved at me, but I was still upset with him for not warning me about the whole "you might be an alto and won't be able to go to Italy because we have all the altos we need" thing. Still, true to his word, he had come through and was paying me equivalent wages for my time in rehearsal so I could afford to quit my busboy job. My uncle hadn't seemed upset in the least about me quitting and the waiters were relieved to see their short singing careers go by the wayside.

My mother seemed almost as disappointed as I was about not being able to go to Italy. While she held no special interest in seeing my dad's hometown the way I did, the idea of a Summer of Love in Italy with Douglas Rasper, her personal Roger Moore, appeared to tickle her. It was nice to see her this way. Her daily hair poofing and beauty regimen suddenly took on Olympic-training intensity.

I couldn't believe the effect Rasper had on her. I think she was trying to figure out a way to go to Italy as badly as I was. When she dropped me off for my first rehearsal, my mother had decided to stay in the car. She'd discovered a blemish on her nose that morning and didn't dare have Rasper see her in her be-zitted state. She drove home instead to tend to her skin.

Hicksville was fairly central to Long Island's geography. There were members of the choir who could walk here from Plainview, the town next door, and others who traveled as far as Ronkonkoma and Riverhead to the east and New York City and White Plains to the West and beyond. To me, if you were coming from towns like White Plains, you might as well have been coming from Iowa. Some of these kids came from so far away, they spoke with an accent.

During the summer, most rehearsals were scheduled during the late afternoon. When school was in session, rehearsals were every Tuesday and Thursday night as well as every other Sunday afternoon. When the Performance Season arrived, we'd continue to rehearse in addition to our three to four concerts during weekdays and two on weekends. It was so exciting; I couldn't stand it. I felt like my life was just starting to course-correct and get me to where I needed to be. Now I just needed to figure out a way to become a permanent, touring tenor instead of a one-week-only alto.

We took a break after the first hour of rehearsal. With so many eight-year-olds, bladder control was a major consideration. I wandered the hallways of my old school thinking how I always felt bad for those kids who had to take summer school classes. And here I was.

Other than Charley, only Terrence, an alto, came over to say hello. I think the rest of the kids knew I was just a substitute and not worthy of their time. Terrence was one of only two African-American boys in the choir. He was friendly and, I think, eager to make a friend with a fellow alto who was older than him.

As I went back into the rehearsal room, I bumped into a large mound of fur that made me think I was backstage at the zoo. I excused myself. A royal voice from the mound of fur said, "And you are?"

"Eli. Eli Mitchell. And you?" I said in an equally regal manner, thinking she was kidding.

"I'm your elder."

She was still huffing as I looked for a seat. I sat in front of Charley who was seated with the tenors on the second-tier platform. Charley tried to smile at me again and made a cross-eyed face. I knew I couldn't stay mad at him for long.

Rasper's accompanist, Hubert Breggleman, sat down at the piano and paged through some sheet music. Hubert was a twerpy forty-year-old and, according to Charley, didn't have much of a social life. His subscription to the Battlestar Galactica fan newsletter was as spicy as his life got. He had black, greasy hair, a nervous disposition, and was often mistaken for a fellow choirboy. His most surprising feature, however, was his wedding ring.

Hubert's wife, Florinda, stood next to him as she had for the entire first hour of rehearsal. Florinda was beautiful, flirty, twelve years Hubert's junior, and dressed in tight clothes. The latter quality alone ranked her high in my book.

Rasper stood majestically in front of the piano, ever the choral director, with his sleeves rolled up and his eyes scanning us for possible physical or vocal flaws. He was our Field Marshal giving careful instructions as we prepared to trudge through the rocky and sometimes muddied landscapes of Schubert, Bach, and Irving Berlin. He reminded us to use our head voice and sing from our diaphragm. Under no circumstance were we ever to sing from the back of our throat. These orders were received with Patton-like urgency.

As we dutifully took out our sheet music for the next song, Rasper introduced Dolores Querrel. My elder in fur. I looked at Charley questioningly, my eyes offering a stay of his execution. He leaned over and explained in whispers.

Querrel, one of the main benefactors of the choir, was a mean old bitch whom everyone called Lady Bear behind her sizable back. She had gotten her nickname from her reliable insistence on never being seen in public without her enormous silver-blue fur coat.

Querrel was squat but her fur coat added immeasurably to her stature. Her facial features were pre-ordained to be eternally sculpted in a scornful, disapproving frown. With her surgically lifted eyes, brows, and jowls and bright-orange dyed hair, the effect of being imperious and permanently cranky was sealed. Charley said she never once smiled nor laughed. It finally occurred to me that she resembled Richard Nixon had he been born a furry, female leprechaun.

No one was sure where she had gotten her money. One envisioned a long line of deceased robber-baron-husbands; each having sampled the dubious pleasures of the Lady Bear matrimonial bed-deluxe.

She had provided her matronage since the choir's inception. Word around the choir piano was that Rasper had some special arrangement with Lady Bear. She had used her society contacts to arrange for annual concert events at certain exclusive Ladies' Clubs, charity fundraisers, and the like. I'm not entirely sure what she got out of it, but she certainly seemed to enjoy having several dozen boys be her audience as if she were royalty.

Lady Bear rose grandly and addressed the choir, her fur draped regally over her broad shoulders. She stared at us with a look that fully expected genuflection toward her glory.

"Boys, I know you're awaiting my decision about where in Italy we'll stay this summer. But, due to circumstances even I can't control, there will be no summer tour through Italy this year. For that, I am deeply sorry."

For an uncomfortable period of time, Lady Bear gazed at us for good measure. Then she turned with a dramatic flourish and exited, knowing when to leave them wanting more.

There was a great flood of shocked murmurs around me. Before the choirboys could revolt, clearly feeling a sense of entitlement to their annual summer European tour, Rasper calmed the crowd.

"Now, boys, you know we would if we could. Mrs. Querrel has done all she can for us. She assures me there will be other opportunities. I dislike discussing finances with you, but these trips are impossible without our sponsors. Concerts do not pay what they used to. I mean, there were times when even the Vienna Boys Choir couldn't go on tour," said Rasper.

"Yeah," I whispered to Charley. "And for the same reason: Nazis."

I was mostly upset I couldn't go to Italy and research the town where my dad had grown up. Sure, there was personal pleasure in this trip but my whole life, I had fantasized about either long-lost relatives in a quaint Italian village that were related to royalty or finding out my dad was secretly Fellini's brother.

I felt a cold stare. It didn't take a trained Navy dolphin to locate the source of the stare.

"Mr. Mitchell, this is no laughing matter," said Rasper, having heard my utterance.

This had the unexpected effect of making Hubert laugh. His wife placed her hand over his mouth to try and plug the disobedience from chuckling out further. I soon found myself laughing with him in contrapuntal harmony.

"And I expect never to hear such backtalk from you again," Rasper boomed over our fizzed-out laughter. "Now, since you're green here, why don't you go into the hallway and practice scales with Mr. Breggleman."

Charley leaned over and whispered, "Still think this is living the dream?"

I left dejected, having only sung for an hour before being placed in choral detention.

Hubert followed me out in a manner reminiscent of a bailiff escorting a condemned prisoner out of the courtroom.

"You have to learn to be respectful," mumbled Hubert, shuffling out into the hallway. I couldn't tell if he was talking to me or himself. Florinda followed us, making tiny clicks with her heels on the school hallway tile.

Hubert had been the Long Island Boys Choir accompanist for as long as anyone could remember. To hear Rasper tell it, which, I would learn, he did ad nauseam with the elderly patrons at the fundraising cocktail parties that preceded many of our concerts, Rasper had selected Hubert with the same drama and flourish that David O. Selznick used to select his Scarlett O'Hara.

Florinda sat down at Hubert's left at the extra piano that was rolled out into the hallway during rehearsals.

"Florinda," Hubert said meekly. "This is Eli. He's new."

"Well, hello to you," she said.

"Hi. Pleasure." My eyes were drawn to my shoes which had suddenly become fascinating.

"Let's get started," said Hubert quietly. "How about some Bach?"

Florinda took out the sheet music and placed it on the piano. As Hubert began playing with his right hand, Florinda played the bass notes with her left hand while turning pages with her right.

I learned that a few years earlier, after a late choir concert, Hubert went home and had gotten drunk. He ended up falling asleep at his piano; his head and the majority of his body's weight leaning on his left arm. When he awoke, a fluke of nerve damage caused him to lose all mobility in his left arm. The non-playing arm hung at his side like an understudy that would never go on.

To compensate, Florinda, filling in the role of the dutiful wife, played all of Hubert's bass chords. It astonished me that Rasper's loyalty extended to employing what was essentially a one-armed pianist and his wife. During pre-concert meals, Florinda could be found curling or straightening Hubert's left-hand fingers so he could grasp utensils.

The rehearsal room opened and one of the baritones—a big, tough, brooding African-American kid—stepped out into the hallway. He winked at Florinda. She excused herself from Hubert's piano and headed down the hallway behind him.

"First note," said Hubert, prompting me with a nod of his head.

With Hubert facing me, I saw Florinda put her arm around the baritone while he grabbed her ass. Florinda and the baritone disappeared around the corner. All the while, Hubert continued playing scales.

"Ahh... AHHH..."

"Eli, let's try again," said Hubert patiently.

"Mr. Breggleman, I need some fresh air. Sorry. Must be the jitters. Be right back."

I raced through the nearest exit door to investigate Hubert's wife and the baritone's tryst. I took a deep breath of the summer air. What the hell was going on? Florida was the dutiful wife. Adults were supposed to act like, well, adults.

I couldn't find them and felt out of my element. Suddenly, serving Nachos Alfredo all summer didn't seem so bad. I decided then it was better to pass the olive branch to Charley since he seemed to know everything about everyone here. As I headed back into the building, I caught the sight of a large hairy object floating down the sidewalk in my periphery. I realized it was Lady Bear. Impetuously, I followed her. She walked into the Capri Bar.

Rasper required the choir parents to drop off their kids precisely on time. The parents were then expected to disappear and pick us up a few hours later. There weren't many options in Hicksville when it came to killing time.

The Capri Bar was the gathering site of choice for the waiting choir parents. They would crack open the doors of the small bar, break through the smoke and bourbon haze, and deposit themselves onto cracked leather stools to sip away the day's responsibilities, knowing they were doing their part for culture. Most parents were three music sheets to the wind by the time they picked up their kids.

I snuck in and took a seat in a dark corner near Lady Bear where no one could see me. Happy Hour was just getting started. Lady Bear was speaking conspiratorially with an older woman. This other woman wore a Puritanical buttoned-up sweater, thick glasses, and was crowned by a haircut that could only be described as a "Moe."

Without giving away my position, I moved closer to get a better listen.

"Calm down, Eunice," said Lady Bear. "He's just a kid."

"Wrong, Dolores," said Eunice. "I'm telling you this cop has been watching me. It's always the same one, too. Large mole under his right eye. Disgusting. He's practically a kid, alright. But I'm telling you he's a cop. I know it."

The two of them finished their drink and were approached by a waitress.

"Another round, Mrs. Clancy? Mrs. Querrel?" said the waitress.

"Why not?" said Lady Bear. She waited until the waitress was out of earshot. "Now Eunice, you just keep purchasing those little books of yours."

"Did you retrieve the stolen ones? I tell you, it's the DEA."

"Calm down, Eunice. I was able to get half of them back. Little pricks."

"Bart is against this whole thing, of course," said Eunice.

"Bart doesn't fart without getting scared," said Lady Bear. "And speaking of kids looking like adults, I've got it all arranged with Eddie."

"That little punk kid?"

"Don't be such a prude. We need the little drug dealer to go to Rome and pretend to be Hubert. There's just no other way around it," said Lady Bear.

"Heaven knows we don't have the funds to go," said Eunice in a self-pitying tone.

"We need that inheritance," said Lady Bear.

Eunice spun around, and I thought she heard me breathing. But she couldn't have because I couldn't breathe. This was all too much.

"What?" said Lady Bear.

The other bar patrons turned around at the sound of the agitated Lady Bear.

"I'm sorry," said Eunice in a hushed voice. "You ever get that paranoid feeling? Maybe it was this cop following me. I don't know. This makes me very nervous. Look, are we really going through with this?"

"Go through with it?" said Lady Bear, lowering her voice. "Honey, we're already doing it. We're playing past that now. Hubert's aunt is dead and left everything to him. You heard what Bart said. We need that key."

"You're right, Dolores. Of course, you're right. A shame we can't go to Italy too, that's all I'm saying."

"We just keep this hush-hush so Douglas keeps his nose out of it," said Lady Bear.

Their drinks arrived. The two of them clinked glasses, celebrating some unspoken covenant.

I picked up my jaw from the beer-soaked floor and slinked away from the bar, feeling queasy.

I had known Rasper for only a week but suddenly felt as intensely loyal to him as he did to poor one-armed Hubert. His benefactors were using the choir for some illicit scheme in Italy and that seemed supremely unfair.

My mission was all too clear. I needed to ensure Rasper saw Rome this summer and that no harm came to him or the choir. Rasper in Rome meant the Long Island Boys Choir in Rome. And that meant me in Rome. Somehow, I would explain this to my mom and find the money. And figure out a way to be invited. As I walked back to rehearsal, a plan came to me.

I found Hubert in the hallway tuning the piano. His wife was thankfully elsewhere. I sat down with Hubert and practiced scales.

"You know, Mr. Breggleman," I said casually. "This music reminds me of the Elmer Bernstein score for The Ten Commandments. Why, Charlton Heston's a good friend of my mom's cousin. And he's filming in Rome this summer."

Hubert perked up and gave me his undivided attention, knowing this bit of court gossip would win him favor with the King.

I placed my cherry on top of the sundae.

"And when I told Chuck, sorry, Mr. Heston, that we'd be touring Italy this summer, he said he'd meet Mr. Rasper for dinner and possibly be a choir sponsor. But since we're not going, it would disappoint Mr. Rasper to hear, so don't tell anyone, please."

"No," said Hubert, an astonishingly bad liar. "Of course not."

CHAPTER SIX

***Contralto**—Lowest female singing voice.*

Things were bad but could have been worse. At least my mother didn't tell my father about the Great Clit Lit Robbery. At first, our mothers wouldn't tell April and me why they were smiling when they discovered our heist. Our awkward, blushing, hypothesis was they were too embarrassed to go into the dirty bookstore in Hicksville to buy Clit Lits. Now, they had access to a stolen stash. And even though my stash had mysteriously vanished, there was plenty left in April's stash to keep them satisfied, even after a few of the books had been burned.

It was no fun to be a teenage castaway. A week after I was ostracized from The Wall, word had reached my parents about my Wall activities. They felt it necessary to saddle me with one of their lectures. They chose the dinner table in front of a box of take-out pizza.

"Jane, we just don't want you to end up like your cousin Anna," said my mom, serving my dad two slices.

Whenever my parents brought up my errant cousin Anna, battle stations were generally at full alert.

"Anna's fine," I said.

I was adopted when I was an infant, but my parents still treated me like they were holding the purchase receipt and might decide at any moment to return me.

"Because she was sent to a convent and became a nun," said my dad.

Although Anna and I had never met, pre-nun Anna was a true hero of mine. Her family lived a few towns away and her legendary exploits were still spoken in reverent tones around her neighborhood. This enthralled me to no end. Anna was only two years older than me which inspired me to believe there would be adventure in my life as well. True, we weren't blood cousins, but I still felt the same thrill coursing through my veins. A few years ago, Anna was sent to a convent in Rome after a few too many late nights and morning-after hangovers. She stayed on and became a nun, completely repentant of her wicked ways. That was the part of her story I never enjoyed. I always wanted to hear the full story of Anna and her relationship with the Italian nuns. Had they been able to show her the proverbial light or had Anna simply faked piety?

I knew the right thing to do was end the trajectory of this conversation by changing the subject. But I couldn't let go of my fear.

"Are you going to give me up like Anna's parents did?"

My parents, clean-cut suburbanites, flustered easily. "We're just so worried about you."

"If you've been good parents, you shouldn't have to worry!"

Okay, I went a bit far. But at that point, the tense silence in the air made it impossible to take it back.

"Young lady..."

I stormed off before they could finish. I left the house, hoping things would simmer down in a few hours.

I went out exploring. In my little suburb, exploring meant walking to the mall. I wandered around by myself, window-shopping the smaller mall stores, waiting for my life to begin. I wanted it to explode with passion and excitement. I wanted adventure and hijinks.

And just as I was thinking of hijinks, I found myself in front of the new Tobacconist Shoppe. I had heard rumors that the back of the store operated as a head shop. Well, this was too much mystery for me to handle. I had to know.

I innocently made my way into the store. A few respectable-looking customers milled about, inspecting silver lighters and mahogany pipes. No one made furtive glances to the back of the store, so I assumed they were either shopping for legitimate tobacco purchases or were paranoid of narcs arresting them for trying to get high.

I screwed up my courage and made a bee-line to the back. Past the shelves of foreign tobacco paraphernalia, I was confronted by an enormous Grateful Dead beaded curtain and Indian sitar music. Glass cases displayed bongs of every shape and size. There was a revolving pillar of rolling paper samples. Groovy, tie-dye lighters were arranged beside paisley bandanas and hemp blankets. Vials of patchouli oil mingled with multi-colored incense sticks. Wood and jade Buddhas observed the proceedings from meditative poses.

I thought I had died and gone to Stoner World.

"Can I help you?" said a familiar voice.

I turned around and there was Eddie.

"Eddie, what are you doing here?"

"I work here part time. Great employee discount."

I unconsciously combed my hair with my fingers.

"So, you think you're the Lone Ranger?" I said with a kidding lilt.

"More like the Stoned Ranger," he said and laughed. "Weed." He laughed some more at the sound of the word.

My notion of Eddie took on a different feeling. Perhaps I had been wrong about him.

"So," he said. "What brings you here?"

"Browsing."

"No one ever comes back here to just look. You're either lost or buying."

"Actually, I'm kinda screwed," I said, immediately regretting both the intimacy of my confession and the word choice describing my circumstance.

"Really?" said Eddie, moving toward me from behind the counter, where he had been taking bong inventory.

"You know, it's sort of because of you. But not really. My parents busted me. They're threatening to send me off to a convent in Italy."

Eddie's eyes widened. "Italy? Seriously? Where in Italy?"

"Near Rome. Why?"

He moved in closer, looking around conspiratorially. Our common paranoia bonded us in the back of the head shop.

"You need to let me know when you're going to Rome. I have a big package that needs to be picked up," he said.

"Hold on. I'm not going to Rome. My parents were just kidding. At least I hope they were."

He relaxed and the look of intensity that overcame his face regressed back to the stoner façade.

"Just promise me that if you ever go to Rome, I'm the first one you tell. I got big business with guys over there," he said.

"I can't imagine how I'd go. And if my parents send me to Italy, there's a pretty good chance I'm not coming back. So don't hold your breath."

"No problem," he said. "I have another courier that's going soon, anyway."

Eddie ducked behind the counter and rolled a joint. He popped back up and offered it to me. "On the house." He was getting cuter by the second.

The beaded curtain parted grandly and Mrs. Querrel, sporting her ubiquitous bright orange-dyed hair and fur coat, entered grandly like a suburban Norma Desmond. She immediately began wiping her eyes and coughing.

"Shit," whispered Eddie. "Come here."

I hurried behind the counter. Eddie grabbed my head and pulled me down.

"Hey…" I said.

"I'll explain later. You don't want to get busted."

"Not that. Watch my hair."

I tucked myself into a ball behind the counter and positioned my head for maximum eavesdropping. Now, this was more like it. This was the sort of adventure I sought.

"Good afternoon, Lady… I mean, Mrs. Querrel," said Eddie. "What brings you to this fine establishment?" For a stoner, he was remarkably composed.

"Cut the crapola, Eddie," said Mrs. Querrel. "I'm here to square away the details of your trip."

Eddie looked down nervously at me. I pretended to be more interested in the joint in my hand. Classic eavesdropping technique.

"I can't, Mrs. Querrel, I..."

"You do not want to say no to me, Eddie. We need you for this transaction."

"I can't get a passport, okay? I have a record for dealing and they won't give me one. Believe me, I tried. Plus, I got a narc following me, okay? I can't go. Sorry," said Eddie. He sounded sincere. This was turning out to be quite a juicy afternoon.

"A narc? What does he look like?"

"He's, like, my age, maybe."

"Oh my God," said Mrs. Querrel. "Listen very carefully. Does he have a large mole under his right eye?"

"Jesus, how did you..."

"Never mind," said Mrs. Querrel. "You're right. Until I can figure out who this cop is, you're not going to Rome."

"Mrs. Q, I'm way ahead of you. I paid this other kid to go in my place. Charley Welsham. He's going with that faggy boys' chorus you bankroll. He don't know what the real deal is. Only that he's got to pick up a package for me in Rome when he's there. It's beautiful. If he gets caught, I deny ever knowing him. Pretty smart, huh?"

There was a silence between them. No wonder Eddie wanted me to duck under the counter. This was major illegal and major exciting. It was weird about the cop with the mole under his right eye.

"And you thought of this all by yourself, did you?" said Mrs. Querrel.

"Yup. You're still taking that choir with you as cover, aren't you?"

"You're a much smarter boy than I give you credit for, Eddie."

"Thanks."

"Except the choir trip is off, you idiot," said Lady Bear. "I told you we couldn't sponsor the trip."

"Well, you've got lots of money," said Eddie. "Like, you can figure this out, I'm sure. And there's one more thing."

"What is it now?" said Lady Bear, in disbelief that she was transacting in the back of a head shop.

"It's nothing. Actually, it might be good. This Charley kid was nervous about picking up the package by himself, so he got some other kid to go with him. I think Charley is going to pay this other kid to do the pickup, so we're even further removed from the situation. If you know what I mean."

"That's very good, Eddie. Now, someone else knows our business. Do you know the name of this other kid?"

I took a hit off the joint. Not wanting to give away my position, I opened a cabinet under the counter and exhaled into it, quickly closing the cabinet door. I looked up and saw Eddie squinching his face as if he was thinking very hard.

"Got it. It's Eli. Eli Mitchell."

"Eli?" said Mrs. Querrel. "Really? Well, well. Thank you, Eddie. I'll be in touch. Do tell me if this narc comes to call."

I heard the beaded curtains tinkle and knew the coast was clear.

"What the hell was that all about?" I said, standing up and straightening my clothes.

"It might be better if you don't know," said Eddie. "Could get too hot."

"What do you mean?" I asked. This Rome business was eating away at me. Here I was searching for adventure and Eddie had business connections with Italian dealers. Plus, he mentioned Eli who I desperately wanted to meet.

"Don't worry about it. Hey, how's that joint treating you?" said Eddie, clumsily trying to change the subject.

I opened my purse. "Well, here," I said, handing Eddie the Roman opera ticket I had found in one of Mrs. Clancy's Clit Lits. "If you need proof that I know my way around Rome."

"Where'd you get this?" he said.

"You're not the only one with secrets," I said in my most seductive tone. I was just getting a buzz so the tone might have come out more spacey than seductive. Either way. Eddie leaned in, interested.

"You know," he whispered. "Business here is up, but all these guys keep coming in looking for drug deals and it's making me paranoid."

"But it's a head shop. What the hell do you think all that rolling paper is for? How many cowboys live in this town making their own cigarettes?" I asked.

A man in his early thirties came into the back of the shop, avoiding eye contact.

"See what I mean?" said Eddie.

I walked over to the front of the store to wait out the customer. I watched Eddie selling him some rolling paper. In his nervousness, Eddie accidentally dropped the Clit Lit bookmark into the man's shopping bag. The man walked past me on his way out of the store. Something about this man seemed off to me. Instead of continuing my conversation with Eddie, I followed the man out of the store. He made a left toward Macy's. I stayed in front of the Tobacconist Shoppe and kept an eye on him. The mall wasn't that crowded. The man did a strange thing a few stores down, near the pretzel cart. He gave the shopping bag to another man. I couldn't get a look at the other man but as soon as he had the bag, he ran out of the mall.

I re-joined Eddie who was back to counting bongs.

"So, Eddie," I said coyly. "What's in Italy that you need so badly?"

He looked in every direction to make sure no one was around.

"You ever hear of Romatene?"

CHAPTER SEVEN

***Grandioso**—Indication that the entire composition is to be played grandly.*

My Uncle Jacob told my mom that business was actually picking up at Tijuana Meatball since I had left. That pronouncement encouraged my mom to let me stay in the choir. She seemed sad that she wasn't seeing much of Rasper when she dropped me off or picked me up. Parents weren't allowed in rehearsals. Rasper would come out of the school occasionally and wave to her or stop by her car to talk briefly, but there was a room filled with choirboys and always dozens of other parents clamoring for his attention. My mom knew she wouldn't be spending her August with Rasper in Italy and that didn't help her mood. She felt entitled to that trip. I knew how she felt.

I got her to agree over a chicken stew dinner a few nights earlier that if I could figure out a way to pay my way for the Italy trip, I could go. My mom smiled and said fine, and she would do the same. Her tone told me she might as well have agreed to send me to the moon for Hanukkah.

I had two problems that kept me from Italy and the search for my dad's past: the money for the trip and the fact I was still a damn alto in the choir and needed to become a tenor just to be invited on the tour. At least I had parental consent to go if I came up with the money. I had a plan cooking for my alto dilemma.

As I walked into rehearsal, I met up with Charley. We had let bygones be bygones. I asked him if his parents were back from their travels yet. I didn't understand why his parents, who were so wealthy and connected, couldn't sponsor the Italy tour.

"Sorry, Eli," said Charley as we took our seats. "My folks have bigger organizations to sponsor."

"Do they know Lady Bear?"

I figured rich people hung out together. Then Charley clarified something about rich people I hadn't known.

"My parents really only deal with New York City people. The burbs are considered community service for them. They're slumming here. What do they say? It makes them feel grounded. Just like sending me to public school and letting me be in the choir."

So, there were different striations of rich. Only Charley's parents would consider Lady Bear middle class.

Rehearsal began. We sat in a self-inflicted caste system: sopranos, altos, tenors, and baritones. Like four mini-gangs clustered in the same room, reading new sheet music while Hubert and his wife played it through for the second time. The new piece, a coronation mass in Latin, was fairly complex which was the reason for the second read-through. Typically, we'd be expected to sight-read the music on the first pass. The rest of the time associated with a new song was devoted to harmonizing and phrasing.

At the first break, I noticed some of the kids had gathered around Big Francis. He was the baritone I saw with Florinda at my first rehearsal. Usually, Big Francis kept to himself or joined a few of the other exceedingly large and ferocious-looking kids in a jolly and sporting game called Atomic Wedgies for the Weaker Kids.

Big Francis had been a soprano years ago. I'd seen pictures of him performing with his thick afro, wide-open moon face, innocent eyes, dark brown skin, and beautiful expression, as if his most wicked thought involved farting nuns.

From what I understood, he had grown up fast and hard. He was eighteen and on the verge of being a full-fledged hood. His parents had divorced a few years earlier and rumor was he had no parental guidance. His mom had moved out and his dad was a traveling salesman. Big Francis was a senior but only went to school when he wanted, had a part-time job loading furniture into delivery trucks, another part-time job as a sous chef at a Greek restaurant, and regularly went to bed after midnight. Subsequently, he could juggle couches or souvlaki with ease and was rumored to never having lost a fight. He also turned to professional wrestling as a part time means to pay bills.

We were in awe of him and there wasn't one choir boy who didn't consider him, in some fashion, a hero. In a choir filled with outsiders and weirdos, the act of Big Francis showing up for rehearsals and blending his voice with ours was downright astonishing.

I think he needed this choir to keep some kind of balance in his life. He knew he would never run into his own crowd at rehearsals or any of our concerts and that anonymity brought him some level of comfort and satisfaction. He was only one of two African-American kids in the choir. The other was my fellow alto, Terrence, who was always smiling. Terrence was still one of the few choir boys who was friendly with me.

Big Francis was a tenor and, truthfully, I didn't think he deserved to go to Italy. He had way too much other cool stuff going on in his world. He could easily have missed this trip and not lost out on any awesome memories. He'd be having too much fun wrestling for money and spending it all on his girlfriends. I really envied him. Italy was all I had to cling to. With Big Francis out of the way, the choir would be short one trained tenor and Rasper would practically beg me to go. At least, that was my plan.

During the rehearsal break, I approached the gang of altos and tenors that had congregated around Big Francis, whose head bobbed slowly from side to side as if he was sparring with some unknown force in slow motion.

"Eli," he exclaimed. "Great. Here."

He handed me a combination padlock and walked off. Everyone followed this Pied Piper out of the rehearsal room into the hallway. I went after them, trailing behind.

"We fixing a locker?" I said.

No one answered. Some of the kids looked scared. Regardless, they continued following Big Francis; his tight afro acting like the flag of a tour bus guide. He led us out of the school and into the dark June night.

Just moments earlier, we had been choirboys, joyously singing in the Hicksville Junior High School rehearsal room. Now, we stood in the middle of a damp and humid football field at night.

Charley menacingly waived a recorder—the poor plastic cousin of the flute. I looked at the other boys. Some of them held combination locks in their hands while others held dusty, gray music stands as big as lunch trays. Three kids held rocks. They all squeezed their weapons, hoping that tightening their grip would release courage.

Big Francis reached into his jacket pocket and took out a switch blade. With practiced ease, he let loose the thin, steel blade. Even in the early light of the stars, it glistened with ominous purpose.

The only one missing from our makeshift gang was Little Francis.

We called him Little Francis since Big Francis demanded we do so. Big Francis moonlighted as a professional wrestler with the stage name of Tiger Claw but was insecure enough to believe someone might confuse the two of them.

Little Francis was a slightly more wooden version of Howdy Doody. He even looked like the little dummy if you performed surgery on old Howdy and removed any semblance of personality, defiance, or charm and just left an angel's voice. In short, Little Francis was a perfect vocal instrument.

He'd always cry from sitting too long. Sometimes, he'd wet himself, having been too timid to ask Rasper for a bathroom break. But he could sing like a sweet bird; his voice a honeyed wave of light that made you feel the presence, if not the very existence, of a higher power. That's why no one bothered him. There was a running bet, however, that once his voice changed, Little Francis would get the snot beat out of him on an alarmingly routine basis. Nine out of ten times, beautiful soprano voices didn't morph into beautiful tenor or baritone voices. His voice was going to be average, statistically speaking.

In general, sopranos were strictly off-limits when it came to being the brunt of practical jokes. No one was allowed to Super-Glue their butt cheeks shut and pop them open by having them fall backward on a hard surface.

You needed to have your voice start to shift a bit downward in scale to partake of that singular pleasure. You had to be an alto like me. Luckily, Big

Francis was not amused by my ass-cheek-popping prowess and moved on after the first week, shark-like, in search of more entertaining prey.

Altos were the oddity of the choir. For a full, traditional choir sound, you needed the angel voices of the sopranos, the desperately longing ache of the tenors, and the cavernous reassurance and harmonics of the basses. Altos were window-dressing. Filler.

Altos were a no-man's land between child and man. Their voices cracked. Their parts could be sung by burly, Hungarian women. Rarely did the melody come our way. And that was fine with me since I was unjustly placed with the altos. I was biding my time before I got promoted to a tenor.

Rasper's genius was to gather some of the toughest, surliest sons of bitches from after-school detention rooms, high-school football teams, and, in the case of Big Francis, professional wrestling and make them sing. Rasper would recruit with the passion, savvy, and finesse of a seasoned college admissions officer to the point parents had no choice but to simply transfer custody of their child over to him. These potentially future convicts quietly and slowly disappeared into the folds of the choir's robes, molded by Rasper and his respectability.

"What's going on here?" said one of the altos.

"Shut up," Big Francis said. He looked past us into the dark outer circle of the junior high football field, expecting to find something.

Charley leaned over to me, temporarily putting his recorder back into its cloth case which hung off his belt like a scabbard.

"It's a gang fight," Charley explained with utter surrender. "This kid, Daryl, sent a note to Big Francis, challenging him to a fight and the kid turned out to be this big gang leader. But you know Big Francis. He told this kid to bring his whole gang."

"So, we're waiting out here in the cold for a gang to come and beat us up? Like 'West Side Story?'"

"Big Francis said he found out the other gang only has eight kids. We have more than that," Charley said in a surreal logic.

We both smiled faintly in recognition that from a distance, we did seem treacherous as a group, just as long as you didn't take a close look.

Big Francis walked over to see what all the whispering was about.

"Sorry, Big Francis," Charley said.

Big Francis looked us over the way a drill sergeant inspects his troops.

"Welsham, where's your weapon?" he barked. Charley took out his recorder and instinctively started playing it. Big Francis slapped it away from him.

"No noise, moron. We want them to think it's a big-ass knife fight, not the fuckin' town parade," whispered Big Francis.

As Charley reached down to search for his beloved musical instrument, Big Francis directed his unstable and cold eyes at me.

"Eli, let me show you how to hold that thing." He grabbed the combination lock out of my hands and demonstrated its purpose tonight. He slipped the lock's clasp over his middle finger, holding the lock itself in the palm of his hand. He wrapped his hand tightly around the lock and held out his hand to me.

"Brass knuckles, Eli," he said quietly. "The poor man's brass knuckles."

When Big Francis walked away, Charley whispered, "Eli, can I have the brass knuckles?"

I gladly handed the combination lock over to Charley. I stepped back when Charley said, "Here. Trade."

He handed me a four-inch switchblade in the shape of a Venetian gondola.

"Charley, where the hell did you get this? The Godfather gift shop?"

"Shut up and keep it. I like the combo lock better."

"Stick to the recorder," I said as he walked away. I pocketed the gondola blade. It was times like this I was certain Charley had a whole other life I wasn't aware of.

There was a rustling noise in the distant field by the hole in the fence that led out to the Chevrolet dealership.

"It sounded like a twig breaking," said Kenneth, a tenor.

"Maybe it's the gang of kids," said Charley.

"I bet it's the largest kid in the gang climbing through the fence, forcing it open," said Terrence, an alto.

"Or a twig. Probably, the noise was a twig," I said.

We all looked up, trying to filter out the wind and passing traffic. Our ears, ordinarily attuned to discerning minor chord differentials in Beethoven symphonic movements, hunted for any potential sound of threat. We quietly shifted closer together. Without any direction or prompting from anyone, we had moved into our choir performance positions: sopranos to the left in front, altos to the right, tenors behind the sopranos, and baritones behind the altos. Rasper would have been proud.

We waited in that wet field for what seemed like hours. The whole event only lasted three minutes. There was a pattering of feet running behind us. We spun around in unison.

It was Little Francis.

"Hey, you guys, Rasper is calling us," said Little Francis with sweet innocence. "Break's over."

And with that, it was over.

"Pussies! Fags!" yelled Big Francis into the darkness toward the fence. There was no response. We assumed he was calling out to the rival gang. He turned to us. "Let's go inside. It worked. We scared them off."

"Francis," yelled Rasper. Big Francis actually flinched when he heard the bark. Rasper had stepped outside to search for his missing choir. We all averted our eyes from Big Francis getting busted.

I remained a respectable distance away but still leaned in to hear.

"Sorry, Mr. Rasper, I was just fooling around with the other kids," he said, suddenly demure.

"I have spoken to you before about this. These kids look up to you. Decorum, my boy. Decorum."

And with that, Rasper walked away, waving his hands to herd us back into the rehearsal room. Big Francis trotted happily along with the rest of us.

I turned to Charley and we held back from the others. "What the hell just happened?"

"What do you mean?"

"Charley," I whispered. "I paid this guy Daryl to pretend to be a gang leader. There's no rival gang. We live in the suburbs. It was a fake threat to get Francis kicked out."

Charley let out a small, surprised laugh. "You should have checked with me first," he said.

"Why?"

"Because Big Francis is Rasper's favorite. Rasper's even paying for his tuition. He won't ever be kicked out."

I was beside myself. All my hard work and planning were ruined by a freak coincidence of kindness and circumstance.

Charley and I made it back into the rehearsal room and we all took our seats.

Before we began, Rasper walked to the rehearsal room door and opened it grandly. The Great Dowager Empress Lady Bear waltzed into the room, draped in her fur. She scanned the choir, looking for someone. Rasper stood by the piano, deferring to her like she was the monarchy. He let out a little cough when Lady Bear's eyes met mine. Her scanning ceased. I was the target she was trying to acquire.

"Mr. Mitchell, we have not formerly met yet," said Lady Bear. "I pride myself on meeting all new choir members. I am Mrs. Querrel. I have been associated with this choir throughout its entire existence. You have heard of me?"

I didn't know how to answer that. That was like the sun asking the beach if they had previously had the pleasure.

"It's an honor," I said in my most obsequious tone.

"Very good," said Lady Bear. "Douglas?"

Rasper took a step forward and cleared his throat. "Boys, I have very good news indeed," he said. "We have found a sponsor for our Italy tour after all. The trip is back on. The Welshams have graciously offered to sponsor the entire tour. Let's all thank Charles and his parents for their generosity. Thank you!"

Charley turned red in disbelief.

CHAPTER EIGHT

Impromptu—*A short piano piece, often improvisational and intimate in character.*

April was grounded for two weeks for her part in the Great Clit Lit Robbery. This had no small effect on my social life, never mind on April's. My first mission was getting April a boyfriend. It would give her something to look forward to and would be my way of making up for the trouble I helped get her in. April was naturally shy and would never admit to the need for a beau, but I knew in my heart she was desperate. So, for that matter, was I.

I spotted that tall boy, Eli, from the diner, walking around my neighborhood a few days earlier and my heart instantly melted. It made me forget all about Eddie. I decided I just had to meet Eli. I mean, April wasn't the only one in need of a beau. I was on constant lookout.

Two days after I decided to help out April with her boyfriend problem, I found a boy for her. His name was Daryl, and he was a former Wall member. Although, from what I heard, he left voluntarily as part of a self-imposed policy to clean up so he could get into a respectable college. We met at the mall, and he sounded interested. He seemed perfect for April who was equally conservative and studiously minded.

I invited April and Daryl over to my house so they could meet. Part of the delight of this plan was that it would be a blind date. How good a friend was I? And how lucky for Daryl I had run into him and arranged for this meeting.

The doorbell rang.

Daryl stood at my front door. He wore suburban-issue summer clothing: Billy Joel concert t-shirt, cut-off denim shorts, and sneakers. He looked younger than his eighteen years. But mostly, he looked kind and happy to be here. I invited him in.

"Nice house," he said. He seemed nervous, which struck me as odd. I wondered for the first time if he had a girlfriend and whether this whole April set-up would be a washout.

"How's about we sneak off to the backyard? It's so much nicer there," I said, leading him through the house.

"When's everyone else getting here?"

I recalled my fabricated story that got Daryl here. Something about a summer barbecue while my parents were at work.

"Oh, they'll be here in a half-hour. You're early," I said. "No one's here but me."

"Great."

I escorted him to my backyard. The built-in swimming pool glistened in the afternoon sun. The cabana next to the pool gave me an idea. We never used the cabana. In the summer, it was just an empty cedar structure barely tall enough for an adult to stand in. It had one door on the pool side and a small window on the opposite side that faced the street. In the winter, it became a storage shed.

"You know what would be fun?" I said. "If you hid in the cabana and jumped out to surprise everyone when they got here."

My plan was to let April know I had a surprise for her. I'd take her to the cabana and Daryl would pop out. Perfect.

"Cool. But you hide in there with me," he said. "I'm kinda scared of small places."

There was something innocent about him. I figured I could still pop out and surprise April with her summer gift.

The inside of the cabana was hotter than I expected. I closed the door and opened the small window which let in the only light. I peered through the small crack in the doorway, waiting for April.

"This is going to be a blast!" I said, trying to maintain Daryl's spirit for the thing.

"I like that we're alone in here," he said. I turned around. He had removed his shirt.

Oh dear. I knew that look in his eye.

"Now, Daryl," I said calmly. "You have this all wrong. We're not here to..."

Suddenly, I heard April's voice outside by the pool. Thank God. I was about to ask Daryl to stay put so I could have a chat with April when I heard another voice. A man's voice. I peered out through the small crack between the door and the jamb.

It was Eddie. What was he doing here? I squinted and saw him talking to April. They were both giving the back of my house a good survey in search of me.

Daryl, bare-chested, was slowly making his way toward me.

"Daryl, wait here while I have a quick talk with April. Do you know April? She's great."

I was just coming around to the idea of this impromptu double-date when I heard yet another voice. Another peer through the crack.

Oh my God! It was Eli, the cute boy I had seen a few days ago. For whatever reason, I could not get him out of my mind. What was going on? I listened closely.

"Eli, what's up, man?" asked Eddie.

"Looking for you," said Eli.

Apparently, April had invited half the neighborhood to a party that I never agreed to. Of all the nerve. How dare she try to set up a gathering behind my back?

But wait. I couldn't come out of the cabana now to meet Eli. Not with Daryl in the cabana. Not with the look in Daryl's eyes, not to mention his denim-covered erection. Too much time had now passed and our presence together in the cabana would seem entirely suspicious. Especially if I didn't convince Daryl to put his shirt back on.

There was only one true and adult course of action.

"Come on Daryl, we're going out through the window."

"Huh?" He didn't seem especially pleased by this development. "Why?"

A fair question but one I didn't have the time to answer.

"Later. I'll explain later."

"No way."

"Look," I said, suddenly conspiratorial. "There's a narc out there and I wouldn't want you wrapped up in my business. The window faces the street so no one will see us."

That about seemed to do it. He opened the window and helped me up through it. I wriggled through with minimum embarrassment. I imagine I may have given Daryl a bit of a show during my exit as well. I stood outside and quietly asked Daryl to come through. I grabbed his hand to help him.

"I can't do it," he said, breathing heavily.

"I'm sorry. You can fit."

"It's not that. I'm scared of small spaces."

"But you're already in a small space and you're trying to get to a big space."

This last comment flew towards Daryl's head but made no purchase. I needed another tactic.

"Daryl," I said quietly, still holding his hand through the window. "Do you happen to be a Cesarean baby?"

"I have no idea. Why?"

"Same concept here."

Somehow, this seemed to do the trick. I began pulling him through. Halfway, he got stuck.

At the same time, I overheard Eli telling Eddie, "I'd love to go to Italy but don't have the funds. Sorry."

"Come on, Eli," said Eddie. "I hear you're great at coming up with schemes. Charley's always telling me about stuff you're cooking up. You can figure out a way to go."

"Wish I could," said Eli.

"Well, I gotta go find Jane," said Eddie to Eli and April.

"Jane? Is that the tall girl with, like, the really nice green eyes?"

Oh my God!

With a sweaty heave, I birthed Daryl through the window and onto my lawn. He lay in a sweaty clump, disoriented. I took off and ran around the house, entering through a side door that led to the den. Thankfully, no one was home. Now I could pretend I had been inside all along. Then I thought of Daryl and how he might spill our little adventure. I couldn't have him ruin my chances with Eli. I ran out my front door and across my front lawn towards the cabana. I hadn't gotten so much exercise in an entire year's worth of gym class.

When I got there, Daryl was gone. I rushed to the back of the house by the pool. No one was there. Where did they all go?

The doorbell rang. I ran around the house and ducked inside through the side door again. Out of breath, I opened my door, trying to appear calm.

"Hello," I said.

It was my old boyfriend, Morgan. The one I had gone out with for three months, the one who had broken up with me badly, the one who had broken my heart. He was still obsessed with me. He had lied about his age. It turned out he was four years older than me! I found that romantic and creepy, all at the same time.

"Jane," he said. "How are you?"

This was awkward.

"Fine," I said coolly. My eyes were darting back and forth in search of my recent party guests. "What do you want?" The last statement came out a bit crueler than I wanted. He still had the large mole under his right eye. It didn't seem as sexy now in the harsh light of not dating him.

"Looking for Eddie. Thought I saw him walk back here. I asked this Eli kid, but he didn't know. You know Eddie?"

"That's all you have to say to me?" I asked and slammed the door on him.

I ran upstairs to my room and closed the door. I looked out the window and saw Morgan driving away. If it was summer adventure I sought, I didn't need to leave the confines of my house.

Where did everyone go? And why were people always running out on me?

CHAPTER NINE

***Portamento**—A mild glissando between two notes for an expressive effect.*

There was this awkward three-week period when my high school was still in session and the Long Island Boys Choir would transition from rehearsals across the street at the junior high to performing summer concerts in New York City and around Long Island. What I hated most about the mid-week midday concerts was the boys' locker room. The choir allowed boys from ages eight to eighteen. That put two-thirds of us in junior high or high school. The good news was we got out of school early. Generally, concerts started around 7:00 p.m. which meant we needed to get on the road at 3:00 p.m. at the latest. This was mostly due to horrible traffic driving from Hicksville into Manhattan. Rasper was maniacal about punctuality.

Rasper had a strict and diligent work ethic that considered allowances for traffic, forgotten music, sick children, re-arrangements of harmonies, staging, re-assigned solos due to said sick children, stage parents, bathroom breaks, and any other possible distractions. His schedules always included arriving early to our venue to receive payment for our non-denominational entertainment and uplifting services, investigate the acoustics, assess the audience demographics, evaluate the theatrical potential of our performance by checking lighting cues, whether there was a proper stage, backstage, curtains, and whether said received payment would pass muster with its originating fiduciary establishment. After Rasper did all this, he would have his dinner of a half-quart of scotch.

Rasper, I came to understand, was insane. But the alcohol seemed to keep his already exuberant energy and attention to detail down to a somewhat humanistic manic level. His slicked-down shock of hair, sharp facial features, and deep, penetrating eyes convinced anyone who spent more than a passing moment with him that he was the genius in residence.

I was in my eleventh-grade science class peering through a microscope at something that looked like it had been coughed up by a smoker. An announcement wafted over the rusty P.A. system.

"Elias Mitchell and Charles Welsham. Please report to the office. Thank you."

The class laughed and began to whistle at me until the teacher, in the middle of repairing a Bunsen burner, poked his head up and hushed them. He nodded at me for dismissal. That wasn't too bad. Until we complained recently, they used to announce our names and say we were to report for pickup in front of the school for a choir concert and that we were free to get changed in the boys' locker room. They might as well have strung blood sausages around our necks and thrown us into a hyena den. You had to love public school.

I didn't fit in with most of the kids in my high school. But I was also indifferent to my outsider status. I knew high school was a temporary thing and most of my life lay in wait outside the doors of graduation. I imagined I got this optimistic view from my dad. I figured that's how he was able to endure hardships in his little village in Italy before coming to America. My attitude regularly drew the scorn and consternation of less secure boys. And all because I had a deep appreciation for the arts. Well, not only an appreciation. I participated fully, whole-heartedly, and unashamedly in dramatic productions, musicals, community theater, and church productions (despite being a Jew). I sang in chorus, played cornet in the school orchestra, and had absolutely no interest or clue about sportsball.

This tended to single me out. Now, unfortunately, what didn't help my social situation was that I was precocious as a prince and smart ass as a pauper. The sports team getting ready in the locker room derived enormous pleasure and not insubstantial joy at pummeling the crap out of me.

Despite my interests in the arts, I was straight, but the sports team always assumed I was gay. I attributed their behavior to being heathens.

So, there we were, Charley and I, in the locker room, putting away our public-school street clothes, and donning our crisp white shirts, black polyester pressed pants, black rayon socks, shiny black dress shoes, plaid bow ties, plaid cummerbunds, and creamy white dinner jackets.

This particular afternoon, as we dressed in the locker room, we were lucky there were just some straggling kids late for gym and the football or rugby team wasn't in full barbaric attendance.

"Did you get a hold of your parents yet?" I asked. I was fascinated by this latest development that, out of nowhere, Charley's parents had sponsored the entire Italy tour. Most of me was excited but, I have to admit, a peevish part of me was disgusted the choir was going without me. It also burned me that adults had that kind of money and sway over other people's lives.

"Yesterday. They're still in Tahiti so the reception wasn't great," said Charley. He sat down on the wooden bench in the middle of the lockers rows to put on his shoes. "They said they might be sponsoring this. They couldn't remember."

"Honestly?"

"They said they just can't keep track with all the things they sponsor."

"Can you just ask them to adopt me?" I said.

"My dad said to check with our accountant and then the line went dead."

We stood up and faced the mirrors to tie our bow ties. Rasper took great pride in having his little soldiers know how to tie real bow ties. He always envisioned us as mini-men about town, Cole Porterettes, roués, and cads.

"What did the accountant say?" I said.

"I have no idea. Do you know how many accountants they have? Rhode Island has fewer people."

We finished getting ready and headed out of the locker room. The two of us proceeded down the hallway toward the main doors of the school. This drastic transformation in appearance always drew attention. Over time, we developed a protective stance that involved us walking back-to-back, protecting each other; fox-hole buddies with a common purpose. We would walk in this fashion while we circled so we each had a full 360-degree view of any village raiders.

As always, for just a few, naïve, innocent moments, I was a secret spy or a superhero in his bat cave, answering a distress call with a license to kill. I was suave, debonair, capable of ridiculously muscular feats, and courageous as a wolf with hair-trigger instincts to match. I wasn't just an eleventh-grader trying to get through his school day and extra-curricular activities. I wasn't even an exceptionally lucky eleventh-grader with the drive, pluck, grades, and voice sufficient to be in this professional choir. I was removed from my life for those few seconds as I donned my cool white dinner jacket, prepared for world adventure.

Then my head got slammed into a locker door by orangutan paws and I momentarily dropped the superhero and spy angle. The paws belonged to some sportsball player senior who used to be friends with me in first grade. But around third grade, he was twice my height and by sixth grade, twice my weight. Now, his life's greatest pleasure was apparently trying to crack my head open like a coconut.

Charley ran toward the front door. I got up as orangutan-boy laughed himself silly. I was a bit wobbly but did my best Harrison Ford to dash out of the evil mastermind's lair before it blew up. If only.

Charley and I waited in front of the school in our full regalia, thankful that Rasper was rarely late. We looked like waiters on our way to a Club Babaloo convention hoping to get Ricky's autograph. Even the teachers would open their classroom windows and yell out disparagements with all the wit that comes with serving within the public-school system in a blue-collar neighborhood.

The Maxivan pulled up, already filled with other white-jacketed boys. "The Long Island Boys Choir" was painted on the side of the van in a fanciful font, like some strange version of the Partridge Family bus, so as not to be confused with a van filled with boys who are ready and equipped to provide one with catering services.

The door opened and Rasper barked something about getting our hindquarters inside the van since there was time to make up. Most of what he said sailed past me and didn't really register. To me, he was simply the gatekeeper to this world I truly loved.

As the Maxivan left the school grounds, orangutan-boy had gathered his fellow primates outside the school and they chased us. I felt victorious, albeit temporarily, when we left them all in the dust.

As we proceeded into New York City, I left my student world and rejoined this magical one. The Long Island Boys Choir had thirty members. We were generally split equally among sopranos, altos, tenors, and baritones although there were usually more sopranos and altos than the rest. Tenors and baritones tended to quit the choir when they got their driver's licenses or discovered some vice that offered more wicked pleasure than the choir had to offer. I was frustratingly still an alto.

The kids were all white except for Big Francis and Terrence. Of the current members, I was the only Jew. In addition, I was one of only nine that were straight, as far as I could figure. It's hard to tell with some of the eight-year-olds.

The choir was billed as non-denominational but near as I could see, everyone but me was very denominational. That suited me just fine. I was an outsider in a group of outsiders so, in a strange way, I felt comfortably at home in my usual role of social oddity.

I was still consumed with how I was going to afford this Italy trip. I had no savings and there wasn't enough time to actually work for the money. Well, there may have been, but the consideration was fleeting at best. This was the time in my life when I wished I had a wealthy aunt or at least a wealthy aunt's inheritance.

"How's your head?" asked Charley. We were sitting together in the back of the van.

"Spongy," I said.

I was still amazed Charley persisted in the public school system and withstood Rasper's orders. He had the social position to put it all behind him. He had the kind of wealth and resources I yearned for and yet he chose every day to live the life I lived.

"Tell me again about the orphanage?" I said. "It's not like 'Annie,' right?"

Charley had been providing me tales of this legendary Italian girls' orphanage outside Rome and how the choir was scheduled to perform a concert there. This was something out of my wildest fantasy. The idea of a sea of beautiful Italian high school girls watching and listening intently as we melted their hearts with our voices and harmonies was almost too much to bear. And I wanted to go to Italy more than ever.

"If I could learn about my dad and kiss an Italian orphan girl, my life would be complete," I said.

"I think my grandmother once knit that on a sampler."

We trudged through traffic into Manhattan. Our concert was at the Metropolitan Club, a members-only society where I was sure the membership application asked how many islands you owned. We disembarked from the Maxivan and met the rest of the choir members who had been shuttled to our destination by their parents.

The Metropolitan Club building was a multi-story, classic marble-column-and-granite-façade affair designed to bring to mind a homey visit with the emperor. We, of course, entered through the servant's entrance. An elderly tuxedoed black gentleman, wearing white cotton gloves, led us through a dark passageway into a large room. A long table was laid out with baloney sandwiches on paper plates and water in paper cups. This was either dinner for us or they were expecting a visit from Rikers Island convicts.

After we ate, there was still about an hour before our concert. Rasper, never to waste idle time, collected us all and held a quick rehearsal. We performed a cappella since there was no piano in the dungeon mess hall. Hubert stood in the corner during our rehearsal for moral support although I found it odd he kept looking at his watch. Florinda stood by his side in case he needed anything.

As soon as the rehearsal was over, Hubert bolted toward the door. He made a left out into the hallway though I knew the men's room was to the right. I stealthily left the choir and followed Hubert down the hallway and watched as he exited the building into the busy downtown Manhattan streets.

Once out in the street, it was harder for me to stay incognito. While I was surrounded by thousands of men in suits heading to bars or their homes, the fashion of the day was more deep blues, browns, and blacks, not bright, creamy white jackets, and plaid bow ties. Still, I managed to stay half a block behind Hubert as he turned down one street, then another. Finally, he tapped a buzzer and was let into an office building. I didn't dare to ring the buzzer when I got to the building. Mostly, I couldn't think of an excuse as to why I should be allowed entry. But I did get a chance to look at the building directory in the lobby through the front door glass. The building was an exclusive law office.

I retraced my steps back to the Metropolitan Club. Rasper never even noticed I had disappeared. Thirty minutes later, Hubert joined us as well. He whispered something to Florinda, but I couldn't hear it in the din of the rehearsal room.

The concert itself went fine. Polite applause surrounded us from the city's elite and I felt cultured and special. I also had the feeling the Metropolitan Club members would have been just as appreciative if three trained circus seals came to play bicycle horns.

It was customary after our concerts to go out and mingle with the audience. In the case of the super-rich Manhattanites, they felt it was part of their community service to pat our heads and nod approvingly that we came to sing for our suppers.

Rasper encouraged us all to make our rounds and say thank you to everyone in the room. After ten minutes, I noticed three patrons whom I expected to be there were missing. Lady Bear and Mr. and Mrs. Clancy were nowhere to be found. I asked the elderly man who had let us into the building earlier if he had seen them. He smiled and leaned down so he could whisper in my ear.

"Never mind those biddies," he said, almost cackling. "They're no longer members here. Can't step into this place and be broke at the same time."

CHAPTER TEN

***Development**—Where the musical themes and melodies are developed.*

April and I each leaned back on the swings in my backyard. I thought again how the more I believed I understood adults, the further off-base I was. The sun was shining and there was such a light, summer breeze that the birds couldn't help but sing. A few days had gone by and our moms, sitting at our backyard picnic table, had decided to lecture us about Clit Lit.

April's mother explained the Clit Lit books belonged to her, my mother, and assorted other neighborhood housewives. They had founded a bit of a secret book club. Not that they were getting together over tea and crumpets and reading aloud. It was like my friends and pot. One of us usually bought it and shared with everyone else.

We found out that usually April's mom bought the books but sometimes the other mothers would venture into Manhattan for a literary purchase. When I asked April's mom where she bought them, she went silent. This was the most adult conversation I had ever had. It wasn't just the content, although that was certainly exciting. It was the first time my mother spoke to me like an equal. I had always looked forward to that day. I just never thought it would be regarding the subject of masturbation.

Our moms' attitudes had changed in the past few days. Maybe some time had passed and they felt this was a rite of passage. Maybe they stopped thinking of us as little girls.

"So, one day, Mrs. Clancy overheard our conversation at the market," said April's mom. "About the books," she added in a whisper.

"And she asked us to borrow one. She even paid me five bucks," said my mom. "Well, we were just startled that a woman like her would be remotely interested in this sort of thing."

Our moms giggled and sounded like they were standing near their high-school lockers again. April and I looked at each other like we had stepped into the Twilight Zone and were watching ourselves in the future.

"But the woman kept coming back for more and more," continued my mom. "She became addicted."

"Jeez. And she paid us five dollars for each one," said April's mom. "She kept them from her husband. The new Mr. Clancy, whatever his name is. And she couldn't get enough. It was like she was buying the reefer and we were her reefer seller."

"Mom!" yelled April. There was only so much of this she could take. She was clearly uncomfortable with this whole scene and kept looking at our garden gate for a quick exit.

"Oh, April, please. Grow up," said her mom.

"So, what happened?" I asked, riveted to this story like it was one of my soaps.

"Well," my mom continued, "we decided we needed to put a stop to it. Although it was good money we were making. But it was getting, excuse the expression, out of hand."

Suddenly it occurred to me. Our moms weren't just burning the books, they were burning their guilt. They were starting fresh.

"But Mrs. Clancy had other plans," said April's mom. "She bought all the books. From everyone. At least from everyone willing to sell them. Now girls, you can never repeat any of this to anyone, you understand?"

"Wow," I said.

"We finally figured Mrs. Clancy was being puritanical and trying to cleanse the town of sin," said my mom.

"She paid us top dollar," added April's mom.

Then everyone got quiet. April stopped swinging which made me slow down. Eventually, our backyard was very still. Even the birds stopped singing.

"What?" I said.

"I don't know how to tell you," said my mom.

I suddenly felt like running away. I shifted in my swing and tried to prepare myself for bad news.

"We were hoping, that is, your mom and I, were hoping that we would make enough money from selling these books to Mrs. Clancy," said April's mom. "Because we had so many books, you see, we wanted to make enough to send you girls to Italy in August."

"To stay with your cousin Anna in Rome," said my mom.

"And we would get to spend our Summer of Love with our husbands," added April's mom.

"Oh my God," I said. April remained quiet, staring at the ground. I got the feeling none of this was news to her.

"We thought we'd have enough money, but Italy is more expensive than we imagined. Even staying at a convent," said my mom. "I know you must be disappointed. I'm so sorry, sweetie."

"We shouldn't have told them," said April's mom.

Our moms got up and headed inside.

"Let's go take a walk around the block," I said to April, taking her hand. As soon as we left my yard, I burst into laughter.

"Oh my God," I said. "Why would they even tell us that?"

"I'm so sorry, Jane," said April. She wasn't laughing.

"What's the matter?"

"You really want to know?" said April.

"Tell me."

"Even without the Clit Lit money, my mom says she can afford to send me to Italy. I don't think yours can."

I searched for something to say. "But, you don't even know my cousin Anna."

"I don't want to go without you," said April. She cried and hugged me.

I know it sounded selfish, but I was relieved April felt this way. And I really wanted to go to Italy now with her. I'm sure I could figure out a way to pay for it. After all, it was just airfare. Anna and her nuns could provide food and shelter. I'm sure they were all friendly like the ones who helped out the Von Trapps.

April and walked around our neighborhood for a while but I could tell she was getting sadder the more time we spent together. We said goodbye and she walked home. I continued pacing around the block trying to think my way through this.

Then it occurred to me. What was the one thing that, when presented to the rest of the Wall gang, would instantly allot me a lifetime membership and all the smoking, drinking, music, and bonking pleasures commensurate with enrollment?

Romatene. The magical, mystery drug. It was a myth, an urban legend. Romatene was the kind of drug kids in schoolyards joked about. It was cheap, nearly impossible to detect using conventional dog-sniffing techniques, and gave you a rush more powerful than cocaine followed by a paranoid-free mellowness that made pot seem like smoking caffeine.

In its natural state, it resembled a basil plant. It was non-addictive and pliable in its applications. You could smoke it. Hell, you could boil it into a drink. RomaTea.

My key to Romatene was Eddie. He mentioned an Italian courier earlier and the thought that he had a local connection intrigued me. How could a Lone Ranger-badge-wearing goofball like him be involved with such a delicious enterprise?

I went to Eddie's house but no one was home. His parents worked in the city, which was how Eddie had so much free, unsupervised time on his hands. I thought about his schedule. He seemed to have so many jobs.

The next day, I took the bus to the mall. April was working in the ice cream kiosk, making chocolate chip cookie ice cream sandwiches. I stopped over and asked when her next break was.

Fifteen minutes later, I walked into the head shop with reinforcements.

"What is it exactly we're doing here?" April asked.

"I need to ask Eddie something."

"Eddie? Eddie-Eddie?" she asked, appalled. "The one who got you expelled from the Wall?"

"And he's going to help me get back..." My voice trailed off.

Oh my God. It was Eli.

He was browsing in the head shop but was obviously waiting for someone. Probably Eddie. Eli was even cuter than I remembered. He saw me, smiled, then turned and bumped into the counter. He looked around as if he was embarrassed. I smiled back.

"What's going on?" asked April.

"It's him," I said.

"Eddie?"

"Eli."

At the mention of his name, he walked over.

"Hi," he said. "I've seen you before."

"Maybe at Debbie Dombrowski's Sweet Sixteen?" I asked.

"Maybe," he said. "I feel like there's a Sweet Sixteen every weekend. And they're all..."

"In someone's basement and kinda' blend into one another?" I asked.

Eli laughed. "You're funny, Jane."

"You know my name?"

"Of course. Well, yeah," he repeated. "I mean ... I'm..."

"Eli. Yeah, I know. You're friends with Eddie? You're taller than he is."

"You're tall too," he said. His face turned red. "I mean, I wouldn't exactly call Eddie and I friends," he said.

April cleared her throat.

"Oh, I'm sorry," I said. "And this is my friend April."

April smiled but knew enough to stay in the background and play the supporting role of the best friend.

"I don't think Eddie's here today," said Eli.

"Come on, man, the arcade's waiting," said Eli's friend from the front of the store.

"Alright, Charley, in a minute."

He turned to me and said, "It was so great meeting you, Jane. Hope to run into you again." He smiled and took a few steps away. Then he turned back and said, "Us tall folks have to stick together," and continued on his way.

Well, I just melted.

April dragged me away before I could make a complete ass of myself. We floated back to April's kiosk. Actually, I floated, April tugged.

"What the hell was that about?" she asked.

"Oh my God, wasn't he adorable? Oh my God!"

"I guess. You still didn't tell me what you needed from Eddie."

"Eddie has a Romatene connection," I said.

April stopped dragging me and looked me in the eyes.

"No," she said sharply. "Just all sorts of no."

"April, please."

"Jane, do you know how dangerous Romatene is? Not just to take but to deal it? It's against the law. You could, like, end up in jail with no TV and stuff. Promise me you won't do anything stupid."

"I promise."

Then I saw Eddie walk into the head shop, holding a pretzel.

"Well, gotta go," I said to April, following Eddie. My head was swelled with thoughts of Eli. Also, it was stuffed with thoughts of how I was going to score Romatene.

CHAPTER ELEVEN

Dissonance—*Harsh, discordant, and lack of harmony.*

"I simply don't have the money, Eli," my mother announced. We were at the beauty parlor where she worked. I came to plead my case, but her attention was being divided between killing my dreams and dyeing her customer's roots. "I'm sorry," she added.

I didn't doubt what my mother was saying. I just didn't like it.

Invoking my most earnest, reasoned, and working-class look, I said, "I have a proposition. If I raise my $350, can you match it with your $350? Like they do on the PBS pledge drives. That's cheap for your only child's Roman adventures."

"Jesus, you let your son talk to you that way?" said the customer.

My mother's eyes glazed over after I mentioned the $350 like she usually did when I waxed on rhapsodically.

"He's very precocious, this one," said my mom.

"It would mean everything," I said. "Think of my lifetime of memories."

"But what about that business of you not being a tenor?" asked my mom. I was hoping she had forgotten that snag. "I've discussed it with Douglas, sorry, Mr. Rasper, but nothing's come of it."

"When did you discuss it with Mr. Rasper?"

My mom put down her dyeing materials. "Alright, I'll agree to matching your funds. If you can raise the money."

I think she agreed to my proposal because it was still a lost cause. I had one month to come up with my half. Logic dictated I find a part-time and weekend job with a lot of flexibility that paid at least three dollars an hour. Something all-American, dignified, respectful, and time-honored.

I came up with a better plan. I mean, after all, that Jane girl might become my girlfriend and I would need the extra leisure time.

There was a new restaurant opening over in the next town. I had just finished reading an article about it in Newsday. The reason for my interest was that this was a Greek restaurant aimed at kids. It was called Athenos, and was advertised as charmingly authentic. They were trying something new at this family restaurant. The kids would dine in their own sections, fashioned after the Greek Islands, while the parents ate in relative peace and quiet on the mainland, updated regularly about their children from the wait staff. Their chef was actually from Greece. If this idea took off, I had read, the owners were going to start a franchise and had investors already lined up.

Now, apart from the thrill of adventure I knew was awaiting me in Italy, particularly the girls' orphanage and the chance to sing in every major cathedral, I was looking forward to this trip because of the food. At sixteen, I was a self-taught food snob. Some kids had sports, some had weird bug collections, I had theater, film, and food. The Holy Trinity of my childhood. And Greek cuisine served to me authentically and directly from the motherland was a pleasure too perfect to miss.

I had begun my intense fascination with food quite by circumstance. My mother always worked late, and I didn't like having to wait for her to feed me. I learned to cook for myself after school. At first, it was basic kid stuff: peanut butter and jelly, mac-and-cheese, that kind of thing. Having gotten quickly bored with that rotation, and always being on the creative side, I began to experiment.

The food shopping budget was limited at first but once I showed my mother a delicious and ambitious meal awaited her after a long day, she was happy to sponsor the procurement of my ever-growing grocery ingredients.

And so began my relationship with one of my best friends: self-reliance. Cooking also afforded me a relationship with world travel, time travel, responsibility with fire and spices, time management, and the marriage of flavors, textures, colors, and temperatures.

As I stepped off the bus and walked into Athenos alone on the second day of its opening, it was not without a passing knowledge of regional Greek cuisine. Also, I didn't want to put the miserable experience of bussing tables at my Uncle Jacob's restaurant earlier this summer to waste. I wore my best suit and carried a small but prominently displayed notebook.

"Table for one, please. Children's side," I told the hostess. "Santorini, if you can manage." She looked at me oddly, then told me it would only be a few minutes. I moved to the side and let the other customers put their names on the list. Periodically, I opened the notebook and jotted a note or two. The hostess, assisted now by the Maître d'Athenos, eyed me suspiciously, as if they weren't used to the sight of dressed-up sixteen-year-olds dining by themselves on a weekday. The hostess approached me tentatively.

"Did you get stood up?" she asked sympathetically. "Like on a date?"

I put on my most business-like and indignant look.

"Hardly."

I followed her to a small table. This side of the restaurant, that is the kid's side, had been optimistically decorated as a mini-Athens, complete with a little Parthenon you could crawl under. It was built to such a scale as to make each dining tyke feel like a Grecian King Kong. A bright blue sky was painted on the ceiling and various Greek island landmarks dotted the walls. Waiters were dressed as Greek peasants while the music system poured out "Zorba the Greek."

Opa!

Could an enterprise be both mind-numbingly tacky and remarkably splendid at the same time? I walked slowly, noticing every detail. My pace and body language made it clear to the waitress I was someone important. Or at least someone with a lot of time on their hands. My table, situated near the little Greek boy and girl facilities, afforded me a view of the dining room's activities as well as a perspective of the waitstaff's operations.

I was reviewing the menu when the waiter approached. He had been forced to wear a pronounced fake mustache and was decked out like a fisherman.

"Are we dining alone tonight?" he said.

I met his question with a dignified silence.

"Parents in the other room?" he asked.

I shook my head.

"No siblings, then?" he asked nervously, realizing suddenly kids don't tip.

I made a small entry in my notebook.

"May I order now?" I asked, looking up.

"Of course," he said, raising his pad and poising his chewed pencil.

I considered the menu with the utmost seriousness.

"Is it possible to prepare a sample platter arranged by region, beginning with Crete?" I asked. "And then move regionally from south to north?"

The waiter, clearly used to writing down Fried Cheese was taken aback. "I'll see what I can do." And with that, he put down his pencil. Before he turned his heels towards the kitchen, I made sure he saw me take out a pocket watch and place it on the table.

"Thank you," I said, dismissing him with a casual wave.

There was a large window that looked out onto the restaurant parking lot. This had the effect of ruining the illusion you were touring the Greek Islands. A familiar car pulled into the parking lot. Lady Bear got out of the car with Hubert and Florinda and the three entered the restaurant.

Intrigued, I waited a few minutes, then wandered over to the adult side of the restaurant. I didn't want them to see me since it would blow my cover. I hid behind a Doric column and spotted them seated at a corner booth. I listened as best I could. The restaurant was doing a brisk business, so it was hard to pick out exactly what they were discussing.

Lady Bear seemed stressed, as if trying to untangle a Gordian Knot of a problem. It seemed the crux of their conversation had to do with the advice Hubert's attorney had given him. I concluded it was the same attorney he went to see in Manhattan. The gist of the attorney's recommendation was that Hubert had to personally go to Italy. I didn't think that was big news or helpful advice since he was already going to Italy to accompany the choir on the tour.

Then I heard Lady Bear mention the word "inheritance" and my ears perked up. Hubert had to go to Italy to receive his inheritance. I would have stayed longer to overhear more of this intriguing mission, but I saw my fisherman waiter approaching. I casually walked back to my table.

"Just inspecting the rest of your operation," I said as I passed him.

The food came twenty-three minutes later, and I immediately noted so in my ever-present notebook. The waiter, accompanied by the Maître d'Athenos, placed the platter at my table. They were trying to assess this strange situation at Table Nine in Santorini.

"Yes, may I help you?" I asked, getting a bit nervous but trying not to let it show.

"Is everything alright?" asked the Maître d'Athenos.

I grumbled indignantly, hoping it would suffice as a haughty response. They left me to my lunch, but I could see them spying on me. I tasted the melitzanosalata first, made a thoughtful face, then entered a note in my book. I did the same with the other regional samplings on my dish.

During my main entrée, I watched Hubert and Florinda leave. I walked back to the adult section and saw Lady Bear sitting with an old lady. As much as it pained me, my options for going to Italy were getting thin so I took a deep breath and approached Lady Bear's table.

It was with deference to her regal character that I approached Lady Bear while she enjoyed her second lunch. She might not have the funds to be a Metropolitan Club member, but I was willing to bet she still had rainy day funds squirreled away. My plan was to appeal to her better nature and show how deserving I was of her charity. In short, I was stooping to panhandle the wrinkled broad so I could afford the Italy trip.

The elderly woman that sat across Lady Bear looked mannish in an unwholesome way; the kind of person I didn't expect to see dining in public in this sort of establishment. She looked like she would be more at home in a truck stop or greasy spoon. But one could never tell with the rich. They lived by their own rules of conduct and decorum. Still, there was something familiar about her. Then, it struck me. It was Mrs. Clancy. I realized I had last seen her clink glasses with Lady Bear at the Capri Bar.

"Hello," I said, walking by their table. "Funny meeting you here," I spoke in my best raised-eyebrows surprise.

Lady Bear and her butch companion looked at me as if the busboy union had suddenly decided to pursue the option of revolution.

"Beg pardon?" said Lady Bear in her throaty, imperious voice.

"Sorry, I'm Eli. Eli Mitchell. We've met before. I'm in the Long Island Boys Choir. Anyway, I just..."

"What do you want?" said Lady Bear, cutting to it.

"And why are you interrupting our lunch?" said Mrs. Clancy.

This wasn't going as planned. I held on with my reserves of courage.

"Well, the tour this summer. To Italy. I've been invited to go. But my mom doesn't have the money and..."

"And you want me to pay your way," said Lady Bear astutely. These wealthy society matrons had a way of getting down to the plum pit in one quick bite.

"Maybe..."

"I'm sorry but I can't help you," said Lady Bear, sounding very final on the matter.

"Can I just..."

"Is this the boy helping us?" said Mrs. Clancy to Lady Bear.

"Eunice!" said Lady Bear. She turned to me. "If I can't pay my own niece's way..."

"Sorry," said Mrs. Clancy.

"Your niece?" I asked.

"Florinda. Married to that nincompoop, Hubert," said Lady Bear.

Florinda was Lady Bear's niece? How did I not know this?

There wasn't much else I could offer at this point in the conversation unless I could suddenly produce a juicy bit of gossip for the Ladies who Lunch.

"Okay, then," I said. "Thanks anyway." I slinked my way back to my table.

I was served dessert. I ate while mulling over this new information about Florinda. Finally, the Maître d'Athenos walked over with purpose, checked on my progress, then left the room. He returned shortly with what I assumed was the House Manager. He was a portly fellow who looked a bit like the man on every pizza box.

"Everything to your liking, sir?" the House Manager said. Apparently, between ordering and eating, I had acquired the title of "Sir."

"Fine, thank you," I said, reviewing my notes.

They looked nervously at each other, not knowing how to broach the subject. Finally, the House Manager broke the silence.

"May we relocate you to a more hospitable table? One further from the lavatories?"

I had two bites left of my baklava. "That would be nice," I responded. I relocated to the center of the restaurant, amidst the help of three waiters and two members of management. Lady Bear and Mrs. Clancy were already gone.

"There. How's that?" asked the Maître d'Athenos.

"Wonderful." I began to eat again, ignoring their company.

The House Manage couldn't resist. "It is very important to us that you have a memorable dining experience with us, Mr...."

"I'm sorry," I said. "I'm really not supposed to reveal my name."

"Of course, of course. Merely making conversation," the House Manager added lightly.

"I mean, if my editor at Newsday found out…"

"Yes. Well." And with that, they were off.

The meal was wonderful. Three out of four Acropoli.

My dishes were cleared and my waiter waved the Maître d'Athenos over. I was given a large leather-bound folder; the type that typically contained an equally large bill at the end of the meal.

"I think you'll enjoy the after-dinner mint," the Maître d'Athenos said conspiratorially and walked away.

I slid the folder under the table and slowly opened it. A small, white piece of paper fell out. No crisp hundred-dollar bills. Not even a few twenties. Just a bill for thirty-three dollars.

And a Greek mint.

CHAPTER TWELVE

Chord—*Three or more notes played simultaneously in harmony.*

My fate that summer was sealed with the clanging of the mailbox door. I was alone in my room, listening to Paul Simon and thinking about Eli. I ran downstairs, hoping in the most romantic way it would be him, sneaking a love letter to me.

Our mailbox was affixed to our house. I opened the front door, leaned over, and grabbed the mail. I scanned my street to see if Eli was hiding somewhere, wanting to see me open his anonymous love letter. I didn't see anyone hiding so I brought the mail in.

Hidden within the stack of bills was a letter. My breathing became labored. It was an international envelope addressed to my parents. The return address was Convento del Sacro Cuore, Aprilia, Italia.

The living room clock told me it would be hours before my parents had dinner and settled in to watch TV. That was the officially sanctioned time when my dad would open the mail. I tried to figure out how I could possibly wait that long. The envelope was made of onion-skin paper that was incredibly thin. But somehow, no matter how much I held it up to the light, I couldn't make out its contents.

I had to burn off this nervous energy, so I decided to walk to the mall. It would kill some time and I might run into April or Eli or at least someone happy to see me. No dice. There wasn't anyone there I recognized. I stopped into the record store and picked up the 45 of the Village People's "YMCA." Maybe I could go home and dance away my anxiety.

Later that night, after dinner, right on schedule, my parents settled down in front of the TV in the den and put on "Happy Days." The den was my dad's space and was decorated with dark-paneled walls and a fluffy leather couch. It always smelled of his cigars.

I brought in the mail, like I usually did, and handed bills and such to my father who would open and read them during commercials. This was proceeding in accordance with the usual itinerary when I handed my father the international postal envelope. I knew he would have asked for the bills if I had handed him the international letter first so I figured I would save it for last.

My father didn't know what to make of the letter at first. He simply held it up to the light as if hoping to divine the source of the letter's great power. I didn't want to tell him I already tried that. He turned off the TV, so I knew this was important. Few things interrupted my dad watching the Fonz. Flummoxed, he handed the letter over to my mother. She quickly turned it over and read the postmark.

"Aprilia," she said, slightly surprised. "That's near Rome."

"Italy?" inquired my father.

"That's where they're keeping Rome these days, Daddy."

Normally, he'd give me a stern stare at such a remark, but he was so taken with this letter from another land, he let the comment slip by.

"I wonder if this is about your cousin Anna?" said my mother.

"Well, open it and find out," I said.

My mother gave the letter back to my father with the delicacy of a bomb squad handoff. He took out his pocketknife and carefully sliced open the top of the envelope. He widened the envelope's slit and blew inside it, forming a sort of paper balloon. He looked inside hopefully, as if expecting a little Italian bicycle messenger to come pedaling out. My heart was pounding. I didn't know how much more of this I could take.

He removed a small paper packet from the envelope. As he unfolded it, it blossomed into a two-page letter. We had never received such a letter from across an ocean. My father began to read it. The paper was the same microthin type they used for the envelope but I couldn't see the backward handwriting as my father held the letter against the living room light behind him. My mother leaned in, curiosity getting the best of her. He finished reading and put the letter down on his lap.

"Well?" said my mother. "What does it say? Who's it from?"

"You were right," said my father.

"About what?" said my mom.

I looked for meaning in my father's face, but he just took a long drag on his cigar and slowly blew out smoke.

My mother gently took the letter from him and read it. A sad smile lit her face. She and my dad nodded to each other.

"Jane, you remember we spoke of your cousin Anna, right?" she said. "The nun?"

I nodded.

"She wants you to spend a few weeks this August with her in Italy."

"What?" was all I could manage to say. I couldn't believe what I had heard. This couldn't be happening. "Can I see the letter?"

My mom handed it to me. Sure enough, my cousin Anna was asking permission to send me to her convent in Aprilia, Italy so I could spend the first three weeks of August with her. All expenses were paid for, and she would soon be wiring the money for airline tickets to my parents. We just needed to send her a telegram accepting her invitation.

A drop of water landed on the letter and made a crinkling noise. I realized I was crying. My mother hugged me.

A brief thought suddenly crossed my mind: the letter was a fake. After all, who knew what a real letter from Italy looked like? Could this have been Eli's handiwork? Eddie mentioned briefly Eli was good at coming up with schemes and Eddie did need me to go to Italy to score Romatene for him.

My father grabbed the letter from me and re-read it again, looking for a catch or any fine print.

"You can't refuse a nun," said my mom. And my father actually smiled.

"Looks like our girl is going to Italy," he said.

My mom hugged me again. As she did, I whispered to her, "And you get your Summer of Love."

CHAPTER THIRTEEN

***Fermata**—To hold a tone or rest beyond the written value at the discretion of the performer.*

Charley had invited me over to his palatial house. Though his parents were still halfway across the world, Charley's house was abuzz with staff tending to every need. I rang the bell on the security gate and was let in.

As I entered and walked around to the back of the mansion, I thought about Charley's tax bracket. It's been said only the poor and the rich can be found barefoot at home in the middle of the afternoon. Everyone else was middle class. I'd often seen Charley's family unshod at 3 p.m. enjoying martinis.

Charley and I sat poolside in his backyard, dipping our feet in the warm, chlorinated water. He had asked the lifeguard to wait inside. The pool was surrounded by large evergreens which created a cozy privacy amidst the sprawling estate. It was a warm night, and the lightning bugs were out in force. Charley's dog, Peebee, barked at us from inside the house. Charley had named his furry paramour Peanut Butter Cup. He said it had something to do with the dog's coloring. I told him it was because he and the dog were nuts inside. Charley loved his dog and kept insisting we let him out, but I asked him not to. That dog was a classic leg humper and I wasn't in the mood.

I finished telling Charley about what I overheard at Athenos.

"Holy crap. Lady Bear is Florinda's aunt," said Charley. He had always prided himself on knowing everything about the choir. "That makes total sense. I always wondered why Lady Bear put up with Hubert and his one-armed playing."

"What about Rasper?" I said. "Is Hubert the choir's accompanist just because of Lady Bear?"

"Oh no, Hubert is actually pretty talented," said Charley. "Rasper really does love the way he plays."

It was getting dark. The pool lights went on. This was shortly followed by the backyard lights which were positioned high above, in the trees. Apparently, Charley's backyard doubled as a movie set. I waited for a fake backdrop of the Eiffel Tower to appear.

Charlie was backlit and I considered his worried look. I knew he held his big secret close to his heart but I keep waiting for him to trust me enough to tell it.

"You hear from your folks?" I asked.

"That's funny," said Charley. "I sent them a telegram and just got their response today. They're fine."

Charley threw one of Peebee's tennis balls into the pool. "You want to hear something weird?"

"What?"

"It's about Rasper. He told me to ask you about your mom. Your mom!"

"What about her?"

"I don't know. That's all he said. 'Ask Eli about his mother.' I mean, do you think...?"

"They got together last week. I keep telling myself it wasn't a date," I said. A thought occurred to me. "Wait, do you think Rasper picked Italy for this summer's tour because Hubert has to go there to pick up his inheritance?"

Charley stood up and walked around toward the deep end of the pool. "He might have. I know Lady Bear was putting all kinds of pressure on him to go to Italy."

"Maybe she's using the choir as cover for something," I said.

Charley laughed and dove into the pool. He swam around for a while. The quiet gave me time to think.

"Charley, can I ask you something?"

"Shoot." He was doing laps now.

"Are you muling drugs for Eddie?"

"Am I what?"

"Forget it," I said.

"No, what?"

"You know. Like you're bringing illegal drugs here from Italy. Maybe Romatene? Is that why you're going on this trip? For Eddie? I mean, if you are, it's okay with me."

"No, Eli, no way," he said indignantly. He dove under and didn't come up for several seconds.

I waited for him to come up and tread water. "It's just I've been talking to Eddie…"

"And you thought I was involved in drug dealing?" he said, clearing his ears.

"No. Well, yeah. Sort of."

Charley thought about this as he drifted over to the shallow end near me. He made little ripples in the pool.

"Cool," he announced with a smile on his face. He got out of the pool and dried himself off. He sat down across from me on a lounger.

"Sorry," I said.

"No, it's totally cool you thought of me like that. So, about Italy…," he said.

"Looks like I'm out. Lady Bear was my last idea for money."

"Eli, the telegram from my parents. I asked if I could bring you. You're my best friend. The trip isn't going to be half as much fun without you. You figure out how to be a tenor and you can be my guest in Italy."

He said it so simply I didn't hear it at first. Then, after a few minutes of silence, it sunk in.

"Say what?"

"You heard me."

"Are you sure?" I couldn't breathe. I was light-headed.

"What are friends for?" he asked.

CHAPTER FOURTEEN

Expressionism—*Atonal and violent style used as a means of evoking heightened emotions and states of mind.*

"April, we're going to Italy!" I shouted when April opened her door.

"Say what?" she said.

I explained about my cousin Anna and her letter. I told her it was destiny. Her name was April, and the town was Aprilia. I was so ecstatic and felt I was talking too fast. She put on her shoes and we took a walk.

"But," said April as we walked around the block, "I don't want to spend my summer in a convent. I mean, what do they even do in there?"

"It's just like the 'Sound of Music,'" I said. "We'll have a great time."

April turned to me with a serious expression. "I need you to do me a favor, Jane."

"Anything." I didn't know what type of favor April needed but in these perilous teenage times, one never asked. She certainly had helped me out plenty of times and was the one true friend I still had left.

"Wait till we get to the woods."

We turned at the end of her block and approached the woods at the end of the development. April stayed close to me. The sky was silver blue and the air was fresh. But in April's eyes, apprehension was afoot.

"What is it?" I finally asked.

"It's a boy."

"Of course."

"The one who works at the mall at the leather belt stand. You know, the one with Jackson Browne hair," she said dreamily.

I knew who April referred to. He was a new employee at the mall and was quite mysterious. Most likely, he was like everyone else, but for now, had the cache of being unknown and therefore exotic and romantic.

"What about him? And where are we going?" I asked as the voice of reason.

"I finally asked my co-worker to talk to the assistant manager at the Leather Hut, who he had driver's ed with, to talk to the new kid. I found out his name is Robert. Not Bobby. Robert."

"Robert. Got it," I said, trying not to rain on her insane parade. But I knew the feeling.

"He told his friend he liked me and would leave me a note in the woods. Taped to an elm tree or something. You know how creeped out I get in the woods, so will you go in there with me?"

"We're going to Italy and this is what you're worrying about?"

"Please."

"Of course," I said. Who was I to get in the way of a relationship that involved more modes of communication than Western Union?

We arrived at the end of the street and the start of the woods. The woods were not supposed to be there, at least according to the town planner. Twenty years ago, two new roads were supposed to have been built, followed by rows of Levittown-type houses. But the town ran out of funds and a rare species of bullfrog was discovered living in the woods. Or perhaps, as local legend had it, developers found out the woods were haunted and could never be trespassed. I didn't believe it for a minute, but April ate this type of stuff up with a spork.

"How do we know which elm tree he might have left a note on?" I said.

"He *did* leave a note," she said, already defending her boyfriend-to-be. "It's supposed to be one of the old elms by Tiny Tim's stump."

Years ago, one of the oak trees in the woods grew to a disproportionately enormous size. It became a town landmark. During any given time of the day, Tiny Tim's shadow would fall over some part of the town. After several decades, the giant tree fell under its own weight. The ragged stump still stood twenty feet high and was at least six feet in circumference at its base. I wasn't the first kid who thought of digging out the middle and moving in. Now, Tiny Tim's carcass was a major feature of the town, often acting as a compass to lead brave kids in and out of the woods.

I took a step into the woods. April grabbed my shoulder.

"I can't," she said.

"You can't what?" I said. "He's cute and you need a boyfriend."

"I can't go in there."

All this talk of Tiny Tim and the woods had given her a bad case of the suburban heebie-jeebies. So, I did what any good friend would.

"Fine, you wait here. I'm going in."

"Wait, this is like one of those horror movies. You'll be killed and then I have to go in to find you and then I'll be killed and then…"

"April, shut up."

I proceeded into the woods, leaving a nervous April by the sidewalk. I walked directly to Tiny Tim's stump. The white noise of the woods was refreshing. During the entire time I was in the woods, I tried to think about the white noise and how friendly and harmless it all was. Then I thought about Italy and smiled. I saw a folded piece of paper crudely attached to a low-hanging twig a few feet away. I emerged from the woods with a note from the Leather Man.

"Oh my God!" said April. "What took you so long?"

"I was gone for, like, two minutes," I said. I handed her the note. She ripped open the envelope and read it. Her face became a bit longer. She read it again. No mistaking the contents during her third and final read. Definitely bad news.

"What is it?" I said, trying to preserve her dignity and providing her with an opportunity to lie and save face.

"He wants to know if I can get him some good weed. That's all he wanted. That's it," said April, balling up the note and throwing it back into the woods.

"April," I said. "Please come to Italy with me. We'll have the best time. There are, like, a million Italian boys who love American girls like us. Can you imagine? They'll flirt, pinch our butts, buy us drinks. Did you ever think a boy would pinch your butt? I promise you a wild time. Romance! And when you're really old, this Italy trip is what you'll remember."

There. A compelling speech to rouse the blood of any dormant romantic. Plus, I desperately needed a friend on this trip. How could she resist?

"No," she said and walked away.

I pursued. "But April, it's your last chance for fun. Your parents said you could go."

"Sorry." Her pace picked up as she proceeded down her street. I followed closely.

"In Italy, they don't have woods. They were all cleared away by some Roman Emperor centuries ago. Please go with me."

April took in a deep breath. "But the convent," she said. "It's not like 'Sound of Music.' I bet it's like one of those Vincent Price movies."

"Oh," I said. "I should have been way clearer. You think we're staying with my cousin the whole time? We're only paying a quick visit to the convent. We'll spend less time there than I was in the woods. We're having a great Italian adventure. But it only works if you come with me."

April smiled. After a minute, she said, "Okay."

We hugged and I went home to think about what I would pack.

Now that I had gotten April on board, there was one thing left to do before we flew to Rome. The day after my woods adventure with April, Eddie told me where Eli lived, and I found the courage to knock on his door. I needed to meet him officially and see if he really liked me. I wanted to know if he would be waiting for me when I returned from Italy. I needed to know if I should look forward to him.

There was nobody home. Dejected, I walked to April's house. She was swinging in her backyard. I joined her and let her know about Eli. Friends like April were hard to come by. There was nothing more valuable than throwing my trouble monkey on the back of my friend and watching as she not only domesticated the damn furry thing but taught it tricks.

"I've got it," she said.

April's plan was simplicity itself and yet brilliantly conceived. We taped a note to Eli's front door asking him to meet us at the Wall at 8:00 p.m. It was signed by April and me. I didn't want to be so forward as to have the note just from me. The Wall gang usually didn't congregate until it got completely dark, about 9:00 p.m. If they saw me, they'd be sure to kick me out. We would be safe until then.

April and I crouched behind the Wall, silently waiting. Being back at the Wall brought back so many wonderful memories. It also made me wistful for the good old days when I swam in the right social circles. As the skies darkened and it approached 8:00 pm, I snapped myself out of my melancholy, reminding myself the need to legitimately return to this spot was what drove my destiny.

And meeting Eli.

Suddenly, April grabbed my shoulder. We stood up and saw Eddie walking down the street towards us. What was he doing here?

He waved weakly to us as if not all that excited to be here. Or maybe he was nervous.

"Hey," said April.

"Hey," said Eddie.

"Hey," I said.

Well, now that all the pleasantries were behind us, the meeting could come to order.

"So, what's going on?" said April, holding the note behind her back and breaking the ice.

I was searching for something to say but Eddie interrupted my thoughts.

"So, Jane," said Eddie, using his best business voice. "No chance of you doing me that favor we talked about?"

"Favor?" said April.

"Oh, it's nothing," said Eddie. "Jane and I just got some history, and she was going to do something for me." He turned to me. "After all, I gave you Eli's address. You owe me one now."

"No, Eddie. I haven't changed my mind," I said.

"Jane," said Eddie. "Can we talk in private?"

We walked down the block, leaving April at the Wall in awkward silence.

"What is it?" I said, annoyed.

"Your friend, April. Is she seeing anyone?"

"April? You're interested in April?"

"Yeah, I guess."

"Jane! Come back!" yelled April from the Wall.

I saw Eli running away, turning the corner at the end of the block. I rushed over to April.

"What happened?" I asked, as Eddie caught up to me.

"Eli. He told me he was going to ask you out but didn't know you were with Eddie. Then he just ran off."

"Eddie?" I said, incredulous.

"Yes?" he said, sidling up to us.

"Why the hell did you screw that up?" I said, pushing him away.

"Screw what up? Hi, April," said Eddie.

April rolled her eyes. Her heart was broken because her best friend's heart was broken. Suddenly, a car pulled up and flashed its headlights at us.

"Shit," said Eddie and jumped behind some hedges. He got up and bolted down the street. I missed all the intrigue that happened every night at The Wall.

"What the hell was that?" asked April. The car's headlights turned off and we saw the driver get out.

"Oh my God," I said. "Morgan."

"Jane? What are you doing here?" asked my old boyfriend.

"Same to you," I said.

"I'm looking for Eddie. Listen, it's important. If you see him, tell him I'm looking for him."

"Stop following me," I said and took April by the arm.

April and I didn't look back. We walked down the street, arm-in-arm, broken-hearted. Only an Italian summer adventure could warm our spirits now.

CHAPTER FIFTEEN

***Serenade**—A lighthearted piece, usually performed as background music for a social function.*

The rehearsal room felt hot and stuffy. It was late July and this public school room had never been intended for human occupation in the stifling summer months. We were into our first hour of rehearsal and were a bit withered. Rasper did his best Leonard Bernstein in the front, showing no signs of heat stress. Hubert had sweated through his shirt and Florinda, faithfully turning the pages for him, tried not to notice.

I hadn't really made any new friends here. I think it was partly due to me still being an alto and that I wasn't a permanent member yet.

Little Francis sat in front of me with the rest of the sopranos. He didn't talk to anyone and was still intimidated by the choir. We didn't know Little Francis that well. He mostly kept to himself which I found odd. Most of the sopranos banded together like little hobbits on a quest. He had joined the choir this year although he had spent over a year in the Long Island Boys Choir Eastern Preparatory choir. Unless you had spectacular innate talent in addition to self-mastery of seventeenth- and eighteenth-century music, a grand working knowledge of music theory, and uncanny ability to sight-read complex music cold, you weren't ready for our major leagues. I bypassed the prep choir apprenticeship program and was placed directly into the choir due to my reference from Charley, his rich parents (always an attraction to

Rasper), and the fact I was over twelve years old. Plus, I'd like to think I had some talent.

The prep choir was for younger kids who were still moldable. Rasper liked that these kids were putty. He could instill in these little musical sponges a work ethic, music knowledge, and healthy fear of him at an impressionable age.

Many parents, thinking their little male prodigies were ready for prime time, were appalled to find that they would be paying tuition for just a prep choir. Then Rasper, and solely Rasper, would determine when their young heir had been properly seasoned. But Rasper always did an incredible and charming job of convincing each parent this was by far the best decision they could make. He'd play to their egos, their insecurities, whatever it took. He wasn't conning them; he was molding a professional-caliber choir and negotiating with his talent pool and financiers.

There was now a two-year waiting list to get into the prep choir. Eight- to twelve-year-olds hoped to get into one of three locations. There were no conditions to join the prep choir other than a willingness to attend every rehearsal and the ability to pay the tuition.

It was genius on the part of Rasper. Not only did he manage to gain enough income from the prep choir tuition to quit his day job as a public junior high school music teacher and concentrate on the Long Island Boys Choir full time, but he essentially created a fully-funded research and development unit. He could hand-pick his future stars, molding them exactly as he saw fit.

After the investment made in the prep choir, a potential boy's desire and aspirations to gain admission into the choir proper were quite high. Auditions were required. Rasper was the gatekeeper. But, by then, they were all hooked. Rasper used tactics typically favored by cocaine dealers and their ilk.

It still amazed me Rasper could hand out sheet music that we'd never seen before, give us a few minutes to look it over, have Hubert play it over once, then raise his hands in the air and, on the downbeat, we'd sing it in almost perfect harmony. Sure, the music was broken down into soprano, alto, tenor, and baritone parts, along with the piano accompaniment, but we were performing high-caliber sight reading and musical performance. It wasn't a bad way to spend a summer. Although it would have been better if I had a girlfriend, was a tenor, and could go to Italy.

We were on the third run-through of this particular new sheet of music. Each time we'd finish, Rasper would give us notes to tweak the sound in the same way a recording engineer would turn up certain instruments and turn down backup vocals. We listened to him intently. The real art to choir singing wasn't the singing, as odd as that sounded. It was the listening. If we all just sang to the loudest and best of our abilities, it would be a cacophony. We listened to each other and Hubert's accompaniment, watched Rasper dictate the volume and tempo, and maintained our portions of the song. After a few weeks with the choir, it was incredible how I could modulate what I sang while simultaneously listening to the sea of voices that surrounded me.

We finished the song and Rasper let his arms down, which was the signal we could sit. The heat had made us wobbly, and we were thankful for the rest. Little Francis looked shaky, and his skin had been turning perpetually paler by the minute. He had come into the rehearsal looking like the Coppertone baby and had transitioned over the past hour to Eddie Munster-level whiteness.

I watched the back of Little Francis' well-combed head, which didn't move, possibly in fear of attracting any attention. Rasper had his back to us as he sifted through the pile of sheet music on the piano, discovering what we could practice next. Little Francis let out a moan that did not sound like vocal warmup exercises. Did I say Eddie Munster white skin? Little Francis had turned a Linda Blair green. With no further warning, Little Francis deftly turned around in his seat, faced behind him, and proceeded to vomit.

On me.

Voluminously.

I was wearing my favorite jeans. They were my Sergio Valentes and had a yellow star on the right back pocket and another on the front left thigh. It appeared the yellow star on my lap served as a homing beacon and target for Little Francis's recent dinner.

I had never been thrown up on, so I wasn't sure what etiquette dictated. I jumped up and the vomit made a second splat as it slid off my lap and onto the vinyl tiled floor. Little Francis held his belly and groaned.

"What's going on?" demanded Rasper, banging a lower C on the Steinway. The other altos had already moved a measurable distance away from me after quickly calculating potential future splatter trajectories.

"I think I'm sick," moaned Little Francis. He went down on his hands and knees as if auditioning for choir mascot.

"I'll second that," I said.

"I'm sorry, Mr. Rasper," whimpered Little Francis.

Rasper looked pathetically at Little Francis, then at my dripping pants, and motioned for a fifteen-minute break. He then abruptly left the rehearsal room and down the hallway. No one followed him.

Rasper never took the role of caregiver or parent with us. He was more of a drill sergeant: giving orders, pushing us, rewarding us, and pointing out our flaws. We, in turn, took care of each other. The seasoned older tenors and baritones, and one too-old alto, acted as big brothers to the younger ones. In general, the walking carried the wounded.

At every break, depending upon the rate of vomiting per choirboy, Rasper would disappear upstairs to an office in the junior high school. We were never allowed to go with him. Rumor had it he was making long-distance phone calls while tucked away in a dark office. We knew he was also running off dittos on the old mimeograph machine in that comforting, faded, dull purple lettering. Word around the piano was Rasper was stealing the school blind on supplies he used for the choir.

Which was fine by me. It made me like Rasper that much more. How many people would I ever meet who had been trained in Vienna, received their doctorate in music, and yet were still interested in sticking it to the man?

Florinda stepped in as den mother. She helped Little Francis up and gave him a glass of water. She told him to lie down until his grandparents could come to pick him up. Little Francis' parents had died in a car accident, and he lived with his mother's parents. Florinda left to place a call to Little Francis' grandparents. He huddled on the floor near the piano.

No one seemed concerned with the status of my saturated Sergios. Luckily, Charley had been playing tennis earlier and brought his gym bag to rehearsal. He handed me a spare, clean pair of gym shorts. I ran into the boys' locker room to get changed, glad to be alone in there. I threw away my Sergios. I wish I had more time for a proper ceremony, but they were simply dismissed into the trash can for the janitor to find in the morning. I didn't think it prudent to carry around my jeans and their rancid smell in a bag for the rest of the evening.

When we returned from the break, Rasper almost tripped on Little Francis. He paused, considered Little Francis, and lifted him up onto the piano. He patted him on the head, then turned around to face us. He announced he wanted to add yet another song to our repertoire. Rasper loved, above almost all else, fashioning a musical program that was different for each performance. He lived for crafting a unique concert based on who the audience was. Weddings, charity events, Christmas celebrations, Jewish Temple openings, fundraisers for hamsters with three testicles in need of companionship: dammit, the man wanted options.

"It's a solo, I believe," said Rasper. We sometimes did solos for variety. It broke up the choral monotony. It was always an honor to be chosen since they only happened once or twice each season. "Yes, a solo," Rasper said.

He took out a piece of sheet music and handed it to Hubert who played the instrumental through once, with assistance, as always, from Florinda. It was a beautiful, quiet piece and lent itself to a soprano or alto.

"For His Lord's Tenderness Keeping," Rasper said, announcing the title.

"Wasn't that a James Bond movie?" I whispered to Charley who sat a few seats from me.

"Well," Rasper continued. "We'll see who gets it."

He said it in a way that made me want it more than anything. How did he do that?

Before Rasper could continue, the rehearsal room door opened and an elderly man appeared. He was dressed in an expensive-looking overcoat and his hands looked like they had never known toil. In short, the man was loaded.

"Hello," said the man. "I'm Bart Rollins. Francis' grandfather. Francis!" He rushed over to his grandson in the fetal position on the floor near the piano. Mr. Rollins picked up Little Francis with the fragility and tenderness usually reserved for handling radioactive eggs. They left the room together without any acknowledgment from Rasper.

"Who's that?" I asked Charley in a whisper.

"That's the guy everyone calls Mr. Clancy."

"The one who married Mrs. Clancy? Our Mrs. Clancy?" I said.

"The same," said Charley.

Rasper seemed annoyed about this interruption and for having an elderly man temporarily assume an alpha position that distracted our attention. He took a deep breath and raised his hands, indicating we were to stand and sing.

"Excuse me. Is there an Eli Mitchell here?"

We all looked up. Standing at the front door was Bart Rollins again. He wasn't holding Little Francis and I assumed he had deposited his grandson in either the car or the school library lost-and-found. I looked at Rasper, who nodded at me.

"I'm Eli," I said.

He waved me over. I could feel the eyes of the entire chorus on me, but especially Rasper, as Little Francis's grandfather led me out into the hallway. The rehearsal room door shut behind me.

"Francis tells me he got sick on you," said Bart Rollins.

"Just around the edges," I said, still not quite sure what this was about.

"Yes. Are you alright then?"

Ah, I thought to myself. *So, it's lawsuit-prevention time, is it?*

"I'm fine, I think. My favorite jeans are ruined though. I had to throw them out in the locker room."

"That is regrettable. Perhaps Mrs. Rollins and I could assist you in some way as a form of apology?"

"Mrs. Rollins?" I said.

"My wife. Some people still call her Mrs. Clancy. She and I are chaperoning the choir's tour to Italy this summer. Although I'm not sure if that's quite public information yet. Keep it to yourself until Mr. Rasper makes it official, will you?"

"Of course," I said.

We approached the front doors of the school. Outside, I could see Little Francis in the back seat of Mr. Rollins brown Toyota Corona. Mr. Rollins turned to me. "Tell you what, it's hot as hell in that room. That's no place for boys to be spending their summer nights. How about I take you and Francis out for some ice cream?"

"Thanks," I said. "But I really should get back to rehearsal."

"We'll be gone fifteen minutes tops," he said. "Live a little." He headed to his car.

I liked this guy. He had a casual way about how he conducted himself that made you respect him. I followed him toward the car. He opened up the door and Little Francis got out.

"Come on, Francis," said Mr. Rollins. "We're walking. It's just around the corner."

We walked to Vinny's Gelato Palace which, by its very location, was a school hangout. No one knew who Vinny was and no one ever ordered gelato. It was all soft-serve ice cream. The gelato sign made me think of Italy. I longed to taste real gelato.

The line was short, and we waited to order. Little Francis held Mr. Rollins hand and was typically quiet. It made me miss my dad.

"Sorry again about Francis," said Mr. Rollins.

"I'm sorry," said Little Francis.

"No problem," I said. "So, you're chaperoning the Italy tour."

Mr. Rollins smiled. "I haven't been to Italy in years. Used to live there, you know. Long before I met Mrs. Clancy, er, Rollins. You wouldn't know it to look at me, but I was a hell-raiser in those days."

"Really?"

"But I got tired of my outlaw life. Yes sir, Eli, take it from me, you want to conduct your life on the straight and narrow. It makes everything so much easier." Mr. Rollins was lost in his memories, staring into the middle distance.

"Thanks for the advice."

We walked up to the window and ordered three vanilla cones with sprinkles.

"So, any favor I could do for you?" said Mr. Rollins. "I worry about Francis and would hate for this incident to sour his experience with the choir. Boys can be cruel."

"I don't know," I said.

"I mean, anything shy of paying for your trip to Italy," said Mr. Rollins and let out a laugh. Little Francis rolled his eyes.

Our ice cream was ready, and we ate as we walked back to the school.

"I've already got the money for the trip," I said. "Well, my best friend is paying my way as a gift."

"That's a good friend."

"Only I can't go on tour because..."

I stopped and smiled. Mr. Rollins turned to me, a vanilla cone in one hand and Little Francis on the other. "What's on your mind, young man?"

"I have a favor, but I don't know if you could do it," I said.

"Now you're insulting me," said Mr. Rollins. "You have a girlfriend, Mr. Mitchell? Boy your age should have a girlfriend."

"I wish. There is this one girl."

"There's always that one girl. Mine was in Rome before I met Mrs. Clancy," he said, smiling. "But don't tell her that." He laughed again.

I took a deep breath. "Is there any way you could talk Mr. Rasper into making me a tenor right away?"

"Pardon? You want me to give him a ten?"

"Make me a tenor."

"A tenor. Of course, I can do that. Mr. Rasper owes me big time. That's the least I can do after you've been thrown up on."

I was beside myself. "If you do that, I'll spread the word Francis is not a chronic upchucker. Deal?"

We walked back to his car. He placed Little Francis into the car and walked with me back to the rehearsal room.

"It would be nice if you could ask the other boys to make it easier for Francis," said Mr. Rollins.

Rasper was in the middle of a show tune with the choir. I took my place with the altos and sang. When the song was over, Mr. Rollins asked to speak to Rasper. The two of them stepped out and everyone looked at me. I just shrugged my shoulders, ever the innocent. After a minute, Rasper walked back into the room, gaping at me. I couldn't tell if he was amused or irritated. Mr. Rollins wasn't with him.

Rasper handed some sheet music to the first choir boy he could reach from the piano. "Please provide this to Eli," said Rasper. Ominously and silently, it was passed down to me. I looked at it. My first solo. It made me surprisingly nervous.

"Okay, Eli?" asked Rasper with a rare stab at faux collaboration.

I had gotten the solo. It was probably because I was new and this was the equivalent of a mob guy making his bones. Who would I be singing this to? Wealthy patrons of museums, churches, and foundations. Nothing to fear in the least.

"Absolutely," I responded.

"And Eli," said Rasper. "You'll be singing it as a tenor. Better move into their section."

I opened my mouth and out came the Lord's tenderness keeping.

CHAPTER SIXTEEN

Piano*—An instruction to play softly. Abbreviated by a "p."*

April and I held hands as our plane took off. It was a show of friendship and an acknowledgment we were young, free, and about to embark on a wild, madcap adventure. Once we had decided to go together, it was a whirlwind. I wrote back to Anna that I was accepting her invitation but I was bringing a friend. Passports were taken out of bank security deposit boxes, luggage was purchased, and dollar-to-lira conversions were strictly monitored daily. Our parents walked us to our gate and our moms cried. My mom packed my cousin Anna's letter in my purse in case I needed to show proof I wasn't some pretender when I arrived at the convent.

Shortly after takeoff, April was struck with nausea that increased as the cabin air became more pressurized.

"Maybe if you sucked on some nuts," I advised her absent-mindedly. I had brought my sketch pad and was drawing to keep my mind calm.

April looked at me with mischief peeking through her sickness.

"Story of my life," she said.

I swear we giggled halfway across the Atlantic.

"Bollocks," I exhaled. I had decided to pretend to be from England for this trip. When do you ever get to reinvent yourself with no consequence?

April nodded, agreeing with our predicament. The flight had already gotten dreary. I put away my sketches, which weren't as good as usual. Probably something to do with altitude or already feeling homesick. I mean, what was I thinking? It was one thing to dream about going to Italy with my best friend but here we were! I had no idea what I was going to do with all this freedom. Then again, we were staying at a convent.

To save money on airfare, we were forced to take this rather low-budget flight from LaGuardia Airport in New York to Ireland before switching planes. Our flight then left Ireland, stopped in Milan, then finally reached our final destination: Rome. After we landed at Shannon Airport in Ireland so the plane could refuel, we wandered a bit to stretch our legs and enjoy our buzz.

The plane we got onto for Milan and Rome was much bigger. April and I were seated in the back of the plane, reading through some Irish magazines we had bought. Then we looked up and saw the plane was filling up with cute boys. Most of them had already been seated but just from the backs of their heads, I could tell they were cute.

We took off again, but April felt better about this ascent. After we reached our cruising altitude, we took turns getting high in the bathroom. We were careful to let all the smoke go down the toilet, followed by constantly flushing. It was merely an exercise in hydraulics. Who knew studying Bernoulli's Law in Physics would pay off? When you sat down on the toilet and shifted ever so slightly, you created an opening in a vacuum which made a rather embarrassing sucking sound as air rushed into the toilet. Voila.

No smoke. No smell. Nice high.

At one point, a gravelly-voiced old lady pounded on the door and demanded, "What's going on in there? Hurry up!"

We were now out of pot except for the stash we had packed. But our bags were deep in the belly of the plane. We had smuggled our pot on board in a small Ziploc bag that was rolled up tight and stuffed into a tube of suntanning cream. If only we could get paid to be so inventive and allusive in a way that would benefit society.

I was looking forward to the in-flight movie for a few reasons. My mind was whirling, being deprived of oxygen in all sorts of ways at 14,000 feet. The darkness would help that. So would the quiet in the cabin. And I'd be able to focus on one image. They announced there would be no movie.

And then the most extraordinary thing happened. April and I were high, so it was possible we were sharing the same delusion. But this pot wasn't that good. Still, in our stoned haze, the sight was remarkably mirage-like.

The flight attendant announced, "We are looking into the movie difficulty and will keep you posted," with no impression of remorse. Then, a handsome, older man stood up and said, rather loudly and definitively, to no one in particular, "No matter." Then, he gestured to everyone around him. "Boys," he commanded.

He strolled up and down the aisle and tapped all the cute boys of various shapes and sizes on the shoulder. Unbelievably, they each stood up, extricated themselves from their confining seats, and followed him down the aisle. They were mice following this Pied Piper of the airways.

April turned to me with eyes half-closed.

"Oh my God. It's one of those mass suicides," she whispered with a hint of excitement in her voice. "They're going to pray, open the door, and jump out." Then, after a pause, she yelled, "I'm so fucking high!"

April had a brilliant talent for stating the unelusive.

I sat up, intrigued by this thought. The effects of the pot were just starting to wear off which meant we wanted more. An overwhelming feeling of rapture came over me as I thought about the few weeks of adventure that lay before us. And our Summer of Love would start with young virgin males flinging themselves into the North Atlantic, compelled by their knowledge they could never have me. Well, it was a hell of a way to begin a vacation.

They stood in the aisle single-file, facing the front of the plane and the rest of the seated passengers. The boys arranged themselves in order of height with the shorter boys in the front and the taller boys in the back near us. Their leader, the one who had clearly corrupted and brainwashed their trusting minds, forming them into this parachute-less sky-diving cult, stood in the front near the cockpit. They eagerly faced him. April and I were so far back, I couldn't make out most of their faces. Two of the taller boys looked a lot like Morgan and Eli. I told April and we both laughed.

"This is totally weird," yelled April, unaware she had no self-editor.

I was in complete agreement. They sang "Go Tell It on the Mountain." All the boys in the aisle. These random passengers. Despite the plane's loud engines, their voices were so clear. They sang in perfect harmony, and it was beautiful. Angelic.

Their leader raised his hands to conduct, and it was like he was teaching us all to swim in the air, the way his arms danced with the music.

The other passengers were equally moved. All other noises were silenced. We couldn't even hear the engines. Just this beautiful choir singing. They moved into "There Is Nothing Like a Dame."

My eyes grew wet with tears, and I was six years old again and able to believe in God and Santa and love and miracles. And it was because of their music, not because we weren't going to watch virgins sacrifice themselves.

They sang for twenty minutes and only our seatbelts and the limiting overhead luggage compartments kept us from accompanying our thunderous applause with a standing ovation.

When they were done, I realized my face and shirt were drenched with tears and I was breathing irregularly.

They took their seats and I wished at least one of them was seated near me.

April tapped me on the shoulder.

"We've got to get high again. That was so cool!"

April handed me a small bottle of sun-tanning cream from her purse. I looked at her in surprise. She giggled.

"In case of emergency, break glass," she giggled.

This was indeed going to be a memorable trip. Roma, here we come!

CHAPTER SEVENTEEN

***Tutee**—Passage for the entire ensemble.*

We were at our gate at John F. Kennedy airport and our flight was leaving in about an hour. All the parents were there giving little speeches, hugging their kids, taking photos. Rasper was walking around with a clipboard like a summer camp counselor checking off items from his prodigious list.

My mom was crying as she hugged me. I was trying to pull away, but she kept hugging me closer. It was embarrassing. Especially in front of the choir and strangers getting ready to board the plane. I know she was disappointed she wasn't going but I was hoping the time she spent by herself would help her. Mostly, though, I couldn't wait to get on that plane.

My mother pulled me aside and leaned down to look me in the eye. I had been getting taller recently, so she didn't have to lean as far. "Eli, I have something important to tell you," she said.

"Mom, this can't wait?"

"I tried to tell you earlier, but you were so busy getting ready."

"What is it?"

"You know money is tight. I got offered a job in Rahway. They want me to start after Labor Day."

"Rahway?" I said. "Like, New Jersey? We're moving?"

"I haven't said yes yet. I don't know. We'll see."

"I don't want to switch schools for my senior year. Can't this wait?"

"I don't know, Eli. I thought between working at the beauty parlor and helping my brother at the restaurant, things would be okay. But you saw where the restaurant's going."

"Just promise me you won't decide until I get back," I said.

"I promise. I love you. Now you be good and enjoy yourself." She kissed me on the cheek.

"Ah, Phyllis," said Rasper, smiling.

"Douglas." My mom giggled like a girl at the junior high prom being asked to dance.

"You should be very proud of Eli," he said. "He's a fine addition to our choir."

"All he does is talk about you and the chorus," she said.

"I wish there was a way that you could join us," he said. "Perhaps we can continue discussing Eli's future when we return," said Rasper.

"I'd like that very much," said my mom, beaming.

"Mom!" I interjected.

"Now, Eli," said Rasper. "Your mother is concerned about you. She's also very special herself."

"Oh stop," she said, blushing.

Rasper took her hand and kissed it. "When I return…"

He smiled again, turned around, and went back to his clipboard, disappearing into the crowds.

My mother looked like she needed a minute, so I disappeared too. I went to go find Charley.

Hubert and Florinda were seated quietly next to their faded, brown leather carry-on luggage. Lady Bear refused to take off her fur and was wearing it proudly. Her face was more intensely made up than usual, bringing her entire look to what could only be described as DEFCON 4. Bart Rollins and his wife, Eunice Clancy, strolled around with Little Francis, trying to keep him engaged so he wouldn't cry or get sick.

"Boys," said Rasper in a voice that cut through all the ambient, busy noise. We all disengaged from our parents and stood at attention. Even the parents stood and listened for further instructions. "Boys, I have two pieces of good news. One: we have someone new joining the choir. Mr. Ponte, please step forward."

A young-looking man stood up and waved at us. He had a large mole under his right eye. He looked too old to be in the choir but too young to be doing anything else.

"Mr. Ponte will act as our interpreter throughout our tour. He isn't an official choir member and won't be expected to actually sing. But he will help us navigate more efficiently through Italy. Please make him feel at home."

No one seemed surprised or excited by this. I actually hadn't thought about the language barrier. It did strike me as odd that Rasper would spring for the extra expense of an interpreter. But Charley's parents might have kicked in the extra money. I looked over at Charley and felt bad for him. His parents were still away so he was there with his valet. How embarrassing.

"And now," continued Rasper. "The second surprise. Anna Bond and her Channel 2 Eyewitness News team will be here any minute to interview us and provide press coverage of our trip. Please be on your best behavior."

There was a joyous murmur in our group. We were going to be on TV! Unfortunately, we wouldn't be around to watch ourselves later that night. My mom turned to me and promised she would watch. It was the first week of August and TV was filled with reruns. I hoped my friends would all see me anyway.

"I'll even take a Polaroid of the TV so you can see yourself on it," said my mom.

A few minutes later, right on cue, Anna Bond and her news crew arrived, walking toward our gate with purpose.

Rasper snapped his fingers and we all got into our choir positions. The parents and chaperones moved to the side. "We will sing one song for the cameras," he said to us.

Anna Bond interviewed Rasper under the bright camera lights for about ten minutes. We remained in the background like window dressing. I wondered if we were going to be interviewed or even get to sing. Then Rasper walked towards us and raised his hands. We sang a chorus of "God Bless America" for the cameras.

The news crew thanked us and packed up. The airline announced boarding and I said a last goodbye to my mom. I walked with Charley onto the plane with the feeling this was one of life's greatest moments.

We left JFK on time, bound for Ireland. We were then switching planes and taking a flight to Milan. I think the plane was continuing on to Rome. We would eventually get to Rome ourselves but by train via many city stops in between.

It was a big plane with a wide aisle down the middle. I got seated next to Hubert and Florinda. Hubert was smoking furiously. Half the passengers were smoking and it was amazing our young, singing lungs didn't collapse in protest. The poor passengers in the non-smoking section were starting to complain about their red eyes and coughing so the stewardesses were throwing complimentary vodka their way as quickly as they could scoop up the little, glass bottles.

"I just love the initiation of new tenors," said Florinda. She and I sat in the middle seats with Hubert staring forlornly out the window. This was a conversation I didn't want to get into. Everything about Florinda spelled trouble to me. Plus, Big Francis was just a few rows back and I could feel his meaty eyes on the back of my head. I didn't want her to appear too friendly to me. It seemed dangerous getting in the middle of whatever was going on between Florida and Big Francis. Instead, I leaned across her towards Hubert.

"Mr. Breggleman, are you looking forward to the trip?" I asked.

He sighed and Florinda looked like she was squeezing his hand tighter.

"I'm looking forward to getting back," he said.

"Sorry again to hear about your aunt," I said. "I know what it's like."

"How do you mean?" said Florinda.

I didn't want to get into this. But it was going to be a long flight. "My dad died when I was three so..."

"Do you remember him?" asked Hubert, turning to look at me for the first time on the flight.

"Sort of," I said. I didn't want to share my plan to go visit his hometown. That was not adult-appropriate information.

He took a deep drag on his cigarette. "I never knew my aunt. I hear she was wealthy and..."

"And we're excited to be chaperones for your tour," interrupted Florinda.

Even though I had overheard Hubert's plan to receive his inheritance in Italy, it was still a surprise to learn Hubert was making the trip. Charley told me he rarely traveled with the choir outside of the New York area. He had a thing about being away from home too long. Hubert was generally quiet, particularly around Florinda, when he was out in public. Florinda would always accompany us to our concerts, sitting next to Hubert on the small piano bench. She seemed to be devoted to him despite her flirtatious nature with Big Francis. And she was Lady Bear's niece which no one talked about. They were quite a puzzle.

I wondered what the big mystery was with Hubert's inheritance from his aunt and why Lady Bear and Mrs. Clancy cared so much. I was pretty sure it had to do with Romatene. At least in my fantasy. And speaking of fantasies, I kept thinking about Jane and wishing she was on this trip with me.

I had sat next to Hubert and Florinda for over an hour and still hadn't come close to unraveling their mystery. Periodically, she would laugh out loud about something she was reading in her magazine. She'd point it out to Hubert who would just smile politely. She'd then turn to me and roll her eyes conspiratorially, as if to suggest we were in cahoots to reform Hubert's sense of humor. When I'd politely smile back at her, bewildered, she'd laugh ever louder and poke Hubert in the ribs. He'd hold her hand and sometimes kiss it. I sat there and watched this routine as we crossed the Atlantic and thought, *This is how crazy people behave.*

I got up to find Charley. Big Francis, who had been sitting next to Charley, gladly switched seats with me so he could put in his own face time with Florinda.

"Eli, I can't believe you think Florinda is involved with some drug deal," said Charley.

"You don't believe me?" I asked, trying to sound hurt.

"Bingo."

"Well then," I said, "I have to report this to Rasper. He'll believe me and get her kicked off."

"No, Eli," said Charley, suddenly alarmed.

"What's wrong?"

"If you tell Rasper, he'll place a curfew on the whole choir. That's what he does for stuff like this."

"A curfew?" I said. "I was just kidding around."

"I can't have a curfew."

"Then how about you go along with something else I have brewing," I said.

Charley rolled his eyes. He fidgeted with the airplane window shade. There wasn't anything to see outside but cloudy darkness. Inside, the smoke-filled cabin was making everything hazy.

"What?" he asked, finally.

"What if I told you that Rasper is a CIA agent?"

"Eli," said Charley.

"And he booked us on Evergreen Airlines as a cover." I handed Charley my newspaper so he could catch up on current events.

Before we took off, I read in the paper that the airline we'd be flying on, Evergreen Airlines, was facing charges of conspiracy and failure to cooperate with the FAA. The FAA was alleging that Evergreen may have acted as a front for the CIA and may have been used, according to some Byzantine plan, to shuttle the Shah of Iran to America via Evergreen's home base: Shannon Airport in Ireland. As if the Shah of Iran was a critical person to world peace.

Leave it to Rasper and his legendary cheapness to find this airline deal for his beloved singing boys.

"Alright, I'm in, whatever this is. Just don't piss off Rasper. I can't have a curfew," said Charley.

"I'm going to talk to the rest of the chaperones to see if they are CIA as well," I said. "Cover me."

Charley went back to reading his book.

I saw Mr. Rollins, Mrs. Clancy, and Lady Bear seated together. The only choir boy sitting anywhere near them was Little Francis. They didn't once look around to check on the choir. They were too involved with smoking and reading. Even Little Francis was being ignored. I could already tell what kind of chaperones they were going to be.

There was nowhere to sit next to them, so I stood in the aisle next to Mr. Rollins.

"Hi, Mr. Rollins," I said.

"Bart. Call me Bart, Eli."

There weren't too many adults who wanted me to call them by their first name. I tried his name on for size. "Hi Bart," I said. It sounded good.

"Ready for your Italian adventure?" he asked. "I know Francis is very excited."

I looked over at Little Francis and he gave a weak smile. It was abundantly clear he'd rather be eating Cap'n Crunch in front of the TV and watching Tom and Jerry.

"I can't wait," I said.

"Prepare yourself for romance and mystery," said Bart in a mischievous way.

"Bartholomew," screeched Mrs. Clancy. "Stop filling the boy's head with such foolishness." She turned to me. "And you, go sit down somewhere and leave the adults alone."

Bart looked apologetically to me as if he was powerless to do anything about this. Mrs. Clancy didn't wait for me to leave. She just turned back to continue the clandestine conversation she was having with Lady Bear.

We deplaned in Ireland while the plane re-fueled. In our first taste of international freedom, Rasper announced we had one hour to wander on our own in the international terminal.

"Don't waste any of your spending money on duty-free anything," he warned as we slowly stole away from his circle near Gate A-16. "And Hubert will assign chaperones for the sopranos."

Hubert began pairing sopranos with the baritones. Lady Bear and Mrs. Clancy took the opportunity to steal away and leave the homesick kids to stew in their own juices for a while. Some of these kids, mostly sopranos, were even weeping for their parents. Little Francis grabbed Bart's hand tight and didn't let go.

I breathed a sigh of relief as Charley and I ran away. Some of the tenors were clustered around a bank of pay phones looking for loose change. A gaggle of high school girls were desperately trying to get their attention, but these girls were barking up the wrong tree.

Suddenly, Charley stopped running.

"What is it?" I asked.

"I was just thinking," said Charley, slightly out of breath. "A few hours ago, we were just a bunch of geeky kids from Long Island."

"Aren't we still?"

"Not here. Not anymore." Charley pointed to the crowds rushing in all directions on their way to everywhere in the world.

"These people don't know us," continued Charley, his ninety-eight-pound frame trembling with excitement. "We could be anybody. Quarterback of the high school team."

I looked incredulously at him. He made perfect sense. "Well, I don't know if I even want to pretend to be a jock. But we could be famous theater actors, taking our Tony awards on tour."

We sighed deeply.

The high school girls across the terminal walked off toward the cafeteria. We looked at each other and knew we would be following them in there. We'd sit across from them, send an order of orange juice to their table compliments of the young millionaires just in from the Coast. There would be sparkling conversation, something like, "We'd love to have your phone numbers. And we promise to stop in whenever we're in … where are you from again? Sweden? Ah, yes. Well, what about a kiss to remember you by? One at a time, ladies. Tongues? Well, when in Sweden…"

Charley and I laughed at our communal fantasy and went off to buy whatever overpriced Irish duty-free chocolate crap they had. We sat down on the floor in some unpopulated concourse next to a newspaper stand. I stared at the headlines and decided to share my secret information with Charley.

"I have something big," I said.

"Is this a dick joke?" Charley asked.

"Shut up, Charley. No, listen. I've been thinking about this trip. The people on the plane with us."

"Who? Us and the chaperone dorks?"

"The CIA."

"Shut up," said Charley.

"Evergreen Airlines and the Shah of Iran and the CIA. It all makes sense. Follow me."

Charley rolled his eyes. I stood up and Charley followed me through the crowds. We walked to the departures board and I pointed to our Evergreen flight leaving in half an hour.

"We land in Milan," said Charley, not putting it together yet.

"Exactly," I said. "And where does it go from Milan?"

Charley searched the board. "Rome," he concluded. "But we're going to Rome later by train."

"Right. And what's in Rome? The Vatican," I said dramatically. Then, I pointed to the newspaper headlines. "Where he lives."

The new Pope.

The thirty-day Pope, John Paul, had died. I liked the one who died. He was half the Beatles.

"Yeah, so?" remarked Charley, unimpressed. "The Pope is in the Vatican. That's where they keep him. What's this have to do with us?"

I lowered my voice. "Don't you get it? The Pope's political views have made him enemies," I said, showing Charley the front pages.

"What politics?" said a voice behind us.

It was Ponte, our mysterious translator. He carried a gym bag slung over his shoulder and was wearing sunglasses inside the airport.

"Nothing," I said, walking away. "We're just messing around."

"See you back on the plane, Mr. Mitchell," said Ponte.

Charley caught up with me. "How does he know your name?"

"Who knows? Maybe he's part of the CIA too," I said. "Come on, better get back to our gate."

Charley looked at me and nodded his head condescendingly. "Eli, this is bullshit. Your imagination's going way over board this time. Come on, let's go have some fun. We still have a few minutes."

He walked off but I quickly caught up with him.

"Wait, I know it sounds crazy, but look," I said emphatically and pointed to a well-dressed man in his thirties talking on a pay phone. "That guy has been watching us the whole time."

"You're right," said Charley. "I was hoping it was a coincidence."

The man sported a trim beard and had a look of efficiency and urgency about him. He wore a fedora hat and paisley scarf around his neck that told me he wasn't from America. His sunglasses reflected the terminal fluorescent lights and hid his eyes from us.

"And look," said Charley.

Ponte approached the man and the two of them got into an intense discussion.

"That's the guy. The one making the arrangements," I said. "Just watch. And he's talking to Ponte. They're both with the CIA," I said.

"Eli, I know you were kidding around before but…"

Ponte walked off towards our gate. Just then, the man with the fedora hat checked his watch. His jacket came away from him and something in his inner jacket pocket was revealed. Something shiny that also reflected the fluorescent lights. Perhaps something metallic.

"You see that?" I said. "Right there."

Charley was speechless.

"Say it, Charley. You saw it too."

"A gun," he finally said. "Jesus."

We looked at each other and we were scared.

"What do we do now?" said Charley.

"I don't know. I was bullshitting you before."

"Asshole."

"We need more evidence. We can't go to anyone with this yet. I mean, you didn't believe me," I said.

"Yeah, but that was when it wasn't true," said Charley with a little too much logic.

"Let's wait and see what Ponte does on the plane," I said.

"What about this guy?" asked Charley, indicating our armed friend.

"Ireland can have him," I said.

And with that, we walked back to the plane. Ireland had forged a deeper friendship between Charley and me. We weren't just going to Rome to sing in cathedrals. That was officially our cover. We were going to lay bare a CIA conspiracy. Or something. We weren't really quite sure what was going on.

When we boarded the new plane to Milan, I looked for Ponte. He was in a window seat reading a book. Charley and I sat down together. A few minutes later, Charley elbowed me. The man with the fedora hat, our spy, sauntered in and sat three rows in front of us at a window seat. I started sweating. Were we in danger? This was ridiculous. My own imagination was getting the better of me. Still, luck had placed him at a safe distance where I could keep a careful eye on him.

The plane engine rumbled and made my teeth chatter. The plane was filled with people, so I had to focus on his activities and not let myself be distracted by the conversations around me or the curious backs of people's heads. Charley got bored quickly with the spy game and moved on as my spy partner and co-protector of the free world to more dubious activities. He was throwing peanuts at the old lady in front of him.

The man trapped in my surveillance net was doing his damndest not to appear suspicious. He smoked cigarette after cigarette and occasionally blew smoke rings at the non-smoking section in front of him. Rasper had managed to obtain seating for most of the choir in the smoking section. Just what we needed. Most of the smoking adults were, of course, seated in the non-smoking section.

Behind me, Lady Bear chattered on to a total stranger. No one else in our group wanted to sit next to her. Even Rasper surprisingly avoided her on this flight. According to Lady Bear, somewhere in her travels, although she was vague on details, she learned she may have been actual royalty. Maybe she was a real Lady Bear. Her opinions were expressed loudly, as if undisputed fact, in that gravelly voice of hers.

From what Charley had told me, Rasper had charmed her years ago, had poured out his dreams and unfulfilled promises, and Lady Bear responded appropriately. She lavished him with small gifts at first but when she saw he was serious about this boys' choir business, that it wasn't some passing fancy or some line to get hold of her money, she adopted him as a charity. Charley once overheard Rasper say it legitimized her.

"They should always leave at least one first-class seat open," Lady Bear proclaimed again for the whole plane section to hear. "In case someone shows up. Someone who really deserves it."

The poor man seated next to her tried fake sleeping but his regular breathing gave him away. Lady Bear gave him a shake as if he were a pinball machine she was trying to tilt.

"I mean, it's one thing to sit back here with the cattle when you're used to it." Finally, she sighed. "Ah well. It's my cross to bear." She got up from her seat, still wearing her fur coat.

"Excuse me," Lady Bear ordered the faux-sleeping man. As she shimmied her way from her window seat, her hand slipped and smacked me in the back of my head with her large diamond ring.

"Pardon," she said, no doubt an expression she learned from the butler who put too much cream in her afternoon tea. *Why couldn't she afford to sponsor this trip?*

No one moved for her. She was, at worst, a source of irritation and, at best, a snide source of distant amusement, depending on where you were sitting.

"I need to use the ladies, if you please," Lady Bear said sharply to the still fake-sleeping man next to her. She gave him a genial yet firm shake that told him she meant business.

He slowly opened his eyes, stared at her for a while, then finally lifted his knees to his chest, allowing a small corridor of passage for her.

"A little wider please," she insisted like a dental assistant.

"Lady," the man said, fully opening his eyes, "this is all the room the cattle are giving you."

I made a little, silent cheer, as I'm sure everyone did. Lady Bear awkwardly maneuvered her way out of the small enclosure. I imagined her only similar experience was getting through the Christmas crowds at Bloomies.

I felt the ping of her giant diamond ring on my head once more before Lady Bear went to have a cattle-class pee. She returned to her seat at the same time the movie screen lowered. The flight attendant at the front of the cabin walked down the aisle handing out headsets to everyone. Just as I was opening up the plastic bag to let my headset out, the projector made a terrible crackling sound. The movie screen folded up into the ceiling.

"I'm sorry," said the lead flight attendant, "but we're experiencing technical difficulties with our in-flight motion picture system. We are looking into the difficulty and will keep you posted."

Great. Three more hours of the complaining society dame behind me. And still, the spy hadn't moved. He just smoked and smoked.

Just then, Rasper stood up and tapped the choir boys on their shoulders.

INTERLUDE

In the 1940s, the Liscio Corporation was a mid-sized cigarette company based in Rome. They mostly sold their coffin nails domestically. With war in full swing, Italian soldiers demanded lots of voluntary ways to kill themselves and smoking was at the top of their list. With the Italian smoking population growing and outpacing the rest of the breathing world, Liscio cigarettes were in steep competition with dozens of other Italian manufacturers. They needed an angle, a hook. Something to make their cigarettes stand apart.

They had already tried advertising to different markets. No luck. People were loyally entrenched with their cigarette brand. Liscio then hired an advertising firm who suggested they run a year-long campaign aimed strictly at women. Another complete failure. Italian soldiers noticed the prominent ads and associated Liscio cigarettes with being effeminate. The advertising firm was fired and Liscio went back to the drawing board trying to unravel the puzzle of how they could stuff more of their cigarettes into the lips and lungs of the smoking public.

During the year of the *"Liscio Sigarette per le Signore"* ("Cigarettes for the Ladies") campaign, a Liscio research scientist, Enzo Gabrizzi, was spending all his time in the research lab. He preferred the lab to his childless home. Home was where his wife made a cuckold of him with a minor Corporal at least once a week and all his neighbors knew it. Gabrizzi had been eating his lunch one day at his lab, staring at the tree out his fifth-floor window, when the idea struck him. Oddly, it was while watching two squirrels perform their mating dance, circling each other in a storm of fur. He thought of his wife and wondered what he was going to do with his life. Gabrizzi was a short, balding man in his forties and knew he wasn't any kind of prospect for attractive women. The army hadn't wanted him either. This idea of his had the power to transport him to a better life. A life without her. A life where, perhaps, an attractive woman would welcome him.

He cleared his lab bench and began working out the formulas necessary to make this idea work. He didn't share his idea with anyone. He needed to see if it was sustainable first. Gabrizzi worked on his experiment long after the other men had gone home to their wives and weekends. No women were working in the research lab. Gabrizzi studied Liscio's tobacco leaves and played with grafting other plants to the tobacco plant.

After nine months, Gabrizzi presented his findings to the Liscio Board. Gabrizzi told the Board his data pointed to an incredible innovation.

An edible cigarette. A cigarette you could eat or smoke. Or both. His charts and formulas were laid out on the conference room table like menus to hungry trattoria customers. He requested funding to continue his research. The marketing team latched onto the idea immediately. They dreamed up different flavors of cigarettes and how they could now sell them to kids. You'd eat them as a kid, then smoke them as an adult. Italian soldiers, miles away from fresh supply lines, could eat their cigarettes when their rations ran out. The Liscio Board was desperate enough that they granted Gabrizzi his research funds on the spot. They gave him six months to produce results.

Gabrizzi, never a social animal, always found it difficult to make friends at work. He found himself with a need and budget to hire staff. He discovered the process intoxicating. He realized the missing ingredient in his life: power. Once he realized he had control over who entered his life and worked for him, he found work relationships to be easy. His wife certainly never listened to him. In the Gabrizzi lab, everyone's job was to listen to everything he said. He built an entire secure lab and hired his dedicated staff, each sworn to secrecy to avoid trade secrets from being revealed to competitors. They all worked with purpose for six months, giving up weekends and most evenings. The staff included the only woman in the lab.

Sofia was a thirty-something, red-headed woman with a Master's degree in Chemistry. He always assigned Sofia to work at the opposite end of the lab so she wouldn't distract him.

At first, the experiment results were predictable for the intermediate products that resulted. Grafting different vegetable leaves onto tobacco proved relatively easy but getting that new plant to the next step proved elusive in practice. Like his marriage certificate, on paper, Gabrizzi's formulas marked the path towards success. He mostly stayed away from home, hoping to make his monumental discovery before announcing he would be leaving his wife. And thought of maybe asking out Sofia. Every day, the lab filled with smoke, and the smoke dissipated, leaving little progress but many more questions. Gabrizzi and his staff were disheartened. Then, occasionally, someone would make a little breakthrough, and everyone would be bucked up and productive work would continue.

One day, Gabrizzi went back to his original calculations and formulas. He was drinking his morning espresso when he had another revelation. It was the caffeine molecule. He had written it in shorthand originally but had forgotten to include a carbon chain. He went back to the microscope and began experimenting. Later, during his daily briefing, his staff gathered around and took copious notes, hungry for good news. He noticed Sofia, in particular, hung on his every word. They were all sure they were on the brink of discovering a product that would revolutionize the world. No one was surer than Gabrizzi.

Except it didn't work. The caffeine-augmented tobacco leaves were an utter failure. The lab mice wouldn't eat the minced tobacco leaves no matter how much the leaves were processed. The leaves smelled pleasant enough. But Gabrizzi couldn't improve on the basic tobacco leaf. After six months, they gave up on the last trial and the staff slowly resigned, one by one, including Sofia. Liscio's Board pulled Gabrizzi's funding, thanking him for his efforts before firing him.

Gabrizzi went home to find his wife had left him for the Corporal. She had been thoughtful enough to leave him the house but took every single possession in it except his clothes. A week later, Gabrizzi called on Sofia, having written her address down from her employee file. She slammed the door in his face. Now that he wasn't her boss or ticket to fame and fortune, the value of Gabrizzi's currency in her life had plummeted. Gabrizzi moved back into his empty house. He never invented anything again. The spark of imagination, driven largely by revenge for his wife's infidelity, never returned. He died alone years later in his home watching two squirrels chasing each other up a tree.

Liscio needed Gabrizzi's lab the day they fired him. They discarded all his notes and experimental leaves in the bin behind the lab.

One of Gabrizzi's lesser lab workers, Salvatore Piccolo, waited for the janitors to finish their job cleaning out the lab. He was in his twenties. His girlfriend, Nella, also in her twenties, thought he had a handsome face ever since the two had first dated when they were sixteen. His black hair stuck straight up, always giving him the appearance of someone who was in a constant state of shock. When Piccolo was sure the janitors were gone, he reached his long arms into the garbage bin and rummaged. He found the dozens of glass jars of minced tobacco leaves from Gabrizzi's final experiment and placed them carefully in his leather satchel. He also took the three-ring binder filled with Gabrizzi's lab notes.

He lived a short train ride away from Rome in a modest house in the small town of Frascati. Nella lived with her parents on the other side of town. Frascati was a quiet town whose only points of interest were the train station and the girl's orphanage run by a convent of strict nuns based in the town of Aprilia. Piccolo knew the train station well but always steered clear of the orphanage. He thought it was bad luck to go near it.

Piccolo biked from the train station to Nella's house. She opened her parents' front door and radiated warmth. Her smooth, olive skin glowed and made her broad smile and beautiful almond-shaped brown eyes shine more than usual. She had her long brown hair in a ponytail and wore a simple house dress with an apron. When she smiled, little dimples around her mouth added to her appeal. She kissed Piccolo warmly and asked him to come inside. He smiled shyly and said he couldn't. He told her he had some matters to attend and would see her in about two weeks. She had lived through his schemes before and knew better than to question them.

Piccolo biked home and parked his bike on the side of his house. He entered through the back door. It was a one-bedroom house he had inherited from his parents. He walked upstairs to his bedroom and opened the satchel. He carefully laid out a tablecloth on the floor and poured out the minced augmented tobacco leaves from the first glass jar.

Piccolo couldn't afford to eat out and Frascati didn't have many dining options. When Nella wasn't over making him a meal, he learned to cook for himself and saw a direct correlation between cooking and his science experiments at Liscio. He took out his mezzaluna chopper and wooden bowl, usually used for finely mincing herbs, and worked the tobacco leaves. When he was pleased with their shredded size, he took out a small sheaf of rolling paper.

The lab experiments had been so focused on eating the processed leaves, no one had thought to simply smoke them. He lit his homemade cigarette and inhaled deeply. Salvatore Piccolo didn't come out of his house for nine days. The high was like nothing he had ever experienced. He was flying, he was swimming. He was a supersonic jet circling the galaxy that had suddenly converted to neon lights, a bursting submarine piercing the dark envelope of the ocean lit only by radiant fish.

On the tenth day, his mind still hazy and wild with creativity, Piccolo opened Gabrizzi's lab notes and devoured the information. He thought of smoking the pages but decided it was better to keep them intact for now. He had resigned from Gabrizzi's team but still held a job at Liscio. He called them and quit his job. He went to dinner with Nella but hadn't told her his discovery yet. He just smiled all evening, and she knew he had struck gold. She trusted him implicitly.

Piccolo called family and friends and borrowed money from everyone he knew so he could purchase equipment for his basement. No one asked what the money was for. They thought they were just helping out Piccolo in between jobs. *He is a bright fellow,* they thought, *and will get another job at a chemistry lab soon.*

Piccolo plunged full time into homemade Romatene production in his basement.

He knew it was never going to be for personal use only. In fact, he made himself a schedule of when he could smoke it so it wouldn't impact his manufacturing. He would visit the rainbow stars and luminescent bottom of the ocean once every ten days. He made Romatene in the form of half-cigarettes since he figured most people couldn't handle their potency in larger quantities. When his garden was filled with the augmented tobacco plants and his house overflowed with foil-wrapped half-cigarettes, he went into distribution.

He started in the alleyways of Rome. When word quickly spread of this miracle drug, Piccolo was forced to hire some kids to help him with the demand. It was at this point that Nella approached him and demanded to know what his secret was. He knew she was the only one he could trust in this world, and he told her everything. Nella smiled when he showed her his home laboratory and discussed his finances and operations with her. Nella told him she loved him and they were married a month later in a private ceremony with no family. Piccolo had paid back all his investors so they wouldn't ask to be included in his business.

He amassed a quiet fortune within three months of his first sale. Piccolo sold his house and bought a larger one in Rome for him and Nella where he could concentrate on mass production. By this time, he had silent investors and a growing cult of users and followers.

He was careful who worked for him. There were rumors Romatene was cutting into the usual drug trade in Rome. Piccolo didn't want to make enemies and kept himself anonymous as best he could. He always kept Nella directly out of the business. He was wary of people in general, always suspect they were after his Romatene, or worse, his Romatene formula.

One evening, on a rare night off, he and Nella were in Rome, sitting at one of the outside tables in the piazza, sipping white wine in the cool night air. Their life had properly begun and they smiled at each other. Piccolo ordered a second wine and noticed that Nella asked for water. He looked at her and she smiled back, her hands folded against her smooth belly. He knew she was carrying his child. They toasted to their luck and success.

On the way home, she wanted to tell her parents the good news. He dropped her off at her parents' house and drove back to theirs to check on the Romatene harvest and production.

When two hours went by, with no sign of Piccolo, Nella got a ride back to their house from her father. They were still a mile away when she saw the flames and smoke in the exact direction of their home. Her father stopped the car, but Nella insisted they drive on and advance toward the blazing house and farm. Nella could only get a few hundred feet away before the smoke choked her. Nella's tears wouldn't permit her to get any closer. Nella had to wait until the next day before the fire and smoke had completely cleared.

Piccolo's remains were strewn among the ash and rubble that used to be their home and garden. All traces of their Romatene crop and production had been set ablaze.

Nella knew calling the police was futile since they were probably in on it. Various competitors, corrupt police, and underworld figures were obvious suspects in the death of Piccolo and Romatene. They had reached out to Piccolo previously to convince him to share the formula for half his profits. The violence was sudden and short-lived. The Romatene war Piccolo had feared was over before it began. The mob had unknowingly blown up all traces of Romatene when they set Piccolo's house on fire.

False reports of Romatene continued to surface from time to time. No one took it seriously. The drug trade went on as before. Now, instead of Romatene spreading wildly, its rumors covered the planet.

Nella escaped with her parents the day after the fire. She didn't know if anyone was after her, but she didn't want to take any chances. She had her baby in a small Italian village two hundred miles away. Years later, she returned to Frascati. She missed her town too much and figured enough time had passed. That's where she fell in love for the second time in her life with a visiting American named Bart Rollins.

PART TWO
ITALY
AUGUST 1979

CHAPTER EIGHTEEN

***Gregorian Chant**—Singing or chanting in unison without strict rhythm.*

The difference between America and Italy, or at least between Long Island and Milan, was that in Milan, sixteen-year-old boys were treated like men. I was allowed to drink beer, stay out late, ogle women, and get a job. I would have been doing all these things, maybe even at the same time, but I was a visitor. With chaperones. Lots of chaperones.

The adult chaperones, six in all, were seated around the fountain bench in the center of the Piazza del Duomo in Milan, sipping espresso under the early morning salmon sky. Birds sang all around, replacing the plane engine noise that had been embedded in my brain. Seventeen choir boys made the trip, including me. We sat on the ground like a little supplicant army. Rasper stood in front of us, assuming his post as commander-in-choir, going over his travel plans for the upcoming week.

"This itinerary sucks," someone whispered from the back row. Probably Big Francis. Rasper heard it and looked annoyed.

"Who said that?" he asked, interrupting his own speech. He clearly knew who said it. He could identify each of our speaking and singing voices at forty paces. But even overseas, Rasper had a sweet spot for Big Francis and let it slide.

The problem was all the choir boys thought the itinerary sucked. We had flown into Milan yesterday to find our hotel wasn't expecting us until today. Rasper slammed his fist on the hotel registration desk but they were simply booked solid for the night. We were generally sleeping four to a room and the chaperones had the usual adult accommodations. Instead, last night, we all slept on the street. It took the shine off the trip and a lot of our illusions of a fantasy life were slapped away by the cold, hard concrete of the Milanese gutter. And we were disappointed there was no media to greet and interview us like when we left New York.

Lady Bear, of course, went ballistic. But out of all of us, she was the only one who had gotten a decent night's sleep. It became a survival advantage when you walked around with a furry sleeping bag draped around your shoulders all the time.

"Pay attention," said Rasper. "I want you all to start relying on Mr. Ponte, our Italian liaison. He used to live in Rome and even sang with a local choir in his younger days. Besides being an interpreter, he will be acting as a sort of guide."

Ponte smiled weakly, stepped forward, and nodded. Travel, jet lag, and sleeping in the street had not agreed with him. He looked disheveled and irritable. In other words, he looked like part of our choir.

Rasper continued with the first week's itinerary. Our entire tour took us through Italy for three weeks but apparently, we were only trustworthy enough with one week of information at a time.

"Can we sit on the stairs?" asked Big Francis, indicating the marble steps that led to the upper tier of the piazza.

Rasper considered the move from the street the way a general considered moving his troops through enemy territory at midnight. After a dramatic pause, he acquiesced. We all stood up, stretched, and sat down on the steps. Rasper approached us while the other five adults stayed put. I imagined they were more upset than we were about the sleeping arrangements last night. After we artfully arranged ourselves on the steps of the pigeon-crowded square, Rasper proceeded with further instruction.

Hubert and his wife Florinda sat in the middle of the adult cluster. Hubert was the closest tie to the choir power structure and the one most familiar with the rigors of touring with a team of unruly, gifted, and precocious boys. Hubert and Florinda held hands but faced in opposite directions. They were in silhouette against the sun which gave the illusion they were some odd two-headed monster. It didn't seem they were speaking to each other but that may have been due to the lack of sleep.

Lady Bear sat next to Hubert, tightly clutching the lapels of the fur she wore as if she was deathly afraid of it being stolen. She was chatting Hubert's ear off while puffing smoke indignantly in everyone's general direction. She had already made changes to our plans in Venice, requesting to stay in a better room with a grander view. She wanted more stars added to her hotel's rating.

"One that doesn't quite reek so much of fish and sewage," Lady Bear had imperiously demanded of Rasper.

Venice was in three days. I was sure Rasper was trying to figure out how drunk he needed to get the old broad so she'd agree to pay the difference for a better Venetian hotel.

"My grandparents are already bored," said Little Francis, mostly to himself. He stood in front of me so I could see his short, wiry eight-year-old frame balancing his crooked haircut. His grandparents, Bart and Eunice Rollins, although we still referred to her as Mrs. Clancy, generally looked more anxious than bored. They must have been on the distant side of sixty. No one knew exactly how they were allowed to chaperone us or how they beat out less geriatric candidates for this position. I was also not quite sure why they were interested in joining their eight-year-old grandson on a singing tour. Mr. Rollins still liked to be called Bart and was friendly enough. Mrs. Clancy was too friendly with Lady Bear for my liking. I always kept an eye on her.

Bart Rollins leaned on his wife's shoulder while she read a travel brochure. On closer inspection, he was sound asleep, and his snoring would startle the Milanese pigeons and cause them to flutter away to less thunderous pastures.

My attention was momentarily drawn to a man watching Hubert from a distance. I noticed him because he had been staring at Hubert for several minutes. The man also looked like a pirate. He had an intense, penetrating stare and black curly hair. He wore khakis and a loose white linen shirt the way pirates did in movies. After a few minutes, he disappeared into the crowd.

Hubert massaged the small of his back. When we found out there was no room for us at the inn the previous night, part of me had hoped this trip would be canceled so we could fly back home tomorrow and I could find that Jane girl. I found myself thinking about her a lot.

"Eli," demanded Rasper.

My daydreaming ceased and my attention snapped front and center to our choirmaster. He had that kind of effect.

"Thank you," he said. He looked at us, his head swaying from side to side like a spectator at a tennis match, making sure all eyes were on him. "Now," continued Rasper with a slight change in his tone, "the hotel here in Milan and the one in Venice are already paid for. But hotels in Florence and Rome and a few towns in between aren't yet. We'll be singing for our supper to earn our keep after Venice. Just thought you should all know."

Lady Bear made a clucking noise with her tongue and I knew something was afoul. We were told back in New York that everything was covered. We were being bait-and-switched. I mean, I still would have gone to Italy if I had known our lodging was non-existent, but it felt good to have something to complain about.

"Rehearsal at the Milan Cathedral tonight at nine," continued Rasper. "Adjust your watches to Italy time, no running around, and remember, we're not only guests here but representatives of our country."

"As long as there's no pressure," I muttered under my breath.

Charley added, "We're like Olympiads." I elbowed him in the ribs.

"And finally, the topic of free time," said Rasper with a dramatic flourish. "Our itinerary allows a certain amount of time when you are on your own. Baritones and tenors, look after the altos and sopranos as always. Francis, please stay out of trouble."

Big Francis shrunk in his skin.

"Mr. Ponte is here to help," continued Rasper. "Stay within four blocks of the hotel. Buddy system is an absolute requirement. Watch your spending money and be back in an hour."

"For God's sake, just let them loose," yelled Lady Bear. It was the first sensible thing she had ever said in her life.

We burst out of there in every direction like scared pigeons.

It was the first time any of us had been on our own with no parental encumbrances in a foreign land. Hell, for some of us, this was the first taste of freedom ever. We had an hour to find adventure, work out our demons of attachment and apron strings, find independence, see if it was true that Italian men practiced a common ritual of cute-girl-ass pinching, have an official Italian gelato, and hurry back to the hotel. And, I suspected, one of us also had to find a Romatene dealer for Eddie.

Charley and I wandered off a few blocks and were captivated by the display window at a bakery. It was early in the morning and the smell was irresistible. Terrence walked up and asked if he could hang around with us. Charley rolled his eyes, but I knew what it was like to be an alto who wanted to be with the big kids.

"Of course," I said.

We stared at the pastries like we were ogling a Playboy centerfold.

"Anyone exchange their money for lire yet?" I asked.

"I'm going to go do that right now," said Terrence, reaching for the wallet in his back pocket.

A man in his twenties wearing a blue newsboy cap breezed by, reached into Terrence's back pocket, grabbed his wallet, and took off down the street. Terrence stood frozen, unsure of what had happened.

"Hey!" I yelled.

"Let's get him," said Charley.

The three of us took after the guy in the blue cap.

"Oh man, oh man," said Terrence, crying, all his money stolen on the first day.

The man in the blue cap ran into the square, crowded with tourists, shoppers, and pigeons. He was sprinting in a zigzag fashion, trying to avoid the human obstacles. We were doing a pretty good job at catching up to him. He turned a corner at the square and we lost sight of him.

"No, that's it!" said Terrence, sounding defeated.

We kept running at full speed and headed to the corner. When we made the turn, we practically ran over the blue cap. The former blue cap wearer was dangling in the air, his feet kicking but not making contact with the ground. The man grasping the pickpocket from the neck was the pirate. The pirate slapped the pickpocket with his free hand which caused Terrence's wallet to fly to the ground.

"Thank you," screamed Terrence, overjoyed.

"*Ora di che ti dispiace*," said the pirate to the pickpocket.

"Who are you?" I asked.

The pirate shook the pickpocket menacingly.

"*Spiacente!*" said the pickpocket to us. "Sorry."

"Now you go from here, boys," said the pirate.

We ran off toward the comfort and security of the choir.

"I can't believe that happened," said Terrence. "That was so cool!"

"Who was that guy?" I asked as we made it through the square again.

"Mob," said Charley calmly. "Clearly, the mob."

CHAPTER NINETEEN

Fugue*—A composition written for multiple voices. Beginning with the exposition, each voice enters at different times, creating counterpoint with one another.*

As soon as we landed in Rome, I found an airport payphone. It was late in the evening. I took out my cousin Anna's letter and called the phone number she had included. April stood next to me, still in disbelief that we were actually here.

"Do convents have phones?" April asked. "Is there, like, a nun receptionist?"

There was no answer. I let it keep ringing. Finally, I hung up. This trip was not starting out like I expected.

"Now what?" said April.

"I don't know."

We waited another hour in the airport and tried the convent again. No answer. We pooled our money and checked into the airport hotel. Our first night in Italy and we hadn't even breathed Roman air.

We had breakfast the next morning and tried again at a different airport payphone. Maybe the first payphone was jinxed. It rang three times before someone picked up.

"*Ciao*," said a female voice.

"It's Jane! Your cousin! April and I are in bloody Rome!" I was still sporting this truly stupendous and authentic Brit accent! "How posh," I added.

"Hello," said the female voice. "Who is this? Jane?"

April looked worried and leaned in so she could hear the phone call directly.

"Yes, it's Jane!" I said with a bit too much enthusiasm. "Your cousin! From America. You sent for me. Jane?"

"Ah, Jane, yes! How are you? You arrived safely? Where are you now?" Anna sounded delighted to hear from me. April seemed relieved by the new direction of the conversation.

"We're still at the airport. We called last night but no one answered."

"I'm so sorry. I wasn't expecting you until later today. Very good," said Anna. "Welcome to Roma." She sounded nice enough. Her voice was smoky and foreign, but she might have been thinking the same about mine. I wasn't sure if she had reconsidered hosting us for the next few weeks.

"I didn't know nuns had phones," I said. April turned to me with an odd look. I suppose it was a strange thing to say.

"I have many privileges," said Anna. "I live in Frascati which is less than an hour away from Rome."

"Remember I'm with my friend, April. What if we met you in the city somewhere?" I asked, speaking slowly to make sure Anna could understand my English. I couldn't speak any Italian but at least I could speak British and American English. April didn't even know how to order veal parmigiana.

"That can be arranged," said Anna.

"You know, like at a bar with cute boys and statues and shit," I urged her helpfully.

Silence on the other end. April slapped me on the shoulder.

"Sorry about the last bit," I said.

"Jane, I'll pick you and your friend up at five this evening at the bar by the Piazza del Campidoglio."

I nodded to April who made a little cheer. "That's perfect. Love it. Just one thing," I said, holding my mouth close to the phone. "Where the bloody hell is the Piazza del whatever?"

Anna gave me directions and information on getting a taxi and exchange rates. She could have been detailing the mating habits of the local mollusks for all I understood but it was good enough.

Before we left the payphone, we realized we hadn't called our parents yet and feared they had the American Embassy out looking for us. We each called our parents to tell them we were alive and in Italy. I'm not sure which parts of that surprised our parents more. Overall, they seemed happy. At least I hoped they were because we hung up on them pretty quickly since we couldn't wait to get out into the fresh air.

We finally stepped out into the sunshine. April handed me a lit cigarette and I took my first drag on Italian soil. I decided right there I wanted to take a maiden drag from every country in Europe before I died.

April looked at me inquisitively. Her hopes were my hopes: that our Roman hostess would understand our need to drink and ogle Italian boys. We hoped she would be the understanding kind of nun. It was a good thing we had showered, blow-dried, and primped this morning.

An hour taxi ride from the airport later, we were in Rome and exploring the streets and people. We had stepped into our own personal movie. Around five, we were sipping Campari at the bar Anna recommended under the beautiful and hectic Roman sky.

Children ran after pigeons in the Piazza and parents ran after children. Tourist groups walked in a phalanx clustered around a tour guide. The air was filled with the fragrant mist from the grand fountain in the center of the Piazza. The sound of rushing water intertwined with concertinas, strolling guitarists, clanking of glasses, and arguing waiters. It was organized chaos and not unlike a symphony orchestra warming up.

April and I sat silently, waiting for our ride, and wearing ever-broadening smiles. The plane hadn't taken us across an ocean and a continent but across time. I felt older, more mature, independent. And I knew enough to appreciate the moment and recognize I would always remember this afternoon. This felt like the start of something. Like I would be making better decisions from now on. Decisions that would have a positive impact on the rest of my life. I hoped this would be the first of many

Campari-sipping afternoons on this glorious adventure. Life couldn't get any sweeter.

And then we saw him. April nudged me under the table. She spotted him first and gave a small, unobtrusive, orgasmic sigh. I knew what that sound meant so I spun around to catch a glimpse of the man that had so easily made April excited.

Into the activity of the Piazza stepped the masculine object of our attention. April and I collectively gasped.

"Christ, he's perfect," whispered April.

"April, there's no way this is the first guy we hit on."

"I won't be able to take it if the whole country is filled with guys like him," said April.

"Maybe he's the ugliest guy in the village."

"I can't stand it here. My heart can't take it. How does Sophia Loren do it?"

"Because she's Sophia freakin' Loren," I said.

"Either way, I'm moving here," she responded.

He wore khakis and a loose white linen shirt that gave us ample information about his lean and tanned body underneath. His hair was dark and curly, and his face was at once harsh and masculine yet tender beyond his years. His eyes were crystal blue and looked brighter than the grottos on the postcards they sold.

"Oh my God! Sexy Pirate is coming over," yelped April, barely able to contain herself. She played with her hair, then switched to her shirt. April couldn't decide what needed adjusting and shaping. To anyone who didn't know her, it appeared April had suddenly gone into convulsions.

"You are the Americans," he called in a thick accent. He was walking toward us from the fountain. We looked around to assure ourselves he had indeed recognized our presence.

April shifted from convulsion to full epileptic fits.

Oh my God, oh my God, oh my God rattled inside my brain.

"The two of you. Americans?" he said again as he approached closer, this time with a smile that could melt marble.

We didn't know what to say or how to react.

"I am Angelo," he said. "Anna, you cousin, sent me for picking up the Americans. That's you, yes?" He sat down next to April and put his arm around her chair. His attitude reflected a familiarity with us, as if he met us every afternoon at this bar and was only pretending he didn't know us.

"I am Angelo. I drive from Milan this morning to come here. For you. I am Angelo," he insisted, pointing to himself. Well, did he think we were mentally deficient? Maybe. Probably. We hadn't said anything yet and continued to stare at him with slack-jawed blankness.

"Hello," I managed. "I'm Jane."

April giggled and muttered, "Holy shit."

"And that's April," I said.

He smiled at us and took a sip of April's drink.

"Angelo, where's my cousin?" I finally asked.

April kicked me to indicate she was in no rush. I knew she was much more interested in Angelo's status than the whereabouts of my relatives.

"Are you Anna's boyfriend? Do nuns have boyfriends? Maybe you're her neighbor? Nuns have neighbors, right?" April asked, trying to sound sophisticated. She took a sip from her drink and let the glass linger on her mouth a little too long. Some Campari spilled out onto her shirt, staining it red. She grabbed a napkin and wiped the stain on her shirt with one hand. With the other hand, she took Angelo's linen shirt tail and tugged it. She saw his shirt wasn't going to help with stain removal and let it go. She let out a laugh which made her sound even more insane.

I suddenly thought about Eli.

Angelo, sitting across from me with his languid charm and arm around April's chair, looked at us. He was sizing us up. A serious tone crossed his chiseled face.

"You cousin," he began, taking a deep breath as if to start a long story. "You cousin is stuck."

"Stuck?" I said. "Stuck where? Like, traffic?"

"No," he said. "Is no stuck. She is, how you say, stalk."

"Like corn?" said April, helpfully.

"Yes, April," I said. "My cousin Anna, the nun, is an ear of corn."

"No," said Angelo with an earnest tone. "No is corn. Is stalk."

We continued to smile at him and our good fortune. He could have told us the world was ending by an asteroid collision and we would have sat there smiling at him.

"She is...," Angelo continued, fumbling for the words. "Someone follows her. Stalk. I am bodyguard for her."

"Who the hell is following her?" I asked.

April took another sip from her drink. "Is it a full-time thing? 'Cause we're being followed too."

I turned to April. This didn't make sense. Maybe it was the language barrier. "Why would a nun need a bodyguard?"

"Maybe she's one of those flying nuns," said April. "Like Sally Fields."

"I am her bodyguard," repeated Angelo.

"Guarding bodies," said April. She took another sip of her Campari.

"I explain on the way," said Angelo. He slapped the table and stood up. The slap was a cue for us to follow him to his car. It worked perfectly because that's exactly what we did.

His car was a pale green two-door with a little motor that sounded like a child's toy. April insisted on sitting in the front while I shared the backseat with our luggage. We left the piazza and headed out of the city.

April seemed so happy staring at Angelo and the Italian countryside. Then it occurred to me. Who was this guy? Maybe he just overheard us at the airport talking to Anna and followed us to the piazza. Maybe this is how he made his living. Maybe we had just been kidnapped. Oh crap.

CHAPTER TWENTY

***Ornaments**—Tones used to embellish the principal melodic tone.*

After three days, our tour of duty in Milan was coming to an end and was lamentably uneventful. Our days had been spent with little precious free time. We mostly rehearsed and sang in what the locals called "small churches." These places of worship were like Gandalf compared to the American Frodo churches.

To be honest, I'd be happy if I had never seen another cathedral. At first, the novelty of them was not lost on me. I was a Jew, after all. But after a while, the idea of oohing and aahing at the same tea-light candled apse with another alabaster face staring down piously in front of a stained-glass, grief-stricken martyr seemed like homework.

Initially, I was entranced by the staggering size of the cathedrals, the intensity of their detail, the impossibility of their scale. Each stained-glass window was more magnificent than the last, whether it depicted some monumental or incidental milestone in Christ's life, or simply a serene moment that had somehow been captured by God's photographer. It seemed to me only God would think of painting and coloring with intricately leaded glass.

And the silence of each cathedral contrasted sharply with the stony resonance of the giant structural space. We would all sit in awe at the sheer magnitude; so beyond human.

Until about the sixth or seventh cathedral. Then, it was enough already. How impossible could building these cathedrals be if they seemingly had sprung up like weeds along the countryside? Every hick burg with no indoor plumbing had a cathedral that would put the grandest church in America to shame.

I'm sure the first person who ever encountered a glazed doughnut immediately dropped to his or her knees at the impossibility of its perfection. But, by the second box of a dozen doughnuts, the thrill was gone. And I'd about had my fill of the Catholic crème filling and historical sprinkles that seemed to make up all of Italy.

During one of these visits, boredom had seeped in. I sat in a pew in the middle of the cathedral with Charley and Little Francis. It was one of the rare times when Little Francis was without a chaperone. He was mortified to learn his grandparents had made a covenant with Rasper that they would focus their chaperoning responsibilities exclusively on their grandson. It was fine with me since it thinned the remaining chaperone-to-choir boy ratio.

I could tell by the furrowed brow on Little Francis' face that he knew he'd be recounting this entire emasculating portion of his life to his much visited-upon therapist one day as an adult. His grandparents were either in a bathroom or gift shop. We gazed straight up into the flying buttresses and enormous chandeliers.

I said something about how the view made it seem anything was possible.

Charley, in a bored daze, thought out loud, "Makes me glad I live in this century, you know? We can just sit here and look up and think about how it must have sucked to work so hard back then."

"I agree," I said in the cloud-watching whisper we had assumed.

There was a palpable silence where Little Francis's observation should have been. His worried look was still present.

"Little Francis?"

"I don't know," Little Francis said finally. "Makes me feel small."

"Little Francis."

"Really," Little Francis continued. "What's the point?"

"Well, maybe your grandparents will buy you a lolly," Charley said.

Francis laughed for the first time since we had left New York.

"So," Little Francis said. "What kind of dog would you be if you could be any kind of dog?"

Charley and I looked at each other before returning our gaze to the magnificent ceiling.

"Not Peebee," I said.

"Hey, I love that dog," said Charley. "What's your favorite number?"

"One," said Little Francis.

"One?" I said. "Nobody's favorite number is one."

Bart Rollins walked down the aisle and sat next to us.

"Hello boys," he said. He was followed by his wife.

"Francis, darling," said Mrs. Clancy. She reached into the gift shop bag and pulled out three lollipops for us. Charley, Little Francis, and I burst into laughter.

Later that night, we returned to our hotel. Rasper was in a good mood since he had received a note that my mom had called, asking him to call her back. All I got was a note from her saying she hoped I was fine.

We were rehearsing in the stale air of our Milan hotel parlor. We sounded stale too. Rasper persisted and we went through about two-thirds of our extensive repertoire. There was no room for a piano in the parlor, so Hubert played in the hallway outside while Florinda banged away on the bass chords, turned the pages and relayed messages back and forth from Rasper.

Ponte joined us for the second half of our rehearsal and it was clear he had lied on his resume. He had no vocal or music training. Mostly, he mouthed the words and was another tall presence in the choir which made us look more formidable and less like the Little Rascals. After rehearsal, Charley kept stealing glances at Ponte. When I asked him about it, Charley said he thought he recognized Ponte from somewhere. I thought he looked familiar too. It added to his mystery.

Charley and I would have continued our Ponte speculations, but Rasper clapped his hands and requested our attention. He called the chaperones into the rehearsal room as well, so we knew this was important.

"I have some very good news," announced Rasper. He was never optimistic but seemed bursting with cheer. "You already knew we were going to Rome. You may have even surmised we were going to sing in St. Peter's Square during the Pope's Wednesday audience mass." Rasper waited and raised an eyebrow; surely a sign of something miraculous to follow. "We have been invited to sing Sunday mass at the Vatican for the Pope himself! And half the world's Cardinals will be in attendance. We are the first American boys' choir to ever be given such an honor."

The information landed on our ears in stunned silence. I couldn't believe it. Even the adults appeared shocked. This was beyond our wildest dreams. Then again, silences made me uncomfortable.

The room erupted in cheers, and we hugged and slapped each other on the back. I envisioned this was what sports people did when they made it to their sports finals. Rasper then released us for our free time.

Charley, Terrence, and I ran through the streets. We might have even skipped. The news about our Vatican concert made us giddy. We only had an hour. I wanted to get into harm's way, find glory, risk something in Italy. I also wanted to meet girls. Italian girls. Girls with curly brown hair that fell on their olive-skinned faces. With arms that were fashioned akimbo on peasant-skirted hips. Instead, we ran around the town square, occasionally running into other choir members and waving at them. An hour later, we returned to the hotel to get ready for the concert.

It was difficult to focus on the minor Milanese concert after the Vatican news, but we were professionals and did what we could. The Cathedral of Milan was beautiful to an American's eye. To a native, it was just the local church, just another building on the cityscape, like the grocer or doctor's office. The cathedral's Saturday night mass was half-filled. The audience was made up of devoted Catholic regulars and curious local on-lookers that came to view the lucky American boys that were on their way to perform for the Pope. Rasper had made sure to get the word out.

Before mass began, we sang a mini-concert to warm up the audience. We sounded professional, enthusiastic, and properly respectful. Rasper even had us sing a song in Italian for which we rehearsed unmercifully until the proper inflections and accents were attained.

After a short break, we gathered in the back of the cathedral to sing for the Saturday night mass proper. We wore white robes with red collars and looked like proper altar boys. At least that's what I imagined. Being Jewish, this was like Halloween to me. Each of us held lit candles in our innocent hands and sang in angelic voices on high. Our chaperones all sat in the same pew; the aisle seat reserved, of course, for Lady Bear. She had pulled out the good fur and the best jewels for the occasion. Her face had more plaster than the ceiling of the Sistine Chapel. It probably had more cracks to hide. The vast cathedral was decorated at the ground level to celebrate the visiting American choir. The rafters were filled with our echoes, incense, and the perfumes of the worshippers that crammed every pew.

At the start of his Mass, the priest gave us our well-rehearsed cue. We began our procession from the back of the cathedral, walking in single file to the rhythm of the organ music, past the pews filled with parishioners. We held our lit candles before us, making sure to keep enough distance from the boy in front of us. We proceeded forward in this solemn manner down the center aisle, singing in perfect harmony. The acoustics were beautiful, echoing and resonating throughout the church. It was like our voices gained power and volume with each note.

Within a few minutes, a traffic jam had developed near the altar. We stood in the aisle and continued to sing. Apparently, the priest was not given right-of-way by the visiting Bishop, who had unexpectedly showed up for the celebration and screwed up everyone's choreographed plans. Plus, from what I could see, the bishop had chosen to arrive sporting the Big Hat just to show everyone up.

As I craned my neck to get a better view of the two bearded, wise, old Holy men wagging their fingers at each other like professional wrestlers, I suddenly smelled something odd. A wet raccoon smell. A smell like an old lady's hair was on fire. I looked down.

Lady Bear's hair was on fire. It had been lit by my candle. The smoke rose high above the crowd like we were sending signals in the Old West. Big Francis, standing in the back of the church, saw the smoke and looked for the closest extinguishment device. He quickly grabbed the large bowl of Holy Water and passed it down to the boy in front of him. The bowl continued to be passed down the line with the efficiency of an 1860s country fire department.

The entire time, we never stopped singing.

The heavy bowl of Holy Water was handed to me.

This turned out to be the exact moment Lady Bear bolted up and shrieked. Apparently, there was a bit of insulation between her skull and hair and she couldn't feel the heat. The bowl of Holy Water dipped away from me and splashed her head and fur coat. The water put out the fire but left her head a smoking, sizzling dome. Lady Bear continued to scream, trapped in her aisle by a line of robed, pyromaniacal, singing boys.

Heads, naturally, turned toward us in a curious and not-so-reverent fashion. All I could think to do was to snuff out the remaining smoke with the hem of my robe. With one deft movement reminiscent of Ginger Rogers' dance partner, I threw down the candle and put it out with my foot while I whipped off my robe. Working quickly, I wrapped the robe around her dumbfounded head like a turban. If only I hadn't been wearing denim cut-off shorts and a Billy Joel T-shirt underneath. It seemed a tad disrespectful. Rasper said it didn't matter what we wore that night since our robes would be all anyone would see.

Lady Bear stopped screaming. She was breathing heavily as the music from the organ and our song swelled to a crescendo. Lady Bear looked upon me as one would a madman. I smiled and removed the robe cocoon from around her head to assess the damage.

She was bald as a freshly laid egg. I peered into my robe. Nestled within the folds was a smoking, charred wig. I realized, even at my young age, Lady Bear had experienced an inconvenient evening. With her fur coat soaking wet and her makeup-smeared face looking like an Impressionist painting, she reached up to her now vacant scalp. When she felt a smooth head that made Kojak seem positively hirsute, she let out a shrill noise approximating a high-pitched scream that only Milanese dogs could hear.

Thankfully, at that moment, we began a new song and the traffic jam at the altar cleared up. I put the robe back on though it was soaking wet. I placed Lady Bear's wig remains in the inside pocket of the robe that was reserved, I was sure, for more holy purposes. The procession began to move and we sang angelically, "She is Blessed." Lady Bear cried while the rest of the choir passed her Buddha-belly of a head. I imagined they resisted laying their hands on her head as they walked by. I smiled and thought Italian trips just don't get any better than this.

Afterward, we went as a group to the Piazza del Duomo. Rasper was nursing Lady Bear. Luckily, she hadn't been able to place the face of the choir boy who had made her a human matchstick. There were advantages to her thinking we all looked alike. Rasper let us loose and told us to meet back at the hotel in two hours.

The Piazza was lit by a thousand candles on a thousand outdoor tables. Small blue, yellow, and green globes, strung together with a loosely knit tangle of old wire, hung overhead, casting a pleasing and almost mystical glow and strange hum.

Bound in white aprons, waiters rushed around with trays of food and drinks serving the laughing and clinking clientele. Dogs and birds danced between the crowds, avoided being stepped on, and picked up stray scraps of dropped appetizers.

Charley and I went off our own way. I was starting to feel guilty about Lady Bear. She'd had a rough evening. I was also worried she would eventually figure out which one of us ruined her wig and tell Rasper. Rasper would easily kick me out of the choir if it came down to a decision between her and me.

Charley tapped me on the shoulder. I turned around and saw his face was gushing with excitement. He grabbed my elbow and led me away down a busy alleyway.

"What is it?" I asked.

"Ponte," he said.

I looked in the direction where Charley was pointing. Ponte was walking in the Square toward us. It appeared he was following us.

"Maybe he's CIA," said Charley. "Maybe your whole story is true and something shady is going on."

"The Pope will save us," I said. "I mean, we're practically pals now. He's, like, invited us to hang out with him."

We hid in the alleyway until we were sure we lost Ponte. After a few minutes, we strolled back into the crowded Square. Charley and I walked up to the first counter we saw. We were starving and itching to spend money. The bistro was as crowded as any other.

"*Birra*," Charley said confidently.

The bartender behind the counter looked at us suspiciously.

"*Duo birra*," said Charley, this time holding out two fingers. Then, he turned to me. "Eli, slap your money up there."

I took out a few thousand lire and slapped it on the counter, feeling like I was in an old Western. The bartender quickly replaced the lire with two beers.

"*Mille grazie*," said Charley, taking his beer and ambling away. I looked at Charley like he was a stranger. I had never seen him so brazen and confident. I grabbed my beer and followed him.

I took a sip of the beer and thoughts of Charley's newly displayed chutzpah disappeared. I had only tasted beer once before, at my uncle's barbecue, and thought it was just awful. This Milanese beer made my uncle's beer seem like sweet nectar.

"Charley, this is horrible," I said as I spit out the beer, much to the disgust of the nearby outdoor diners.

"Come on, Eli, live a little." Charley continued to walk toward an outdoor table that wasn't well lit. We sat down, eager to make believe we were adults. We raised our glasses and I watched Charley take a sip. I pretended to drink but slowly let the beer dribble out of the glass.

"God, this is piss," I said.

"A little respect please," said Charley. "Besides, you don't drink it for the taste. Nobody drinks beer for the taste except people on commercials. It's to get drunk."

"I think I read that on a Budweiser billboard once," I said. I tapped Charley and pointed across the Square where Ponte was crossing with two beers.

It was exciting to be on our own, drinking locally brewed goat urine and relaxing in a pubescent bubble of free time. Then someone put his hand on my shoulder.

"Mr. Mitchell," Rasper said loudly.

My hand jerked upwards in surprise, sending a fountain of tepid Milanese Piss into the air. Charley was frozen.

"Mr. Mitchell," repeated Rasper. "What are you and your cohort up to? Hmm?"

He didn't seem to be aware of our alcoholic consumption. I hated when he spoke to us like children.

"Careful boys," he said, smiling at us.

And then he winked at me in a way that made me reconsider everything I knew about this odd man. Did he know we were drinking beer? He walked off alone.

We turned our attention back to Ponte who disappeared into the crowd. I watched Charley dump the rest of his beer on the ground. Then something caught my eye. From my vantage point, I swore I saw Big Francis and Florinda ducking into an alleyway together. I shook it off.

"Come on, Charley, let's get something to eat."

"I know where I've seen him before," said Charley. "Morgan."

"What?"

"Ponte. He's Morgan. From back home," said Charley, waving his hand in the air.

"You're right," I said a bit too loudly. "Didn't he graduate a few years ago? Why's he hanging out with us?"

"I heard he became a narc," said Charley.

"Why's he here?"

We both looked at each other and were thinking the same thing. I said it first. "Romatene."

This was one of those moments we knew we weren't talking of childish things.

"You know Eddie back home, right?" said Charley.

"Eddie. Right."

"He wanted to make you a Romatene mule. You know I was never going to ask you to do that, right?"

"Are you bringing some back for him?" I asked. My voice was quiet, scared.

"Originally, I thought I would. But not now."

"Screw Eddie."

"Yeah," said Charley. "Screw him. Let's go get something to eat."

We came to an old pizza stand. It seemed to be crowded mostly with the local waiters from the other trattorias and bars. This was a good sign. The man behind the counter appeared round and happy as if he had never outgrown being a newborn. These were exactly the physical attributes I enjoyed in my pizza makers. As we approached the counter, the smell was almost too delicious to believe.

"Charley! Real Italian food!"

My nostrils were soon filled with the pungent smell of garlic, olive oil, basil, and sausage. The pizza was thick and cut into a huge square. It was the size of a baby's crib mattress. It rested on a wooden board and steam floated away from it like a fragrant ambassador of good will.

"Maybe we can buy the whole thing and raft down the Grand Canal," said Charley.

I asked for one slice by offering some money and holding one finger, hoping it didn't mean anything rude. Charley and I watched as the pizza maker cut a huge rectangle about the size of an ironing board out of the mother pizza. He placed it on a thick piece of paper and folded it in half lengthwise.

"Italian origami," I said to Charley as I took the pizza. This couldn't be the way pizza was meant to be eaten. I waited to see if Charley's order would be any different.

"Can you make mine into a giraffe?" said Charley. He got the same folded slice as I did. We each stood there holding this clumsy, saucy, folded thing. Charley took one bite and the pizza filling fell out and landed on his shoes.

"Shit," he exclaimed as he shook the pizza sauce off his feet.

"Wait," I said. "Mr. Rollins, Bart, he was telling me how to eat this the other day."

I balanced the folded pizza and carefully took a bite.

"That guy's alright," said Charley.

"Looks like you boys haven't had pizza here before," said a man's deep voice in a slight Italian accent. It wasn't a voice I recognized.

We turned around. The man was tall, thin, and wore a fedora hat that made him look old-fashioned. He was young and old at the same time. He looked to be in his mid-thirties, but I was always a poor judge of these things. He held a gelato in a paper cup.

"Can always tell the new Americanos in town from the pizza sauce on their shoes," he said seriously.

He licked his gelato with such delicacy as if to illustrate his point of local tidiness. He drew closer to us.

Charley broke the tension of the surreal moment in his typical elegant fashion.

"Who are you, mister?" Charley demanded loudly, dabbing his shoes with a napkin.

"Armand Buccenti," the man in the fedora hat announced. "See, strangers no more."

Charley and I nodded to him the way you nod to a complete lunatic. We slowly departed without making direct eye contact or sudden movements.

"Aren't you forgetting something?" Buccenti inquired as he took another delicate lick of his gelato. In any other circumstance, I would have suggested he and the gelato get a room.

Buccenti's voice was calm, reasonable, and suddenly without accent. We knew he wanted something from us. He spoke with a purpose. He gave off the air of someone used to getting what he wants.

"Wait," I said finally. "You're the guy from Shannon airport. The one on the plane with us."

He just stared at us and continued to lick his ice cream cone.

We were officially scared shitless.

Charley tried to look as menacing as he could. Altogether, we were about as intimidating as a plate of eggs to a truck driver.

"Who are you?" I asked.

"That has already been established," Buccenti stated plainly. "Now, if you're acting coy with a mind to change the deal, boys, it is ill-advised."

"Deal?" said Charley.

"More of an exchange, wouldn't you say?" Buccenti responded in that matter-of-fact tone.

"Charley, I think this guy...," I said.

"Did Rasper send you?" asked Charley.

"Boys, let's complete this transaction so you can go change your shoes," said Buccenti.

"Wait a minute," I said. I turned quickly to Charley and we nodded to each other. We took off down the street like the Three Stooges at the end of every film.

"Oh shit, oh shit, oh shit," Charley kept saying in rhythm with his running. I turned back. Buccenti just stood there, getting smaller, licking his gelato.

"The CIA plot I made up doesn't seem crazy now," I said.

"Unless he's with the mob," said Charley.

"I think that was the Romatene guy."

"Can't be. I told Eddie we wouldn't be doing this!" said Charley.

"Where are we going?" I said.

"Where do you think? The police."

After getting lost for several minutes, we asked for directions and found the local police station. We caught our breaths outside the station and got our stories straight. As we were about to enter the police station, the front door opened.

Buccenti stepped out and waved at us.

We ran away as fast as possible and met the other choir members at our hotel. Ponte caught up to us and asked where we had gone. We decided to say nothing. We had survived an international drug deal, possibly even a government sting operation. This had been a test and we passed.

Who was I fooling? We were in way over our heads.

CHAPTER TWENTY-ONE

***Pastoral**—A simple and idyllic style suggestive of rural scenes.*

"A little bit more further," said Angelo, the alleged hunky kidnapper, from the driver's seat of his Fiat. April sat in the front seat, entranced by her pirate captor. I was in the back seat with a leg cramp. The top was down so our hair, jewelry, and luggage floated up in hopes of getting airborne and away from the speeding roadster. We constantly shifted our hands from luggage to our hair to holding down our possessions. We had resorted to using our feet to help with our auto organization. It reminded me of a crazy variation of Twister.

We'd left the heavy traffic of Rome forty-five minutes earlier and were speeding through a beautiful countryside. Olive and almond trees covered the mountains and the thin roadside. The darkening sky and burgeoning starlight made the green lushness of the trees and brown fertility of the earth more vivid than I ever could have imagined.

April suddenly became green herself. She hung her head out the side of the car, fully engrossed in the process of losing her Italian lunch.

"Oh God," she managed to say. "Make this goddamn country flat."

I tapped April's shoulder, trying to communicate to her our kidnapped predicament. Her focus seemed to be on not throwing up again.

"You are in good luck," said Angelo. "We are here."

The car screeched to a halt, and I thanked God. The last part of the drive had been the most religious experience of my young life. We flopped out of the car. The gravel driveway led to a small terra cotta two-story house under a canopy of trees. Smoke billowed out from the chimney. A dog lazed herself on the front porch. Even at night, it was stunning.

Angelo helped us with the bags. He had stayed quiet during the ride and hadn't provided more information regarding this mysterious stranger stalking my cousin. I was hoping Angelo had been joking.

"This doesn't look like a convent. We don't have any money," I said.

"It look like no one is home. You cousin is back soon," said Angelo.

April looked at Angelo and decided he could be trusted.

"Angelo," she said. "Do you know where we can score some Romatene?"

"Score?"

"April!" I said in a warning tone, as if she'd let out the secret of the grassy knoll.

"Yes," she said to Angelo. "Score. You know, where can I buy some Romatene?"

"April! He might be kidnapping us!" I screamed.

"What?" said April, shocked. I was flabbergasted the thought had never crossed her mind.

Angelo looked deeply hurt. "I no kidnap you. I am working for you cousin. For Anna."

Angelo put down my suitcase and walked over to me. As he approached, two questions traipsed across my mind. One: was he interested in a bit of a shag with a pretend-English-bird once she had a proper shower? And two: where the hell were we? A strange man picked us up, said he knew my cousin, and drove us out to the middle of nowhere to an abandoned house. Treacherous. But mostly, I was thinking about the Angelo-related, post-shower shag. Maybe he could be my first mac-and-cheese? More like spaghetti and meatballs.

He looked solemnly at April and me. "Why you want to get involved in such things? You seem nice girls."

"It's not for us," I said.

"But Romatene...," said Angelo. "Very dangerous. Even to speak of it."

We looked at him with big, kitten eyes like a kid asking Santa Claus for a Barbie doll. We couldn't go into the reasons why we needed Romatene.

He just wouldn't understand the social demands of the Wall gang and why I needed to be cool again.

After a silence, Angelo said, "I know a man in Milano. Buccenti. I spoke to him this morning. I take you to him tomorrow if you like," he said without the slightest hint of horniness or creepy serial killerness. In fact, he suddenly acted as if we'd asked him for a Dr. Pepper. He took our luggage into the house.

"Jesus, who is this guy?" April asked as we stood by the car. "Looking like that and having a Romatene connection? Can he be more perfect?"

Angelo turned to us on the porch. "Tomorrow then," he said. "For now, we go inside for shower and food."

"Yes to everything," said April, feeling a bit better. We followed our Italian host, bodyguard, drug dealer, and object of our unquenchable lust into what I hoped was my cousin's nun house.

The inside was a mess. A homey mess. The kind that looked alive and lived-in. We dropped our bags at the front door. The foyer led into the living room and we wandered in, drawn by the soft glow of a stained-glass lamp. There were large windows with sheer curtains fluttering with the evening breeze. Two large sofas begged to be sat on. The sofas had quilts hung over their arms like waiters tending to the best customers. Oil paintings of the Italian coast adorned the walls. I felt comfortable in this house immediately. It implied to me Angelo wasn't going to chop us up into pieces and freeze us for some wintertime snack.

"Hey, that's you," said April, pointing to a picture of me on the mantel, circa six years ago. "So innocent."

"Yeah, what happened?" I said.

Angelo popped his head into the living room, slightly out of breath.

"You bags are upstairs in you guest room. I bring them. I cook food for you now while you bathe." And off he went to cook us food, leaving us to bathe.

"My God, he's like an Italian Tarzan," I said.

"Funny, since you're Jane," said April.

"I feel like I haven't bathed since this picture was taken," I said.

We tiptoed upstairs, aware this wasn't our house. The upstairs smelled a bit musty but was otherwise as homey as the rest of the house. There were two bedrooms and a small, shared bathroom.

Our guest bedroom was much smaller than the rest of the rooms we had seen. There was one single bed in the middle of the room and a thick quilt and pillow on the floor on either side of the bed. Our luggage was piled high, balanced precariously, on the bed.

A small window let in some moonlight but otherwise, the room was stark and devoid of decoration save for a dead flower in a small, yellow glass vase on top of the dresser.

"Well, this sucks," said April. "Did they think you were visiting with your dog?" she said, giving me a dirty look as if this was my doing.

"April, calm down. It's not that bad. We'll take turns with the bed or something," I said as calmly as I could.

After a late delicious dinner Angelo prepared, he announced he needed to go home. We were disappointed but also relieved. We stayed up as late as we could, but Anna never came. We didn't take turns sleeping on the bed. April said she would take the first shift on the bed, and I took the floor. We were supposed to wake up in three hours to switch but somehow that never happened.

In the morning, we showered and had just finished getting dressed when I heard the front door open.

"Hello," came a voice from downstairs.

It had been years since I had seen my cousin. I was curious to see if Anna was as I remembered: a giggly, shy girl who reminded me of a saintly, yet slightly homely version of me. I was also deadly curious to see what a real-life Italian nun looked like.

We ran downstairs. A beautiful woman stood at the bottom of the steps, ravishingly thin, high cheek-boned, long, curly-haired, chapeau'd in whoever-was-in-fashion, and dressed in a black and white number that made her look more cosmopolitan than a hundred dry martinis.

"Anna," I shouted as I flew toward her. "You look amazing." I hugged her.

"Jane," she exclaimed. "There are no words."

April and I cried. "I'm so glad we weren't kidnapped," I said.

"What?" Anna asked.

"What happened to you?" I meant the question regarding an explanation as to how a suburban, virginal waif could have gone from a nun to a Bond girl in five short years.

"Yeah, is this how nuns are dressing now?" April asked.

"I should explain...," said Anna. She looked at us, confused. Apparently, she wasn't used to being interrogated in her own house.

"Who's stalking you?" continued April, absent of any formal introduction. "And what's the deal with Angelo?"

"This is April, my best friend in the whole world," I said, breaking the silence. The two of them shook hands.

Anna burst out into a contagious giggle that soon evolved into a full-blown laugh. She stepped in and embraced us.

"I'm so glad you're here," Anna said through her laugh. We were all eye-to-eye in a three-way embrace. Anna looked at me. "You both look fabulous. Come with me. We need drinks."

We followed her to the terrazzo. The sienna-tiled floor was shaded by lemon trees. A small fountain gurgled water calmly. The terrazzo looked out upon a spectacular sun-dappled field. April and I sat in the cushioned wrought-iron chairs at the table. Anna arrived with a tray of Bloody Marys.

Anna gave one to each of us and raised her glass. "My American ladies," she said. "To your Italian adventure."

We clinked glasses and I knew this was the best moment in my life.

"As you can see, I am no nun," said Anna. She had changed into a sundress and large-brimmed hat. In fact, there was a fine line between a small beach umbrella and her hat. "I'm a model now. Very busy," she said confidently. "And nobody's stalking me," she said to April. "I'm in no danger. Angelo just likes to feel important."

Anna leaned in closer to April. "He's my agent's son. Learning the business. He's not my bodyguard and, I have to say, he's not interested in either of you. Or me."

"But how..." April's brows squeezed together.

"He likes boys," said Anna.

"No," said April, shaking her head. "Just no."

"A model?" I said. "How?"

"I will show you tomorrow. You're going on a modeling gig with me."

"Just no," repeated April.

CHAPTER TWENTY-TWO

***Glissando**—Sliding between two notes.*

I was standing on the balcony of my hotel room, holding my room key, and taking in Venice. Venice was another planet. Charley and the rest of the choir boys had gone down for the continental breakfast that the hotel offered. We had been starving since the previous night. Apparently, Rasper wasn't great with managing our funds. Dinner the previous night had consisted of us sitting on one of Venice's stone bridges that crossed a canal. A gigantic wheel of cheese was passed down from boy to boy along with three or four loaves of crusty bread. The food was gone before it reached me. I thought life would be better as a tenor.

I peered out at the maze of rivers and streets and pondered how they intertwined. The whole city floated and everything in it had to float as well. Even my hotel key had a large wooden bob attached to it. I never wanted to leave here. I could see why my father must have loved it. At least, that's what my mom told me.

I knew Rasper had sent my mom a few postcards which made me uncomfortable. I tried to sneak a peek before they were mailed but the Italian postal service was intensely secure.

I breathed in the scenery once more before heading downstairs to join the others for breakfast. At least, there was enough toast and Nutella for everyone. The adults must have been on a different meal plan entirely because I never saw them eat with us nor complain about going hungry.

After breakfast, we headed to the hotel lobby for a quick rehearsal. Hotel guests and passersby were treated to an impromptu concert punctuated with screaming from Rasper. Bart Rollins stepped into the lobby and gave me a nod. Last night, he and I had worked out a little plan for this morning. Bart stepped over to Rasper in between songs and whispered in his ear. Rasper looked at me and furrowed his brows. Momentarily, he seemed to acquiesce.

"Mr. Mitchell, I'm allowing you to take leave of us only because Mr. Rollins has agreed to personally chaperone you. I find the entire venture suspect. I have told your mother I would keep you safe. Nevertheless, remember to be back at six sharp tonight. I have a surprise for all of us and the train won't wait."

Bart waved me over. As we left the rehearsal, I peered back. Little Francis cried at the sight of being left behind by his grandfather. Mrs. Clancy was not around. Probably out somewhere with Lady Bear. We walked into the Venice sunshine.

"Is he going to be okay?" I asked Bart.

"Francis has to learn he's not the center of everything," said Bart. "Besides, you have important matters to attend."

We walked over a few bridges and down some twisting alleyways. Bart stopped to catch his breath. I used the break to take out my map and make sure we were on the right path. Bart nodded and we proceeded.

Our first stop was *Vetro Doratothe*, a Venetian glass shop where one could take a glass-making and blowing tour. We entered and proceeded to the tour desk. The store itself was filled with glass objects in shapes and colors I had never seen. I would never have thought much about the details of glass making. But it's what my father did as a kid to earn a living.

I reached for my wallet to pay the tour fee, but Bart raised his hand and insisted on paying.

"After all," he said as they tore our ticket and we entered the first room of the tour, "if I can't do this kindness so you can reconnect with your father's past, what good am I?"

A guide escorted Bart and me down a hallway. The wall to our left was made entirely of glass which was so perfect it could have been air. Through the glass, I saw craftsmen blowing glass at the end of long, steel pipes like they were playing the strangest instruments. They spun blobs of molten bubbles and bent glass with metal pipes like it was peanut butter. It was fascinating and I pictured my father working under the intense heat, turning out objects of beauty from the center of the sun.

I asked the guide if they had any glass made by my dad. I hoped my dad had been an especially gifted artisan and his work would still be held as the standard. The guide told me she had never heard of my dad.

At the end of the tour, we ended up in the gift shop where black-and-white framed photos of former glass artisans hung on the wall. I reviewed them intensely, but my dad was not among them. Bart placed his hand on my shoulder.

After the glass tour, Bart and I walked seven blocks to the street where my dad grew up. I had gotten the address from a little memory box my mom kept of my dad's stuff. My dad's street was long and twisting, stuffed on both sides with skinny, two-floor row houses. The houses were all the same color and indistinguishable from one another. We arrived at my dad's door. Bart tapped me on the arm.

"Aren't you going to knock on the door?"

"I don't know."

"Don't you want to see the inside? You came all this way. What's three more feet?"

I didn't want to see the inside of the house. I was afraid of finding nothing special in there. I didn't want to discover there were no photos of him in his own house. Even the glass factory, with all its glorious colors and shapes, didn't provide me the clues I was looking for. They didn't tell me my father was unique, talented. I needed to know he was special. Because then, one day, I might be too. I would rather make stuff up about him than be confronted with the emptiness behind his childhood front door.

I turned and ran. Bart tried to catch up, but I lost him after a block. I returned to the hotel and ran to my room. Staring out the window, I saw Bart arrive fifteen minutes later, wheezing. I knew he was disappointed in me. I went back down and told him I was sorry and he hugged me. Mrs. Clancy and Lady Bear approached us and asked where we had been. Bart let me go and escorted them to the other end of the hotel. I felt ashamed and hoped my dad was not looking down on me. It made me miss my mom.

Later that day, we boarded the train and were assigned compartments by Rasper. I was teamed up with Charley and Terrence. The compartment was small and had been designed for six passengers. I was grateful it was just the three of us. The compartment door opened, and Big Francis walked in. He plopped down next to me. I shifted across from him.

One of these things was not like the other and he was a hulking presence that was happy to beat the snot out of the other three. Thankfully, Big Francis fell asleep as soon as the train left. I was glad Ponte hadn't been assigned to our compartment. Ever since we realized he was here under false pretenses, we were ducking him until we could figure out what he was up to.

Ten minutes into our journey, Rasper stepped into our compartment and explained why we were currently heading from Venice to Frascati by train on our second week here. For publicity reasons, he had arranged for us to perform a benefit concert at the Santa Teresa Orphanage and Reform School for Girls. I had also overheard Hubert mention he had distant family he wanted to visit near Frascati.

I was clearly much more interested in the first reason for our side trip. We had been in Italy for too long and had seen little adventure and even fewer girls. The image of an entire building filled with beautiful Italian girls was all too much.

My mind was also a bit preoccupied from what I had seen at the hotel front desk that morning. While waiting for the hotel manager to make me change, I saw a postcard under a pile of mail. The postcard was from Rasper to my mom. I couldn't read the whole thing but the part I could make out was enough to intrigue me and make me feel a little nauseous. Rasper was writing to tell my mom he was quite fond of her and thought she was beautiful inside. He wished she could be here. He said he hoped he was worthy. It was the most inappropriate note a teacher ever wrote to a parent.

The train ride was different from my experience in America. The trains here were luxurious and broken-down at the same time. Our compartment had cracked leather seats that held six comfortably. Well, it would have been comfortable but Big Francis was stretched out, sleeping, in an entire row while the three of us sat opposite him like chickens facing an ax. The olive and lemon tree landscape whirred by, ignoring my hungry eyes as I tried to feast on its escaping scenery.

Charley sat next to me in a groggy state. He still wasn't used to the time change or all the hustle and bustle. He was trying to write a postcard to his dog. Charley was nuts about his dog and missed him more than he missed his folks. I don't know what kind of services this cocker spaniel provided to Charley, but it clearly had Charley enthralled. All he talked about was that goddamn dog.

"Tell Peanut Butter Cup I say hi," I said to Charley.

"I absolutely will," said Charley, assessing the remaining available real estate on the postcard so he could squeeze in my kibble of a salutation to old Peebster.

"I hate dogs," said Terrence. Charley glared at him as if Terrence had just admitted to poisoning the world's water supply.

Big Francis woke up and stretched.

"Where the fuck are we?" he said in mid-yawn.

Big Francis didn't care what he said in front of anybody. Except Rasper. For some reason, Rasper tapped into his inner self-censor.

Big Francis' eyes darted back and forth and up to the compartment door window, making sure the coast was clear of Rasper.

"Yo, are we in fuckin' Florence or whatever yet?" he asked, rubbing his face.

It was amazing that this tough-talking, mean-looking, burly kid looked like a proper angel in his Long Island Boys Choir dinner jacket, bowtie, and cummerbund. He sang in a melodious tenor with none of the raspy, cartoony street toughness.

I was doubly intimidated by him since last week in Milan. He had shoved me into a corner, looked me right in the eye, and demanded I swear to him I wouldn't say anything to anybody about him and Florinda. I must have uttered something pleasing to his ear because he let me go and allowed me to continue living. If I had been born a Christian, Big Francis would be the cross I'd be bearing.

"We've got an hour or two to go," I said. My hand was in my pocket and I rubbed the little metal gondola-shaped switchblade Charley had given me back in Hicksville during the fake rumble. The smooth metal gave me courage.

Big Francis slid down in his seat, closing his eyes. "Well, wake me up when we get there," he ordered. Then, after a pensive pause, he muttered, "Orphaned Italian reform school chicks."

"He's like black Fonzie," said Charley. Then, turning towards Terrence, he said, "Sorry."

"No, it's okay," said Terrence. "I definitely feel like black Potsie around him."

I turned and gazed out the window. The sun was setting against the landscape which raised and dipped with endless variations of beauty. An olive tree orchard would give way to acres of grapevines which transitioned into pastures for cows and sheep.

"Charming," whispered Charley.

I thought Charley was a little afraid of Big Francis. Not me. Hell, no. I was shit-in-my-pants petrified of the crazy bastard. And also in awe of him.

Big Francis fell back asleep. All the adults were no doubt having fun somewhere on the train and we were stuck in this compartment with time to kill, scenery to contemplate, and the tattered, red curtain framing our door.

"Charley, why did you join the choir?" I didn't know where the question came from.

"What do you mean?" he asked, his window gaze interrupted by my question.

"I joined because my momma said she wanted to keep me on the right side of the tracks," said Terrence.

We didn't know what to say to Terrence. It must have been hard to be a black kid in the choir. He got picked on a lot by the older choir boys. I guess that's why he attached himself to us.

"I'm glad you're here, Terrence," said Charley.

Terrence smiled. "What about you?" he said.

"I don't know. I like to sing, I guess," said Charley.

"No, we know that," I said. "We all like to sing. But that doesn't mean you join a professional boys' choir. Like if you enjoy making eggs doesn't mean you become a chef."

Blank stares from Charley weighed down my curiosity.

"My momma had to take an extra job just so I could stay in the choir. I hope she thinks it's worth it," said Terrence.

"She's probably hoping you think it's worth it," said Charley.

"I know we're not allowed but I'm going to call her when we get to the next town," said Terrence.

"My father," I stated softly. "I think I do this for my dad."

We all stared out the window and were soothed by the clickity-clack of the train.

"What do your folks say about all this?" I asked Charley.

"What do you mean?"

"Come on, Charley."

"Well, they're probably happy to be rid of me for three weeks," he said.

"I guess so," I said. "Although they're never home long enough to know if you're gone."

An orchard of lemon trees dotted the hillside below. I took in a deep breath and could almost smell the lemons in the air.

"So, what's with your dad?" asked Charley, tentatively.

My gaze broke and I looked directly at him. "What's with my dad? Well, you know he was from here, right?"

Charley nodded, taking keen interest in this rare admission of my family history.

"His mom, my grandmother, wanted to be an opera singer. She was pretty good, from what I heard."

"They've got that gigantic opera house in Rome," said Charley.

"*Teatro dell'Opera*," I said. "Well, her dream was to audition for the opera company there. But she knew she had to practice with the local opera groups first. Kind of like our prep choir.

"So, she was, like, seventeen. And everyone encouraged her to get married. Instead, she decided to join this small opera company. And the first guy she met was the manager. When she auditioned for him, he told her that in this opera company, all the members were also the producers."

"Jesus," said Charley.

I checked to make sure Big Francis was still sleeping. "I know," I whispered. "So, she gave him whatever money she had, and he ran off. But not before getting her pregnant."

"Your dad?" said Charley, incredulously.

"That's the story. So, my dad, who could never sing himself…"

"Sorry."

"Never heard me sing," I said.

"My daddy left when I was young too," said Terrence, more for camaraderie.

There was a silence.

"And now I got Rasper making moves on my mom," I said.

"What?" said Charley.

The train came to a screeching halt. Big Francis rolled off the seat and landed at our feet. He jumped up like a caged animal that had been released, punched me in the shoulder, and bolted out the door.

With our compartment door open, we could hear a commotion down the hall. It sounded like Mrs. Clancy was screaming. We poked our heads out but had to bring them back in quickly since Rasper was racing down the hall.

"What happened?" I asked as he ran by.

He stopped and turned to us. "It's Mr. Rollins." Then he turned and ran towards Little Francis' compartment.

CHAPTER TWENTY-THREE

Rococo—*A musical style characterized as excessive, ornamental, and trivial.*

Anna was a wild driver. She didn't believe in using brakes, relying instead on the friction caused by her screeching tires as we banked sharply along another extreme turn on the gravel mountain road. Her roadster mostly stayed on the planet but was occasionally airborne. It was a convertible, naturally, and she wore a scarf around her head that magically stayed put, its tail whipping enthusiastically behind her, smacking April in the face. April was the sole passenger in the back, and she held on for dear life. I was in the passenger seat and held the bottom of my seat so as not to projectile out of the car into the mountainside. The roar of the engine and the wind rushing by made it difficult to collect my thoughts, never mind make conversation.

Angelo had an errand to run that day, so Anna insisted she drive us to her modeling shoot in Rome. We missed Angelo terribly, or at least his calmer driving habits. Perhaps he was out scoring some Romatene for us.

We careened down the mountain and the road spilled into a small village, narrowing into a one-lane cobble street. We were grateful for this regression in infrastructure because it required Anna to downshift and drive at a human pace. At last, I could hear myself breathe and knew I was still alive. I loved when my heart beat fast with adventure but Death was a dance partner I wasn't ready to tango with quite yet.

"My God," said April through heavy breaths. "Are you trying to kill us?"

"I know," said Anna, beaming. "Isn't this wonderful?" She really was happy here and had carved out quite a life for herself.

Now that we could hear each other, I asked her, "So Anna, why do our parents think you're a nun?"

"They still do, don't they?" she said. "I think it's good for them. I bet their friends are jealous."

April leaned in after composing herself. She was glad not to be doing battle with the back end of Anna's scarf. "Were you ever a nun?"

"Ha! Never," said Anna. "I don't know about you, but my parents were never very ... how would you explain it? Their focus was never really on me."

"That sounds like a dream," I said. "All my parents do is obsess about me."

"I think it was a combination of a language mix-up and a bait-and-switch ad," said Anna. "The brochure advertised a convent in Rome, but it was really a reform school in Frascati."

"Wait," said April. "Your parents never came to drop you off or see if this place was legitimate?"

"They weren't child-centric," said Anna.

We drove through the quiet small town and watched the shopkeepers opening doors and sweeping entrances. It was so peaceful here. I wondered if sixteen-year-old girls here were facing the same troubles as I was. Did they have a Wall here that everyone aspired to be the queen of?

"So, while I was sent to reform school, my parents thought they had placed me in a convent. The reform school is run by an order of nuns, but they're based in Aprilia. Not too far away. After a few months, it was easier to tell my parents I was going to be a nun. I think it gave them peace. Plus, they sent me more money to keep up my studies. I don't think they have a clue what it takes to be a nun."

"How do you solve a problem like Anna?" sang April.

"The year I spent in reform school? I did a lot of growing up," said Anna. "That's where I met the Bella Donnas."

"The Bella Donnas?" I said.

We came to the end of the small town and the road opened up again. Anna gunned the engine and we were off in a cloud of rushing wind. April grabbed the tail end of Anna's scarf and held onto it, determined not to be dominated by Italian fashion. We drove for about ten minutes and in the distance, I could make out Rome.

We parked outside a windowless one-story building on the outskirts of Rome. A security guard walked out of the building and gave Anna a hug. Anna whispered to him and pointed at us and he wrote something down on his clipboard. Anna hopped out of the car and waved us in. The security guard nodded his approval as we trotted by.

We entered the building and were surrounded by activity. Men were moving lights and white screens to arrange the next photo shoot. Tables were arranged in the corners that acted as impromptu makeup rooms for the models. Racks of clothes were pressed up against the sides of the room. Women with clipboards raced by us, barking orders at their harried assistants. It was chaos of the highest degree and I loved it.

"You two stand over there for now," said Anna, indicating one of the makeup tables. "I'll be right back."

"Are we being made up?" April asked. "You know, like, to be photographed?"

April and I smiled longingly at Anna, suddenly seeing a lifelong fantasy come true that we didn't even know was a lifelong fantasy until a few minutes ago.

"Not so much," said Anna. "You just watch. And don't touch anything."

We walked dejectedly to the losers' table past tall, beautiful women and felt like we were in high school all over again. A middle-aged woman with a clipboard approached us. She had a lit cigarette in her mouth but reached past me for a pack of cigarettes. She took one out and lit it.

"*Sei un modello?*" she said.

"What?" said April.

"We're with Anna," I said in my best British accent. "Isn't she fab?"

The clipboard lady took a deep drag from her cigarette. "*Sei americano?*"

"We're from England. Great Britain? You know, The Beatles? David Bowie?"

The clipboard lady looked at us and smiled. "I like Ringo," she said and continued with her work.

We watched Anna get ready. I had always wished to have that kind of attention lavished on me. Men checked her light levels constantly; women brought her fabrics to see how they glistened against her perfect skin. And all the time, a team of makeup artists applied the trendiest makeup and worked on her hair. She would take two steps forward and they would take two steps forward. She was like a shark with fashionable pilot fish.

After an hour, it came time for the photo shoot. Anna was posed on a Styrofoam rock with a painting of a beach behind her. She put the back of her hand on her forehead like she was about to faint. She arched her back slightly and the cameras popped and clicked. The clipboard lady who liked Ringo barked out orders and the photographers switched positions and continued taking shots.

Once the photographers covered her in every conceivable angle, they waved their hands in the air, indicating it was time for a break and change in scenery. Anna came over to us. I noticed she was using her model walk. She clapped her hands to get the room's attention.

"Everyone," she said, in English for our sake. "These are my dear cousins. Treat them like family."

April sat up and whispered to me, "I'm family!"

"Hullo," I said in my best British accent. The crew and photographers approached us and did their best with their English. They asked April and me about our trip from America. I don't think any of them were buying that I was from Great Britain. They were fascinated by American culture. But after you got past Farrah, Saturday Night Fever, KC and the Sunshine Band, The Love Boat, and Star Wars, where were you? But they seemed impressed I knew all about Mr. Roarke and Tattoo.

I always had the ability to get along with any group I was thrown into. It proved an especially useful skill in high school where everyone was segregated by popularity and interests. I got along with the rich kids, the jocks, the rockers, the burnouts, and the nerds. I think it was because I hadn't found myself yet. I tried on different personalities like I was trying on lipstick. It was also an easy way to avoid the fact I was still a virgin. If I didn't stay too long with one group, they wouldn't have time to ask that question.

Anna stayed for her shoot a few more hours. Then she whisked April and me off to pick up dinner. We raced back up the mountain at a crazy pace and landed at her hustle-and-bustle-free house. Angelo wasn't there but it was nice to have a quiet girls' night in.

"So, you want to know how I became a model?" said Anna as she poured us some limoncello after dinner.

"More than anything," I said.

"The answer will not impress you," said Anna.

"Trust us," said April, sipping her first limoncello. "My God, this is good. How have I never had this before?"

"I just worked hard," said Anna. "Yes, I had great bone structure, but I worked my ass off. It was hard at first. I made enough from modeling recently to buy this house."

"I want to be you when I grow up," I said.

"You are grown up," said Anna. "Haven't you noticed?"

It was the best limoncello ever.

On the third day of Anna's modeling shoot, actual British models arrived. I thought I could work on my accent and learn more phrases from them. I secretly hoped I might make a British friend and have a British summer adventure next year. The British models made me out to be a phony in two seconds. While Anna was being photographed as a matador against a painted bullfighting arena, I was suffering my own personal British invasion. The British models treated me like an American, which is to say with kindness and curiosity. But they did not include me in their social circle as one of their own. I was crushed. It was the first time in my life I didn't fit in with a clique.

I didn't get around to asking Anna what the heck the modeling shoot was for until the fourth day. I chalked up my delayed question to being dazzled with Rome along with the chic modeling sub-culture. During one of her photo breaks, I approached Anna. April had begun to flirt with one of the lighting guys and I could tell he was toying with her. I think she knew it too.

"So, what is all this for?" I asked Anna.

"Book covers," she said.

"Book covers? What kind of books?"

"It's all the same author. They sell her books in America too. She is a legend around here. Very reclusive. Perhaps you have heard of her. Gina Puttanesca?"

CHAPTER TWENTY-FOUR

Grazioso*—Indication that the entire composition is to be played gracefully.*

Here's how I knew something was wrong with Bart Rollins.

I had learned a life lesson with my uncle's father when I was eight. My Uncle Scott was married to my mother's sister. My Uncle Scott's father, Ernesto, was always sickly. He looked wrinkled, sallow, and weak for as long as I knew him. He was like the "after" picture of an anti-smoking campaign. With his slight, wiry frame, slicked back, dyed-black, thinning hair, he never had to work hard to leave a strong impression on me of what getting sick or old would be like.

During family get-togethers, he'd typically be in great spirits, usually because he was imbibing great spirits. He drank heavily despite his lung cancer. I'd overhear him talk about his latest doctor visits and hospital test results. This sterile information held great fascination to my adolescent mind.

"Eli, those bastards gave me a seventy percent chance of full recovery," he'd say to me as I walked by. "I like those odds." Or, "Damn chemo's making more of my hair fall out. Figure I have to go wig-shopping. Is it called a wig if a man wears it? Besides, I have a whole closet of hats I haven't worn in years."

He was resilient, feisty, and in full battle against the devil in his body.

Later on, though, something changed. He got cheerier and his conversations turned to more of the small-talk type.

"My new pulmonologist is so accomplished," he'd say to whoever would listen. "He graduated first in his class. And every Saturday, he takes off to ride his Harley. Imagine that. A Harley!"

That's when I knew he was dying without hope. His conversation focused on his doctor's personal life, as if this was some medical TV drama unfolding before him and he was a detached observer. Gone was the talk brimming with the sparkle of grit, optimism, and recovery. It was replaced with a car salesman's smile and façade intended to distract and fractionate the grim reality that awaited sweet Ernesto.

He died two weeks after telling me about the goddamn lung doctor's Harley.

Bart Rollins talked like Ernesto when we got to Italy. He never acknowledged his health; just talked about the weather.

The train had stopped in Florence when we all received the bad news about Bart Rollins.

Mrs. Clancy seemed to experience the unexpected death of her husband as some type of mild annoyance. She did not seem terribly shaken and, in fact, appeared to take this in stride, as if she expected her husband to die on this trip. She cried in public and wore black, but I knew bad acting when I saw it.

We were in Florence at our two-star hotel eating a one-star breakfast. I still hadn't gotten used to these European continental breakfasts. Toast, weak jam, plain milk, and toast. That was it. Every morning. I was convinced these breakfasts were the reason Europe had the highest suicide rate in the world. By lunchtime, we were zombies: cadaverous and ravenous. We were Americans raised on fat sausage, thick oatmeal, rich eggs, and sweet cereal. And chocolate milk. And all of it covered with maple syrup and bacon.

I was having breakfast with Charley and Ponte. Ponte was hungover again and trying his best to hide his condition from the ever-watchful gaze of Rasper. We didn't feel like making conversation with Ponte, so I was glad he just moaned and stared into his toast.

Hubert's wife, Florinda, was sitting with Little Francis, Mrs. Clancy, and Lady Bear. Little Francis was devastated and red from crying. The choir boys channeled their grief by taking turns patting him on the back or just holding his hand while he cried. Mrs. Clancy, dressed in black, was trying to spread the whatever-berry jam on her bland toast.

There was an empty seat next to Mrs. Clancy that was just unbearably lonely. Hubert stumbled into the room as if he hadn't slept. The wrinkles on his shirt were outmatched only by those on his face.

"Coffee," he mumbled. Hubert plopped down next to his wife and Mrs. Clancy, causing the spillage of various glasses of juice, coffee, and water.

"Not in that chair," said Mrs. Clancy, sharply.

Hubert sprang up and surveyed the room for an empty chair. He had unusually pudgy, pink fingers like sausages. I had always thought so; this wasn't just driven by my hunger for real breakfast food. His fingers were at odds with the rest of his skinny frame as well as his vocation as a piano player. He'd plink the keys in a way that, miraculously, wouldn't touch the adjacent keys.

They were the complete opposite of Bart Rollins' fingers. Bart's fingers looked like ghost hands. They were white and thin. His hands used to tremble slightly, and his frail fingers had left no doubt in my mind of his health and his poor judgment to chaperone us on this trip.

When Bart had taken me to the glass factory where my father had worked, I first noticed his sickly digits. He saw me staring at his fingers and offered a weak smile. An Ernesto smile. That wasn't that long ago. And now he was gone. He had just been here. I already missed him.

Abruptly, Hubert got up and dashed out of the room. Florinda looked awkwardly at the rest of the table, as if deciding whether to go after him or finally eat her hard-won victory over the jam and toast. She stood up and chased after him.

Rasper was buried in his itineraries and contracts for the upcoming few days and didn't notice the activities unfolding. He was, of course, bereaved about Bart. But he was also trying to keep everyone calm, especially the more emotionally unstable boys. And he was upset we were running out of money. I overheard one of the towns had stiffed him on the bill for one of our concerts. He was constantly muttering about how he was going to feed all of us. Something in his character told me he really placed importance in appearing rich regardless of whether he actually was wealthy. While he had his nose buried in his itineraries and checkbook, he neglected to notice me get up to eavesdrop on Hubert and Florinda.

I sneaked down the hallway and heard voices by the small lobby. Creeping stealthily along the ragged carpet, I came upon Hubert and Florinda sitting on the lobby couch. I ducked around the corner. I could barely make out what they were saying. Something about an aunt. I shifted slightly. Something about Capri. Something about a dying old house.

Then I felt bad. I stepped outside myself and examined the situation. What was I doing? This had nothing to do with me. I had enough to worry about. Besides seeing what else I could find out about my dad, there was getting ready for the girls' orphanage concert, hoping Big Francis wouldn't beat me up, and, lately, thinking about Jane. I couldn't believe Bart was gone.

As I turned around to head back to the breakfast room, I overheard Hubert say, "I'm taking a cab this afternoon."

And his wife returned with, "You're going alone then."

"I'll go with you."

Who said that? It sounded like me.

Jesus.

Hubert looked across the lobby and spotted me. He nodded thankfully.

CHAPTER TWENTY-FIVE

Presto—*An indication the tempo should be played very fast.*

After our first week in Italy being chaperoned by Anna, April and I were ready to have a Roman adventure on our own. This was sparked not by a sudden wave of courage but by Anna's announcement she and Angelo had pressing business to tend to, and we were free to stay at her house for the day. Unfortunately, the phone was out of order so if there was trouble, we really were on our own.

We waited for an infinity after they left, easily five minutes, before we grabbed our things and headed off to Rome. We walked to the train station and were transported to our personal Audrey Hepburn fantasy forty-seven minutes later. Now if we could only find our very own Gregory Peck.

As we walked through the city streets, the men in Rome did notice us. That was the good news. But they mostly just watched us walk by. The older or uglier ones would walk behind us for a block or two, catcalling or whistling. One even approached us and slapped my butt. This was not what I expected, and it frightened me. We decided to go sightseeing so we could avoid the gaze of these creepy men.

We walked up the one-hundred-and-thirty-five steps of the Spanish Steps. That stopped the old guys from following us. We were a bit winded ourselves, so we sat near the top and gazed out at the city that surrounded us. The sun was shining brightly without a cloud in the sky. In the distance,

I heard church bells ringing mixed with doves cooing overhead. It was the most perfect moment in my life.

"Now what?" said April.

She obviously didn't appreciate the grandeur the way I did. "Well," I said, "We could go about the business we came here for."

"Shopping and postcards?"

"Romatene," I said. Angelo and Anna had been silent about their Romatene connection. I wasn't sure if they had lied to me or if they were holding out.

"I don't think that's such a good idea," said April. "It's been so nice not being arrested or deported this whole trip."

"What would you have us do?"

"I was thinking we need to get you back to the Wall, right?" said April.

"Double quick."

"What if we became famous models?" said April. "And our pictures were in every magazine in America. I'm talking TV Guide. They'd have to take you back. That's our ticket back to the Wall."

Oh, sweet April. I loved her so much at that moment.

"That's possibly the nicest thing you have ever said," I said. "And the dumbest."

April's smile disappeared and her face went long. "Why?"

I searched for an answer. "Because you have to have your own TV show to be on the cover of TV Guide. Otherwise, your plan is flawless."

"Oh good. Could you imagine if our moms bought the latest Puttanesca book and saw their daughters on the cover? They'd shit a cow!"

"Could you imagine if we ever got to meet Gina Puttanesca? I'd shit a cow," I said. I stood up and stretched. "Come on, let's go get a gelato. And then to the farmers market." I bounded down the stairs and April followed.

"What's at the farmers market?"

We walked with our lemon gelatos to the outskirts of the city toward the farmers' market. I had brought along my little English-Italian dictionary which fit nicely in my purse. We made sure none of the creepy men were following us. There was one man, dressed in a suit with a paisley scarf and a fedora hat, who kept popping up. He looked familiar, but he might have been a businessman on the way to the farmers market as well. At least he didn't pinch my ass.

We arrived at the crowded farmers' market. Immediately, we were tempted by the crates and tables filled with pastries, necklaces, glass ornaments. We were less enthralled by the dead chickens and weirdo vegetables displayed.

The secret to getting this operation right would be to ask the right question in the right way to the right person. After that, I figured we were on easy street. The farmers' market would have delighted me any other day but this morning, we were on a mission. April stayed close by my side.

We found a man who was selling tapestries and hookahs. It was the closest approximation to the mall head shop back home. I smiled at him and took out my dictionary. He picked up some linen placemats and waved them in the air to demonstrate how light they were. Just the quality I was looking for in placemats.

"*Ciao*," I said.

"That's a good start," said April.

"*Ciao*," said the vendor. He was a young man of about twenty with curly, brown hair and a mouth too large for his face.

I paged through my dictionary, piecing together my intent.

"*Stiamo ... cercando ... erba.* Yes, definitely *erba*," I said.

"*Non capisco*," said the vendor, staring blankly.

"I think he wants money," said April.

"For what?" I said. "He doesn't even know what we want yet." More dictionary pages turned. "*Abbiamo bisogno di erba.*"

"*Erba?*" said the vendor.

"*Si,*" said April with a wink. "I think we're getting to him," she said to me.

"*Siamo muli,*" I said.

"*Muli?*" said the vendor.

"*Si,*" I said, getting the hang of this. "*Muli erba.*"

"Ahhh," said the vendor, and a little bong light must have gone on in his head. "Aspettare." He took out a piece of paper and wrote down some instructions in Italian. He pointed us towards the man at the far end of the aisle standing alongside a horse. He smiled and wished us a good day.

Now we were getting somewhere. I held April's hand tightly with excitement. We approached the man with the horse. The man and horse were both gray at the muzzle and both appeared to have been ridden too hard and needed to be put out to pasture. The horseman smiled at us and we handed him the note and pointed to the vendor. He looked at the note, then us, then back at the note. "Okay," he said and shrugged.

He moved around next to the horse and opened up the back gate of a large, wooden cart. The cart was filled with hay. He invited us to sit in the cart while he tied his cart to the horse. April and I regarded each other, then got in, sitting on the floor of hay. We had no idea if this was how things got done here.

There was an abrupt shock and we were off. We craned our necks and saw the gray man perched on a little wooden seat that was attached to the cart and the gray horse. The horse was happily pulling all of us towards Romatene. I'm sure if we were arrested, the horse would plead not guilty.

The city gave way to the gorgeous countryside and the undulating fields of green and yellow we had grown to admire so much.

"This is not good," said April. "Not good at all."

"We'll be fine," I said. "We'll go to this guy's shop, get our Romatene, and he'll give us a ride back to Anna's. My plan is perfect."

"No, not that," said April. "I'm sitting in shit." She was afraid to move for fear of spreading it around or actually looking at it. "I think I'm going to be sick."

"From the jostling and the shit?" I said.

"No, from the ending of 'Grease.' Yes, from the jostling and the shit!"

I held her hand and April gave me a sour look, still trying not to move.

One fifteen-minute horse-driven cart ride later, we arrived at a small farm. The man led his horse and our cart towards a small stall. He jumped down and detached the horse from the cart, then led the horse away for a drink. The moment of truth had arrived. I hopped off the cart and held out my hand for April. She stood up and a patch of hay stuck to her bottom. I grabbed a handful of hay and wiped it away.

"Actually, it's not that bad," I said.

"You're buying me new clothes when we get back to Rome," she said.

A short boy of about fourteen approached us, pushing an enormous wheelbarrow filled with hay. He rested it in front of us, took off his hat, and smiled.

"I speak English so no worry," he said. His voice hadn't changed yet. "Is good, the English, yes?"

"Perfect," I said.

"I am Domenic," he said.

"I'm Betty and this is Veronica," I said, not wanting to use our real names.

"Do you have any paper towels or a hose?" said April, still using the hay to wipe off her dress.

"You tell my uncle you here to buy?" said Domenic. He seemed chipper for someone involved in a drug deal. Then again, so did I.

"Yes. We'd like to see what you have," I said.

He pointed to the wheelbarrow.

"It's in here?" I said, confused.

"Is this," he said, reaching and holding up the hay. "You say you need grass for mule. Is good grass. The best. Delicious. Your mule will be very happy."

Domenic was at least nice enough to give us a ride back to the city, once April made him clean out the cart.

April and I went straight to a modest dress shop, and I purchased her a new dress. My funds were quickly being depleted by this Romatene excursion and we had nothing to show for it. We should have stayed at Anna's house.

That reminded me her phone was out. We found a payphone in town and checked in with our folks. My parents told me they had sent a telegram to Anna's address. I hadn't received any telegram. My mom told me to check with the local Western Union office. One cab-ride-with-no-shit-on-the-seat later, we found the Western Union office. They had a whole stack of telegrams for April and me. April's were all from her parents. Western Union wasn't sure why they hadn't delivered the telegrams to Anna's yet. I sifted through mine. They were mostly from my parents. But several were from Eddie. The gist of all of Eddie's was the same: "How's it going with scoring Romatene?"

CHAPTER TWENTY-SIX

***Obbligato**—An extended solo, often accompanying the vocal part of an aria.*

Rasper had given me the stink eye when Hubert told him I was to accompany him on this road trip.

"I don't think it's advisable," said Rasper to Hubert. Hubert shrugged his shoulders. I didn't understand their secret language as accompanist and conductor. I think Rasper grasped that Florinda had refused to go. "I'll tell your mother you're fine," said Rasper to me. "Go."

Rasper seemed more panicky and stressed after breakfast. Was it the finances? The pressure of our upcoming Vatican concert (which I had recently taken to calling Popestock)? The fact that Big Francis had redirected his bullying from me to Terrence? Or was it the recent death of Bart Rollins? Probably an all-of-the-above situation with an emphasis on the latter.

Hubert and I headed to downtown Florence in a cab. He was quiet during the drive. While Hubert and I waited in line for the rental car, I asked him about Rasper. Hubert stared into the distance and shrugged. The shrug told me he just didn't give a shit any longer.

Here's what I learned. Or at least how I processed what Hubert told me. It turned out Rasper wasn't just feeding my mom a line about him being a country boy.

Douglas Rasper was born around 1935 in South Carolina on a duck farm, of all places. His parents had been duck farmers all their lives. He led a fairly Huck Finn, all-American childhood until the age of eleven. Then his father died.

Rasper's father had been enlisted in the Navy during World War II, leaving behind his wife and young son to run the farm. Rasper had no other siblings so without his father to direct and assist him, the farm slowly fell into disrepair. The ducks kept escaping or got eaten by local dogs. The pond where the ducks swam dried up inexplicably one day. Basic maintenance was ignored since Rasper didn't know how to mend a fence or install a new roof to the barn.

When Rasper was sixteen, he and his mom decided they needed to bring in some help. They hired six men, all over the age of forty. They were all black, all native South Carolinians, and all sons of former slaves who had never wanted to leave their home state. The sun-drenched land, rich with fertile soil and moist air, could not have been a more perfect place to live or raise a family. The six men, who all knew each other from previous jobs, were great farmers but knew nothing about ducks.

Rasper got to know these men slowly. He was shy at first but, over several months, opened himself up to their friendship and accepted them as father figures. He enjoyed being around them and was shocked at their stories of folk tales. He had heard his parents talk about the Old South but to hear these men talk about their perspective was like hearing about another world.

Soon, the ducks were dying and Rasper's mother grew more and more desperate. She found it difficult to make decisions that would have a great effect on her life or those around her. She often wrote to her husband knowing he could never answer.

Rasper's mother had been hardened by her life of toil on the farm. Her hair was gray and pulled back tightly in a practical bun. Her face had aged from worrying about duck disease, ducklings being eaten, and paying the monthly bills. Her formerly cheerful eyes had been burdened by her husband's absence.

One of the six farmhands, Taylor, came by to see Rasper's mother one afternoon. He came from half-black, half-Hispanic heritage and was a large, friendly-faced man with creamy brown skin and a deep baritone voice.

Rasper's mother sat at her kitchen table going over some bills while little Douglas tuned the radio to get better reception for the classical station.

Taylor, wiping the sweat from his brow, walked into the kitchen and spoke to Rasper's mom. Douglas pretended to ignore them.

"Mrs. Rasper?" Taylor said quietly, trying to get her attention.

Rasper's mother didn't look up.

"Mrs. Rasper, the other men and I been talkin' and seein' as how the duck business is goin' down, pardon the pun," he said, pausing slightly. "Not that any part of it is your fault. No Ma'am."

Rasper's mother looked up and caught his eye, as if she had just noticed his presence in her kitchen.

"Just what do you want, Mr. Taylor?" she said. Her mind was elsewhere.

Taylor shuffled back and forth, his eyes sweeping the floor. He swallowed hard.

"It's just that me and the boys, we was all thinkin' that we should be movin' on. That we should..."

"You're leaving me too," she cried out with a cutting tone. She sobbed, her shoulders heaving under the stress. "You're going to work for another farm," she continued. "A better farm. Where they've had the goddamn forethought and planning to raise something other than ridiculous ducks!"

There was a deadly silence. Douglas had stopped moving, hoping to become invisible. He knew what was coming. He had discussed it with Taylor and the other men a week earlier.

"Actually, ma'am," said Taylor, looking at Douglas. "We're starting a traveling choir."

"A choir?" said Rasper's mother.

"And we want to take Douglas with us. He'll be well taken care of."

"What?" she said.

"We'll always provide him food and a bed, and he'll get to see the country and..."

"You're all leaving to start a choir?" she said. "I am mystified. You're going to sing?"

"Yes, ma'am."

"And you want to take my Douglas with you so he can be a gopher for your choir?"

"No, ma'am. We need him to be our director. He's a natural."

"Why, Douglas doesn't know the first thing about being on the road. He can play music, sure, but..."

"Ma'am," said Taylor. "I don't mean to interrupt. But Douglas already got us a contract with the National Road Show..."

Just then, Douglas ran upstairs into his room, leaving behind his stunned mother. The tension enveloped the entire house. Douglas ran back into the kitchen holding a small sack. He dropped it on the kitchen table. It landed with a metallic thud.

"Douglas, what's this?" his mother said. "Not you too."

"Open it, momma."

She untied the brown cord and unfolded the top of the bag. Cautiously, she reached inside like she did when she would gather the fragile duck eggs from the coop. She pulled out several sheaves of sheet music. Pages after pages were filled with completed compositions, all written in Douglas' distinctive handwriting with the fountain pen she had given him for Christmas. It was the same fountain pen she had used to write her last letter to her missing husband.

"Douglas," she said, looking up in wonder, her eyes welling. "You always loved music. It's a gift that the Lord gave you."

"Not that. Reach inside again, momma."

Rasper's mother reached in and pulled out a wad of twenty-dollar bills. Reaching in with the other hand, she produced a handful of coins. Each shiny disk slipped through her fingers.

"You're right about your son, ma'am. He truly has a gift. He made this just writing music," said Taylor quietly.

Rasper's mother sat in bewildered silence, stroking the corner of a twenty-dollar bill like a security blanket.

"And he'll make more directing us," Taylor continued.

Rasper walked up to his mother and held her hand.

"Can I, momma?"

She looked at Taylor, then at her son. "You grandfather was a golfer, Douglas. When I was little, he used to take me out with him. He'd explain the magic and secrets of the game. 'Always play through the ball,' he'd say."

"Momma?" said Rasper.

"Took me years to understand what he meant. Your grandfather meant to not just live in the present but look forward to the future; to see past your nose."

The money on her table would get her out of debt. She could sell the farm and finally be with Cooper Stephenson, the miller whom she had been seeing for years. Rasper would find out years later that his mother's relationship with Stephenson was the real reason his father had moved out and enlisted in the Navy. Rasper supposed his mother had always felt guilty about driving his dad to the war and death. Years later, after Rasper graduated with full honors from his studies in Vienna, he went to the battlefield where his dad had been killed. That night, he went to a restaurant and ordered duck in his honor.

"Go, Douglas," said Rasper's mother. "Go see the world."

CHAPTER TWENTY-SEVEN

Legato—*Indication that the movement is to be played smoothly.*

The train made a pleasant vibrating hum beneath us. Anna and I sat opposite each other, having the compartment all to ourselves. Anna had placed a calf-skin suitcase between my feet. The suitcase made a rattling sound as the train moved along. April had wanted to do some sightseeing and had been more than thrilled when Angelo smiled and offered to escort her around town in Anna's car.

The porter had just taken our tickets so I knew we wouldn't be interrupted.

"Can I ask why you sent for me?" I said to Anna. "I mean, all the way from America. I'm totally grateful."

Anna nodded. "I was wondering when you were going to ask," she said. "Is there anything wrong with wanting to see my cousin?"

"I always did like you," I said.

"Me too. And I miss my family. But they would never understand my life. I thought you might."

We rode in silence for the first two stops, and I let the flying scenery hypnotize me.

"Your life is good in America?" Anna asked.

"It's okay."

"Your parents treat you well?"

"I guess. I think it would be different if I was their real daughter," I said. The scenery was whizzing by so fast I couldn't make out details. "It's complicated."

"It's always complicated," said Anna. "Besides April, you have many friends?"

I leaned in towards her. "Anna, if you have a Romatene connection, it would be great to meet them soon. I have a guy at home who I need to do a favor for."

"He's your boyfriend?"

"Oh God, no," I said. "It's to get my friends back."

"Romatene. You're living very dangerously."

"Please," I said.

"I have a connection. You will love my connection," said Anna.

The Santa Teresa Orphanage and Reform School for Girls was an odd place for Anna to take me. Anna had been sent there by her parents in an effort to tame the wild horse that was quickly inhabiting the space formerly leased by their daughter.

"What happened to you at Santa Teresa?" I asked. I knew the major points but wanted to hear the details.

"It's a long story."

"We have time," I said.

"Very well," said Anna, applying lipstick. "At the Reform School, what I refer to as *La Grande Casa*, while I did my time, I fell in love. Not with a boy. With the Bella Donnas. They were a group of long-timers. Eight girls. Between fourteen and eighteen years old. True orphans. Surly.

"On my first day at *La Grande Casa*, I instantly knew how I would survive my year here. There was a hierarchy. The orphans lorded over the reform school girls. Reform school girls were there by choice. Not the orphans. So, I told the Bella Donnas my parents had recently died."

"You did what?" I said.

"I put on my best tough girl face and told them I was an orphan too. The Bella Donnas were intrigued by me. I was this beautiful, lost American thing to them.

"I found the girls' company comforting, not threatening. I even felt oddly at home. To help my social standing, I might even have hinted to the Bella Donnas that I had a hand in my parents' death."

"Oh my God," I said. "This is the best story ever."

"The Bella Donnas believed every word. I think they thought I was exotic. By the end of my second month in *La Grande Casa*, I became their unofficial leader. Some of the girls were interested in my beauty. I never played that hand. But I did use my influence for the betterment of *La Grande Casa*.

"For a brief period, the Santa Teresa Orphanage and Reform School for Girls held art classes, made attractive uniforms, and had access to cigarettes. I used my charm with the nuns and guards to arrange these things. I also helped organize the Bella Donnas, so they started working together."

"I'm so impressed," I said. "I could never even run for Student Body Treasurer."

"It was around this time the statue of Santa Teresa, which stood watch over visitors in the grand marble foyer of the main building, went missing. It had been blessed by no fewer than three Popes.

"The nuns went crazy in the way that only nuns can. Besides the usual interrogations, the nuns instituted a policy of absolute silence until the little stone statue of Saint Teresa crawled back home on the ancient mantle.

"All the Bella Donnas? We didn't crack. We never revealed the whereabouts of Saint Teresa."

Anna snapped her compact mirror shut and deposited it back into her leather purse.

"Did you know that Saint Teresa is the matron Saint of Feminine Joy? That irony was not lost on us," said Anna.

"Feminine joy," I repeated.

"Shortly after Saint Teresa went missing, so did I. I found some loose wall stones near the end of the hallway by the bathroom and figured out an escape route. The Bella Donnas covered for me during inspections, saying I was at the medical ward or in the bathroom. The nuns were so confident in their lockdown, it never occurred to them that I escaped."

"Where did you go?" I asked.

"To meet with photographers. I did this about once a week. I was serious about becoming a model. When word would get to me that a modeling shoot worthy of the risk was available, I'd gather the Bella Donnas. Sister Henora usually worked security at night. If you could manage to get past her without detection, fool her into thinking you were asleep in your bunk, loosen the stones in the wall, shimmy down to the ground, and manage to get past the locked, iron gate, then you had a chance to escape. I had this down to a business."

"You are officially my new religion," I said.

"At around nine at night, Sister Henora would start her lockdown walk. When she'd reach the rooms upstairs, where the Bella Donnas slept, I'd slip outside after knocking on the door of one of the younger girls downstairs. The girl would bound upstairs through the servants' steps and slip into my bed.

"Then, one day, I finally got my big break in Milan. But I knew I owed a great debt to the Bella Donnas. That's why I stole the statue of Saint Teresa."

"What?" I said.

"Actually, I smuggled out Santa Teresa many times as I pursued my modeling career. To me, stealing the statue made perfect sense. And it wasn't really stealing since I would return each night to the orphanage and place it back in its proper spot."

"Then why take the risk?"

"Guilt mostly. I guess I loved my parents and wanted to please them. They needed to believe I was in deep contemplative contrition at the convent. They wanted me to be a nun. Going on modeling assignments with Santa Teresa made me feel less guilty.

"Even though I had steady modeling work, I couldn't afford to live on my own yet so I would go back to the orphanage to live there. My disappearances from the modeling world added to my mystery. The statue was my bridge between both worlds.

"Anyway, eventually, I left the orphanage for good although I still keep in touch with the Bella Donnas."

"That's the most spectacular story I ever heard," I said. "And the nuns never found out? What about the statue?"

Anna pointed at the suitcase between my feet.

"No," I said. I opened up the suitcase. Little Saint Teresa looked up at me. "What are we doing?"

"It's time I put Santa Teresa back on her mantle for good. I no longer need her comfort."

"That's why we're going to the orphanage?"

"One of the reasons," said Anna. "Look, if you are worried, I can go by myself."

There was no way I was going to commit the international, cultural, and religious faux pas of screwing up a modeling career, depriving teenage orphans of their contraband, or rob zealous nuns of their savior.

"Oh, I'm so going with you," I said.

The train rattled over the twisting countryside, occasionally making our compartment bump violently. The suitcase bearing the statue fell over flat. Anna instinctively reached down to check on Saint Teresa like a protective young mother. The sun decided to stream in through the overcast sliver clouds, past the thin train window and directly onto Anna's face as she bent over to attend the fallen suitcase. It completed the beatific Madonna image and took my breath away. I felt in awe of my cousin and her easily-achieved beauty, chosen schizophrenic lifestyle, and affinity for danger and good deeds. I was also a bit intimidated.

"Any chance I could meet your Romatene connection soon?" I said.

"Very soon."

We were due at *La Grande Casa* in a few minutes. We were transporting to the Bella Donnas three cases of American cigarettes, assorted candy and cookies, fresh joints, some Vogues, and, of course, Saint Teresa.

"Tell me again what's happening tonight?" I said.

"There will be a formal dinner, some speeches, and entertainment from a visiting American boys' choir."

"American boys?" I said.

Saint Teresa was smiling down on me.

Feminine joy indeed.

CHAPTER TWENTY-EIGHT

Elegy—An instrumental lament with praise for the dead.

Despite hourly changes from tightly negotiated schedules, Rasper's itinerary was our travel bible. On this particular day, it allowed for an entire afternoon of free time. That happened to coincide with the road trip Hubert and I were about to embark upon. Rasper was busying himself with making plans for Popestock and was okay with one less choir boy to keep tabs on. He hadn't provided me any updates on the burgeoning relationship with my mom, which gave me relief.

I still wasn't clear why I agreed to go with Hubert, but we found ourselves in a rental car driving on a road the Devil built and God had forgotten. Maybe I wanted to be alone, or at least away from the crowds. Bart Rollins' death had affected me in a way I wasn't expecting. I hardly knew him. But he had extended his kindness to me and made me feel more like an adult. He had shown me what it would have been like to have a father. And now he was gone. Memories of my Uncle Ernesto also refused to escape.

My mind was jarred back to the rocky country road as Hubert maneuvered past some potholes the size of Delaware. I was riding shotgun.

"Careful," screeched Lady Bear from the backseat. She had imposed herself on the ride, apparently thinking my chaperone needed a chaperone. I figured Rasper had sent her to get her out of his hair and to make sure Hubert came back on time. "Hubert, are you quite sure you're not Italian?

You drive like the locals," she shrieked in her best impersonation of a fishwife. "They're all mad. It's all that olive oil, I tell you. Not enough butter in their diet."

Hubert shot her a weak smile through the rear-view mirror, then plodded on through the pocked, dusty road. The day was a bit overcast which mirrored Hubert's melancholy mood. Lady Bear asked me to close my window. Something about noise or dust. She never addressed me by name.

"Which one are you, anyway?" Lady Bear asked after a half-hour of silence. Boredom must have really set in with her if the conversation had degraded to this level.

"Tenor, formally alto," I said.

"No, I mean your name." Something about her made everything she said sound imperious.

"Francis," I said. "But everyone calls me Big Francis." I figured if I did say anything truly offensive and punishable, let old Francis take the heat.

A small smile formed in the corner of Hubert's mouth, which I found comforting. It was good to know he could still enjoy a schoolboy conspiratorial game of "Screw the Old Lady."

"Francis," said Lady Bear, disdainfully.

"Alright then," said Hubert. "We're almost there."

I thought of telling Lady Bear her makeup looked fine, seeing as how her undead breed didn't cast reflections in mirrors. But I decided to let circumspection get the better of me.

A small village peeked out through the mountains. It was as if someone had once imagined a town in this remote land amongst jagged hills in some type of drunken mirage, sobered up, and decided to build here anyway. What else could explain the improbability of the village's chosen location but a grappa-induced delusional bender?

"Finally," squawked Lady Bear.

We drove into the center of the small village which somehow managed to pull off the delicate trick of getting smaller the closer we got to it. The place was devoid of tourists, which made a nice change. It occurred to me that every tour, every train, every pizza shop we had visited had been crawling with people from other countries. Pasty people with camera-laden necks, pockets stuffed with extra flashcubes, postcards, and unacceptable currency that needed spending. In short, those places were filled with us.

This village, Bovarti, as I understood it to be called, seemed like an actual Italian village; a place actual Italians called their actual home. There were only three places in the world such a quaint, perfect village could exist: here, on TV, and Disney World.

Hubert parallel parked and I noticed his hands trembling slightly. I purposely had not asked Hubert about where we were going or why we were going there. Lady Bear had hinted at something regarding Hubert's inheritance, but her information was mostly embedded in insults hurled at Hubert or me. Hubert's shoulders shuddered and I knew he wasn't looking forward to whatever awaited him at the end of this journey. Personally, I couldn't wait to find out what it was.

"Now, how long exactly will you need again?" said Lady Bear, extracting herself from the car.

"As long as it takes," replied Hubert. "And there's one more stop after this."

"Oh, I haven't forgotten," she said. "Because I have shopping to do. I've heard there's the most exquisite jewelry market nearby."

So much for my theory that Lady Bear was here to lend Hubert support and to make sure he got home safely.

"Mr. Breggleman," I said. "Can we all meet back here in one hour? Is that enough time?"

Hubert looked at Lady Bear, then gave a nod which I interpreted as agreement.

"Very well, one hour," announced Lady Bear regally, as if the idea were hers. "And not one minute more." Before we could say anything, she was off on her jewelry shopping excursion.

Hubert and I watched her until she turned the corner of the cobblestone street. We didn't move for a while; long enough for it to be awkward. I think Hubert was waiting for me to go my own way. Finally, he looked down at me.

"Eli, go find a bookstore or something, will you?"

"Really?"

"Promise me you'll be safe. That you won't do anything stupid."

"I'll try," I said.

And with that, I was on my own. Hubert shuffled up the street in the opposite direction of Lady Bear. And I was left to my own wits with some money in my pocket in a place where nobody knew who I was, where I was, or when I would ever return. The possibilities were staggering.

I had never felt so alone. Standing on the side of the street, I considered all my options. Then I did the only thing that made any sense.

I secretly followed Hubert.

By the time I made it to the end of the street where Hubert turned, he was gone. The street was mostly lined with two- and three-story houses with small food markets on the street level. The awnings and hanging baskets made it difficult to see around the bend. The few villagers on foot and bicycles obscured my vision as well but in a picture postcard way.

I caught a flash of Hubert's blue coat in the distance and I stealthily pursued, using the local color as camouflage. Luckily, the townspeople all seemed to purchase their clothing from the same drab tailor, so it was easy to spot Hubert while maintaining a safe, anonymous distance in a sea of earth tones.

He turned into a street filled with row housing, each five stories high. Except for the occasional tattered awning or broken window, each house looked identical. The air smelled of salami and sharp cheese which reminded me I hadn't eaten recently. Italy, in general, made you feel like you needed to eat. America, in general, made you feel like buying something you didn't need or subjugating a small country.

Just as I was deciding to give up trying to chase Hubert and sate my hunger instead, I spied Hubert ducking into one of the houses halfway down the block. As soon as he was inside, I burst into a full run like OJ in an airport. Maybe this was nothing like a sportsball player's run. I don't know. Nevertheless, I sprinted rigorously past the villagers with their baskets of fresh bread and cheese and the roaming dogs picking up scraps dropped from the heavens above.

The front door of the house had almost closed when it met my shoe at its kick plate. I held it open long enough to discretely enter and escape detection from anyone who might gaze my way.

Inside was a dark hallway that led to a set of back stairs. There was a staleness in the air as if no one had lived here for years. As I walked down the hallway, I noticed all the windows were closed. Each room was ghostly empty. The only sound belonged to the groaning floorboards I had walked on and the footsteps above from Hubert.

I reached the end of the hallway and peered up the wooden stairway. It spiraled up to the fifth floor. I took a firm hold of the smooth, wooden banister and began my ascent. I was slightly dizzy, which is typical when I'm climbing up and looking up at the same time.

The light seemed to be coming from the third floor. Before I alighted the stairs, I took one more glance to make sure no one was following me. This wasn't much different from when I would sneak up and spy on Rasper during rehearsal breaks back home.

Halfway down the hall, I noticed one of the peeling-paint doors was open. A muffled, warbling sound spilled out into the hallway like a drunk in an alley after last call. This room was also the source of the light. The warbling had a rhythmic, dull ticking sound underlining it. I approached the room and peered in.

The room had two closed windows without curtains. There was no furniture on the worn, hardwood floors. The walls revealed several layers of peeled paint. Hubert sat on the floor in the middle of the empty room in front of an old reel-to-reel tape recorder. Its cord snaked across the barren, dusty floor and went off under a closet door where I assumed it was connected to a hamster-driven wheel.

The tape recorder made the ticking sound as it slowly fed an old tape through its mechanism. The sound emanating from the tape machine was a boy's voice.

"And, well, let's see," the recorded sweet voice said over the ticking sound. "Oh, I know, Auntie, I got a B in spelling today! And piano classes are going okay. Thanks again for paying for them."

Hubert sat cross-legged, tears streaming down his face, suppressing an outburst so as not to drown out the taped voice. Maybe the tape was old and only had one good spin left in it. Or maybe this was some kind of "Mission Impossible" code and would self-destruct and Hubert was really a spy. A weepy spy.

I quietly turned around and walked down the stairs. I discreetly left the old house. I was more bewildered than when I entered.

"And now I suppose you'll want to know what this is all about," said Lady Bear, standing outside the house on the sidewalk, stepping out her cigarette.

My instinct was to run away but something about Lady Bear's tone was different. It was as if she was an entirely different person at the moment. The pretentiousness, the fussiness, the high maintenance demeanor had all been shed.

Lady Bear actually took my hand and led me down the street.

"Let's walk this way," she said. "I don't want Mr. Breggleman to see us when he walks out."

I actually let her hold my hand. After what I'd seen inside, it felt comforting.

"Are you alright?" she said.

"Have you been following me?" I asked as we turned the corner.

"Little boys. Such imaginations." She took a breath. "I was keeping an eye on Mr. Breggleman. Douglas is very concerned."

"What's going on?" I said. "What's Mr. Breggleman doing up there?"

It occurred to me that she hadn't asked me why I was following Hubert.

We arrived at a coffee shop and went in. She bought me a hot chocolate and ordered a high-maintenance espresso for herself. It was nice to know certain things hadn't changed in this topsy-turvy day. We sat down at a table by the window.

"I spoke with my niece this morning," she said. "Mrs. Breggleman."

I listened attentively.

"The thing is, Hubert will be retiring after this tour." She took a pensive sip. "Hubert is about to inherit some old junk from his dear departed aunt." Her voice broke off. She took another sip and gathered herself. "Such a dear woman. Such a shame she passed on. And Hubert was so close to her. Sometimes when someone gets bad news like that, they tie up loose ends or try to re-capture their youth."

I had a feeling Lady Bear was lying about Hubert and his aunt.

She stared out the window and something caught her eye. I looked out and saw Buccenti walk by the other side of the street. He did not look like a local villager.

"How do the police work in this country?" I asked.

Lady Bear appeared startled. "What ever do you mean?"

"Like, from movies, I know the mob extends into different towns. What about the police?"

Lady Bear cleared her throat as if to erase the image of Buccenti and his fedora hat following us.

"We're all gonna miss Mr. Rollins," I said, slicing through the silence.

She gazed at me coldly.

"You never met my late husband Jonathan, did you?" she said quietly as if I was an old country club tennis partner. "He was…"

"Mrs. Querrel, you were telling me about Hubert."

"What? Ah, yes. Right. Hubert. Hubert misses his family. His childhood. Do your parents have lots of pictures of you?"

It was a strange question. "I guess," I said.

"Did you know that Hubert's family never took pictures of him as a boy?" she continued. "He had to start working very young."

"Probably why he hangs around with us," I said.

She stared at me, and a smile crossed her lips. "You're very perceptive for one so young, Eli."

So, she did know who I was.

"This is the whole reason why we're here in Italy. For this very visit from Hubert," she said.

"I don't understand."

"Hubert insisted on it and threatened to quit. Told Douglas that. Can you imagine? The mouse that roared," she said. "I thought my niece married a subdued, quiet man. Who knew he had such determination?"

"And Mr. Rasper relies on him. He couldn't afford Mr. Breggleman to quit."

"Precisely," she said. "So, Hubert came because his aunt lived in this town. Some of her things are still in storage. And her apartment is still under her name."

"That's where Mr. Breggleman is sitting right now?" I said.

"Yes. He used to send his aunt updates on old reel-to-reel tapes."

"So that was Hubert's own voice he was listening to," I said. The street suddenly seemed small and cluttered, and the sky looked gray and rainy. "He just wanted to hear his own voice again one last time."

"I suppose," she said. She was distracted by the image of Buccenti as he paced by again.

"And he wanted to imagine his aunt sitting there listening to him," I said.

Lady Bear took out her compact and artfully plastered her face with more makeup.

I suddenly missed my mom and wanted to go home.

"Can you understand all of this?" she said.

I didn't know how to answer that.

Lady Bear sipped her espresso and kept an eye on the window. She knew we were being followed and I could tell she was trying to see how much I knew. She added some sugar to her espresso, stirred, and gently put the spoon down. It made a pleasing metal sound against the ceramic tabletop. She peered out the window and my eyes followed hers.

There was a shadowed figure outside pressed up to the café window looking right at us.

"I have to go to see the lawyer," said Hubert, muffled, through the glass.

Lady Bear and I gave a sigh of relief. Lady Bear's expression quickly changed to her usual sour puss.

"Lawyer? Right now?" she said. There was something about her that was more excited than surprised.

Hubert shuffled into the café but didn't sit down. He had cleaned his face but was otherwise disheveled. It was evident he was in a hurry.

"Any souvenirs from your aunt?" said Lady Bear.

"My aunt's attorney is in the next village. About a ten-minute drive," said Hubert. "Do you want to come with me, or should I pick you two up here afterward?" I couldn't tell if he had a preference. He mostly just sounded sad.

"And how long will it take for you to wrap up your affairs with this solicitor?" said Lady Bear, pretending to be interested in her espresso.

"I don't know," said Hubert. "Maybe an hour. I have to go now. I just want to get this over with."

Lady Bear turned to me. "Well, Eli, what say you? Shall we accompany Mr. Breggleman in his hour of need?"

My face went flush with panic. I didn't want to get involved in these adult games. I had a suspicion of what was going on but wasn't entirely sure. I knew Lady Bear couldn't be trusted and Hubert needed a friend. I thought about my dad growing up in this country and how I wished he had been a remarkable man. Maybe he was. Maybe he had helped a friend once.

"I think we should go with Mr. Breggleman," I said in as clear a voice as I could manage.

"Then it's settled," said Lady Bear, standing up.

We found the car and left the village of Bovarti. We drove around another mountain until Bovarti had completely disappeared from view. Soon after, another town, which looked like a replica of the one we had just left, appeared at the next bend.

Hubert parked a block away from the lawyer's small office building. We got out of the car and looked at the building. Hubert didn't say anything. He gave us each a quick glance and entered the building.

"Well," said Lady Bear. "Let's not pretend we're not interested in what is going on in there."

"You mean, you're not going to look for jewelry?"

"Come with me," said Lady Bear. She marched into the lawyer's building and I followed. Somehow, this seemed less fun than sneaking around.

It was a two-floor building which was once a house. The lawyer's office was upstairs. I heard Hubert finishing his ascent on the wooden stairs. I got to the top much quicker than Lady Bear, given our age difference and her insistence on wearing eight pounds of makeup and two hundred pounds of fur.

There was a waiting area at the top of the stairs outside the lawyer's office. I saw the lawyer's door closing and caught a quick glimpse of Hubert entering and being greeted by the lawyer and Buccenti.

Lady Bear, a bit winded, sat down on the wooden bench in the waiting area. The bench groaned but accepted this intrusion on its privacy. I paced the room, trying to figure out why Buccenti was following us and what he was after. I thought it wise not to share my discovery of Buccenti's presence with Lady Bear.

"Tell me, Eli," said Lady Bear. "Do you know a boy back home named Eddie?"

I stopped pacing. "There are a lot of Eddies in my class. Shapiro, Quinn, Dursing, Locatelli. Why?"

"You joined the choir rather recently, didn't you?"

I nodded.

"You got in so quickly. This Italian tour was like the cherry on top."

I continued pacing. Every time I walked past the lawyer's office, I picked up snatches of conversation. I walked by again and heard the attorney telling Hubert in broken English there would be more boxes later.

"Eli?" said Lady Bear, annoyed.

"Yes?"

"I was saying that I was curious who your cliques were in school. The computer people? Drama club? The burn-heads?"

I thought of her burned wig. "Yeah, the burn-heads, that's me."

Lady Bear inspected herself in her compact and re-applied makeup for the umpteenth time. "He's in there discussing his inheritance, you know. Rather silly, I'd say. His aunt was poor. Most valuable thing she probably left him was that tape recorder."

"I wonder what Little Francis will get," I said. Lady Bear looked up at me, trying to figure me out. "You know, inheriting stuff from his grandfather."

The lawyer's door opened, and Hubert walked out. The door closed behind him, the lawyer and Buccenti choosing to stay within its protected walls. Hubert carried two small cardboard boxes, one under each arm.

"Well, we're all set here," said Hubert. "Here, Eli." He handed me one of the boxes and made his way downstairs. "Let's go."

We rode in that clunky, stuffy car back to Rasper and the choir. Lady Bear sat in the backseat, more annoyed than ever. Hubert had placed his cardboard box in the back seat with her. The other one was at my feet. Hubert didn't say a word. Neither I nor Lady Bear asked him a single question. Through the side-view mirror, I could see Lady Bear secretly slipping her hand into the cardboard box, rummaging through its contents. She looked out the window and made disparaging remarks about the poverty and corruption, but she seemed focused on the box's contents. By the look on her face, I could tell she was not thrilled with what Hubert had inherited from his aunt.

We returned the rental car and took a taxi to the hotel. There were a police car parked outside the hotel with its lights flashing. As we entered the hotel, a policeman walked past us, got in his car, and drove away. In the lobby, all the choirboys were sitting quietly on the floor. Florinda was sitting on an old, upholstered chair, crying. Lady Bear stood up when she saw us. She ran to Hubert and hugged him. Rasper and Little Francis weren't there. Neither was Mrs. Clancy.

"What in heaven's name is going on here?" said Lady Bear in a thunderous voice that echoed across the marble walls.

I went to Charley, but he just shook his head. I sat down next to him. "What's happening?" I said.

Charley looked at me gravely. "Mrs. Clancy died."

CHAPTER TWENTY-NINE

***Soprano**—The highest female voice.*

"You know, Jane," said Anna. "This is where your Nonna Nella was from."

I had such a rich mix of feelings. Here I was, in the town where my biological grandmother had lived. It was hard reconciling my dim memories of my Nonna with this convent and orphanage. The orphanage was far less gloomy than she described. While it looked medieval and was built with rough stones and metal, it seemed well-appointed and freshly painted. The lighting also emphasized the detailed decorative moldings and fixtures.

Anna escorted me down the large hallway.

The nuns certainly had put thought into the overall ambiance of their wards. This made my thoughts and impressions go the other way. If these orphans were here waiting to be adopted, and if the primary role of the nuns was to find good homes for them, it struck me as odd that the orphanage was designed with such residential permanence.

We arrived at a massive wooden door. Anna pushed it open and led me into a large living room where the Bella Donnas greeted us. They were all in their late teens and looked just like my friends back home. They were a little behind the times as far as hairstyles were concerned. Their fashion sense was muted by their white blouses and long, gray skirt uniforms. I could see why Anna loved them and had bonded so strongly with them.

The Bella Donnas surrounded Anna and hugged her the way a returning heroine gets praised.

The orphanage seemed to exist for this group of girls who would never be adopted. They were rough around the edges and had probably something in their history that made them unwantable in the eyes of potential parents. That's why the orphanage, this colossal catholic lost-and-found, was designed the way it was. I was sure each of these girls, pretty in their individual way, had aspirations when they were three or four years old that they would be adopted. But as they hugged Anna, their eyes and the tones of their voices revealed this was their forever home.

It was easy to say why Anna had adored her time here so much. This was her family. The Bella Donnas talked to her in Italian, but I couldn't make out what they were saying since they were speaking so fast. Anna raised her suitcase and they all laughed.

Anna introduced me and they all gave me a curtsy like I was visiting royalty.

"Could you please show Jane where she'll be sleeping tonight?" Anna asked Alexandria, a broad, tall girl with long, brown hair like a horse's tail. "And remember, the nuns aren't expecting her."

Alexandria smirked and led me down the dark hallway to the next room. She kept peeking at me and smiling the way people who don't speak your language do. I turned back to Anna.

"I'll be right back," said Anna, patting her suitcase. She disappeared down the hallway.

I entered the room Alexandria had pointed out. It was small, had one single bed, a narrow window with a tattered curtain that revealed little light, and a spare dresser someone had thought to place in this broom closet. I walked on the bare wooden floor and touched the peeling plaster wall. The room smelled of mothballs.

"Did someone die in here?" I said, placing my purse on the bed.

Alexandria didn't understand English any better than when we were in the hallway and just smiled.

"Die," Alexandria repeated and nodded.

And, with that, she leaned down and picked up my purse. She opened it and stuck her hand all the way in.

"Uh, excuse me," I protested.

"Ah," she exclaimed, pulling out a pack of my cigarettes. She opened the pack, plucked out a Newport, and popped it in her mouth.

"You want a cigarette?" I said sarcastically.

Alexandria put the pack back in my purse without any sign of remorse and placed the purse back on the bed. She turned on her heels and left the room, closing the door behind her, leaving me alone in a Roman orphanage, shy one Newport.

The lonely bed seemed like a prisoner in here. Were they expecting me to take a nap? Anna was supposed to return Saint Teresa to its rightful location, then come back and fetch me in a few minutes so we could get ready for the choir concert and dinner.

I was feeling anxious. I tried to think about the Romatene, but my mind kept coming back to this little room. I went to the window, pulled aside the thin curtain, and peered out at the overgrown garden, still green and lush. There was a large marble fountain statue of cherubs that spit water occasionally. Moss grew on the cherubs and it was apparent no one had cared for the grounds in years. I didn't hear any birds outside. It was suddenly quiet.

I thought about April and wondered what she was doing now. Whatever it was, it had to be more fun than this. At least she had Angelo. At least she wasn't surrounded by mossy cherubs, nuns, and the Italian road company of "Annie."

What was taking Anna so long? I was sure she was doing her stealthy best to circumvent the nuns' security system. Did she say anything about guard dogs here? No, that was crazy. They wouldn't have guard dogs at an orphanage. They weren't keeping the Lindbergh baby here.

Whenever I got out of here and met up with April, I promised myself I would score my Romatene right away so I could focus on just having a good time. There was no way I was going home without seeing local ruins, shopping for Italian leather, and making out with a Roman boy or two. The only thing I had done since I had arrived was continue to travel on trains, cabs, cars, and more trains. What kind of vacation was this?

I continued gazing out the window. And then another thought crossed my mind. What if this was all a set-up? I usually needed to be high to get so paranoid but the ease with which I succumbed to this change in my vacation plans made me worried. Somehow, I ended up in a small room in an Italian orphanage.

Had my parents given me away? Did they discard me? Maybe they didn't have the heart or nerve to send me away to an orphanage so they sent me to Italy so my cousin could do the dirty work. I had been a pain-in-the-ass lately. Maybe my parents saw the writing on the wall and decided to cut their losses. They couldn't look me in the eye and explain their betrayal, so they called Anna. That would explain a lot.

And Anna was in desperate need for validation and connection to America. Maybe she wasn't a model after all. I mean, maybe the whole photo shoot was like the fake moon landing. Were all her friends in on this scam? It could be. I read "The Godfather." No one could be trusted.

Oh no. Maybe my parents decided to do the old switcheroo and trade me in for their beautiful Roman model niece. Maybe Anna agreed to participate in this devious crime in exchange for passage to America, complete with free room and board in my old bedroom.

That was it. My parents were trading up. They had been setting this up for months.

Wait a minute! Maybe Anna wasn't really my cousin at all. Maybe she was just someone looking to take my passport. But why would my parents want to trade me for a perfect stranger? Trapped in this orphanage, I'd never know.

But hold on! April! She was my savior. I instantly felt better when I thought she was on this trip with me. She was my link to the real world. Her presence here in Italy with me completely crumbled all my crazy notions.

Except...

What if April was in on it? No. Never. Not April.

What if her parents sat her down one day and said, "You're on a dangerous road that can't lead to anything good. And it's all because of that Jane. Now, we're giving you a choice. We can send you to reform school or you can help Jane's parents send Jane to an orphanage in Rome where you'll never hear from her again. And you'll then begin to lead a productive, happy life without her evil influence on you. Plus, Anna, who may or may not be

Jane's cousin, would be trading places with Jane. So, you'd have a new friend. Someone who is beautiful and may or may not be a Roman model. Or a nun. Think of the makeup tips alone! Pookie, Anna's like a free lifetime subscription to Vogue!"

Or what if April's parents had also decided to disown April and she was locked in her own orphan room at this very moment? Oh God, how could I have been so stupid?

I hated this room's view. I went to close the curtain. Just then, a deer pranced across the garden. A blazing blue bird landed on a nearby tree branch. It brought me back to reality and I smiled. This was getting ridiculous. I had to stop smoking pot. It was really having a negative effect on me. I breathed in the mothball air and sighed deeply.

I heard a click behind me. I went to the door and tried to open it. It was locked from the outside. I pounded on the door as my head suddenly felt feverish and all my fears resurfaced. I heard faint footsteps walking away. No one came. No sound penetrated my jail cell.

Merda.

CHAPTER THIRTY

Nocturne—*A musical composition that has a romantic or dreamy character with nocturnal associations.*

We rode the rickety train through olive tree valleys to the outskirts of Frascati. Little Francis was in a state of shock. He had lost his parents and just lost his grandparents. He was only nine.

I was in the compartment with him, Florinda, Hubert, Charley, and Big Francis. Little Francis sat on Florinda's lap and whimpered. His body was crumpled as if his bones had melted from all the grief. The air was thick with sadness. We were on the way to an orphanage for a concert and the irony wasn't lost on us.

Eunice Rollins' death, always and forever Mrs. Clancy to us, had been ruled a suicide associated with the grief of the recent death of her husband. She had been found on her hotel bed with an empty bottle of pills and spilled glass of water on the floor. The police investigation lasted a matter of hours. As soon as it was through, Rasper scooped up his choir and chaperones and got out of there. His method of dealing with grief was to push on and continue with life as normal. I think he thought this would all sort itself out, especially after the tour, once we got back to America. I don't think it ever occurred to Rasper to cancel the rest of the tour and just go home.

"Is he staying with us?" whispered Big Francis to me, indicating Little Francis. I was sitting in between him and Charley.

I shrugged my shoulders. "I don't think there's anyone back in New York for him. Besides, we can't exactly mail him home."

"Damn," said Big Francis. "Kid's got nobody." It was the first time I had seen anything resembling empathy on Big Francis' face.

We sat in silence as the train rolled on. Hubert watched the scenery roll by with a blank look on his face. He had packed up the contents of his two cardboard boxes from his aunt. Lady Bear seemed more than a little curious about them. She tried to make it look casual but I noticed. Little Francis continued to whimper, and Florinda patted him on the back, trying anything to soothe him.

Charley elbowed me. "How was the road trip?"

"Weird."

"Any chicks in that town?" Charley asked.

"I didn't really have a chance to explore."

"He can stay with me," said Big Francis. Charley and I turned.

"Are you sure, Francis?" said Florinda. "He's very fragile."

Big Francis stared out the window at the same scenery that was consuming Hubert. "He can stay with me."

This trip was not what I had signed up for. This was feeling more and more like an Agatha Christie mystery. Rasper would have made a spectacular Monsieur Poirot. I excused myself and headed out to find the dining car.

I tried to cheer myself up by reminding myself we were on our way to perform for a reform school for delinquent girls. It was difficult with the gloom that hung in the air. I decided to go for a walk on the train.

"Mr. Mitchell," said Rasper in his booming voice. I had passed his compartment and his door was open. There were some choir boys with him. Terrence sat next to him, looking proud at his place of honor. "Are you alone?"

"Just getting something to eat," I said. The other choir boys smiled, knowing they didn't have the liberty of just getting up to score a bag of potato chips. Rasper demanded attention. He stood and walked out of his compartment. I followed Rasper in between the train cars where he stopped and took a deep breath. The wind was tearing through the small space and it was hard to hear him. His hair never moved an inch.

"Mr. Mitchell, have you called your mother since we arrived?"

"When we first got here. In Milan."

"And since?"

I realized I hadn't in almost two weeks. With everything going on, I had forgotten and that made me feel worse.

"Please call her when we see the next payphone. It would make her feel better to hear from you. You must know that your mother and I, well, we've grown very fond of each other."

"From postcards?"

"From our conversations. Mutuals interests."

"Okay," I said. I didn't know how to respond to this.

"Now hurry back to your seat after the dining car. I don't want anyone else worrying about you."

"Yes sir."

I continued on to the dining car. I opened the heavy metal door to enter it and saw Morgan. It had been days since I had seen him. He was sitting at a table for two, facing me. The gentleman he was dining with had his back to me, but I already knew who it was, even if he wasn't wearing that fedora hat.

Morgan had continued the charade of pretending to be Ponte. He had been showing up and disappearing on this trip for long periods of time. As far as I could see, he was useless as an interpreter. I think even Rasper thought so. Did Rasper know what Morgan's actual intentions were? I was sure it had something to do with Romatene.

As soon as Morgan saw me enter, he signaled to Buccenti, and they stopped talking. Morgan got up, said goodbye to his dining companion, and ambled by me, smiling.

I stood frozen, waiting for Morgan to disappear. I didn't want to go into the dining car with Buccenti sitting there, waiting for me. I turned around and headed back to my compartment.

When I opened the door, I saw Lady Bear in my seat. She had my suitcase on her lap and was in the process of going through my things.

Hubert, Florinda, and Little Francis sat opposite her and just watched her paw my stuff like a rabid raccoon. Charley and Big Francis must have been ordered to leave since there was no sign of them.

"Excuse me?" I said. I reached for my suitcase and closed it, nearly nipping her decrepit fingers.

"That was very rude," said Lady Bear, trying to take control of the situation. "I gave you my comb on our road trip with Mr. Breggleman and you never returned it. I came here to request it back, but you weren't here. I wasn't about to wait for you like a common servant."

I took the suitcase away from her and gave her an accusing look. "I don't have your diseased comb."

I left the compartment with my suitcase and slammed the door behind me. I walked to the end of the car, furious. I think she was looking for her burned wig. I had given it to Charley and asked him to stow it. Charley had three suitcases for this trip and more room in his luggage. I didn't trust Lady Bear and knew she'd come creeping back to get her dead hair. That was a souvenir I would definitely treasure.

We arrived in the town of Frascati. The train station was across the street from the orphanage which told me this was the only show in town. If this had been a thriving metropolis, the train would have been located near the town square or marketplace. Instead, tall solemn wrought-iron gates welcomed us, almost daring us to enter. The orphanage was laid out like a campus with several large, two-story stone buildings squatting like bullfrogs in a swamp, waiting to see which was going to jump first.

We gathered our luggage and exited the train, waiting for it to leave the platform. Once the noise and smoke had cleared, we gathered around Rasper.

"Now remember what you represent and who you are," said Rasper, continuing his traditional pre-concert Tour of Italy speech. "These girls are not used to visits from such distinguished young gentlemen, much less from a foreign country, much less from America."

I had always thought of Rasper as cultured and world-savvy but when he gave these speeches, he seemed arrogant, self-serving, and provincial in a way that much of Europe viewed Americans. I couldn't believe he had the hots for my mom.

We walked double-file, Charley next to me, and entered the orphanage. I was beyond excited by the prospect of meeting these girls. There was something electric in the air that even the gloom of the gothic atmosphere couldn't stifle.

The large wooden entrance door opened and a nun from Central Casting greeted us. She was in the traditional nun costume, or whatever they called them, and had a scowl that rivaled Lady Bear's. The nun bowed her head and turned grandly, indicating with her body language she was to be followed. The only thing missing was her holding a candelabra.

As we walked through the entryway, I noticed there was an elaborate marble mantle prominently displayed. My high school had the same sort of thing by its entrance which was reserved for sportsball trophies. Except this marble mantel was empty. It needed a small statue to be perched on it. Maybe the statue had decided to get up and move away to sunnier pastures.

Nun Frankenstein led us to our rehearsal room where we put down our things in the corner. There was one small bathroom attached and it took a while for all of us to settle in and get changed into our choir uniforms.

Finally, Rasper called us to attention. We stood in a semi-circle around him in the rehearsal room, dressed in our full dinner jackets and bow tie uniforms. I was far less self-conscious about getting dressed in my choral uniform and showing up in public around other kids since we had arrived in Italy.

The room we were in was called the Practice Room rather grandly by Nun Frankenstein because it contained a dingy, broken piano. Hubert took one look at it and quietly chuckled. It was the first time in several days I had heard him make an enjoyable sound.

Florinda skulked about the room, like a bad breeze, trying hard not to touch anything. I never understood why she came along. At the beginning of our trip, I overheard Bart Rollins discussing her and how she seemed to have a strange phobia or condition where she couldn't be alone. She needed someone's company at all times. And so, it fell to Hubert to take her wherever she went. Florinda was so pretty that it seemed like the ultimate irony to me she would ever suffer from loneliness. I could have used Bart Rollins' presence now. In a way, I was glad he hadn't seen his wife dead.

Rasper continued with his instruction before warming us up. He looked at the door behind me for what seemed like the thirty-eighth time for any signs of Ponte/Morgan. No dice. Ponte/Morgan had not reported for duty, and I entertained thoughts he had gone over the wall to relative normality. He must have bailed somewhere between the train station and the orphanage.

Charley, Big Francis, and I agreed to follow Ponte/Morgan the next time he pulled this stunt. It wasn't out of any responsibility towards him or need to protect him from future infractions. We were just so damned curious as to what he was doing when he got to wherever he was going.

It struck me as odd that Ponte/Morgan would be part of this choir, much less join us on this tour. He always kept to himself, was totally anti-social, and was the least curious person I knew. At least until he started taking these unexplained journeys at night. His absences and blatant disregard for Rasper's Rules of Order made him something of an anti-hero to many of us. He just mouthed the words to add bulk to the choir. But secretly, I knew he was with the mob and was following us, knowing we were on Romatene's trail.

Rasper tapped his baton against his portable music stand to gain our attention. He reminded us again we were ambassadors and should act as such in front of the audience. What he meant had nothing to do with our performance. During our concert, we always acted professionally and disciplined and sang like angels. Rasper was referring to afterwards during the reception when we would fraternize and mingle with unescorted, orphaned Italian girls who hadn't seen boys in eight months. At least, that's what I kept thinking about.

As Rasper warmed us up, starting with the sopranos as usual, I was concentrating more on math than music. Only a dozen or so choir boys were old enough to be interested in girls, a few of them were gay, one was AWOL. I liked these odds.

Then I thought of the audience. Seventy-five girls were housed here. Let's say fifty actually attended the concert and thirty of them attended the reception afterward. And twenty of them were old enough to be interested in boys. Twenty to one. Those were odds a Jewish kid from Long Island could live with.

Rasper had been concerned about the acoustics of the performance space. We were scheduled to sing in the orphanage gymnasium. We moved into the performance space for inspection. The nuns had installed some risers so we could be slightly above the audience and our voices would reach the back of the room. The gym was filled with dozens of folding chairs. Hubert worried about the workability of the old organ but felt better after he played around with it for a few minutes. It worked much better than the one in the Practice Room. There were no microphones but when we gave indoor concerts, we didn't need amplification. Our projected voices did everything we needed them to do.

Once the logistics and acoustics had been sorted out, we filed back into the Practice Room and waited. Lady Bear stayed in the gym like a queen awaiting her audience. The rest of us tried to buck up Little Francis. Rasper insisted he continue singing with us; that it would help him. I was pretty sure that particular treatment was not in any psychology book.

A bell rang and told us it was showtime. We entered single-file into the gym: first the sopranos, then altos, tenors, and baritones. The audience applauded as we made our entrance. The room was filled with nuns, dozens of girls ranging from eight to eighteen, and a few civilians. It occurred to me that the girls were of the same age range and number as our choir.

The gym was freezing, and a stiff breeze whistled above the audience applause that I thought, at first, was the organ. Maybe someone had opened a door to let in some fresh air. My plaid bow tie, cummerbund, and crisp white dinner jacket protected me somewhat. I breathed from my diaphragm as I was trained to do. I knew what warriors felt like in battle. I relied on all my past basic training and mock battles so the hill could be conquered.

Rasper raised his hand, and the concert began.

We stood shoulder to shoulder listening to each other with the same intensity as we sang. We watched Rasper with great focus as he waved his arms about in a wild yet calculated way. The choir was not for the weak-hearted.

As the tenors and baritones supported the melody in union with the accompanist, I scanned the crowd for cute girls. It was wonderful looking out and seeing girls my age. Most of the audience on this tour had been a mixture of old people and very old people. The nuns, civilians, and girls all wore earth-tone warm clothing, as if they knew how cold it would be in here. They formed a collective warm, gentle cocoon. It transformed this gym into a stuffed animal collection.

I wanted to melt into them; to disappear into their enveloping embrace. I could live there, enfolded in their insulated pockets and steaming lattes. And as long as I kept singing, they would stay together like this. The concert would never end, and everything would remain perfect.

As I scanned from left to right, I noticed Rasper glaring at me. My face went red with tension as a heat wave rippled across my young forehead toward my skull. His baton seemed to yell at me, "Eli!"

Alright. *Focus, focus, focus.*

My tenor section began in two measures. Hubert looked at us nervously, knowing this was where we sometimes got lost. I took one last look around. Rasper signaled and we began.

Language was an amazing barrier. Since I knew these girls didn't speak English, it somehow relieved an enormous amount of pressure. Knowing it didn't matter what the meaning of the words were, I could concentrate on the music to express myself. The girls loved us. Some screamed like they were watching the Beatles on the Ed Sullivan show.

The reception afterward was in a large hall near the gym. The nuns had set up the room with long tables filled with cookies the girls had baked. Alongside the cookies were large pitchers of some ungodly red punch.

Hubert and Florinda stood in the corner and seemed to be in some type of quiet argument. I couldn't tell what they were saying but I could speculate since Hubert would occasionally point to Big Francis.

I expected Lady Bear to be sitting on a throne while everyone kissed her ring. Instead, she made a beeline for Terrence after the concert and scolded him. There was a lot of noise in the room, and I couldn't hear them either. When I saw Terrence start to cry, I approached them but by then, Lady Bear had moved on.

The girls had not arrived at the reception yet. The nuns wanted to take some time alone to formally welcome the American boys' choir. They cackled with delight as we were forced to mingle with them. I don't think Rasper had informed them that two of our chaperones had recently died. The anticipation of the girls' entrance was unbearable.

Then, Little Francis thought he could pour the red punch from the heavy glass pitcher into the small plastic cup by himself. He was wrong. He promptly spilled red punch all over his white dinner jacket.

Rasper let out a yell that stopped all activities in the room. He composed himself and bowed to the nuns, waving aside any embarrassment. He walked to Little Francis who was already bawling. Rasper spoke to him in an exaggerated whisper and toothy smile so as not to give up his moral position to the hovering nuns.

We were all mingling with the nuns, beaming and nodding pleasantly, putting up with the occasional cheek-pinching and head-patting. It was something we were used to. After a concert, we suddenly became potentially adoptable pets to our audience. The nuns, who spoke little English, were taking the opportunity to cluster three or four of us together so they could get us to perform again.

"Sing," they'd say, the one clear English word they knew. Apparently, they felt entitled to an encore. Depending on the tone of the nun's request and the sense of fun in their eyes, we complied with their wishes. When Rasper wasn't around, we even burst into a four-part harmony version of "On Top of Spaghetti" which seemed to delight the nuns.

In between all this activity, I was really just stalling for time. I kept watching the doors at the opposite end of the room where the girls would be making their entrance. As we expected, they were late. Most likely, they were still primping or simply trying to drag out the anticipation and thus make themselves more desirable.

This tactic was totally working on me.

Sure, they were a captive audience and sure, they were orphans, but how often did I get a chance to meet girls my age who were interested in meeting me?

As I was listening to one of the nuns talk about her ravioli, she stopped in mid-conversation and joined the other nuns. There was some confusion amongst the nuns, and they momentarily bumped into one another or made little circle gestures with their hands. Their resemblance to a beehive was more than just passing.

From what I could gather, they were confused regarding the protocol of the girls' entrance and whether we should be sitting or standing in line to greet them. Either that or the nuns were about to break out into their rendition of "The Hustle" on the dance floor.

Their commotion came to a halt when one of the doors opened and the girls walked into the room in groups of two.

My eyes immediately fell on a girl that was accompanied by a small nun. I couldn't make out her face through the crowd. There was something so familiar about her. She was tall for her age, about my height. I watched as she crossed the room and I recognized her walk, the way her shoulders moved, the sway of her hips. She was graceful and magnetic. My breathing became shallow. It wasn't possible. Then, I glimpsed her striking green-blue eyes, and I knew. It was a miracle. I managed to make out her name tag from across the room. It read "Jane."

CHAPTER THIRTY-ONE

Natural*—A symbol that returns a note to its original pitch after it has been augmented or diminished.*

I sat in my locked room for hours. No one came. No one even walked by my door, from what I could hear. I had pressed my ear against the door and every wall for what seemed like hours. I cried for the first hour before realizing it was doing me no good. The room was damp and I could imagine my bones melting into the floor for the next hundred years and becoming part of this hell.

I had seen happier days.

This was a situation where I had no safety net. My parents weren't on call to pick me up from my friend's house during a sleepover when I had gotten too sick. They weren't upstairs beautifully threatening to come down to the basement where my friends and I were getting high, listening to Elton John's "Crocodile Rock" for the fifteenth time. My friends weren't here in this gloomy castle to bail me out as they had done countless times. No one was here to cover me and my stupid mistakes.

And I missed them all desperately. And then I cried again.

I was pounding the walls when something else occurred to me. Perhaps I had not been the greatest daughter nor the greatest friend. It seemed I always managed to find myself in the center of some drama or emergency I typically had initiated. Some would say I hung around with troublemakers. We weren't stealing or causing anyone harm. But my behavior, which I always had viewed as free-spirited, open-minded, and indulgent, was, in the harsh, lonely light of this room, a bit self-centered. I was always causing worry to those closest to me.

Well, more than worry. It had gotten so bad, my parents, with the collusion of my friends, had arranged the total and utter erasure of me from their lives. I was never to be heard from again.

But I was too young to inspire such passionate abandonment from people, wasn't I? And I was too old to ignore it. Maybe it was time to gradually leave the life of The Wall.

I knew one thing. I wasn't going to stay here, learn to speak Italian, become a professional orphan, eventually cocoon into a nun, and wear those habits and black robes of theirs. I hated hats. And those robes would be so unflattering for my cute figure.

I heard the latch on my door unlock. The door creaked open slowly and for a second nothing else happened, as if an unseen ghost was passing by. A small nun finally poked her head in. The top of her face was hidden by her habit, but I could see she was smiling. She approached me with open arms. The light from the hallway outside, along with the dusty air, clouded my ability to see her face.

She moved toward me quickly as if she was young. I didn't know how to react since I had never been tackled by a nun before. She hugged me deeply. A feeling of complete release suddenly overcame me. My body shuddered and let go buckets of tears and sobs. I was bawling like a baby. She just kept hugging me and rocking me gently.

She whispered softly in my ears some Italian words of consolation. I didn't understand a word but was sure it was some kind of prayer. Though her face was still shrouded by her habit and the room's shadows, I thought she was the prettiest nun I had ever seen.

She continued her Italian chanting as we stood in my cell. My head rested on her shoulder as I held onto her like a life preserver in the middle of the ocean. She was so beautiful. What a pity her beauty was wasted. What a life she could have had.

Suddenly, I realized she wasn't speaking to me in Italian. It was a sort of mock-Italian mixed with complete gibberish and pig Latin. And her perfume smelled familiar. Wait, perfume?

"Are you ready to meet some boys downstairs, you big baby?" she said in a voice all too familiar.

"April!"

I pulled back, wiping my tears away. There stood my best friend in the whole world.

"Why did you lock me in here?" I demanded.

"I had nothing to do with this. Angelo found out from Anna," said April.

"How did you get in here? What's going on?" I said.

April laughed, then saw how scared I was.

"I'm sorry."

"I was petrified," I said but couldn't help laughing a little as well. April looked so strange dressed as a nun.

"What's all this?" I asked.

"Come on," she said, grabbing hold of my elbow. "We don't want to be late."

I gave a quick look around the room, making sure I didn't leave anything behind. I left the room quickly; this room where, just minutes ago, I was contemplating my life as an orphaned nun and had relegated myself to eternal residency.

April closed the door behind me and we crept down the dark hallway, joining the orphan girls. As the crowd of girls enveloped us, April easily slipped out of her nun's outfit and tucked it into her backpack.

"Well, you never know when it'll come in handy again," April said.

Someone else tugged at my other elbow. It was Anna, marching in line with the other girls. She gave me a big "I'm sorry" look.

I was never so happy to see other people.

As we marched with the orphans, Anna explained to me she had been caught by Sister Katarina as she was trying to return the statue of Saint Teresa. Sister Katarina had brought her to Mother Superior's office where Anna had sat for hours.

Mother Superior and the nuns were busy making last-minute preparations for the American boys' choir concert. Anna eventually realized, sitting there at Mother Superior's office, she wasn't a priority.

So, Anna eavesdropped on the nuns' plans for the evening. She learned about schedules, security, and which nun was responsible for which duty. Anna used the time to hatch a plan of her own. It got more complicated when April showed up, but Anna just rolled with it.

"That sinister guy we kept seeing with the fedora hat?" said April to me as we made our way down the hall.

"His name's Buccenti," said Anna.

"Anna overheard that Buccenti was the one who told the nuns to lock you up," said April.

"Why?"

"Because he said you are too much trouble to follow," said Anna.

"Well," I said. "No argument there. But wait, why is he following me?"

"Guess," said April.

I knew it was Romatene. I wished I had never met Eddie back home. We turned the corner.

"I have so many questions," I said.

"First, I stole the nun's habit and robes and gave them to April," said Anna. "I knew that the nuns were angry with me. I mean, getting caught red-handed with their sacred statue. They absolutely had to make an example of me. I overheard them saying they were going to make my life hell. Like they could keep me here against my will. I don't think they realize I'm no longer a child. They were going to keep me in their office tonight while the boys were singing. Now, isn't that just what Jesus would do?"

Anna lowered her voice as we passed a small phalanx of nuns marching down the hallway in the opposite direction.

"After the concert, they're going to notice you've gone," said April.

"I know. And they've arranged to have all the doors locked except where the boys' choir comes in," said Anna. She and April looked at me with concern.

"Have you been crying?" said Anna.

"She was just playing along with the whole nun masquerade," said April, defending my honor.

I was embarrassed. And I suddenly felt young and stupid.

"I thought," I said quietly, making my way down the crowded hallway. "I thought that everyone I knew..."

I couldn't say it.

"What?" said Anna.

"Forget it," said April.

I gave April's hand a squeeze, glad to be among a gaggle of girls marching toward a gaggle of boys.

"Stay close," said April. "We're busting out tonight."

"How?" I asked.

"It's all arranged," said Anna in a giddy, conspiratorial tone. "You have just one job tonight. After the concert, there's a reception. Find a choir boy about your size."

"What?"

"Do it or we may never get out of here," said Anna.

It sounded positively ridiculous, especially with the melodrama with which it was conveyed. What was I doing here? How did I end up in an orphanage with my best friend and a renegade, schizophrenic model, and nunnery refugee? And how were we seriously contemplating bamboozling an innocent choir boy of his uniform in order to escape?

This was more fun than being high while riding the roller coaster.

A double set of doors were opened, and the girls filed into the gym. We took our seats in the back row. The concert had been just what I needed. Half the songs were in English, and it felt so freeing to be in a crowd listening to a wave of male voices delivering sweet sounds to my aching ears in my native language. The jubilation of the songs did to me what only music can do. It helped me right my ship and forced me to take a deep breath of fresh, salty-sweet air.

I had trouble making out the boys' faces. The choir reminded me of the boys April and I had seen on the plane ride here. Everything was fine again. I'd go back to Anna's house with April, pedal my rejuvenated ass back home, and try to restore my once and future glory with or without Romatene.

After the concert, we were asked to stay in the gym for fifteen minutes while the nuns spent some time with the choir. We looked around and every door was locked.

The nuns had given us name tags for the reception which I normally would have resisted even if I were an actual denizen of this place. But April and Anna's rescue of me, our future escape, and the glorious concert had put me in a celebratory mood. I didn't mind the name tags.

We entered the reception hall and I felt like I was attending my prom.

Anna went straight to work, cozying up to a tenor who seemed to be her size. He stood shyly in the corner of the room and looked quite handsome, I must say, in his white dinner jacket, plaid bowtie, and cummerbund. But then, they all looked brutally handsome. It was a sea of tuxedoed testosterone.

Now I needed to find my boy. It was ironic my desire to meet a boy was joined by my need to escape. It was all the same now.

The thought put my mind back on task. I weaved into the clumsily arranged post-concert reception, surrounded by girls and the singing heroes of the evening. The poorly lit room smelled of camphor. A long table at one side of the room was sparsely displayed with sad excuses for snacks. A large bowl held some red punch I didn't even want to contemplate.

A singing boy, much younger than I, distracted me from the giant punch bowl. He was crying like a titty baby, as April was fond of saying, and walking around in circles. He sported a once-crisp, once-white dinner jacket now splotched irreversibly with the crimson punch.

At a closer glance, these boys were very different from one another. I don't know why that surprised me so. Some were clearly intimidated by the nuns while others were scared shitless of us. They tended to cluster in circles, facing towards each other and away from the females of the species.

The choir director and some of the chaperone adults were flattering Mother Superior and the other executive nuns. I imagined it was all part of the standard service.

I scanned the room, looking for a boy about my size. The problem was, of course, that I was a tall, curvy girl with breasts and certainly not a straight-arrow boy. Anna seemed to be flirting quite effectively with her catch and she played the part of an adoring fan with great enthusiasm.

I decided not to pursue my deception with an empty stomach. I made my way through small clusters of boys, girls, and nuns, and finally approached the snack table. I was surveying the snacks, determining which one of the cheeses was going to give me the least chance of an emergency room visit, when I felt a slight tap on my shoulder.

One of the boys was standing behind me. I decided to play hard to get. I kept my back to him. Maybe acting aloof is what women did.

"Is it true most of you don't understand English all that well?" he said. His voice was familiar. He sounded like he was from Long Island.

"Hmmm?" I responded in my most orphan tone.

"Because as soon as I saw you, I thought you were the most beautiful girl in the room."

He said this with utter conviction, completely trusting I didn't understand a word of what he was saying. I was deeply flattered.

"Did I say the room?" he continued. "I meant in the whole world."

Turning around, I saw a handsome boy who was my height and possessed a smiling, open, sweet face.

"Eli!" I said. The nuns shushed me. "What are doing here?"

The nuns walked over, wagging their fingers. I didn't want them to take me away. I tried to play it cool. I decided to be a non-English-speaking Roman orphan girl for a bit longer.

"*Americano?*" I said innocently.

"New York. You know New York?" he said, playing along.

"New York," I said as if I was tasting a new snack for the first time. This was fun. He was cute and had the dreamiest eyes. My heart was beating so fast. He pointed to me.

"And you?" he said. "Where are you from?" He used ridiculously exaggerated arm movements the way every foreign tourist spoke to a native. Well, mock native.

I just grinned, knowing it would suffice as an answer. He looked down at my name tag.

"Jane," he said. "You remind me very much of a girl back home." He smiled slyly. I loved this game.

"I'm sure I'm prettier," I said and giggled.

"Jane, I can't believe it's you," he said.

"I can't believe it's you," I said. I blushed and hoped he wouldn't notice. I looked away toward the snack table.

"I've been in Italy with the choir for two weeks now," he said. "Seen every statue, painting, and ruin there is. A good vacuuming is all this country really needs."

I giggled some more.

"Have you orphans eaten already?" he said and made me feel tingly.

We walked together toward the giant red punch bowl. The din of the room seemed like mild white noise in the background of our conversation. As he poured me a glass of punch, he casually said, "*Mia d'alina, culpa Kyrie. Por ono viva tutti levezzose.*"

He waited for my response with his sweet smile.

I took a deep breath and said quietly and as penitently as I could, "Eli, I don't speak any Italian." I looked away, not able to bear this excitement.

He stopped pouring, put down the glass, and continued smiling.

"Neither do I," he said.

I felt a wave of heat over my face and scalp.

"By the way," he said after taking a deep breath and a slug of punch for courage, "I meant what I said."

"About the Kyrie?" I said.

"Exactly. Kyrie."

My God. In that dinner jacket, he looked like James Fucking Bond.

"I don't live here," I suddenly blurted out. "Obviously. Just visiting. Do you know the Wall back home?"

"I've heard of it. In the town next door to me."

"Got kicked out. This is my penance."

"I'm Jewish," he said, "so we don't really have penance. We just feel guilt all the time. Where are you staying?"

"Why?"

"Because," he said, suddenly serious. "I want to see you again. Here in Italy, I mean."

"You mean, without the nuns?"

"I'm only here for one more week," he said. "Then, it's back to America."

"And back to being our boring selves," I said. "I didn't mean you."

"I know." Now he was the shy one. "You're not like any other girl I ever met."

My breath stopped and he shuddered a bit too.

"Is this really happening?" I said. I couldn't believe it. "We go to different schools," I said. "Different towns. We're here now. What are the chances?"

"It's all about now," he said. "Plus, I hear they have a Wall here that's much bigger than the one back home but not nearly as cool."

"Eli, I..."

Anna grabbed my shoulder and pulled me away. "Let's go, we don't need to leave with the boys. I found a basement door open," said Anna, slightly out of breath.

I slipped out of Anna's grasp. "Wait, wait," I said as I ran back. Eli was there, waiting for me.

"Wait! Where are you going?" he said.

"Busting out, Eli."

Anna was frantically waving me over to the exit from across the room.

"Eli, about the Kyrie thing," I said. "Same to you."

CHAPTER THIRTY-TWO

***Requiem**—A dirge, hymn, or musical service for the repose of the dead.*

And just as soon as she appeared in my life, Jane was gone. My hands were shaking and my heart was pounding from the encounter. We returned to our hotel outside Frascati late at night. Most of the choir and adults were exhausted. I was exhilarated.

I was sharing a hotel room with Charley, Terrence, and Big Francis. Charley was in the bed closest to mine so we could talk without waking up the others. I found myself stuttering, trying to explain the evening. All I managed to do was give him a stupid grin.

"What the hell is with you?" he finally said.

"Jane," I whispered.

"Who's Jane?"

"The girl I met tonight. I can't believe it."

"From the orphanage?" asked Charley. "What are you going to do? Have your parents adopt her so you can date your sister?"

I could always count on Charley to smear some reality into every situation.

"She's from Long Island," I said.

"Shut the fuck up," said Big Francis. "I want to dream about those Bella Donnas." He had been smitten hard by the gang of orphan girls. "Now go to sleep."

I had to figure out a way to see Jane again while we were in Italy. Who knew how long she'd be here?

If we ended up meeting on Long Island, everything would be different. Here, I was mysterious and could be anyone. Back home, she'd know I wasn't worthy. There was a good chance I would end up in New Jersey for my mom's new job. It occurred to me I had no idea what Jane's last name was. Good luck finding her with just a first name. Or where Jane lived on Long Island. I knew she lived near the Wall but that still left several hundred houses. Eddie might know her, but his memory was spotty at best. And I was not about to rely on Eddie's stoner memory for this. It was obvious to me I had an infinitely better chance of finding her in Italy. How hard could it be?

The next morning, I came down for our continental breakfast. I noticed Morgan sitting in the corner by himself. I asked one of the sopranos to move so I could sit near Morgan. Rasper got up to get some coffee, saw Morgan, and sat down next to him. There was a lot of noise in the room, but I overheard most of what they were saying.

Morgan spoke to Rasper in a business-like and methodical manner. He sounded very professional. He told Rasper the police had stopped by while we were giving our concert last night. Following an autopsy requested by Rasper, Mrs. Clancy's death was ruled a murder. An investigation was still on going. The police wanted to talk to some of the choir boys and chaperones. They'd be back tomorrow for more questioning.

Rasper nodded and his eyes quickly darted around the room before resting again on the reality spilling from Morgan's mouth. Rasper looked infuriated and a bit exhausted.

Their conversation hit me like a shock wave. I was trying to make sense of it, hoping I heard it wrong.

"Jesus, Eli, what's going on?" Charley asked, sitting down next to me.

Rasper nodded to Morgan, muttered something to him, and stood up. He marched toward us with purpose.

"Mr. Rasper," I said. "Are you okay?"

"Fine, Mr. Mitchell," he said. "Just tired." He was trying to put on a brave face, but I had seen too much of him lately to know when he was lying. "Have you called your mother yet?"

"Working on it," I said. "Our trip's not going to get cut short, is it? I mean, with Mr. and Mrs. Rollins..."

"We're expected at the Vatican," said Rasper. "By no less than the Pope. And half the world's Cardinals. The tour goes on."

I needed to find a pay phone so I could call my mom. I wasn't sure what I would tell her. I also didn't know if I should ask about her and Rasper.

"I was going to request if you could keep an eye on young Francis," said Rasper. "He's falling apart, you know. We just have to make it one more week."

"No problem," said Charley.

"Oh, Charles," said Rasper, "I wasn't implying you should babysit. You and your family have done enough already."

"We haven't done that much. Besides, the little guy needs us."

"Bless you and your family," said Rasper.

Despite singing in churches and other places of worship back home, my understanding was that Rasper was not a religious man. But this trip had opened his eyes to the fact he wasn't completely in charge of things.

Rasper moved on, approaching another group of boys finishing their breakfast.

I thought about what I had seen and heard and realized Mrs. Clancy's death only made sense as a murder. I didn't know what to do about it. The police were coming tomorrow so I had until then to figure it out. In the meantime, I had to lay low.

Little Francis had been taken to the local church by Hubert and Florinda. Charley and I decided to go see how he was doing. We walked the three blocks and entered the church. Little Francis sat between Hubert and Florinda in the front pew.

Charley and I took a seat near the back.

"I'm worried about him," I said.

"I know," said Charley. "He always seemed too young and fragile to handle anything. Now this."

"Think he blames himself?" I asked. "I figured I would if I was in his shoes."

"Why don't you two fags keep it down. Always yapping." We turned around and discovered Big Francis in the back pew on the other side of the aisle.

"What are you doing here?" I asked.

Charley elbowed me, knowing I shouldn't engage with Big Francis.

"Those chicks we saw last night," said Big Francis. "The orphan girls in that gang. The Bella Donnas. They were about my age, right?"

"I guess," I said. I had no idea where he was going.

"Betcha one of them would want to be with me," he said. He sounded like someone who had just been dumped. I turned to Florinda and realized he had been. Whatever trouble had brewed in their marriage, Hubert and Florinda had been brought together by this horrible tour.

"Come on," said Charley. "Let's get out of here."

"What about Little Francis?" I said.

"He's taken care of," said Big Francis.

The three of us headed back to the hotel. Lady Bear was nowhere to be found. Neither was Morgan. The choir boys were milling about the lobby. We all wanted to call our parents. And our grandparents.

Outside the hotel was a bank of pay phones. I cashed in some money for change and called my mom.

"Is everything alright?" my mom asked. She sounded distant and worried.

I didn't want to tell her two of our chaperones had died on this trip or that one of them was suspected of being murdered. Maybe I was going out on a limb here, but I thought that might trouble her.

"We're doing great. Did you see us on the news before we left?"

"I'm so proud of you," she said. "Did you get my telegrams?"

"What telegrams? Oh, we're singing for the Pope in a few days. In the Vatican."

"The Pope? Which Pope?" she said.

"The Pope Pope. What do you mean, which Pope?"

"They can't have you singing in a nice temple? They have to bring you to the Vatican? I don't like it," she said. "Soon, you'll be Catholic."

"Mom."

"Alright, alright. I just miss you. You know Douglas, I mean Mr. Rasper, he sent me some postcards. I sent him some telegrams too."

I suppose I was glad she brought it up so I didn't have to. I decided to play it dumb. "Really? What does he have to say for himself?"

"Oh, Eli, I'm very flattered but I don't know. What do you think of him?"

"Me? Um, I guess he's okay."

"You know my luck with men…"

"Guess where I'm going today?" I said.

"How can I guess?"

"Tufetto," I said.

There was silence on the phone. At first, I thought we had been disconnected.

"Tufetto?" she finally said. "You know that's…"

"Where you and dad met. I know."

"It's where your father lived when he was a teenager too. He was probably your age when he lived there," she said.

"I'm going there this afternoon," I said.

"I love you," she said. I never found it hard to hang up on my mom when I was at a friend's house or needed a ride from the mall. But this was difficult. I'd see her again in a week but saying goodbye on that call was tough and it surprised me.

I told Charley to cover for me and that I'd be back by dinner. We originally had a concert that afternoon, but Mrs. Clancy's death caused everything to be canceled for the day.

I hiked to a gravel, circular driveway a few blocks from the hotel where the local bus was waiting. I boarded the bus and took a seat. Looking out the window as the bus left, I saw two girls running across a field. I imagined they were Bella Donnas escaping from the orphanage. One of them reminded me of Jane.

I got off the bus forty-five minutes later in Tufetto. It was a small town with a beautiful fountain in the square. My father had rarely spoken of his upbringing here. My mom didn't speak of it either. She had been a tourist that had gotten lost when she came to this town and met my dad.

I strolled the streets and tried to find someone who might have known my dad. I saw a cop and asked him if he had ever heard of my dad, but the cop just shrugged. Maybe it was my mangled Italian. Then, I decided to go into a local bar.

I straightened up and tried to walk more grown up, less hurried. I was a good actor in our drama club so I figured I could pass as an adult for a few minutes. I approached the bar and asked for a beer in a baritone's voice. To my amazement, the bartender gave me a beer. I paid for it and sat at the bar.

The bartender was an older gentleman with leathery skin and polished, blond hair. He seemed like he would be around my dad's age. I reached into my wallet and pulled out a photo of him. I waited until the bartender wasn't busy and showed it to him.

He nodded. He actually recognized my dad. He called over two older guys and they stared at the photo as well. They spoke in Italian, but I couldn't understand a word. I indicated they were talking too fast, and they stopped.

The bartender spoke in a gravelly voice. "Of course, we remember Giovanni. Luckiest man we ever knew."

The other men laughed and brought their hands down in a serpentine fashion, indicating a curvy, beautiful woman.

"Lucky?" I said.

"He was, how you say ... nobody. Nothing, eh?"

The other men nodded in agreement.

"Like us. He was *niente*. And then this *bellisima* Americana comes to town. So smart. So beautiful. She captivated our entire village."

The men laughed in an approving way.

"And who does she fall in love with?" said the bartender. "This vision, this Goddess? Not me. Not Antonio here who was studying law. No, she falls in love with skinny Giovanni."

He poured me another beer.

"The women in this village are known for their beauty. But, compared to your mother, they are all dogs."

One of the men fell down on the floor laughing, barking in-between convulsions.

"And she was a singer. Such a voice. The second night she was here, the power went out, and she stood in the square and sang an aria. It brought tears to our eyes."

Was this the same woman I knew?

"So," said the bartender. "You're Giovanni's boy. How is your mother? Please tell her Segundo says hello." The other men fell apart with laughter.

I thanked them for their time, took back my dad's photo, and ran back to the bus. I couldn't believe what I had heard. What had my mom seen in my dad? Why had she picked him? This whole time, I thought it was my dad who was bound for greatness and had somehow taken pity on my poor mom. I had never thought of her as beautiful and desired. I certainly never pictured her with the world at her feet. She always seemed so sad; not the one who was special. Not the outstanding one. This was all confusing.

Later that night at the hotel, we were sitting in the lobby playing cards. Even Ponte was there. Hubert, Florinda, and Lady Bear were on "counseling detail" per instructions from Rasper. That meant they stayed with us in case we needed an adult to talk to. Rasper was in his room trying to arrange the next gig and wondering when we were getting paid for the last three. I guessed he was also worried about the police interviews the next morning.

We were all fine. Just confused, homesick, and bored. And one of us was confused about his parents. And deeply in love with a girl named Jane. I suddenly understood that "Maria" moment in West Side Story.

Hubert and Florinda walked around the room, checking each boy to make sure we were okay. I noticed Florinda stayed clear of Big Francis.

Big Francis and Charley were playing Crazy Eights and occasionally laughing out loud. Lady Bear strutted up to them and demanded silence. When she turned her back to them, they gave her the finger.

Ordinarily, I would have smiled at the sight. But I felt curious about Lady Bear. She had wanted to be Rasper's benefactor and Matron of the Arts. Instead, she was Haus Frau to seventeen unruly boys.

She sat down next to me. Her eyes scanned the room, and I noticed a faint light of pride and sadness dance across her face. She looked down at me and patted my knee.

"Lady B ... I mean, Mrs. Querrel?"

"Yes?"

"Can I ask you something?" I said, not sure if she was in a conversant mood.

"Please, dear boy. Anything to get my mind off the day's tragedy," she said grandly.

She tried to make it seem like she had been personally affected by the death of Little Francis's grandparents. I saw it as bad acting. When Bart Rollins died, she did seem genuinely surprised. But the news of Mrs. Clancy's death seemed to only cause her irritation. And now she seemed nervous. I know what I overheard her and Mrs. Clancy discussing back in Hicksville and on this trip. Would she be taken away to prison? The silly thought put an inappropriate grin on my face.

"Tell me, Eli, what it is that has you smiling. I could use a laugh," said Lady Bear.

"Nothing," I said, embarrassed.

She looked at me for a moment.

"You know, Eli, I've been watching you. In many ways, you're not like the other boys. You have a quality."

I leaned in toward her conspiratorially.

"Two words," I whispered. "Straight and Jewish."

She belted out a throaty laugh. Everyone turned around to investigate the source of the laughter. Seeing Lady Bear laugh gave everyone permission to ease up and laugh as well.

"You're very quick, aren't you? Very entertaining," she said.

I didn't know how to respond.

"But that's not what I'm talking about," she continued. "I'm talking about a certain empathy beyond your years. A maturity. You're not as self-serving as the other boys."

"Oh, I don't know, Mrs. Querrel..."

"Call me Lady Bear. I know you all do behind my back. I sort of like it."

"Okay. Lady Bear. I can be as selfish as the next tenor," I said, unexpectedly candid.

"Really," she said, intrigued. "Do tell."

"I met this girl today and that's all I can really think about it. I know it's wrong in the middle of all this."

She let out that throaty laugh again which told me she had once been an intense smoker.

"There was a question you wanted to ask me," she said. "You see, I haven't forgotten."

"I just wanted to know what you thought of all this," I said.

"Ah. Well, I feel bad that you boys will have this memory mixed with this wonderful trip. This is a once-in-a-lifetime moment, you know. I hope you realize that. All those other boys in New York are going to camp or playing basketball on their driveways this summer. You're on your way to Rome. To sing for the Pope!

"Douglas, I mean, Mr. Rasper, will get through this. On the other hand, Mr. Breggleman may not. He took this very personally."

"Really," I said.

I looked across the room at Hubert. He was showing some of the younger boys a magic trick. The change in his demeanor in the past few days was astonishing. A great calm had overtaken him. There was an ease in his manner now, as if the storm had gathered and moved on, leaving behind calm waters.

"Still interested in what's in those boxes?" I asked.

"I don't know what you mean," she said. "Why? Did you find out?"

"Mr. Breggleman showed me," I said. It was a bald-faced lie. But I pulled it off.

Lady Bear's eyes widened. Her false, grieving face gave way to her actual greedy one.

"What did he tell you? Did he mention a key?"

"What were you talking about with Terrence the other day?" I asked.

"Terrence?"

I pointed him out. He was sitting with the other altos on the floor, playing gin rummy.

"Oh," she said. "That one. You know, I don't trust him. I personally saw him trying to steal my purse the other day. And I was scolding him."

Terrence was one of the most honest and nicest kids on this trip. He had a rough time on this trip at first but once everyone got to know him, he became one of the most popular kids. There was no way he would steal from this lunatic lady. Lady Bear was lying.

I excused myself and sat down with Terrence and muscled my way into the high stakes gin rummy game going on. I avoided Lady Bear for the rest of the evening. It had been a long day.

The next morning, the police were waiting for us in the lobby. There were two local cops and one from Rome. They asked us all to sit quietly in the lobby while they spoke briefly to each of us alone in the hotel office located next to the lobby. We were told by Rasper to cooperate. He looked anxious like he hadn't slept all night. I didn't blame him.

I sat next to Charley and asked him how this was all going. He shrugged. Big Francis looked irritated, like he had been to a million of these interrogations. Lady Bear, Hubert, and Florinda sat in the corner, drinking coffee, and avoiding eye contact with us.

"Who are they talking to now?" I asked Charley.

"Terrence. They asked for him by name first."

I glared at Lady Bear. "Charley, remember the day I went on the field trip with Mr. Breggleman and Lady Bear?"

"Yeah. You asked me to take a bunch of pictures."

"Is the roll of film still in your camera?"

Charley nodded.

"Go get your camera."

Charley got up and asked for permission to go to his room. Rasper and the policeman nodded. As Charley ran upstairs, I approached Rasper.

"Mr. Rasper, you know that Terrence or any of the boys had nothing to do with this, don't you?"

"Of course not, Eli," he said. There was a sadness in his voice.

"So, what's going on?" I said. The policeman came over to ask what we were discussing and I asked him the same thing. He spoke in Italian so I put my hand up to stop him and gave him the international sign for "I have no idea what you're saying."

I looked around and saw Morgan sitting on the floor next to Big Francis. I waved him over.

"Morgan," I said. "You wouldn't be here if you couldn't actually interpret Italian, right?"

He looked flustered.

"Why did you call him Morgan?" said Rasper.

"A nickname," I said. "Well," I said, turning to Morgan. "Can you actually speak Italian?"

"Careful, Eli," said Morgan.

"Mr. Ponte, I've been disappointed in your performance this entire trip," said Rasper. "Now it seems Mr. Mitchell is asking you a reasonable question given your role with this group."

Morgan took a deep breath. "What do you need?"

"Please translate what the officer is saying."

Morgan spoke to the officer briefly in Italian and the officer started his story over. Morgan interpreted. "He says Mr. Rasper requested an autopsy because he was suspicious. And he was right."

Rasper nodded his head and glanced at the hotel office door where they were still talking to Terrence.

"The autopsy showed there was poison in Mrs. Rollins' system," said Morgan, continuing to interpret. "But that in itself is not enough proof of murder. The poison is hard to detect, and the lab results can be brought into question by the courts."

"How did you know?" I asked Rasper.

"I didn't. I was just suspicious that Mrs. Querrel was so adamant that Terrence was guilty of poisoning Mrs. Rollins. I couldn't abide it."

"What's all this now?" asked Lady Bear, storming into the conversation. "I heard my name. Is this charade almost over?"

Charley came downstairs with his green duffle bag. "My camera," he said.

"Are we taking photographs to memorialize this horrible morning?" said Lady Bear.

Morgan nodded at the cop. "So, our suspicions of foul play were circumstantial," said Morgan.

"I tell you it was that colored boy who had a hand in poor Eunice's death," said Lady Bear.

"That's enough, Dolores," yelled Rasper. It was the first time I had ever heard him raise his voice to her. The room went still.

The hotel office door opened, and Terrence emerged with the other cop. Terrence had been crying and looked terrified. The cop held onto Terrence's shoulder and said something to the other cop near us. Morgan interpreted. "He says Terrence was with the other choir boys when Mrs. Rollins passed away, but he could be lying."

"He is lying," said Lady Bear. "They all lie."

"Enough," said Rasper to her. "Terrence was with us that day."

Charley reached into his duffle bag and produced his Kodak 110 camera. "He was," said Charley. "I took pictures of us and everything." He handed the camera to the cop. "I want my camera and pictures back when you're done, please."

"Children's photographs," said Lady Bear. "Honestly."

"And I asked Charley to make sure to have the daily newspaper in the photo, so we had a record of the day it was taken," I said.

"Why would you do that?" said Morgan.

"You know why," I said.

Morgan nodded. The cop near us spoke and Morgan interpreted. "Our autopsy found something else too. It was why we sought you all out."

"What did they find?" Rasper asked.

"A fragment of burnt polyester fiber in the deceased's stomach."

"Holy shit," I said a bit too loudly.

"Mr. Mitchell," yelled Rasper.

I reached into Charley's green duffle bag and took out Lady Bear's singed wig. I handed it to the cop. "Morgan, tell the officer he'll find the autopsy fibers match the ones on this wig."

"I've never seen that before," said Lady Bear, though no one had asked her anything.

"And if you're wondering whose this is, there's the monogram inside," I said. "DQ. And that ain't the Dairy Queen."

Morgan didn't wait to translate. He grabbed Lady Bear by the arms. She struggled a little, but the cops came over and surrounded her.

"You little sons of bitches," screamed Lady Bear. "Burn in hell! All of you!"

Morgan spoke to the cops. They took off her fur so they could place her hands behind her back. They handcuffed her and led her toward the exit. She screamed the whole way. We were stunned. Just as Lady Bear and the police were about to leave the hotel, I grabbed her fur and chased them down.

"I hear it's cold in prison," I said and threw the coat at her.

Morgan and the cops continued their march outside and stuffed Lady Bear into their police car. Morgan got in with them. They drove away and the hotel lobby was silent again.

"Jesus," I said.

For once, Rasper didn't castigate me.

"Well," said Hubert, breaking the silence. "I think it's time for breakfast." Florinda laughed a little which was odd considering she had just witnessed her aunt being led away in handcuffs for murder. Little Francis, who had been sitting on Florinda's lap, stood up and ran to the dining room. Apparently, this sort of thing made him hungry.

Rasper walked over to Terrence and hugged him. I didn't know Rasper was capable of hugging, but it seemed right. Then he approached me. "Thank you, Mr. Mitchell. Your mother would be very proud of you today."

And it just meant the world to me when he said that.

We were in the middle of breakfast. It was luxurious to be eating with no rush. Rasper had again canceled any plans for the day given the circumstances. Also, he needed to reconfigure our concert schedule and free time since we were down to two chaperones and him. But at least none of them were murderers.

"Excuse me," said a deep voice from the hotel lobby. It didn't surprise me at all.

Buccenti, in his trademark fedora hat, walked into the dining room. Charley put down his toast with Nutella. "Oh no," said Charley. "What's this guy want?"

Buccenti walked over to Rasper and whispered in his ear. Then, he left the dining room into the lobby. Rasper took a napkin to his mouth and dabbed it. He got up and asked Hubert, Florinda, and me to follow him.

"Don't go," said Terrence.

"I'll be fine," I said, though I was feeling nervous.

Buccenti sat in one of the upholstered chairs in the lobby, his legs crossed. We all sat across from him. He took out a cigarette and lit it. "My name is Armand Buccenti. I am with the Italian government. Now, let's play a little game. You will tell me what you know, and I will tell you what I know. And we will see where everything intersects, yes?"

"What we know about what, Mr. Buccenti?" said Rasper.

"Let's start with Mrs. Querrel," said Buccenti.

"They arrested her this morning," said Florinda.

"I am aware," said Buccenti.

"Mr. Buccenti, I am responsible for a room full of children in there," said Rasper, indicating the dining room. "Can we make this quick?"

"Certainly," said Buccenti, and let out a long puff of smoke. "I can appreciate your responsibilities."

"Also, is it completely necessary to have Mr. Mitchell here present with us? This seems like a conversation for adults," said Rasper.

"He needs to be here," said Buccenti. He turned to me. "I want to thank you, young man, for making this investigation easier. You're very resourceful."

"I am?" I said.

"Let us start the game of what we know," said Buccenti.

"I'm not sure what you mean, still," said Rasper.

Buccenti stood up and paced around us. "Let's start with the late Bart Rollins then, shall we? Did you know that, in his youth, he spent some time here in Italy?"

"He mentioned it to me once," I said.

"He was a known drug dealer here," said Buccenti. "That's how he made his money." Buccenti turned to Rasper. "Perhaps you should screen your chaperones better in the future."

Rasper scowled at him.

"Anyway, as is often the case with these things, he lost it all," said Buccenti. "So, he went to America and married Eunice Clancy."

"I don't understand what this has to do with my aunt?" said Florinda.

"Or my aunt," said Hubert.

"I'll get to that," said Buccenti. "Not long ago, Bart Rollins found out he had cancer and was dying."

"I could tell," I said.

"And his wife and Mrs. Querrel knew it too," said Buccenti. "Mr. Breggleman, when you received the letter that your aunt had passed away, you naturally told your wife, right?"

"Why, yes."

"And, Mrs. Breggleman, you, in turn, told your aunt, yes?"

"Of course," said Florinda.

"Well, Mrs. Querrel told her very good friend, Mrs. Rollins. And, you see, that's when the trouble all started. Bart Rollins and Hubert's aunt had been, how shall I put it, romantically involved. Once Bart Rollins found out that Mr. Breggleman's aunt had passed, he decided it was okay to tell his wife and Mrs. Querrel about the Romatene books and key."

"The what?" said Rasper.

"You've heard of Romatene?" said Buccenti.

"Of course," said Rasper.

"Well," said Buccenti. "Bart Rollins knew that certain books had been published that contained the code for the formula to Romatene. One simply had to obtain these certain books, decode with the key, and the world was theirs."

"Romatene," said Rasper. "That's just a rumor."

"To you, perhaps," said Buccenti. "But sometimes ghost stories are real. Anyhow, it wasn't just a ghost story to Mrs. Querrel and Mrs. Rollins. Once Bart told them about the books and the key, that's when Mrs. Querrel and Mrs. Rollins purchased all these specific novels they could get their hands on."

"So, if they have all these books and know how to make this drug, why come to Italy?" said Hubert.

"Because even if you collected all the books and discovered the codes, you still needed a key to make sense of it all."

"Like a decoder ring," I said.

"Exactly," said Buccenti. "So, they hatched a plan to go to Italy."

"I thought I suggested Italy," said Hubert.

"Remember, darling," said Florinda. "Dolores strongly recommended you go and tie up any loose ends with your inheritance."

"Mrs. Querrel needed to have Mr. Breggleman visit his aunt's house and attorney here in Italy," said Buccenti. "That's why I'm sure she was very insistent on your trip."

"But why?" said Rasper. "What was waiting for Hubert here?"

"Mr. Breggleman's aunt was to have left him the Romatene formula key."

"This doesn't make any sense. Why did Dolores and Eunice need this so badly?" said Hubert.

"Because they were both dead broke, despite outward appearances," said Buccenti. "Have been for over a year."

"They were my patrons," said Rasper. "For the choir."

"My apologies," said Buccenti.

"And Mr. Rollins?" I said.

"Died of natural causes," said Buccenti. "Maybe not so innocently. After all, his wife and Mrs. Querrel needed him out of the way. He didn't want them getting involved in Romatene. He knew what it could do to your life. He'd seen it firsthand. Who knows? Maybe they denied him his medications to speed it along. We'll never know."

"I need coffee," said Rasper.

"Please," said Buccenti. Rasper got up and poured himself a cup, then sat down. Buccenti put out his cigarette.

"So, Mrs. Querrel and Mrs. Rollins needed to come to Italy," said Buccenti. "They bring Bart along. But they need a cover. The Rollins' grandson is in a choir. Querrel's niece's husband plays piano in the choir. They will chaperone this choir on an Italian tour. And Mr. Breggleman will collect his inheritance."

"I swear I never even heard of this Romatene," said Hubert.

"I know you didn't," said Buccenti. "That's why Mrs. Querrel and Mrs. Rollins thought they could take the Romatene formula key off your hands so easily. Because you wouldn't even know it was there or what its value was."

"What is its value?" said Rasper.

"Millions," said Buccenti. "Mrs. Querrel and Mrs. Rollins would split the profits and maybe give a little back to Hubert and Florinda here."

"I don't believe this," said Hubert.

"I'm glad I kept that wig," I said.

"Us too," said Buccenti. "That road trip you went on with Mr. Breggleman and Mrs. Querrel. She went along so the two of you could be her alibi for when she poisoned Mrs. Rollins. I suppose she wanted it all for herself in the end. Some friend."

"I don't believe this," said Hubert. Florinda held his hand.

"Oh, and Mr. Mitchell, I almost forgot," said Buccenti. He handed me a stack of telegrams. "They've been following you throughout your trip, but you always seemed a day ahead of them," said Buccenti.

I stepped away from everyone, holding the short stack of thin telegrams. I walked to my room and plopped on my bed. The telegrams were all from my mother. I read them chronologically. There were the usual requests for how I was doing and updates on my mom's daily life. Then my mom mentioned she and Rasper had gone on three dates while I was at Charley's over the summer. I couldn't believe it. She said she was considering dating him when we got back. It was so disorienting. The last telegram was the bombshell. It said she might have to take that job in New Jersey. My heart sank. I couldn't move now. Jane would no longer be the girl next door. My senior year would be ruined. This was so unfair. Rahway might as well be Kansas.

I had to find Jane now more than ever. I thought of the murder investigation, my mom relocating our lives, and Rasper's plight. I tried to wrap my mind around everything happening. It was no good. I kept going back to Jane.

CHAPTER THIRTY-THREE

***Neoclassical**—Movement in music where the characteristics are crisp and direct.*

April and I got ridiculously drunk, just like old times, on Anna's porch. The moon was bright, and the fireflies were out dancing across the hillside, making it look like an upside-down sky. April got smashed, as always, on three serious swigs of limoncello. April and I sat on the bench while Anna sat on her steps. Even though we had experienced it just hours before, we kept asking Anna to re-tell the story of our orphanage capture, entertainment, and escape. We were riveted to this story of ours. It was quickly becoming our legend.

There were some elements in Anna's re-telling of our story that remained shrouded. For example, I didn't understand why she was still so interested in hanging around with the Bella Donnas.

As Anna went on, I quietly smiled, taking alternative sips of wine and drags from my cigarette. I thought of Eli. The idea that I had so randomly met my soul mate—that he was here, totally cute, lived in the town next to mine, sang, and was my age—astonished me. But how to see him again? I couldn't wait until we got home. That seemed like forever.

The air on the porch smelled sweetly of wood and roasted meat. The stars were bright in the night sky and there didn't seem to be another soul for miles. I decided to enjoy the moment, knowing tomorrow was the day for planning the remaining week of my trip.

The bed in Anna's guest room was like coming home. I slept deeply and dreamed of Eli. I awoke the next morning totally refreshed from my temporary stint as an orphan and Bella Donna. My triumphant-return-home hangover, however, was still with me. The shower was hot, forceful, and liberating.

I came down for breakfast a new girl. I felt alive, in love, and full of hope and adventure. Angelo had arrived earlier and fully stocked the kitchen. We had fresh juice, toast, eggs, cheeses, and pancetta. April must have found another place to sleep since she wasn't on the floor when I awoke. She came downstairs and was showing signs of wear and tear from whatever her sleeping arrangements were. She was hungover but still managed to giggle her way through breakfast.

I couldn't take it anymore.

"April, you look like the Cheshire Cat. What is going on with you?" I said.

This inquiry just advanced her giggling into full tee-hees.

"What do you think? She slept with Angelo," said Anna, walking into the kitchen in her bathrobe.

"Really?"

"Many times," added Anna for clarification. She seemed a bit annoyed. "Woke me up too early."

April's tee-hees advanced into the snortling phase.

"I'm sure if you weren't his employer, he'd have slept with you too," I said, patting Anna's hand as she sat down at the breakfast table.

"Of course," said April finally. "He slept with her too."

"At the same time?" I asked frantically.

"Nice," said April, sarcastically.

"You told us he was gay," I said.

"Only to keep you away from him. So, you stayed out of trouble," said Anna.

"That plan worked out well," said April.

"Angelo is a dog," said Anna, matter-of-factly. "Always was. No reflection on you," she said, turning to April. "Me and Angelo? We were ages ago."

April looked at me, still bleary-eyed. "He and I did it this morning after he delivered the groceries," said April, who giggled strongly again. "This is so much better than a souvenir!"

I didn't understand how April could think this was amusing. Still, she got her Italian adventure. Now I was faced with finding an American choir boy in a Roman haystack. High adventure indeed.

I turned to Anna. "So, what's your plan now?" I said.

"I tried telling you last night," said Anna. "But you kept wanting to hear that story again and again. Here goes. I'm starting my own modeling agency. I recently came into some money and am going to create my own agency. I sign the papers today. And all the Bella Donnas will come work with me."

Anna looked beautiful even after a night of heavy drinking and little sleep. She was an incredible goddess.

"Well," I said. "That's fantastic. Great, really. But I was asking what's your plan for today."

"Oh. Well, this place is yours for the next few days, if that's what you mean." Anna sat down and stirred her coffee. "After I sign the papers, I'm off to Milan for a shoot. Angelo is available if you should need ... anything," she said mischievously.

"Dibs," said April, raising her hand.

"Actually, we'll need him to drive us to two places," I said, suddenly the voice of reason in this trio.

Anna seemed intrigued.

"Where are we going, Jane?" April asked.

"Let's ask Angelo first," I said, getting up.

"Oh, Jane," said April. "He's too lovely for such a menial task. Using him for his chauffeur services is like using the Hope diamond for a paperweight."

Ignoring her, I stepped outside onto the gorgeous view of the countryside and sun-soaked sky. The burst of color, crisp air, and smell of earth stung my face, momentarily overwhelming me. I stopped to adjust to the raw beauty.

Angelo was finishing packing up Anna's car. She must have had ten suitcases. He saw me approaching and grinned. The grin told me he was interested in completing a hat trick, a Charley's Angels conquest, with the three women in the house. I didn't have the heart to tell him he'd be sadly disappointed.

Well, maybe I did.

"Good morning, Angelo."

"*Signora* Jane," he said. "We have missed you in the past days."

"Well, I hope you've been able to keep busy." I waited until his grin embarrassed him. "I met a boy, Angelo. I mean, a man. A big man. He loves me," I said.

"I understand, *Signora*," he said. "But this is wonderful! Perhaps later…"

"I am taken. Spoken for. So, we won't be together, you and me. Besides, you have April."

"I'm sorry," he said, shaking his head in confusion.

"No sex!" I yelled. "You and me. No, eh, screwing!"

He backed off, nodding. His hands were raised in defense.

"*Comprendo, comprendo*," he said.

"Sorry," I said, realizing I went a bit heavy on the pepper.

He stared at the car wheels, unsure of what to do or say. Finally, he whispered, "I'm sorry."

"Oh please," I said. "Forget it."

April bounded out of the house in a shiny summer dress I had never seen. She immediately put her arm around Angelo's waist and the two of them became one being like some weird reverse amoeba.

"Great timing," I said. I turned to Angelo. "You have the car all day?"

"That is what Anna instructed to do," he said.

"Great," I said. "We need you to drive us to your Romatene connection, if that's okay. I would love to check that monkey off my zoo."

"That is easy," said Angelo. "He is in town this whole week. Anything else?"

"Yes. I need you to drive me back to the orphanage. I need to see a nun about a boy."

CHAPTER THIRTY-FOUR

Espressivo—*A direction to play expressively.*

We rode the train to Rome and there was a look of shock and sadness on everyone's face as if we were all wearing a Little Francis mask. I sat with Rasper, Terrence, and Charley. No one spoke a word for the first hour. Despite the evening darkness, our shades were drawn in our compartment so not even moonlight could get in.

Periodically, Rasper would shake his head and run his hand through his hair. I got the feeling he would never live this down. He had built this choir all on his own, had hand-picked his singers, charmed the parents, negotiated with concert and tour managers, and had succeeded beyond his wildest imagination. Now it all lay in ruins like the decayed marble fountains and statues in the towns we passed.

I had known something fishy was going on with Lady Bear and Mrs. Clancy. But I never suspected actual people were capable of such dark deeds. I had seen plenty of movies, theater, and TV to know that pretend people acted like this all the time. Real adults were supposed to behave more honorably, at least most of the time. And Mrs. Clancy was Lady Bear's friend. How could Lady Bear kill her best friend? Just for money?

I examined Charley sitting across from me. I couldn't think of a single circumstance where I would actually plan to kill him for the benefit of my advancement. What was wrong with people? Most of me was looking forward to finding Jane and singing at Popestock but a small part longed to return home.

"You're being very brave, Charles," said Rasper.

Charley nodded and closed his eyes. Terrence pretended to sleep as well. Now that Rasper had run out of patrons, he knew he had no one to turn to but Charley's parents. I wondered if Charley's parents even knew what had happened on their son's trip and how they would feel about sponsoring it in the future.

"Your parents have been more than generous," said Rasper.

I guessed Rasper was thinking the same thing.

After the police completed their investigation and arrested Lady Bear, Buccenti had gone back to his office. He told us Lady Bear would stand trial in Italy before being brought back to the States for further charges. Morgan interpreted the whole time. Then Morgan surprised us by adding he was with the New York State Bureau of Narcotic Enforcement and would stay behind to escort Lady Bear back to New York.

Our numbers kept decreasing. It felt like we were fighting a war and only a few of us would make it back home for the parade. I envisioned a version of the Veterans of Foreign Wars for ex-choir boys who had toured Europe. We would be old men talking about our dangerous lives while knocking back scotches and singing scales.

Rasper looked to be in shock from all these revelations pounding on his shore, one after another. I was still ambivalent about him dating my mom.

Hubert, Florinda, and Little Francis weren't with us. Earlier, when we were back at the hotel, Little Francis was told we were boarding a train to take us to Rome. He wailed at the news. I think the thought of an enclosed space that reminded him of his grandparents was too much for his already-bruised and fragile mind. Hubert and Florinda volunteered to rent a car and drive Little Francis. They would meet us in Rome.

Just two hours earlier, we stood in front of the hotel watching them drive away. All I could see was Little Francis's face. Florinda and Little Francis sat in the back of the taxi parked in front of our hotel. The sun was shining down harshly on its way to sunset. Rain and gloomy skies should have been ordered for this occasion. The sun struck the taxi's backseat window while we all watched, feeling sorry.

Rasper slapped the hood of the taxi to indicate it was time to go. Rasper looked away, having never really looked at the cab.

Little Francis didn't wave at us or even acknowledge us. He stared out the window into the blinding sky, eyes wide open. He seemed to be looking for answers.

Back on the train, Rasper reached into his leather satchel he purchased in Venice. He took out his ledger book and a stack of papers. He was performing a financial accounting of our collective funds. I was just starting to arch my neck enough to take a peep at his books when the train came to a stop. The porter made an announcement we would be stopped here while they performed some maintenance on the train.

We all took the opportunity to stretch and get off the train for some fresh air. It was a small train station with no new passengers waiting to board. Even though it was night, everything was brightly lit by the loud moon. When Rasper stepped off the train, he asked us to entertain ourselves for an hour or so. This sounded quite the odd request considering he was our only chaperone. We dispersed into our usual groups. Charley and I went off to the newsstand to buy an American magazine. Lately, we were missing American culture. The train station didn't have any American magazines in English. Instead, we slipped out of the station, making sure Rasper didn't see us.

Next to the train station was what looked like an old construction job site. On closer inspection, they were ancient ruins from Rome's heyday. That was the strange thing about Europe. You could loiter about some broken marble architecture that was three-thousand-years old like Americans hung around McDonald's parking lots.

No one was around so we climbed up a small hill to what looked like a large marble gazebo. Charley and I sat down on the cold marble floor and kicked around marble relics that were older than most of the world.

The conversation turned to the subject that had consumed us since we left the hotel that day. I wanted to talk about Jane instead but didn't think it was appropriate.

Charley had made it his mission to uncover every detail from the grownups regarding this tragedy. I think Charley became consumed by these deaths and this mystery because it filled the gaping hole left by Charley's obsessive relationship with his dog and the long-held secret he kept closely guarded from everyone.

"They'll be back in America by tomorrow or the next day," said Charley. "The Clancys. Or their bodies, anyway. Funeral should be next week." He took a breath, then added, "Little Francis."

"I know," I said. "It's horrible."

"Eli, I'm so sorry I dragged you into all this."

"So, not that it matters now but what is your big secret, Charley? I mean, the whole reason you asked me to cover for you in December so you could get away?"

"Eli, I can't…"

My friend was struggling so I decided to be the grown up on the rubble pile.

"Charley, is it that you have a date with a guy and you're going to go visit him?"

"What are you talking…"

"Charley, I know you're gay."

Charley kicked a small stone over with his foot. "I didn't think you could handle it," he said quietly.

I put my arm around Charley. "Man, you're my best friend. Who cares? Maybe Jane has a brother."

Charley smiled. Then we both broke out in laughter. It felt good to laugh, to have the release.

Tears were welling in our eyes for reasons we understood and for others we didn't. Charley and I sat on Roman ruins, laughing, knowing we were best friends, and kicked ancient marbles back and forth between us. I picked up a piece of green marble the size of an ashtray. It reminded me of Jane's eyes.

"We should probably head back."

We gathered back at the train station and Rasper awaited us. He did a headcount and shepherded us back into our compartments. Big Francis elected himself deputy and was also helping board the smaller kids onto the train.

For the rest of the train ride, Rasper studied his schedules and accounting. I think he was trying to find a miracle.

An hour later, we pulled into Rome. We got off the train and gathered in a circle. Again, Big Francis acted like the choir border collie corralling us. Rasper had gone off to make some phone calls.

After fifteen minutes, Rasper busily marched his way through the crowds. He held an open map of Rome and was immersed in charting some type of course.

Rasper had practically run out of our travel money. This fund was supposed to cover all our costs for the tour, including food, lodging, train fare, museum admission, and entertainment. I was just happy he still had our return airline tickets. I think Rasper had a problem admitting his limitations.

But Rasper was nothing if not resourceful. He changed plans with such adroit efficiency and aplomb, it made me wonder how many times this had happened before.

"Well, good news, boys," he said. "You were such a hit at the Santa Teresa Orphanage and Reform School for Girls that the Sisters there have invited us to stay with their Order in Aprilia."

There was stunned, gaping silence.

"That's funny," I said, not realizing it was out loud. "It sounded like he said we'd be staying at a convent."

"Eli!" shouted Rasper. Then, "A bus is picking us up in twenty minutes."

I turned to Charley. "I thought your parents took care of the finances?"

Charley shrugged. "Might be fun to stay at a convent," he said. "I hear the nuns are a load of laughs."

The bus ride to the convent was blissfully uneventful. It gave me a chance to marvel at the gorgeous scenery around Rome. Even being here seemed surreal. I had seen so many movies and photos of Rome. But nothing compared with actually smelling the air and hearing the sounds. I also hoped Jane was staying nearby.

As we pulled up to the convent, we were greeted with an unexpected sight. It wasn't nuns.

"Now boys," said Rasper, standing at the front of the bus before we got out. "This is your chance to be on your best behavior and really make something of this choir on this tour. The world is watching."

I gazed out the window and saw Hubert, Florinda, and Little Francis waving at us. Next to them was a fully outfitted Roman TV news crew. Rasper had arranged for some free press. The news crew was, of course, interested in talking with us about our stay at the convent, our upcoming Vatican concert, and, perhaps, the recent deaths and murder arrests.

CHAPTER THIRTY-FIVE

***Trill**—Rapid alternation between notes that are a half tone or whole tone apart.*

Angelo was driving April, Anna, and me to Santa Teresa's orphanage. April and I were crammed like olive-oiled-sardines in the backseat. We were all going for different reasons. Anna had promised April she could meet the Bella Donnas again. Apparently, April was quite taken with them. I hoped she wasn't thinking of actually becoming a nun. I'm not sure if I could explain that to her parents back home. Anna had to talk with the Bella Donnas about some modeling contracts. She really was going to make her dreams come true.

And so was I. I was determined to find Eli while we were both in Italy. The wind blew my hair back as Angelo sped down the twisting country road. He insisted on having the top down on the small convertible though we didn't complain much. Other than looking like a fright, the wind whipping around me was exactly what I needed.

When we arrived at the orphanage, Anna made some inquiries and found out the boys' choir had left soon after their concert. No one knew where they were staying or heading next. That wasn't encouraging. I mean, didn't these nuns keep careful records of all visitors for emergencies like these?

We stood in the gothic archway of the orphanage entrance. I didn't know what to do.

"I can help you," said Angelo. "Come with me." He bowed and walked back to the car.

"Go with him," said Anna. "He knows where to take you."

April hugged me. "Hey, don't forget he's mine," she said, smiling. "I hope you find Eli." She and Anna disappeared down a hallway. I turned and saw Angelo revving his engine, motioning me to join him.

He drove us to a seedy little town just outside of Rome. There was a side street off the main square. The houses were gray and hadn't been painted in years. There was no life in this part of town. No plants grew and the lush gardens I had become so familiar with were missing from the landscape.

Angelo stopped the car in front of a dilapidated two-story house. The plaster was crumbling, and parts of the house's wooden skeleton were showing.

"Where the hell are we?" I said.

"We are here for what you seek," said Angelo.

"My American boyfriend isn't in here. He's not a hippie."

"No," said Angelo, caressing the steering wheel. "No is boyfriend. Is Romatene."

"What?"

"You wanted Romatene, yes?" he said. "Inside is man. He will help you. Very rare. I do you a great favor. You will remember, yes?"

I recalled the Wall and how my Romatene score would assure me legendary status. I considered April back at the orphanage. I thought of my parents.

"Thank you, Angelo." I patted his face.

"Of course."

"But I can't," I said. "Start the car. Let's get the hell out of here."

"Your Romatene. You no want?"

"No. I no want. I don't know what I was thinking."

"Because you have something else now?" he said.

"You're right. I met a boy. I don't need to bring back Romatene. I just need to find him. Now let's go."

"Very good," said Angelo and started the car. "Is very good."

We left the shoddy town. I felt so light I thought I was going to float out of the car. I could breathe again. A few miles away from the town, I said, "Where exactly are we going now?"

Angelo smiled. "I know where you answers are."

"I have no idea what you're talking about. But keep driving."

We drove for about a half-hour and pulled into this quaint town. At the end of the road was a small, unassuming house on a large parcel of land. The garden was filled with fig, lemon, olive, and almond trees. It was just beautiful. We rode up the long driveway, Angelo beaming the whole time.

"Where are we?" I said. "Whose house is this?"

He ignored my question, choosing to hum some Italian pop song instead. He parked in front of the house. Angelo hopped out of the car. The blue front door was unlocked and he just waltzed in, closing it behind him. Was this his house? I got out of the car. As I was about to open the front door, I noticed the name on the mailbox.

"Gina Puttanesca."

CHAPTER THIRTY-SIX

Grave*—Indication that the movement is to be played very slow and serious.*

We came running down to breakfast at the convent when we heard the bell ring. This wasn't that different from being in school. I found it strangely comforting. Big Francis had cooked an actual breakfast for all of us, including the nuns. Fresh poached eggs over focaccia and arugula with ham on the side beckoned us. The nuns were ecstatic he was interested in becoming a chef and had experience in a professional kitchen already. They allowed him to cook for us to his heart's content. I think Big Francis wisely neglected to tell them he was also interested in becoming a professional wrestler.

It had been two days since I met Jane at the orphanage and one day since our news conference. During the news conference, the Italian reporter, who spoke broken English, kept circling back to Little Francis. She kept referring to him as "the little orphan *Americano.*" That's when Hubert and Florinda, already holding Little Francis' hands, stepped before the cameras, uninvited, and announced together on national Italian TV that they would be adopting Little Francis.

There was a frenzy in front of the cameras as we, the nuns, and gathered crowd let out a cheer. The news services ate it up. By the evening, the story of Little Francis had graced many of the world's newspapers and TV news programs.

After the news conference, Little Francis seemed at peace for the first time on the whole trip. So did Hubert and Florinda. Even Big Francis seemed delighted at this news. Hubert, Florinda, and Little Francis left the news crew, who were dying to get exclusive interviews, and retreated to the convent for some privacy.

That was all well and good but there was still no word from Jane. I had gone out searching for her every chance we had some free time. Most of our time lately had been taken up rehearsing as we prepared ourselves for Popestock.

The nuns at the convent loved us and pinched our cheeks harder than the ones in Santa Teresa's, if that was possible. I lost count of how many nuns there were here. Maybe a dozen. They all dressed the same and were about the same height. It occurred to me the convent's nun audition process might have been the same as the Radio City Hall Rockettes.

I had my own room in the convent. The small window overlooked a garden. In the distance, I could barely make out the city of Rome, but it beckoned me. After breakfast, we had a free morning. One of the nuns lent me her bicycle so I set out to explore on my own. My interests weren't sightseeing. I checked the nearby hotels to see if there was an American girl named Jane staying there. I was sure that's how a private detective would have handled this situation.

After my third hotel, I noticed the time and realized I needed to head back for rehearsal. Popestock was in two days. As I rode the bicycle through a small town, a car pulled up beside me. Buccenti honked the horn and waved me to come closer. I stopped and leaned down. He was the only one in the car. His fedora hat was in the passenger seat. He picked it up and threw it in the backseat.

"Mr. Mitchell," he said, in a friendly tone. "You're a long way from home."

"I'm alright," I said, trying to sound brave.

"Get in, please. I'll give you a ride back to the convent. Put your bicycle in the back."

I thought about it and decided to trust him. If he had wished me ill, he had plenty of opportunities before. I stowed my bicycle by wedging it in the backseat and got in. He pulled away and proceeded down the road toward the convent.

"It's funny," he said. "You were a big help on my case. A big help."

"Case?"

"Mrs. Querrel and the Rollins'. We've been following them for quite a long time. You were all together the wild card."

"I don't know what you're talking about," I said, trying to piece this together.

"Surely, you know by now that I am working with your government," said Buccenti. "If there was a Romatene formula key, neither of our governments could allow that to get out into the general public. Think of the trouble that would cause. For both our countries."

"Wait, so why were you following us? I mean, I had nothing to do with this."

"We know that," said Buccenti, driving slowly so we would have more time to talk. "But somehow, you insinuated yourself into Mrs. Querrel and Mrs. Rollins' scheme. So, we kept tabs on you. For your safety. And also, in case you stumbled onto something that was going to get you in trouble."

We drove in silence as I dreamed up a million questions.

"And Morgan," I said.

"Of course," he said. "I understand you recognized Ponte immediately. Well, he was the best your government could do on such short notice. Not too many agents who could pass for high school and speak fluent Italian. He was especially well-suited for this unusual assignment."

"He can't sing worth a damn," I said. "No breath control."

Buccenti laughed.

"Hold on," I said. "New York Narcotics would send one of their own to work with you here? And agree to use our choir as cover?"

"Who do you think paid for this whole trip?" said Buccenti.

"My friend, Charley Welsham. His parents…"

"They're in Tahiti. All they know is their son is on a choir trip in Italy. We paid for this trip because we needed to see what Querrel and Rollins were up to. We needed to see what Breggleman inherited."

"To see if Romatene was the real thing."

"Exactly, my dear boy."

"Holy crap," I said.

"What is it?" said Buccenti. "I know this is a lot for you, but I wanted to express my gratitude."

"It's not that. I was just thinking of my choir director. Does he know you guys paid for this trip?"

"We thought it best to keep him in the dark. So, we forged the telegram from the Welshams. After all, I didn't know what kind of relationship he had with Mrs. Querrel."

"He's going to be crushed by this. He thought he had patrons in Charley's parents. I mean, the choir is his whole life."

"Well," said Buccenti as we turned onto the road for the convent. "That problem is out of my jurisdiction."

Rasper and a few of the choir boys were waiting outside the convent gates. I saw Rasper's scowl develop the moment he saw Buccenti behind the wheel.

"Mr. Mitchell," said Rasper. "You're late."

"Sorry," I said as I got out of Buccenti's car. I pulled out my bicycle. Buccenti got out of the car as well.

"If you weren't such good friends with Charles…" said Rasper.

"Mr. Rasper," I said. "There's something you should know." I looked at Buccenti who gave me a nod.

"What is this?" said Rasper. He ordered the other kids to go back into the convent. Hubert opened the front door and let them in. He saw us standing in front of Buccenti's car and approached us.

"Perhaps another time?" said Buccenti.

"No, I'd like to know what you have to say, Mr. Buccenti," said Rasper.

Buccenti looked at me, shrugged his shoulders, and lit a cigarette. He explained to Rasper and Hubert how the Bureau of Narcotic Enforcement and Italian government had sponsored the trip, not Charley's parents.

"But that's impossible," said Rasper. "It can't be."

"It gets worse," said Buccenti. I didn't know where he was heading at this point.

"Worse?" said Rasper. "How could it get worse? Eli, go inside."

I stayed put.

"We got what we came for," said Buccenti. "Or more precisely, we didn't. After going through Mr. Breggleman's inheritance, we confirmed the Romatene key doesn't exist. It never did. So, I'm afraid we're pulling the funding for this operation."

"What?" said Rasper.

"What?" I said.

"We'll fly you all home tonight. The government can't continue to sponsor this singing tour now that our case is closed."

"But the Vatican," said Rasper, finding himself sinking deep in quicksand. Hubert put his hand on Rasper's shoulder to brace him.

I couldn't believe this was happening. I wanted to sing at the Vatican too. I also needed more time to find Jane.

"I may have a solution," said Hubert, stepping between Rasper and me.

Buccenti, who had been getting back into his car, walked around to listen.

"Yes, Mr. Breggleman?" said Rasper.

Hubert looked at each of us, his head turning slowly. "I, uh, don't know where to start."

"You've done enough, Hubert," said Rasper. "It was very kind of you to take Francis in."

"That's just it," said Hubert. "I got my inheritance from my aunt today. I can do a lot more than you think. A lot more than just adopt Francis."

"What do you mean?" said Rasper.

"I'll be your sponsor, Douglas," said Hubert.

"Now, hold on," said Rasper.

"I want to do this," said Hubert. "The choir has been my whole life too. Same with Florinda."

"There, you see," said Buccenti. "It's all settled."

"I can't let you…" said Rasper.

"And I'm not just talking about completion funds for the rest of our tour," said Hubert. "No. I mean I want to be the choir's patron."

Rasper stood there with his mouth open. I had never seen him look that way before, but I got a glimpse of him as a young child. It made me like him again; made me think he could make my mom happy.

"That must have been some inheritance," I said.

"It wasn't bad," said Hubert.

"Hubert," said Rasper, "I'm speechless. I don't know what to say. What this means to me. And to all the boys. Are you sure?"

"Positive. Florinda and I talked about it. It would be our honor and pleasure."

Rasper and Hubert hugged.

"Hey," said Hubert, chuckling. "Now you work for me."

Rasper laughed. It was a day of firsts.

"This is wonderful," said Buccenti. "Now, if you'll excuse me." Buccenti got into his car. I approached his car and waved at him. He rolled down his window. "Yes?"

"Mr. Buccenti," I said. "Do you happen to know an American girl visiting here named Jane?"

CHAPTER THIRTY-SEVEN

***Verismo**—A form of Italian opera where the setting is contemporary to the composer's own time and the characters are modeled after everyday life.*

I heard chatter coming from the kitchen. I was still in the foyer of the small house. I heard Angelo laugh and sensed the kitchen was around the corner. The faded plaster walls were decorated with colorful tiles and small tapestries that were frayed at the edges. The foyer bled into a hallway with the same plaster walls and decoration. Sunlight seemed to stream in from everywhere.

This had to be a joke. How did Angelo know Gina Puttanesca? And why had he not mentioned it before?

I turned the corner as if I was approaching the Pope's inner sanctum. The kitchen was warm and filled with bright colors and cheerful light. A small gray-haired woman faced the oven with her back to me. Angelo sat at the wooden farm table in the middle of the room. Pots and ceramic bowls lined the counters. The wooden cabinets were old and worn from decades of use. Two large windows looked out onto a kitchen garden and, further, orchards of apricots, apples, lemons, and olives.

"Here she is," said Angelo. "We waiting for you."

"For me?" I said. "Angelo, what's going on?"

The old woman put down a large, green ceramic bowl and looked at me, her eyes twinkling. She surveyed me from top to bottom. I didn't know what to do.

"You have no idea how long I've been waiting to meet you," said the old woman with only the slightest accent.

"I'm Jane," I said and stuck out my hand. "It's such an honor. You have no idea."

She wiped her hands on her blue apron and hugged me. She held me tight, and I felt her weeping. Finally, she let go of the embrace but held onto me with her hands.

"Mrs. Puttanesca?" I said.

"I am," she said.

Angelo chuckled and she shot him a disapproving stare.

"Angelo," she said. "Why don't you go wait outside. I'll let you know when the biscotti are ready."

Angelo shrugged and left. I was quite confused.

"How do you know Angelo?" I said.

"He works for me," said Puttanesca, crossing the room. She went into the large, wooden cupboard and brought out a bowl of hazelnuts still in their shells. "You'll help me make biscotti, yes?"

"The only baking I know is with Duncan Hines."

"I don't know who that is. But this will be nice. Go get the milk and butter. In there," she said.

I opened the refrigerator. It was well stocked. "I'm sorry, you said Angelo works for you?"

"And he works for Anna, too," she said as I handed her the milk and butter.

"Anna?"

"Your beautiful cousin. She helped me and, in turn, I'm helping her." Puttanesca added some flour to her bowl and waved me over. "Maybe I should start at the beginning. You look lost."

"Only slightly," I said.

She handed me the bowl of hazelnuts. "Start shelling and I'll tell you a story, my love," said Puttanesca. She grabbed a wooden spoon and together we made biscotti.

"I am Gina Puttanesca. I know you've heard of me. Everyone has but no one wants to admit it," she said. "And it's a good life I've made with my writing. For a long time, I have lived off my crazy imagination.

"But it wasn't always so. When I was a young, foolish girl, not much older than you, I fell in love. His name was Piccolo and he was a mad scientist. Can you imagine? But, my God, I loved him."

"What do you mean a mad scientist?"

"He invented something. Something impossible that everyone wanted. Something no one could have. And I was the only one he trusted with this monumental secret. So, for his troubles, his enemies burned down his house and killed him. My Piccolo."

"That's awful. I'm so sorry," I said.

"Thank you. I knew they would come after me. So, the next day, my baby and I left the village and didn't return for many years."

"His baby?"

"Of course. My beautiful daughter."

Her biscotti dough was ready. She noticed I hadn't yet shelled all the hazelnuts. She took half the remaining pile and shelled them.

"I don't know what to say," I said.

"Then wait," said Puttanesca. "I haven't even gotten to the good part." She let out a guffaw. "A few years after, I moved back to my village. And I fell in love again. Wasn't expecting to. It just happened. So, you see, don't ever let anyone tell you that love won't find you, no matter what your circumstance."

"I met a boy on this trip," I said. I didn't know why I was so comfortable talking to her or why I was revealing anything about myself.

"Of course you did. You're a beautiful girl who is kind and sensible."

I had never been called sensible in my life. I didn't know if I should take it as an insult or a compliment.

"His name was Bart Rollins," she said. "My second love. A visiting American. Just like you." She put down her hazelnuts and turned to me. "Now listen, Jane," she said. "I'm telling you this because I trust you. Believe me on that point."

I nodded but my head was swimming. What was happening?

"My first love," she said. "The father of my child. My Piccolo. The thing he invented? Romatene."

"Oh my God!"

"I know. So, you see why everyone was after him and how he ended up the way he did."

"I can't believe this," I said. I sat down at the kitchen table. She poured me a glass of water and handed it to me.

"Now, with Bart Rollins, I was cautious at first," continued Puttanesca. "After all, maybe he knew who my former lover was, and maybe he wanted to get the formula for Romatene. Maybe he thought I had it.

"But, at that point in my life, I had already become a successful novelist and was making good money. So, I thought, there was no reason to bring up details of my past.

"Well, one day, after we had been together for many years, he betrayed me with another woman. The idiot. I was so angry. I kicked him out of the house, hurling all kinds of insults at him."

"I'm sorry," I said.

"I was so angry, I told him the words he wanted to hear for so long. We had never discussed Romatene. As he was packing his things, I was seething. I screamed out lies that were meant to hurt him. Can you imagine? And he believed my lies. Thankfully, my daughter wasn't home to hear them."

"What did you say?" I asked.

She brushed my hair with her fingers and refilled my water glass.

"I told him that Romatene did, in fact, exist and that only I had the formula to make it. I told him that I had buried the formula in a code in every erotic novel I'd written. That only I had the key to the code. And that he would never have it. Can you believe it?"

"That's awful."

"I was so angry with him."

Puttanesca turned on her oven.

"It was all a lie. The formula to Romatene died with my Piccolo in the fire," she said.

She finished making the biscotti and put them in the oven. I sat at the kitchen sipping water and taking in this story, unsure of how to feel.

"Mrs. Puttanesca, why are you telling me all this?" I said.

"Let's talk about you," she said, wiping her hands.

"Me? What's there to tell?"

"Tell me about your parents."

"My parents? Well, I'm adopted. I don't really remember my biological parents. But my adopted parents are nice. They mean well. Actually, I kinda miss them."

"That's good," she said. A look of sadness had overtaken her sweet face.

Angelo burst into the room. "Okay," he said, heading towards the oven. "Biscotti ready? I only walk for so long."

"Excuse me," said Puttanesca, wiping her eyes. "I'll be right back." She left the room.

"What?" said Angelo. "Was it something I said? Or did I interrupt something?"

"Angelo," I said. "What's going on here?"

He poured himself a glass of water and sat across from me at the table. "She hasn't told you yet?"

"About Romatene? She told me."

"No, not Romatene. She is you grandmother."

"What?" I nearly fell out of my chair.

Angelo's eyed darted around the room nervously. "Merda. Well, is better if she explains."

"How is she my grandmother? Gina Puttanesca?"

"I not the one to tell you," he said.

"Angelo!" I protested.

"Her real name is Nella. And she is you Nonna. You Nonna Nella."

"Nonna Nella." I rolled the name around in my head. It sounded so natural suddenly. As if I had always known her.

"She hire Anna to bring you to Italy. Anna hire me to help. We only mean the best. Please believe."

I got up and paced in the kitchen. "Wait," I said. "Why did you bring me here? What does she want?"

"When you say no to my Romatene connection this morning," said Angelo. "That's when I was instructed to bring you here."

"No," I said. "I mean, why did Nonna Nella send for me at all?"

"That you ask her." He cleared his throat to indicate she was coming back into the kitchen.

"I'm sorry for that," said Nonna Nella. "An old woman has to use the toilet often. Biscotti ready?"

"I'm sorry," I said.

She opened the oven door. "You will only learn by doing. Good. They're ready to be cut." She took out the tray of biscotti and began slicing them.

"Nonna," I said, getting up. She put down her knife and I gave her the biggest hug I had ever given anyone. She hugged me back and we both cried and hugged for what seemed like hours.

"So," she said, finally. "This big mouth told you."

"I'm sorry," said Angelo. "I no have you gift for secrets and, how you say, subterfuge."

"It's okay," said Nella. She held my face. "Like your mother. Beautiful."

"Why didn't you contact me all these years?" I asked. "I thought I didn't have any real family."

"Your parents are real family," she said, sighing.

"I know."

Nella looked deeply into my eyes. "I was ashamed," she said. "The way I had led my life. Writing these books. And my Piccolo's murder. For years, I thought you two would be better off not knowing me."

"Of course I wanted to know you," I said. "Wait, what do you mean, 'you two?'"

"Ah," said Angelo. "More girl talk. I will be in living room watching television if you need me. Please let me know when biscotti are ready." And with that, he was off.

Nonna Nella put the tray of sliced biscotti back in the oven for their second baking.

"How do I say this?" she said. "I always knew you were in America. Adopted. Safe. My sister, may she rest in peace, also had a child in America. I am also his only living relative." She cringed when she said that.

"What's wrong?" I said.

"Bad choice of words. You see, he was mixed up with people who I didn't trust. And I didn't know if I could trust him either."

"But you could trust me?"

"Of course. You are a young girl. He is a man. It's hard to trust a man. Hubert is his name."

"I have a cousin?" I said.

"See, your family keeps expanding," said Nonna Nella.

"So, what's going on that needs so much trust?"

"When my Piccolo died, he had amassed a fortune from Romatene. That fortune was very real. And it was mine. All these years and no one has gotten to it. I never touched it. I never told Bart Rollins about it. I wanted to make my own way in this world. You understand?"

"I think I do."

"It's very important to be your own woman. Anyway, I'm not getting any younger. And I finally realized I need to do something with all this money."

"So, all this time…"

"Yes," said Nella. "I hired Anna to bring you to me. Angelo too. I wanted to see for myself if my only living relatives were worthy of my sacrifice."

I didn't know what to say. I gave her another hug. "Wait," I said. "What about my cousin Hubert?"

"I'm so ashamed. But my history with men. I couldn't trust him at first, like I said. I arranged to have a telegram sent to him telling him I had passed away and that he needed to come to Italy for his inheritance. My attorney would assess if Hubert was trustworthy."

"And was he?"

"Hey," said Angelo, running into the room. "Come in quick."

The television was turned onto the local news. I couldn't make out most of what was being said but the visuals were pretty obvious.

Eli's choir was being interviewed in front of a convent. The choir director was doing most of the talking but the camera was occasionally panning the choir's faces.

"What is this?" said Nonna Nella. "Is this Hubert's choir?"

"There he is," said Angelo, pointing at the television.

"My cousin," I said. "What's wrong with his arm?"

"Two of the chaperones died on this choir trip and one was arrested," said Angelo with glee. As an outsider, this was strictly entertainment to him.

"I'm glad that horrible woman is in jail," said Nonna Nella.

"How do you know about this?" I said.

Suddenly, in the middle of the interview with the choir director, Hubert and his wife jumped in front of the camera, each holding the hand of an adorable little boy.

"We are proud to announce we have decided to adopt Francis," said Hubert. "He will have a great life in America with us and we can help him through this horrible tragedy."

"Well," said Angelo.

"Well, indeed," said Nonna Nella.

"He's a good man," said Angelo.

"Of course, he is," said Nonna Nella with much pride in her voice. "He's my nephew."

On the television, I could hear applause at Hubert's announcement. I imagined he had also passed some test that Nonna Nella had constructed in her mind. Like me refusing to meet the Romatene dealer who didn't really exist. Hubert would now be worthy of her love and fortune.

"What did the news reporter just say?" I asked Angelo.

"That the choir will next be performing at the Vatican."

"The Vatican," said Nonna Nella. "Imagine."

"I'm feeling dizzy," I said.

"Jane," said Nonna Nella. "My love, my granddaughter, I am giving you and Hubert my inheritance. My Romatene fortune."

"Nonna," I said. "I'm overwhelmed. I don't have the words."

"And I want you to stay here and live with me."

I was about to respond when my attention was drawn back to the television. Eli had jumped in front of Hubert and his wife. He stared right into the camera. He looked right at me.

"Jane, if you're out there, I'll be at the Vatican. I love you!"

My heart fainted. So did my brain. I mean, there was only so much a girl could take.

"Jane?" said Nonna Nella. "Are you alright? Is that your boyfriend?"

"Isn't he dreamy?" I said.

"He's a weirdo," said Angelo.

"Shut up," I said. "I think I love him."

Nonna Nella took the biscotti out of the oven and placed them gently in a linen-lined basket.

I walked into the kitchen after her. "Nonna, you're so generous. And I don't want to seem ungrateful. But I can't stay here with you. I need to go find Eli. And I want to go back to America with my friend April so I can be with my parents. And with Eli. Maybe I can come visit you during summer breaks? I mean, I'll have the money now. Oh God, the money. This is crazy. Are you sure you have the right girl?"

Nella handed me the basket of biscotti with tears in her eyes.

"I understand," she said. "Now go, my love. Make me proud. Find that boy."

CHAPTER THIRTY-EIGHT

***Romantic**—A period in history during the 18th and early 19th centuries where the focus was on an emotional, expressive, and imaginative style.*

Popestock had finally arrived. There was a lot of fuss made about us at the Vatican. We had arrived that Sunday morning and sauntered off the bus with a phalanx of nuns like they were our security detail. The nuns at the convent were not giving up the opportunity to see the Pope so they volunteered to be our official escorts. The nuns were, of course, given complete clearance by the Pope and, more importantly, Rasper.

Our white jackets glistened in the blazing morning sun as we marched across the Square at St. Peters Square. Overhead, surrounding the Square from an upper level, enormous white statues peered down at us like disapproving parents. It was easy to imagine Lady Bear had been turned to stone, as penance, and had to spend eternity watching us and other choirs perform.

A Vatican policeman was barking orders into his walkie-talkie. As we proceeded inside St. Peters, priests opened creaky, wooden doors and poked their heads out of their stuffy, marble offices as we marched further down the corridors. Our official Vatican escort led us into a large rehearsal room with a piano. It was there we parted ways with the nuns. They were given reserved seat assignments and fluttered off after pinching our cheeks one last time for good luck. Once the heavy iron doors of the rehearsal room closed, it was a familiar surrounding—sitting in a windowless large space with Rasper in front of us and Hubert and Florinda at the piano.

Rasper looked strangely nervous. His financial troubles were behind him. I couldn't imagine that Popestock and all its inherent publicity were making him unravel. We were well-rehearsed and ready for this audience. We were the first American choir to sing at Sunday mass and the concert would be broadcast around the world. The Pope would be there along with half the world's Cardinals. And, just outside, eighty-thousand or so people, travelers from around the world, were gathered to hear the Mass and our concert through speakers. This was the fruition of Rasper's dreams. Something else was troubling him.

I had bigger fish to fry. In two days, we were flying home. Which meant I only had two days left to find Jane. So far, my TV plea had not produced her or any hints of where she might be.

We were sitting quietly, awaiting Rasper to call us to order. Hubert and Florinda were going through the sheet music.

There was a knock on the door.

Was the Pope himself coming down to wish us well? Was this just the green room for the big TV show?

Hubert opened the door slightly, then looked at me and Rasper.

"She's here," said Hubert.

There was no way. How could this be?

The door opened and there stood my mom.

This couldn't be happening. Maybe one of the Cardinals liked to dress in drag. And had raided my mom's closet. Was there a JC Penney's in the Vatican?

My mom ran over and hugged me tightly, picking me up off my feet. I was swinging like a rag doll, enveloped in my mother's hug. She kept saying my name over and over. I had never been so happy to see her.

"Mom," I said. "What are you doing here?" She put me down but didn't let go of me.

"I missed you so much," she said. She hugged me again.

"I missed you too."

She composed herself when she saw she was surrounded by the choir. "So, this is a nice place. What do they get for rent here?"

And that's when I knew my mom was really here.

"I flew her," said Hubert. "I wanted it to be a surprise for you."

"Mr. Breggleman, out of the blue, calls me," said my mom. "I was so nervous after watching you on the news and the terrible things that happened to you..."

She hugged me again.

Rasper stepped in. He raised his arms and the choir instantly focused on him. "Boys, why don't you give us a minute."

"But, why did Mr. Breggleman...?" I said.

"Where are we supposed to go?" asked Big Francis.

"Just outside in the hallway. Don't stray," said Rasper.

Everyone except the adults shuffled out. Charley gave me a questioning glance, trying to figure out what was going on. I had no idea.

After the metal door closed, Rasper turned to me. "I asked Mr. Breggleman, as his first kindness as a patron, if he would fly your mother here for this concert."

"Douglas," said my mom, blushing.

"It's all he's talked about on this trip," said Florinda. "Phyllis this, Phyllis that."

"It's not as bad as all that," said Rasper. He looked like a junior high kid who had been caught sticking a love note into a girl's locker.

"Don't make me blush," said my mom.

"Too late," said Rasper, moving next to her.

"Oh my God," I said. I wanted to melt into the marble. Things could not have been more awkward.

"Eli," said my mother. "Don't use the Lord's name in vain in this holy place."

"We're Jewish."

"It's still holy!" she screamed.

"I'm so glad you're here," I said.

"Douglas, I want to tell you something," said my mom.

"It's wonderful you're here," said Rasper. "We're supposed to be upstairs for the Mass in fifteen minutes."

"I've flown all this way and I want to tell you," said my mom.

I knew that tone.

Rasper nodded and took a step closer to her.

"You've made me feel good about myself again. Like you see me," she said and kissed his cheek. Now it was Rasper's turn to blush. "And I have a thank-you gift for you."

"You didn't have to..." said Rasper.

"Of course I did," said my mom. "Mr. Heston."

At the mention of Charlton Heston, Rasper stood straighter.

"Mom, don't. You don't have to..."

"But Eli, I wasn't kidding. I do have a cousin in the movie business. She does costumes." My mom turned to Rasper. "And my cousin is doing costumes for Mr. Heston's next picture. She told him what a fan you are. And you know what?"

"What?" said Rasper, completely entranced by my mom.

"She's set up a meeting here in Rome in two days. It's where he's shooting his movie. We're having coffee with Chuck Heston. You, me, and Eli."

I hugged her. My mom really was the special person who had made me what I was.

"Phyllis," said Rasper, taking her hand. "You're a wonder."

I had never seen Rasper so delighted.

They both turned to me and all I could do was smile. It was simply too much to process.

Hubert opened the door, and the choir took their seats. We quickly rehearsed while my mom took her place upstairs. As we were getting ready to leave the rehearsal room, there was a knock on the door. Rasper opened it and stuck his head outside. He was having a conversation with someone in the hallway. His head came back in the room, and he found me with his eyes.

"Oh, Eli," said Rasper. "There's someone here for you."

"At the Vatican?" I said.

Who could this be? What extra ballast could the universe possibly heap on my shoulders? I opened the rehearsal room door.

"Mr. Mitchell," said the man outside. It was Buccenti. He waved me into the hallway. "I have someone I think you would like to see."

I stepped out into the hallway and peered into the dim, marble-reflected light.

"Hello," said Jane.

"How did..."

"You asked me if I knew a girl named Jane," said Buccenti. "I think this is a Jane."

I looked at her and beamed. "That is definitely the Janiest girl I ever knew."

"I can't believe I found you," said Jane.

"You're welcome," said Buccenti.

"Sorry, thanks," I said.

Jane took a step closer to me.

"You have no idea what I went through, what's happened," said Jane.

"I'll be upstairs," said Buccenti. "I can't believe I'm at the Vatican for Sunday Mass."

"That makes two of us," I said to each of them.

Buccenti tipped his hat my way, turned, and walked down the hallway.

I moved closer to Jane. I couldn't believe I was so near her that I could reach out and take her hand. Which is exactly what I did. She took my other one and we just stood there in the hallway, gazing at each other. Her hands were soft, warm. My mind was racing and blank at the same time.

"Decorum, Mr. Mitchell," said Rasper.

The choir was filing out in an orderly fashion with Rasper in the lead. The military had nothing on the drills we had practiced to walk like a singular unit. As the choir walked past us, Rasper stayed behind, leaving Hubert and Florida to lead the parade upstairs to the Big Room or whatever they called where we were performing.

"Mr. Rasper, just this once, can I sit this one out?" I said. "I'm sure the choir will do great without me." I continued to hold Jane's hand.

"I'll keep an eye on him," said Jane to Rasper, smiling.

Rasper sighed. "Eli, I wish I could but the program for the Mass has already been distributed to the Vatican Secretary and the press. The Pope has already approved it."

"But what does that…"

"Mr. Mitchell, it's time you finally sing your solo. 'For His Lord's Tenderness Keeping.'"

"Now? Today?"

Rasper turned to Jane. "Young lady, would you please be so kind as to go sit in one of the reserved pews upstairs? We'll come find you afterward."

And with that, Rasper grabbed my arm, escorted me away from Jane, and shuffled me Popewards.

CHAPTER THIRTY-NINE

Coda—*Closing section of a movement.*

The bloody Pope. I was just about to yell out to Eli where he should meet me when the Popemobile scooted by and whisked my love away. I suddenly understood why men went to war over religion.

April and were surrounded by mobs of people screaming the Pope's name and trying to get a glimpse of him. Most had their cameras out. The electric buzz of Polaroids around me almost muffled the screams. We had made our way up to the barricade on the side of the road where the Popemobile would be driving by. But I had made a major miscalculation. Eli and his choir were on the other side. There was simply no way to cross the road with so much Vatican security around. And now Eli and his choir were running alongside the Popemobile like those New York City marathoners who have their support team throw lemons at them.

I felt powerless. This was a strange feeling considering I had just inherited all the money in the world and found the boy I loved. I had already decided the first thing I would do when I got back home would be to buy old man Dietrich's house so the Wall would be mine. I would be Queen of the Wall and my benevolence would become legendary. I would grow old with Eli, who would become Prince Consort of the Wall, and together we would rule justly and be forever known as those old coots who allowed teenagers to get high and make out in front of their house. It would be glorious.

I'm sure there would be lawyers and trustees involved at first, considering I was only sixteen, but a girl has to start somewhere. At the moment, this girl had to start by finding her Prince Consort. I took April by the elbow and we dragged ourselves against the tide of tourists, away from the Pope. We continued pushing our way upstream and the metaphor was not lost on me. Perhaps at the mouth of this river of humanity, I would find my Eli and we would spawn. Or whatever it was salmon do. I never liked seafood. Mac and cheese was more my style.

With everyone in the Square watching the Pope, April and I easily made it into St. Peters Basilica. I reasoned if we climbed the large marble staircase to the top, we could find some balcony and get a better vantage point so I could locate Eli. April was happy enough to come along.

The marble stairs led to the Basilica rotunda. It was a beautiful dome decorated with mosaic tiles and ornate woodwork. There was a walkway on the inside perimeter that encircled the dome at this level. With its high altitude and handrails, it reminded me of a catwalk in a theater. I didn't see any exits to a balcony or to the outdoors at all.

Just as we were about to leave the catwalk and climb back downstairs to find another way to the roof, April tapped me on the shoulder.

"He's dishy," she said. I had never heard her use that word before.

She was referring to this cute choir boy. I knew he was in Eli's choir because he was wearing the same white dinner jacket, white shirt, black pants, and plaid bowtie and cummerbund. He was black and looked older and considerably larger than Eli. His face was rough and looked like he had seen trouble. But there was kindness there as well. Not really my type. Eli was my type. The choir boy lit a cigarette as we walked down the stairs.

"Hi," said April, approaching him. "Can you spare one of those for an American girl?"

Where was this confidence coming from? I supposed it was the influence of having slept with Angelo.

"Here you go," he said. His voice was silky and didn't fit his grizzled demeanor. He offered me one, but I declined. I wanted my breath fresh when I kissed Eli. "Americans, huh?" he said.

"And we just saw your concert. You were so good," said April. "My name is April. This is Jane."

"I'm Francis. They call me Big Francis."

"I bet they do," said April.

He puffed a cloud of smoke and gave her a hard look. "I remember you," said Big Francis. "Yeah, at the orphanage. I remember you in the audience. And me thinking how gorgeous you were. They let you orphans out for this?"

April blushed. "I'm not an orphan."

"Good to know."

"I don't have a boyfriend," said April. "How about you?"

I was getting impatient. I wanted to be here for my friend but kept scanning the lobby below for Eli.

"Nope," said Big Francis. "No boyfriend."

April laughed and I continued to be amazed at her newly found confidence.

"No girlfriend either," said Big Francis.

"Large Francis," I interrupted. "Do you know where Eli is?"

"Big Francis. How do you know Eli?" asked Big Francis.

"We're from Long Island too," I said, figuring it was an easier explanation than getting into the whole orphanage thing.

"We're probably neighbors," said April to Big Francis.

"No shit," he said. "That's funny. I was just talking with Eli's mom. Her brother owns that Tijuana Meatball restaurant."

"That place is awful," said April.

"I know, right?" said Big Francis. "Anyway, she told me they're re-doing it and getting rid of the Mexican food. Strictly Italian. And they're making me their chef."

"That's so great," said April. "But aren't you, like, still in high school?"

"I got left back a few years," said Big Francis. "I'd rather work anyway. They're advertising it that I'm a Roman-trained chef. Which, I guess, I am."

"I'll have to check it out," said April.

"You better," said Big Francis. He gave her a smile that told her they were definitely going out on a date when they got back.

"And Eli?" I said.

"That's the other weird part," said Big Francis. "Eli was all worried that he and his mom were going to have to move to Jersey so she could take this other job. But with the Italian restaurant thing getting lots of interest, they're staying and she's gonna be a co-owner. So, you could say I'm working for Eli's mom."

"That's great," I said. "But, I mean, where is Eli now?"

"Oh," said Big Francis. "That's easy. Right over there."

I turned and there he was, on the opposite end of the rotunda, on the catwalk. I ran up the catwalk so we were at opposite ends—he at twelve o'clock, me at six. He waved at me. At the same time, we each put up our hand to indicate not to move; that we would come to the other. We both stood there, a few hundred feet apart. I couldn't believe I was looking right at him. It was like the best dream.

And then I remembered reading in the guidebook about the Basilica rotunda. That it was acoustically perfect. That sound traveled around the dome to the other side.

I leaned into the domed wall and whispered, "Eli."

He saw me talking to the wall. This was the moment of truth. He would either think I was a looney, or he would talk back. He took a step towards me and put his ear to the wall, listening, and smiling. He whispered back to the wall. Two seconds later, his message reached me.

"Jane." Even with the echo and distortion, his voice sent shivers through my body.

"You found me," I said.

"I've been looking for you everywhere."

I took a step forward and whispered into the wall. "I've been looking for you my whole life."

We each took a step closer. Our voices were carried across the rotunda and into each other's ears. Our distance kept shortening. The response time for our voices to travel got quicker. So did my heartbeat.

"To find you, I had to escape an orphanage," I said and took another step. This game we were playing was the most thrilling thing I'd ever done. The old me would have run right to Eli.

He took a step closer and whispered to the wall, "To find you, I solved an international murder."

"I became a millionaire."

"I found my family's history here. And my family back home," he said.

"I did too," I said.

We continued toward each other, whispering our secrets and letting them travel and spiral. These walls had heard eons of prayers and plaintive cries of joy and sorrow. We would add ours to the deep history under this dome.

"But mostly I found this boy," I said.

"Mostly, I found this wonderful girl. Then I thought I lost her," he said.

"Never."

"You're beautiful inside. I hope I'm worthy of your love," he said.

I shuddered. Something in me broke loose. Finally, we were ten feet apart. The tension was killing me. I just wanted to kiss him. He reached into his bag and took out a piece of green marble the size of an ashtray.

We finally stood face to face. No adults to interrupt us.

"The color of your eyes," said Eli, holding out the marble for me.

I took the marble. It was heavier than it looked.

"This is your marker. For when you go back home," he said. "To help build the Wall."

"The Wall," I said, tearing up. "You get me."

"I hope so," said Eli.

I put the marble down. I couldn't stand it any longer. We wrapped our arms around each other.

"Hi."

"Hi."

And we kissed.

It was the most perfect moment of my life.

ACKNOWLEDGEMENTS

The events and characters in *Madcap Serenade* bear no actual resemblance to any real boys' choir, nor the adults orbiting their nucleus. However, I must give a deep and respectful bow to Maestro Gerald Barker for creating and directing the very real Singing Boys of Long Island, of which I was a member in my youth. Into the heart of every choir boy, parent, and audience, you provided an inspired love of music, joy, Mozart, Rodgers and Hart, and Billy Joel. You taught your choir boys that focus, dedication, and professionalism are not too much to expect, even when you're nine. My years in the choir, the travel, the city and international tours, the adventures, and the hijinks (most of which was not formally condoned by you) are some of my happiest memories. I'm indebted to you for that once-in-a-lifetime experience.

Thunderous applause to my wife and best friend, Angela, for always supporting my writing and being the most excellent travel companion.

An extra curtain call for Jenn Haskin, my editor extraordinaire.

A standing ovation to Gus the Theater Cat for always supporting creativity and silliness and drawing me out of my shell in my formative years.

Lastly, I'd like to throw a rose bouquet to Pope John Paul II: you sly, old rooster wall.

ABOUT THE AUTHOR

Dan Kopcow's sci-fi noir detective novel, *Prior Futures*, published in December 2021 by Black Rose Writing, won a 2022 Independent Press Award for Science Fiction Distinguished Favorite and was a Science Fiction Best Thriller of 2021 Finalist at BestThriller.com. Kopcow's fiction short story collection, *Worst. Date. Ever.*, was published by Regal House Publishing in March 2020 and was named one of 2020's top 100 novels by the Community of Literary Magazines and Presses (CLMP). The anthology, *Thank You, Death Robot*, which included his short story, *The Cobbler Cherry*, won an Independent Publishing Award for best science-fiction and fantasy and was voted a Chicago Tribune Top Ten Fiction book. Kopcow has had dozens of other short stories published in several magazines and anthologies.

OTHER TITLES BY DAN KOPCOW

Prior Futures

"A smart, satirical thriller with a hardboiled, political edge, hilarious dialogue, and a loopy optimism all its own. As the bodies pile up, sparks fly off the page. A great ride."
—Jon Frankel, **author of GAHA: Babes of the Abyss and Isle of Dogs**

BEST THRILLER FINALIST
BESTTHRILLERS.COM
BOOK AWARDS

Dan Kopcow

NOTE FROM DAN KOPCOW

Word-of-mouth is crucial for any author to succeed. If you enjoyed *Madcap Serenade*, please leave a review online—anywhere you are able. Even if it's just a sentence or two. It would make all the difference and would be very much appreciated.

Thanks!
Dan Kopcow

We hope you enjoyed reading this title from:

BLACK ROSE writing™

www.blackrosewriting.com

Subscribe to our mailing list – *The Rosevine* – and receive **FREE** books, daily deals, and stay current with news about upcoming releases and our hottest authors.
Scan the QR code below to sign up.

Already a subscriber? Please accept a sincere thank you for being a fan of Black Rose Writing authors.

View other Black Rose Writing titles at www.blackrosewriting.com/books and use promo code **PRINT** to receive a **20% discount** when purchasing.

Printed in Great Britain
by Amazon